The Fear of Child Sexuality

The Fear of Child Sexuality

Young People, Sex, and Agency

STEVEN ANGELIDES

The University of Chicago Press
Chicago and London

The University of Chicago Press, Chicago 60637
The University of Chicago Press, Ltd., London
© 2019 by The University of Chicago
All rights reserved. No part of this book may be used or reproduced in any manner whatsoever without written permission, except in the case of brief quotations in critical articles and reviews. For more information, contact the University of Chicago Press, 1427 E. 60th St., Chicago, IL 60637.
Published 2019
Printed in the United States of America

28 27 26 25 24 23 22 21 20 19   1 2 3 4 5

ISBN-13: 978-0-226-64846-0 (cloth)
ISBN-13: 978-0-226-64863-7 (paper)
ISBN-13: 978-0-226-64877-4 (e-book)
DOI: https://doi.org/10.7208/chicago/9780226648774.001.0001

Library of Congress Cataloging-in-Publication Data

Names: Angelides, Steven, author.
Title: The fear of child sexuality : young people, sex, and agency / Steven Angelides.
Description: Chicago ; London : The University of Chicago Press, 2019. | Includes bibliographical references and index.
Identifiers: LCCN 2018058209 | ISBN 9780226648460 (cloth : alk. paper) | ISBN 9780226648637 (pbk. : alk. paper) | ISBN 9780226648774 (e-book)
Subjects: LCSH: Children and sex. | Moral panics. | Teenagers—Sexual behavior. | Intergenerational relations.
Classification: LCC HQ784.S45 A54 2019 | DDC 306.70835—dc23
LC record available at https://lccn.loc.gov/2018058209

♾ This paper meets the requirements of ANSI/NISO Z39.48-1992 (Permanence of Paper).

*For Angelo and Anhtuan,
and in memory of Sandra Eterovic*

CONTENTS

Preface: Under Erasure / ix

ONE / The Uncanny Sexual Child / 1

TWO / Premarital Sex / 21

THREE / Child Sexual Abuse / 45

FOUR / Homosexual Pedophilia / 73

FIVE / Power / 99

SIX / Gender / 127

SEVEN / Sexting / 157

Acknowledgments / 179
Notes / 183
Index / 229

PREFACE

Under Erasure

Lock up your children
Devils in disguise
Lock up your children
Devils in their eyes . . .

—Land of Giants, "Cannibal Dolls," 1982[1]

Perhaps we stay focused on safeguarding children because we fear them. Perhaps we are threatened by the specter of their longings that are maddeningly, palpably opaque.

—Kathryn Bond Stockton, *The Queer Child*, 2009[2]

In May 2015, high-end designer label Miu Miu, of the Prada fashion house, had one of its advertisements for the spring/summer collection banned in the United Kingdom by the Advertising Standards Authority (ASA). The image of a young woman featured in *Vogue UK* was, the ASA decreed, inappropriate because it sexualized a young model they believed appeared to be younger than sixteen.[3] According to news media reports, the ASA felt that the model's childlike "youthful appearance" was enhanced by the use of "minimal make up and clothes that appeared slightly too large."[4] The composition of the photograph was also problematic, argued the ASA, because

> she was posed reclining on a bed, looking up directly to the camera through a partially opened door, which gave her an air of vulnerability and the image a voyeuristic feel. . . . We considered that the crumpled sheets and her partially opened mouth also enhanced the impression that the pose was sexually suggestive.[5]

In some respects the ban is hardly surprising. The last two decades have seen intense and growing anguish about the sexualization of girls by big business, advertising, and the media across the anglophone West. High-profile government and advocacy-group reports as well as inquiries into child sexualization have been conducted in the United States, Canada, the United Kingdom, and Australia.[6] It is not even particularly surprising that the model at the center of the censorship scandal was an adult twenty-one years old at the time of the photo shoot. For what is being at once defended and enforced with this injunction is something very familiar: the *image* of the sexually innocent child. The image of the child (or "childlike" adult) must not be evocative of sexuality. Not necessarily because anglophone societies believe pubescent children to be asexual; in traversing puberty, young teenagers are often seen as both erotic and innocent, although their eroticism is usually regarded to be an undeveloped precursor to mature adult sexuality. Rather, the "sexually suggestive" depiction of children is prohibited because it is widely believed to be a prurient and potentially damaging exploitation of this (erotic) innocence that, as the ASA pronounced, is "irresponsible and offensive."[7]

The Miu Miu ban is just one of countless examples of how controversial is the entanglement of children and sexuality. One reason for this is that sexuality is *the* most highly cherished marker delineating the boundaries between childhood and adulthood.[8] A prevailing narrative of Western cultures is that the transition from childhood to adulthood unfolds according to a series of naturally evolving stages of sexual maturation. Children are generally viewed as latent or protosexual beings whose incipient eroticism must await pubertal development and psychical maturation before the emergence of adult genital sexuality. When the boundaries between childhood innocence (or innocent eroticism) and adult sexuality are blurred or overlap, or when adult sexuality or sexual frameworks are thought to be prematurely imposed on children, usually grave concerns and anxieties about their well-being are voiced. Oftentimes these concerns foment into highly emotive "sex panics."[9] This is a book about a series of child sex and sexualization panics around a familiar set of anglophone social "problems": the sexualization of children in the media and art; premarital teenage sexuality and sex education; child sexual abuse; homosexual pedophilia and intergenerational relationships; and, more recently, teenage sexting. The fundamental worry propelling expressions of public sentiment is a concern with the potentially damaging effects on young people of any untoward or premature encounter with the world of adult sexuality, sexual representation, and sexual practice.

The nature of each of the sex panics studied in this book differs markedly in terms of content and context. However, each is exemplary, I argue, of a rather typical—and tellingly avoidant—response to the commingling of children and sexuality in anglophone societies, no matter the national, regional, and temporal specificity. Scholars have for some time noted how in modern anglophone societies, fear, anxiety, and shame ordinarily have been in close proximity whenever children and sexuality are brought together within the same frame. Usually this is figured as the fear of children's allegedly premature exposure to forms of adult sexuality and the shameful loss of innocence that this occasions. As forensic psychologist Frank DiCataldo summarizes, "Childhood sexuality is an idea deeply engraved in the American psyche as something . . . damaging, scarring, inherently harmful, traumatizing, a warping mark."[10] This is as true of the United States as it is often of anglophone countries generally. Routine scholarly protocol ordinarily demands a wariness of generalization across national and historical settings and boundaries; but with regard to issues of child sexuality and sexual abuse, it is more striking to note, as queer theorist Kevin Ohi affirms, "how little difference national context actually makes."[11] Expressed in astonishingly similar ways, child sex and sexual abuse panics are unswervingly energized by what Ohi describes as a "fetishization of childhood innocence" that is rarely as innocent as it appears.[12] Indeed, it would be "a mistake to take innocence straight," fellow queer theorist Kathryn Bond Stockton cautions, "to believe its benign publicity, as it were."[13]

This book proposes that, like innocence, fear and anxiety (and other emotions such as shame) are also not as unsullied, pure, and straight as they might seem. I argue that the routine public articulation of fear, anxiety, and shame in mainstream media scandals in the face of signs of childhood sexuality frequently serves a particular function: to place the agentive sexual child or adolescent *under erasure*. In public debate we tend to turn away from the child sexual subject, busying ourselves with adult agendas, preoccupations, concerns, and tropes of childhood. Not that the notion of children having sexual subjectivities or agency is necessarily denied or repudiated; rather, where agentive subjectivities are conceded—and often they are—in times of controversy, habitually they are placed under suspicion or discounted and discredited. This is what I mean by being placed under erasure: children's agentive sexual subjectivities are simultaneously acknowledged and avoided (although sometimes just avoided), or they are at once (over)protected from scrutiny and objectified as homogenous Child, exalted in their innocence and infantilized in their transgressions, endlessly spoken about and endlessly rendered mute.[14] R. Danielle Egan puts it this way:

the "sexuality of the child is simultaneously present and absent within discourses on child sexuality."[15] The mobilization of fear, anxiety, and shame and the accompanying erasure of sexual agency are usually done, of course, in the name of *protecting* children and childhood innocence. Children are not always deemed to be innocent *of* sexual impulses, desires, motives, and intentions, but these erotic or sexual drives, aspirations, and apprehensions are typically rewritten *as themselves innocent*: infantile, immature, protosexual, and *un*-adult-like. Often they are just these things, of course. But, as the book will show, young people are not always so easily reducible to tropes of innocence and immaturity, and when insufficient attention is given to the complexities of sexual agency, this itself can be counterprotective and sometimes even harmful.

The paradigms of childhood innocence and child protection are so hegemonic that there are very few legitimate public spaces for acknowledging nonpathological or adult-like forms of child sexuality. Young people's sexual subjectivities are routinely leeched of specificity, complexity, depth, and dynamism in the process of being assimilated to the generic category of the Child.[16] "What can go missing in policy and popular debates on sexualization," as Emma Renold, Jessica Ringrose, and Danielle Egan note in their recent collection *Children, Sexuality and Sexualization*, is "an assumption that children and young people are complex sexual subjects who are actively negotiating sexuality in their everyday lives."[17] Young people are rarely acknowledged as having what Michelle Fine and Sara McClelland call "thick desire."[18] Transgressive and affirmative child subjectivities that talk back—or express "thick desire"—and challenge infantilizing and normative protocols are usually controlled by the terms of the future-oriented convention of child developmentalism. Not yet adults, young people are transitional subjects on the path to future adulthood. One way child sexualities have been stripped of complexity, dynamism, and agency when displaying signs of adult-like behavior and capacity has been to cast them as juvenile and aberrant effects of sexualizing, exploitive, and abusive adult influences.[19] The prevailing assumption, as Egan and Gail Hawkes remark, has been that the "sexual subjectivity of children is generated by some outside stimulus."[20] Following queer scholars, we might call these child subjectivities *queer* in Michael Warner's sense of the term, as forms of "resistance to regimes of the normal," or, as Kathryn Bond Stockton describes, as forms of children's "sideways growth."[21] Such queer or dissident child sexualities are relentlessly displaced, as Steven Bruhm and Natasha Hurley put it, "from the present to the future or the past (that is, the future anterior)," where a child's nonnormative sexual desires, behaviors, and subjectivities "will not have been."[22]

A claim of this book is that, frequently during melodramatic, or what Janice Irvine calls "dramaturgical," moments of child sex panic we come closest to, yet defend against, a direct encounter with the sexual child.[23] My perhaps counterintuitive observation is that sex panics oftentimes seem to be especially histrionic less in cases of forced, violent, or horrific sexual exploitation and abuse than when young people's sexual curiosities, desires, pleasures, motives, intentions, and willful actions—in short, their agentive and assertive subjectivities—are brought into the social frame.[24] This, it seems, is a peculiarly late twentieth- and early twenty-first-century phenomenon. Together the chapters query tropes of threatened innocence, sexualization, sexual exploitation, and sexual abuse, taken for granted and usually presented as emotive drivers of scandals. It is not so much that imperatives of child protection underwriting them are unwarranted, invalid, or necessarily disingenuous (although, to be sure, the rhetoric of anxiety attached to such imperatives is at times inflated, misdirected, and sometimes and in some measure less than sincere.) Rather, overt concern with protecting children from sexualization, exploitation, and abuse is rarely *only* that. Anxieties about the protection of children from abuse by adult sexual practices and representations are usually the public face of sex panic discourses, and the inability to countenance (pre-1980s) ideas of agentive, competent, transgressive, corruptive, disruptive, seductive—even "shameful"—child sexuality are the less palpably confessed and troublesome shadow. A wager of this book is that it is precisely this under- (or other-)side that plays an especially critical even if often misunderstood role in the intensity of the sex panics and the rigid protectionist structures (legal, pedagogical, therapeutic, epistemological) erected in their wake.

Not a comparative account of sex panics across Western societies, the book takes a series of indicative case studies mainly from Australia but also the United States to trace the diminution of child sexuality so prevalent in anglophone cultures and the problems this brings. The contours of some of these sex panics are historicized, but each is presented as a discrete case study (that can be read alone) with its own set of concerns. Some of the chapters deal with sex panics that continue to animate present-day discussions, and notwithstanding the specific geographical location, content, and trajectories of the case studies, that exhibit strikingly similar issues, arguments, logics, and anxieties across anglophone societies generally.[25] The book's overarching framework is not a coherent linear historical narrative. Instead, it offers a series of problematizations located loosely within broader anglophone contexts that together testify to the cultural and political work the mobilization of emotional vocabularies of fear, anxiety, and shame does to endlessly defer an encounter with the agentive sexual child. This, I suggest, is a "strategy" of many child sex panics—although by strategies I am thinking of those aspects of power relations that are, as Michel Foucault famously puts it, "both intentional and non-subjective."[26] Power relations have aims and objectives, and in this way are intentional; but they are also beyond an individual or group's will, consciousness, or control—in that no individual or group *possesses* power and in that power relations have unintended and entangled aims and consequences—and so are nonsubjective.[27] Strategies can thereby also be anonymous and unwitting.

An argument about the denial of young people's sexual agency in moral and sex panics is not new. In addition to my own earlier work, feminists working in areas of teenage sexuality, girlhood studies, statutory-rape law, and sex education have highlighted this for quite some time now, mostly in relation to female sexuality.[28] What I suggest is that the avoidance, minimization, or neutralization of agency has now often become more a first-order aim (or strategy in the Foucauldian sense) than an outcome or side effect of sex panics—an aim now extended to boys, who until recently have been seen largely as agents (if not predators) and benefactors of the sexualization of girls.[29] The term *neutralization* is used deliberately and with more than one meaning, for, as I argue in this book, there has been a shift toward gender neutrality in understandings of child sexual abuse since the 1980s, and this is now unfortunately encouraging conceptions of teenage sexual agency neutered of gender specificity and specificity in general.

If fear—and shame—often functions intrapsychically as a signal of what to steer clear of or get rid of, in mainstream public discourse this dynamic seems to have been twisted and harnessed preemptively, I suggest, as a discursive political tactic not just to warn of impending harm to children. Fear is also exploited (wittingly or otherwise) to avoid, attack, or exile in advance the subject of agentive sexual children and the uniqueness of their individual becomings. The tactics frequently go hand in glove. The term *attack* is also used intentionally, as the vocabulary of fear and anxiety often, it seems clear, act as a (dis)guise for modes of aggression, anger, contempt, disgust, and shame directed at alternative forms of childhood and those who seek to recognize and nurture them.[30] Slut shaming, as feminists have long demonstrated, is but one obvious example of this. As we will see in chapters to come, aggression, anger, rage, contempt, disgust, and shame are rarely far from the surface of many child sex panics. Panics often work, in the service of directly regulating and performatively producing acceptable images and, I would add, ontologies of childhood: as innocent, pure, vulnerable, incapable, and incompetent.[31] To be blunt, those trading in the rhetoric of fear and anxiety sometimes actively serve to mold and create—even if unwittingly—innocent and vulnerable children at the same time as they energetically dismiss and criticize those that contradict these images, including young people themselves.[32]

Although the unifying frame of the book is the idea that child sex panics often have as a principal discursive "strategy" the placing of child sexuality and agency under erasure, this is not each chapter's central argument. However, a prominent feature of this dynamic is the way important experiential and subjective differences and capacities among individuals under the age of consent—such as those captured under the broad rubrics of prepubescence, pubescence, and adolescence—are frequently downplayed, collapsed, or ignored within a unified and age-stratified legal category of the Child. One of the ways this plays out is that the category or axis of age increasingly operates in the West as the definitive, primary marker shaping notions of childhood sexuality and sexual capacity. Age tends to subsume other conventional indices of difference. This diverges from decades of the twentieth century preceding the 1980s, when variances of race, gender, ethnicity, and class were often acknowledged as important factors shaping childhood sexuality and subjectivity. The problem, unfortunately, was that assumptions about racial, gender, ethnic, and class difference often pathologized those children seen to deviate from a privileged notion of sexually innocent and usually white, middle-class childhood.[33] Notwithstanding these serious shortcomings, though, age was not necessarily held up as the only determinant of childhood subjectivity. In the realm of sexuality and sexual consent, then, this book suggests that the prioritization of age and the subsumption of various markers of differentiation underscore the ways gender, race, ethnicity, class, and other axes are often problematically subordinated to, or neutralized by, an all-encompassing category of universal childhood premised on an age-based and linear model of sexual development.[34] Such a model is rather blunt and insufficiently calibrated, often failing to recognize the ways these factors (and many more) shape a wide variety of capacities and subjectivities that do not always correspond to linear and homogenous categories of age.

As puberty largely overlaps with teenage years and is most commonly associated with the transition from childhood to adulthood and the emergence of sexual identity, adolescence is often a particularly fertile site for sex panics. *The Fear of Child Sexuality* focuses mostly on case studies about pubescent and adolescent sexualities. Spotlighting sex panics over the murky domains of pubescence and adolescence illuminates in fruitful ways the fault lines of an undifferentiated category of the Child and the binary division of childhood and adulthood—and the trouble prompted by any blurring or disintegration. Like many other "third terms"—such as *bisexuality* or *intersexuality*—the category of adolescence often functions as a container to house contradictions and anomalies that exceed the rigid oppositional logic of the adult/child pairing.[35] Adolescence is also an overdetermined site for the playing out of dramas of agency and autonomy, and of power struggles over boundaries and practices separating children and adults.

Fear, Sex Panic, and Childhood Innocence

Adults are often more than aware of their own apprehension about confronting the fraught issues of child sexuality and sexual development. Indeed, fear and anxiety are everywhere acknowledged in voluminous advice literature that both names and attempts to dispel them. Parental advice books about understanding and coping with children's developing sexualities certainly testify to these feelings. This is evidenced in titles such as *Everything You Never Wanted Your Kids to Know about Sex (But Were Afraid They'd Ask): The Secrets to Surviving Your Child's Sexual Development from Birth to the Teens* and *How to Talk Confidently with Your Child about Sex: For Parents*.[36] It is also evident in popular press, such as the *Time* magazine cover from the mid-1990s entitled "Everything Your Kids Already Know about Sex: Bet You're Afraid to Ask." Such popular texts have as one of their principal and admirable aims the fostering of knowledge and understanding. They are designed to assist adults in dispelling ignorance, fear, and anxiety and transforming it into knowledge, understanding, and appropriate methods of communication, education, and child-rearing.[37] As such, they go some way toward confirming the presumption of *The Fear of Child Sexuality* about just how widespread is the rhetoric of fear, anxiety, and panic around child sexuality, and how unaware we often are at the level of popular discourse of some of the cultural and political work this rhetoric is performing and the social effects to which it is contributing.

However, it is this point about the cultural work and social consequences of vocabularies of fear, anxiety, and panic that distinguishes this book from advice manuals and psychological research on sexual development. In *Epistemology of the Closet*, Eve Sedgwick famously writes of the importance of deconstructing the category of ignorance. Ignorance is habitually used interchangeably with (childhood) immaturity and innocence; yet ignorance, she says, is not some "single Manichaean, aboriginal maw of darkness from which the heroics of cognition can occasionally wrestle" enlightened truth.[38] Nor is knowledge itself power and ignorance beyond power's reach. Ignorance, Sedgwick reminds us, is but "ignorance *of* a knowledge"; it "is as potent and as multiple a thing there is as is knowledge."[39] Ignorance is often the insinuation of alternative knowledge, alternative truth. It has historically specific meanings. So is ignorance often a political orientation to certain kinds of knowledge and relations of power. Indeed, as it is imposed on children, the category of ignorance shines a floodlight on adult constructions of childhood, and thus exercises of adult power. Unquestionably, much the same can be said of fear (and anxiety, panic, and other emotions). It too has multiple meanings, takes many forms, and is enmeshed in manifold networks of power. Ignorance and fear frequently cohabit, with the latter often said to issue from the former. Taking inspiration from these insights, this book aims not to dispel fear and anxiety (or ignorance) by laying claim to the "truth" of child sexuality (as if there were *one*), but rather to underscore the strategic uses and effects of negative emotional rhetoric. It seeks to expose and track some of the ways in which the language of fear, anxiety, and panic around child sexuality has been harnessed to shape the politics and practices of sexuality and categories of childhood and adulthood throughout the past six decades.

That fear, like innocence, is not always as it seems is evidenced in the rich and growing archive of scholarship on the history of sexuality. Pioneering work by historians and theorists of sexuality has demonstrated how oftentimes sex panics reflect and deflect deeper and broader social anxieties, concerns, and problems than those under direct scrutiny or uttered publicly. Scholars have applied social constructionist ideas to twentieth-century sex crime panics in detailing how changing social and historical conditions often ignite public outbursts of emotion, which serve a number of social functions. Panics work to politicize interest groups in efforts to reform societies, ordain social norms and beliefs, and regulate social relations. For instance, Estelle Freedman, John D'Emilio, George Chauncey, and Philip Jenkins have shown how the American panic over sexual psychopaths between the 1930s and 1960s was not connected to the actual increase in violent sex crimes.[40] Emerging in the context of profound social changes occurring in the 1920s and the Depression, the panic over the sexual psychopath was a way for Americans to renegotiate "the definitions of sexuality normality," says Freedman.[41] Or, as Jenkins observes of child molestation panics, even where "genuine public horror is aroused by sexual attacks against children . . . the problems constructed around these incidents address issues not immediately connected with social violence."[42] The fear is exaggerated and disproportionate to the threat posed, and activists and reformists appropriate the threat or problem to advance their own moral and political agendas. More recently, feminist girlhood scholars have followed suit by interrogating panics about the sexualization of girls to underline the array of sociopolitical agendas served by antisexualization narratives. These include the expression of a range of broader heteronormative anxieties around class, gender, nationalism, the family, purity, and racialized developmental discourses.[43] In their summary of the intellectual history of discourses of childhood sexuality in the nineteenth and early to mid-twentieth centuries in the anglophone West, Egan and Hawkes point to the wider social purposes of child sex panics. "Panics over childhood sexuality serve as metaphors for larger cultural instabilities," they argue. "The need to protect children from sexuality acts as a smokescreen for other social interventions that often go far beyond the bodies and pleasures of children themselves."[44]

Where constructionist scholarship has carefully detailed the shifting historical, social, and political conditions shaping sex panics, poststructuralist, psychoanalytic, feminist, and queer theorists of sexuality have also deconstructed the sexual politics and exposed the discursive structures, fears, anxieties, and fantasies lurking behind them. Central to almost all child sex panics are ideologies of childhood innocence. So mutually entailed are the two that, in *Sex Panic and the Punitive State*, Roger Lancaster declares sex panics to be "less about the protection of children than about the preservation of adult fantasies of childhood as a time of sexual innocence."[45] James Kincaid's *Erotic Innocence: The Culture of Child Molesting* has been especially trailblazing in interrogating our investment in ideologies of innocence. For Kincaid, anglophone cultures are obsessively attached to stories about the abuse of innocent children as a way of denying and projecting our own erotic desires for children and our role in eroticizing "empty innocence."[46] With this he echoes, in part, Richard Mohr's infamous and blunt assessment of the pervasiveness of pedophilic imagery in some of the most mainstream of news, advertising, and cinematic representations of children. Pedophilia panic, he has no qualms in declaring, "springs mainly from adults' fear of themselves, but this fear arises from their half recognition that to admit explicitly, as pornography does, that children are sexy would mean that virtually everyone is a pedophile."[47]

Portrayals of innocent and erotic children are understood in these accounts largely as *projections of adult desire*. Kincaid writes in his other landmark work on the subject, *Child-Loving: The Erotic Child and Victorian Culture*: "What the child *is* matters less than what we *think* it is."[48] Is this because, he asks, the "blank page" of childhood purity and innocence "doesn't interfere with our projections?"[49] On this point, Kincaid's readings resonate with Jacqueline Rose's earlier examination of the role of innocence in children's fiction. In *The Case of Peter Pan, or The Impossibility of Children's Fiction*, she too construes the category of the child as a projection of adult desire.[50] The cogency of these accounts about the centrality of the imaginary child is strangely reinforced in another register when we consider recent incarnations of child pornography laws that prohibit *fake* depictions of childhood sex.[51]

Queer theorists have also taken to task adult fantasies and projections of childhood innocence. Lee Edelman's infamous Lacanian psychoanalytic manifesto *No Future: Queer Theory and the Death Drive* offers an unashamed attack on the ways the figure of the innocent Child in need of protection functions to ensure a heteronormative future and stabilize the political field. The "image of the Child, not to be confused with the lived experiences of any historical children," he declares, "serves to regulate political discourse—to prescribe what will *count* as political discourse."[52] Kevin Ohi's analysis of the erotic child in literature in *Innocence and Rapture: The Erotic Child in Pater, Wilde, James, and Nabokov* also challenges us to think of the broader effects of the "ideology" of innocence. Drawing on Kincaid, Ohi goes further to highlight its broader social impact: the "contemporary insistence on childhood innocence . . . is inseparable from the ideology oppressing all sexual minorities," and the "articulation of erotic innocence structures contemporary sexual ideology in general."[53] With this point Ohi is underscoring an important theme of feminist, sexuality, and queer studies about the various forms of violence perpetrated by the *ideology* of childhood sexual innocence itself. Other groundbreaking texts that unsettle this ideology are Steven Bruhm and Natasha Hurley's collection of canonical essays *Curiouser: On the Queerness of Children* and Kathryn Bond Stockton's *The Queer Child, or Growing Sideways in the Twentieth Century*. While vastly different projects, each invites us to challenge prevailing adult stories told about childhood, sexual development, and optimal growth. As Bruhm and Hurley note, these are "stories we tell to children, stories we tell about children, stories we tell about ourselves as children."[54]

Notwithstanding Eve Sedgwick's well-known critique of "paranoid reading" practices hell-bent on emphasizing knowledge as exposure or demystification, the deconstructive enterprise always has a critical role to play.[55] But caution is advised, as media studies scholar Henry Jenkins notes, with regard to the dogged efforts to unmask adult myths of the innocent child. As important as the historical and theoretical work on deconstructing childhood is "for critiquing the mythology of childhood innocence," he worries that it "often leaves children permanently out of the equation, offering no way to examine the social experience of actual children or to talk about the real-world consequences of these ideologies."[56] Judith Levine's *Harmful to Minors: The Perils of Protecting Children from Sex* takes up just this challenge and leads the way in grappling with the actual impact of the ideology of innocence and our sometimes overzealous protectionism. Through nonfictional case studies she questions the hegemonic presumption that sex is per se harmful to children and child protection from sex inherently helpful. As Levine puts it plainly, the "drive to protect kids from sex is protecting them from nothing. Instead, it is harming them."[57] Lancaster says something similar: "Hypertrophied conceptions of harm have harmful effects."[58] An abundance of feminist scholarship on female teenage sexuality and sexualization discourse, some of it already mentioned, has also challenged the narrative of childhood innocence and identified the tendency in media and popular panics to neglect or nullify the agency of young girls. This research has sought to respond to this dilemma by developing frameworks for making the complex modes of sexual agency of young people (primarily girls) visible in ways that challenge, as Renold, Egan, and Ringrose put it, "a ubiquitous media landscape where children and young people's own experiences of doing, being, and becoming sexual are often sensationalized, silenced, caricatured, pathologized and routinely undermined."[59]

Drawing on this fertile history of scholarship in queer, feminist, and sexuality studies but through a range of different case studies, I too argue that the denial, trivialization, or deflection of childhood sexual agency is often detrimental to young people and society. My particular focus is less on deconstructing innocence than the ways innocence and other related tropes of childhood consistently work to dodge children's sexual agency. Such maneuvering often introduces as many problems as it attempts to solve. On this question of children's agency, Stockton's text encourages us, via fiction and film, to redirect our gaze to the sexual motives (and motions) of children. "How do we see a sexual child as being something other than our own perversion?" she asks.[60] For, as she points out, "our most public image of the sexual child for over half a century has not been a child—not a living child."[61] Stockton invites us to find new ways of making the sexual child visible outside of conventional interpretive frameworks and adult projections of childhood innocence.

The Fear of Child Sexuality examines sex panics for how they play out other interconnected social issues and how they trade in adult projections. However, echoing some of the feminist interventions in the areas of teenage female sexuality and sexualization studies, and opening out in two chapters to case studies of the less-researched topic of boys,[62] the book also wishes to draw attention to what we in the mainstream anglophone West persistently refuse to project onto young people, what we refuse to recognize in some of them. This is not the same as Kincaid's argument about "erotic innocence." For Kincaid, the modern child of anglophone cultures has been eroticized by virtue of having been constructed as innocent, pure, and empty. Kincaid's focus is on adult desires and defenses—specifically, the projection of desire onto the innocent child simultaneous with a denial that we are doing it. Mine is less an argument about adult desires in relation to children than one about dominant responses to *children's complex sexual desires, understandings, and intentions.*

Heeding Jenkins's advice of applying our collective insights to real-life case studies, my aim is to hold the spotlight over the figure of the living, agentive sexual child as he or she appears and then disappears in real-world sex panics.[63] For even when the sexual child vanishes into other preoccupying adult concerns, the absence is only apparent; the child continues to have an abiding, agentive and ghostly presence in shaping both the sexual encounters within which he or she is involved and the enveloping sex panics. This is another way of saying that fear of the sexual child is as much and sometimes more a driver of sex panics and the ways they unfold as concern about exploitive forms of child sexualization and abuse by adults. In order to counter the dominant tendency of placing the sexual child under erasure precisely when making an entrance, it is this agentive role of the sexual child that this book seeks to track—an agency conceptualized in terms of sexual relations *and* social change.

The presence of child sexuality and sexual agency in sex panics that are about sinister adult behavior (such as child sexual abuse) is not often acknowledged within scandals. If at all mentioned, they are usually pretty swiftly swept under the carpet, deflected, or displaced in some way, usually through assumptions about adult manipulation of child protosexuality. This makes a good deal of sense, of course, as the overriding concern is with punishing perpetrators and protecting children, not diminishing their abuse by suggesting their involvement. However, even here, as we will see in chapter 3, there is an important role for the acknowledgment of child sexuality and agency that supports the goal of child protection and the alleviation of harm at the same time as it denounces child sexual abuse. The deflection and displacement of child sexuality is an especially post-1970s phenomenon. As I have argued elsewhere, the gradual erasure of a signifier of child sexuality goes hand in hand with the emergence of an identity category of the pedophile and the discourse of child sexual abuse in the 1980s.[64] This is part a radical transformation of discourses of sexuality in the late 1970s and 1980s that, as Paul Okami has argued and I take up in chapter 3, moved "away from a generally benign [and even positive] portrayal of sexual behavior" to a focus on sexuality's darker, negative and traumatic sides.[65] This shift is also intimately connected to Lancaster's broader observation about the recent historical transformation of the liberal state into a "parent figure" or "paternalistic state whose citizens are conceived as imperiled innocents and infantilized victims."[66] For Lancaster, it is precisely child sex panics that have become the model by which "sexual predation has come to serve as a metaphor for other conditions of injury in the body politic."[67]

As we will also see in chapter 3, it is with the advent of the feminist-led anti–child sexual abuse movement in the late 1970s and 1980s that notions of child sexuality, power, sexual agency, responsibility, and culpability have undergone radical transformation. In earlier decades of the twentieth century, it was not uncommon for anglophone societies to view children as either precociously sexual or innocent, or both. However, as many feminists have demonstrated, the dual notion of childhood innocence and sexual precocity often led to the unsavory scenario of children in the first seventy years of the twentieth century sometimes being blamed for their own sexual abuse. The successful efforts of feminists and child care advocates to reverse this victim-blaming tendency—by bringing the problem of child sexual abuse to public attention and having sexual-offense laws redrafted to ensure this does not happen—are also instrumental in a broader cultural and historical shift. At the heart of this shift is a sweeping socio-legal redefinition of intergenerational sexual and power relations as inherently asymmetrical and one-sided. With young people enshrined necessarily as powerless victims vis-à-vis adults in sexual abuse and age-of-consent statutes, the latter part of the twentieth century has witnessed further moves away from notions of childhood and adolescent sexual precocity or agency—and the possibility of a diversity of youth *sexualities*—to notions of premature sexualization more generally: a transfer from the sexual to the *sexualized* child. The Miu Miu advertising ban symbolizes this broader historical transformation and switch of focus. What we have witnessed is a redistribution of the locus of (sexual) agency further and further away from young people to adults and adult society. Something is being done *to* children and adolescents, as the argument frequently goes (faulty parenting, peer pressure, adult abuses of power, environmentally induced early puberty, corporate pedophilia, media sexualization, to name a few) to awaken or channel their protosexuality *prematurely* and in inappropriate ways, such as through sexting, hypersexualized behaviors, child-child sexual abuse, or sexual relations with teachers and other adult figures. In the landscape of contemporary hyperprotectionism, this often means the sexual child is being reduced to (adult) sexual effect—victim—and generally disappears into debates about the corruption and sexualization of childhood and innocence. One of the problems with tethering power to arbitrary age-bound milestones is that we can lose sight of the Foucauldian insight of power's inherent *relationality*. We tend to apply a model of relational power to adult-adult interactions and a sovereign epistemology of power in which power is the possession only of adults in adult-child interactions.[68] The net effect is a reconditioned notion of childhood sexual innocence for the late twentieth and early twenty-first centuries. Childhood sexual agency has become something of a contradiction in terms, and the model of child sexual abuse has taken a disproportionate hold over notions of youth sexuality generally. This is not always in young people's best interests, be it in terms of their protection, development, or capacity building.

This book adds to the archive of scholarship critical of sexualization panics and attempts to switch the focus of attention squarely toward the *sexually agentive* and not the sexualized child. For we do not need to give up on condemning child sexual abuse when we inquire after child sexual agency. In fact, each informs the other. Extending this work by considering some case studies of boys will also highlight how issues of the sexual agency of boys can complicate a number of gendered assumptions around power and consent that have been mainstreamed within media and legal discourses from dominant feminist analyses of rape and sexual abuse in the late 1970s and 1980s. Childhood and teenage agency are not simply taken at face value, but neither are they necessarily relinquished to notions of ignorance, incompetence, immaturity, or adult manipulation. My aim is to show not only when and how sexual agency is given insufficient consideration, but also the ways in which the very act of minimizing or dismissing childhood agency does young people a disservice in the course of performing a great deal of background work to shore up some less than helpful norms, belief systems, and even laws.

A word on agency. No claim to a universal account of agency is offered in what follows, as I do not see agency as a fixed ontological property or attribute of an individual according to age-stratified models of biopsychosocial development. Instead, following Karen Barad, I see agency as "'doing' or 'being' in its intra-activity."[69] This is another way of saying the inextricable and entangled familial, interpersonal, and social networks and assemblages that constitute and sustain each of us provide the conditions of possibility for agentive action. And these are unique to each individual rather than reflective of a set of age-bound capacities and axes of difference (such as race, gender, class). As a network effect, moreover, agency embodies the dimensions of virtuality and potentiality and, as such, is multiple, mobile, and open to continual change. Not that there are no material, biological, psychical, and discursive constraints shaping the enactment of agency and child sexuality; but how these constraints themselves transform or intra-act with other relational (interpersonal, cultural, historical) forces to produce *unique* agentive and sexual embodiments, expressions, and actions is neither universally set in some developmental stone nor known in advance.[70] However, it is the very specificity and multiplicity of agency—and young people's active participation in such relational dynamics—that is ordinarily given little weight in sex panics. These details, however, are precisely what ought to be considered if we are to better understand and assist young people in navigating sexuality and life.

A caveat is in order about the notion of sex panic. Derived from constructionist moral panic theory, it has been used widely in sexuality studies. Often it is used as an evaluative term to refer to moments of perceived social crisis around sexual practices, crimes, meanings, and identities, such as prostitution, homosexuality, venereal disease, teenage pregnancy, sexual molestation, or pedophilia, to name a few. "What marks each of these social happenings as 'panics,'" notes Gilbert Herdt, "is the level to which the societal and personal expressions are out of proportion with the threat posed."[71] The concept of a moral or sex panic has been extensively critiqued on a number of fronts, including this idea of disproportionality. I have no interest in defending this idea, or rejecting it outright. Nor do I rehearse the intellectual debates about the concept.[72] The term *sex panic* is used in this book principally as a descriptive and not an explanatory or diagnostic concept to draw attention to a politics of emotion that has both manifest and latent meanings. However, this is a conceptualization of latency taken in its broadest sense as *that which is operative but not entirely visible or actualized*. Not reducible to unconscious meaning—although not ruling it out either—this is a notion of discursive latency. The term *sex panic* is not used as a way of dismissing social concerns as unjustified or positing some truth of a problem or issue—sex panics are neither wholly good nor bad; nor are they singular and homogenous—but is used to highlight how the politics of fear and emotion perform a number of social functions (strategies) *beyond* the avowed goals of publicizing and tackling the sexual exploitation of children.

Seeking to diagnose fear, psychoanalyst Adam Phillips points out that "certain defences not only protect us from the supposed object of fear, but also from the knowledge that there is such an object. But what does the way we construct our defences . . . tell us about what we fear?"[73] To twist this psychoanalytic formulation, I pursue a notion of fear less as an affect with unconscious and embodied meaning (although it might be this also, in specific instances for particular people), but as a politico-discursive defense and mode of intervention. No overarching psychoanalytic reading of sex panics is offered (even if occasionally I speculate on particular emotional dynamics and formations), unlike some of my earlier work and that of Kincaid, Mohr, and others.[74] I do not suggest there is some deep reservoir of fear (and anxiety) about child sexuality laying unrecognized in most people or anglophone societies, even if there might well be for some or many people. Nor do I take for granted that discursive expressions of fear in sex panics reflect authentic emotion, as a good deal of the feminist literature on sexualization of girls panics often seems to do even as it recognizes the simultaneous rhetorical mobilization of emotion scripts. Following the example of Janice Irvine, I am interested in what the discursive framing by fear (and anxiety)—and sometimes other emotions—*does* socially and politically in sex panics to the lives and signifiers of sexual children. Emotions such as fear endeavor to do something, to have an effect, to produce some thing, idea, or state of affairs. This is as true of fear as a subjective or intrapsychic phenomenon as it is of fear as a socially and politically generated one. The language of fear mobilized in child sex panics within popular and media discourses and legal court cases is thus performative in a myriad of ways. One of these ways is, to rework Phillips's interpretation, to shield us from the recognition and knowledge of a diversity of child sexualities, especially those sexualities not easily assimilable to uniform images of innocence and immaturity.

But this is no singular fear. The fear enveloping child sexuality is multiple and multifaceted, affective and performative. That is to say, while particular affective incarnations might well be *felt* (meaning different things to different people), fear and anxiety are also, as Irvine would have it, dramaturgically produced.[75] There are, as she notes, discursive rules, norms, and scripts surrounding the display and articulation of emotion.[76] Emotional language and scripts are deployed, in other words, not so much to reflect an unmediated or spontaneous emotional state, but often to generate interpersonal, social, political, and legal lessons and effects. Among these are the enactment and policing of appropriate social meanings, categories, and identities (e.g., childhood, adolescence, adulthood, consent, power, gender, sexuality, citizenship, maturity, abuse); the regulation of young people's sexuality, young people's sexual relationships, and interactions between children and adults; the management of young people's access to representations of sexuality;

the enforcement of laws and policies of child protection; and, of course, *the evasion of childhood sexuality itself.*

For more than two centuries, ideas of childhood sexuality have been closely allied with worry and trepidation, peril and danger. And since the exposure by the anti–child sexual abuse movement of widespread child molestation of the late 1970s and beyond, this alliance has been only further strengthened—so much so that the language of fear and anxiety has become our cultural default, the first thing reached for in a time of heightened risk aversion. Not that an eye toward risk is a bad thing in itself. But when the language of fear and anxiety colonizes the social and discursive landscape and predicts or favors the possibility of harm, it creates an imbalance that makes it extremely difficult to raise questions about child sexual agency, "thick desire," and alternative (let alone positive) outcomes for young people engaging in sex. One of the unfortunate collateral consequences of the success and power of child sexual abuse discourse is that understandings even of nonabusive youth sexual relations are usually framed by or calibrated with sexual abuse diagnostics.

The Fear of Child Sexuality expands our field of vision by incorporating case studies of child sex panics from Australia. Far from unique, these mirror many of the broader underlying logics, rhetorics, and affective and performative anxieties of their anglophone counterparts whenever children and sex become entangled. However, I hope the case studies will enable scholars to interrogate non-Australian child sex panics differently as a result of some of the ideas raised in this book. Following scholars of queer and sexual childhoods, the book will be critical of some of the ways sex panics have been socially managed often to detrimental effect. The enactment of the language of fear (and other "negative" emotion) and the accompanying failure to fully recognize the specificity and multiplicity of gender and sexual subjectivities of children—as a result of assumptions of sexual ignorance, innocence, homogeneity, and immaturity— have at times resulted less in the protection of young people from harm and the promotion of well-being and more in misrecognition, marginalization, exposure to potential harm, and vulnerability to psychic distress.

A comment on terminology is necessary. Because the bulk of the chapters deal largely with pubertal and postpubertal youth, the use of the category of the "child" (instead of "adolescent") in the book's title may at times seem misleading. The category of the child is notoriously unstable, the meaning of which shifts, expands, and contracts according to history, nation, culture, legal statute, context, and discourse. Cognizant of the important differences between and among prepubertal, pubertal, and postpubertal youth, as well as the pitfalls of their conflation, I have chosen to retain the phrases (which I use interchangeably) *child sexuality, sexual child,* and *child sexual subject.* Principally, the reason for this is that the young people who are the subjects of the case studies are defined as children by age-of-consent and sexual-offense laws (and also, in fact, by sex panic discourses). Retaining a legalistic definition of the child even when referring to those between ages fifteen and seventeen is also a deliberately provocative reminder of the ambiguities and contradictions faced by young people in Western societies. Finally, some of the chapters that follow—particularly the ones concerned with teacher-student relationships—take seemingly exceptional and anomalous case studies as their focus. This is also deliberate. For one thing, there is vastly more attention in mainstream and academic discourse given to childhood sexual exploitation. But this is not all. In his account of sex panics, Lancaster uses the term "victimology trap" to highlight a tendency in the neoliberal state "to see victims of injustice as pure, innocent, and good."[77] Child victims of intergenerational sex crime, already deemed sexually innocent and vulnerable by virtue of their age, are usually—and understandably, in many respects—exemplars of this characterization. However, the case studies in chapters 5 and 6 on teacher-student sex crime center on boys not easily consigned to the category of victim. These cases call on us to think carefully about the victimology trap and the ways our judicial systems often seem to be oriented sometimes toward defending ideologies, enforcing innocence, limiting possible adolescent ontologies, and punishing assertive child sexuality as they are toward protecting vulnerable young people from harm. The intentional choice of scandals involving boys is also a means of drawing attention to the *gendering* of the feminist child sexual abuse discourse and the limitations this brings. Often it seems our treatment of so-called exceptions and anomalies more clearly illustrates our investment in prevailing rules, social norms, categories, and power relations when these are transgressed. As Wendy Hollway and Tony Jefferson aptly note, "Single case studies do powerful theoretical work in demonstrating the limits of existing theory."[78] Indeed, the teacher-student sex crime case studies forcefully illustrate the limits of 1970s and 1980s child sexual abuse theory as it has become enshrined into current law, discourse, and social policy—via what Janet Halley has called "governance feminism"[79]—sometimes inadvertently hostile to difference and multiple adolescent realities.

Trajectory of the Book

Chapter 1 opens in the recent past with a sex panic surrounding the artwork of one of Australia's internationally acclaimed artists, Bill Henson. Known for his photography of adolescence, Henson was at the center of a scandal about images of naked teenagers exhibited in Sydney in 2008. The Australian nation has fiercely debated whether these works (one of which depicts a twelve-year-old girl with budding breasts and hairless pudenda) are art or pornography. Then–Prime Minister Kevin Rudd declared the photos to be "absolutely revolting," and child protection and parents groups accused Henson of exploiting childhood innocence. The furor was reminiscent of similar sex panics about nude images of children produced by artists in the United States such as Jock Sturges and Sally Mann. This chapter connects this sex panic to recent alarm across North America, Australia, and the United Kingdom about the sexualization of children by the media and the apparently proliferating images of children in sexual contexts on the internet. This is a sex panic about the corruptive and exploitive effects on children of the adult sexual gaze. While tracing the polarization of debate around art versus pornography, "innocence" versus its "adulteration," the chapter is about what has been much less discussed, even obscured, in the way the scandal unfolded. Encapsulating the principal contention of this book, it argues that what has been obscured, misrecognized, and avoided is the subject of child sexuality and agency, and this is as central, if not more so, to the subject's volatility as the avowed concerns about sexualization and exploitation.

Chapter 2 historicizes the 1960s and 1970s as period of a radical change with regard to anglophone thinking about the sexualization of children and child sexuality. This was a time of massive concern about the earlier onset of puberty, premature sexuality, rising rates of premarital sex, youth promiscuity, sexually transmitted infections, and teenage and "illegitimate" pregnancies. It was also a time of increasing concern about challenges to adult power structures and social and religious norms of gender and sexuality wrought by the commodification of sexuality in media and popular culture, by youth subcultures and protest movements, and by the transformation of the experience of youth itself. Calls for universal sex education of children in schools were being made in this context to avoid what many were forecasting as the rapid rise of hedonism, immorality, and the impending decline of Western civilization. The sexually active adolescent was the primary object of this sex panic. This chapter takes Australia as a case study of the broader anglophone shift toward school-based sex education programs in Western societies. Prompted by developments in the United States and Britain, the Australian government established a Royal Commission into Human Relationships in 1974. The recommendations of the report called for broad-based and universal sex education in all schools as a way of keeping pace with social changes of the 1960s and early 1970s. The chapter tracks the mobilization of widespread anxieties about the introduction of sex education beyond the basic facts of marriage and biological reproduction and the concern that an expansive education on sex and human relationships would only unleash and further encourage, rather than contain and control, adolescent sexual behavior. It argues that the mobilization of fear was a vehicle for advancing several interlinked social, discursive, and political strategies (in the Foucauldian sense). This mobilization was a way of stimulating community action toward controlling the sexualities of young people, enforcing a series of social and moral norms of sexuality, reaffirming boundaries between children and adults, and buttressing adult power. It was also, importantly, a way of undermining young people's claims to sexual agency, autonomy, and knowledge by recasting the teenager as essentially immature, incompetent, and endangered in matters of sex.

There is, I think, something historically significant about this period in history for our understanding of child sexuality, which is why I have included a case study on the 1960s and early 1970s. It was a threshold moment before the child sexual abuse movement gained full momentum, when it was more common for anglophone societies to entertain nuanced and polymorphic images of teenagers as (potentially) at once sexual, blameworthy, capable, and immature—but not exactly or necessarily innocent. Adolescents were endowed by some with capacities for intelligent sexual decision-making and could still be blamed for problem sexual behavior, which was a recognition of their agency and responsibility, at the same time as they were cast by some as immature and unduly influenced by an oversexualized adult society. But this was soon to change with the consolidation and expansion of a mainstreamed feminist child sexual abuse paradigm in which the normative teenager is viewed more and more as vulnerable and innocent in matters of sex, especially sex with those not close in age.[80] Including this case study of the 1960s and early 1970s highlights, by way of stark contrast, the momentous transformation that has swept through anglophone societies in the last forty years.

The idea of premature sexualization and abuse by adult sexual practices is the focus of chapter 3. This is a sex panic about child sexual abuse, spearheaded by the child-protection lobby and feminism in the 1970s and 1980s. Arguably more profound than the Freudian revolution normalizing ideas about child sexuality, the anti–child sexual abuse movement has had, and continues to have, a tremendous social impact. Patriarchal social structures, institutions, and ideas have been overhauled, exploitative adult sexualities and power relations radically challenged; and our reexamination of the dynamics of child sexual abuse and its detrimental effects have generated valuable insights and advances with regard to diagnosis, intervention, policy, law, and policing. Despite these admirable efforts at child protection, this chapter argues that, in particularly significant ways, children themselves have been unwittingly disarmed and disempowered. The expansion of our understanding of child sexual abuse has proceeded at the expense of our understanding of child sexual agency and of nuanced distinctions between prepubescent, pubescent, and adolescent "children." The chapter argues that placing child sexuality under erasure in this way introduces very real problems of its own. First, with the subject of sexual agency minimized and an outdated model of power installed, even actual victims of child sexual abuse are vulnerable to potentially damaging psychological and psychotherapeutic consequences. Second, when child sexuality is installed as something of an oxymoron particularly vis-à-vis adults, its erasure reinforces rather than complicates the inflexible and developmentalist binary opposition of childhood and adulthood that is the subject of so much compelling critique. Childhood becomes unnecessarily homogenized, and our ability to apprehend multiple childhoods and complex relations of power diminishes.

In North America, Australia, and the United Kingdom, sex panics erupted when gay rights movements and homosexual pedophile support groups emerged to challenge age-of-consent laws and agitate for homosexual equality, the acceptance of nonexploitive intergenerational relationships, and the recognition of the sexual rights of children. These campaigns aroused a great deal of opposition about abuse and possible overflow effects, such as the seduction of impressionable children into the "homosexual way of life." Chapter 4 traces the emergence of a pathologized category of the homosexual pedophile as an outgrowth of these sex panics in the late 1970s and 1980s. It examines the raid of the Australian Pedophile Support Group in Sydney and Melbourne in 1983 as an instance of a broader anglophone sex panic over homosexual pedophilia. The chapter argues that categories of the "homosexual" and the "pedophile" were rhetorically conflated by conservative religious and antihomosexual discourses, whose tactics served to deflect attention away from the agentive sexual child and from the distinctions being promoted by gay and pedophile groups between child sexual abuse, child sexual consent, agency, and empowerment. That homophobia has been a structuring feature of pedophile panics of this period in such a way as to scapegoat homosexuals for the problems of child sexual abuse has been widely remarked upon among historians and scholars of sexuality, including myself. However, this chapter draws attention not only to the role of the scapegoat in panic formation, but the role of the sexual child. In focusing on the signifier of child sexuality, I want to suggest that the latent or less acknowledged drivers of pedophile panics were equally the problem sexual boy and how to contain, cloak, and regulate him.

Chapter 5 turns to the first of two case studies on the recent subject of teacher-student sex crime. Throughout the past decade and a half, there has been an explosion of anglophone media reportage suggesting a rise of epidemic proportions in cases of female secondary-school teachers in relationships with underage male pupils. At the center of this sex panic is the widespread disquiet over the abuse of power these relationships are presumed to involve. In fact, it is precisely the assumption of inherent power differentials between teachers and students inherited from 1970s and 1980s child sexual abuse feminism that provides the rationale for positions-of-authority legislation now operative in many Western countries. (The notion of positional-power asymmetries is also the conceptual foundation of recent moves in some North American universities of blanket prohibitions of faculty-student relationships, in some cases regardless of whether a relationship of supervision exists.[81]) Chapter 5 interrogates this sexual-offense legislation that automatically criminalizes sex between teachers and students where the latter are over the general age of consent. Examining an Australian criminal case as a window onto this broader anglophone phenomenon, it critiques the model of power informing such legislation. Highlighting how a notion of juridical, or prohibitive, power forecloses critical questions of subjectivity and intersubjective dynamics, the chapter suggests that these laws function less as a protective mechanism for children from potential abuses of power than as a punitive exercise of adult power. They serve to regulate adolescent sexuality and impose generational norms of age, sexuality, and power. Far from innocuous, the chapter argues that this model of power and its foreclosures often misrecognize the teacher-student relationships under scrutiny and create far greater harm than do the sexual relationships themselves. An alternative model of multidimensional intersubjective power relations is proposed as a way of rethinking power, analyzing interpersonal relationships, giving due weight to modes of adolescent agency and difference, encouraging responsible sexual citizenship, and preventing unnecessary prosecutions and collateral damage.

Consternation about adult-child power differentials and intergenerational sexuality is not the only component of the sex panic over teacher-student sex crime. A second major element is the issue of gender dynamics. Chapter 6 examines the sex panic as it has erupted around the question of gender and the judicial system. Accompanying the media's fascination with these cases has been a highly emotive controversy, staged in almost precisely the same way in North America and Australia, over a perceived gender bias in the sentencing of women. The standard claim made is that many women have received lighter sentences because of their attractive appearances and the apparently outmoded assumption that, as the ultimate heterosexual male fantasy, boys are unlikely to be harmed by encounters with women. The chapter takes a second recent high-profile Australian case as an instance of this broader anglophone sex panic over gender and justice. It is the story of Karen Ellis, a secondary-school teacher who initially received a wholly suspended sentence for engaging in sex with one of her male students. Ellis's sentence aroused such public outrage from crime-victim groups and parent and child-abuse support groups that the decision was successfully appealed; she was subsequently jailed for six months. The case has been held up as a classic example of the judicial system's more lenient treatment of female offenders, and thus of the need for gender-neutral interpretations of sexual offenses. The question posed in this chapter is the extent to which gender, in shaping sexual offenses of this kind, ought to be a factor in criminal proceedings. I argue that the Ellis case, and others like it, is indicative not of the need for rigid adherence to the principle of gender neutrality, but the opposite: a paradigmatic example of when to insist on the recognition of gender difference. Aside from the unique machinations of the Australia judicial system, this is a case that could equally have occurred in the United States. This argument is part of a broader claim that there are serious problems with the principle of gender neutrality as it is being applied within courts and child-sexual-offense legislation and discourse. First, its application is premised on a false image of the adolescent as neutered of gender (as well as ethnicity, race, class, ability, and other dimensions). Second, the conceptualization of gender neutrality is knotted to scenarios of abuse within which a model of juridical power rules, yet this model is being applied inappropriately to nonabusive interactions in which power is much more complex and relational. The imposition of a gender-neutral sexual abuse paradigm legitimizes only one form of adolescent subjectivity: the *victim*. Aside from the fact that not all young people are victims, worse still is that the victim is modeled on the figure of a very particular *female* victim.

Chapter 7, the concluding chapter, shifts focus away from adult-child relations and instead probes another current sex panic concerning activities among young people. The last several years in many Western societies have seen an explosion of anxiety about the phenomenon of teenage sexting. Legislators have been racing to design laws that can keep pace with advances in the use of new technologies for the exchange and dissemination of sexually explicit material. However, in the absence of specific laws covering sexting, prosecutors in many jurisdictions have responded to the practice by charging some teenagers with child pornography, sexual harassment, and indecency offenses. Some of these felonies—even when involving the consensual exchange of self-images to one's sexual partner—may result in adolescents being mandated to register as sex offenders. This chapter examines several recent criminal sexting cases and educational literature on sexting in the early years of the panic in the United States and Australia. Two broad arguments are made. The first is that this sexting panic, like each panic studied in this book, is in significant respects a displaced conversation about teenage sexual agency with explicit and less explicit strategies.[82] On the one hand is the manifest objective of regulating adolescent agency, and on the other are the latent strategies of avoiding the complex realities of teenage agency and enacting a normative and homogenous figure of the immature and inept adolescent. Emotional or affective tropes of fear and shame have been mobilized in the service of these performative strategies. The discussion concludes by probing further the issue of shame's entanglement with child sexuality in order to tease out one of the more distasteful aspects of the sexting panic, and each of the panics studied in the book: all too often there is a great deal of embarrassment of, contempt for, and aggression against, "transgressive" sexual children.

ONE

The Uncanny Sexual Child

On May 22, 2008, the infamous conservative Australian journalist Miranda Devine published what was to be a catalytic opinion piece in the *Sydney Morning Herald*. In it she railed against the sexualization of children in the media. Devine began by announcing the opening that evening of the exhibition of Australian photographer Bill Henson. An internationally acclaimed photographic artist, Henson is well known for his images of adolescents. This particular exhibition, to be held at the Roslyn Oxley9 Gallery in Sydney, caught the attention of Devine and other critics after the circulation among journalists of invitations for the opening night. These featured a single image from the exhibit of a naked thirteen-year-old girl with budding breasts and hands covering her pudenda. For Devine, the photograph is exemplary of the abhorrent depths of a culture out of control in its sexualization of children: "Such images presenting children in sexual contexts are so commonplace these days they seem almost to have lost the capacity to shock." She left readers in no doubt whom she believes to be responsible for this social calamity:

> The effort over many decades by various groups—artists, perverts, academics, libertarians, the media and advertising industries, respectable corporations and the porn industry—to smash taboos of previous generations and define down community standards, has successfully eroded the special protection once afforded childhood.[1]

Devine's article, and the journalistic clamoring of which it was a part, was the catalyst to one of the most infamous and widely debated art scandals to rock the country's history.

The time was ripe for controversy. Widespread concern over the issue of premature child sexualization had been growing steadily in North America, Australia, and the United Kingdom. An Australian Senate inquiry into the sexualization of children in the media was due to report its findings the month following the Henson exhibition. Mirroring developments in the United States, the inquiry was commissioned after increasing public and political pressure was being placed on the Australian government to tackle the problem.[2] In this highly sensitive climate—and in just a matter of hours after Devine's article was released—the Henson exhibition and images were being debated on radio talk shows, the views of politicians were being canvassed, journalists and television news crews were in pursuit of the gallery, and complaints were being made to the New South Wales (NSW) state police. Radio broadcasters had been encouraging the public to visit the gallery website to witness for themselves the "shocking" photographs. Abusive phone calls began flooding in. " 'You're all pornographers'; 'We know where you are'; 'We're going to burn the gallery down.' "[3] By late afternoon police had been called in to investigate both the fracas enveloping the gallery and the exhibition itself. Upon completing their inspection, the police superintendent requested that the Oxleys, the owners of the gallery, "suspend the exhibition 'to allow inquiries of legality of photos.' "[4] Henson and the Oxleys agreed.[5]

The following day, the media and political heavyweights entered the fray. NSW state Liberal Party leader Barry O'Farrell declared that the "sexualisation of children under the guise of art is totally unacceptable."[6] Hetty Johnston, founder of the Bravehearts foundation for sexually abused children, and one of the most high-profile Australian child-protection advocates, was calling for Henson's arrest. "The police should prosecute and the last time I checked it was a crime to photograph children sexually. . . . There is a classification of porn and this falls under it."[7] NSW premier and state Labor Party leader Morris Iemma, who at the time was traveling on government business in China, was quick to prepare a statement for the media. Revealing the depth of the emotional dimensions of the scandal, he unequivocally denounced the images:

> As a father of four I find it offensive and disgusting. . . . I don't understand why parents would agree to allow their kids to be photographed like this. The cornerstone of any civilised society is the protection of its kids and there can be no justification for some of these images. I'm all for free speech, but never at the expense of a child's safety and innocence.[8]

Then came Prime Minister Kevin Rudd's now legendary "gut reaction." It was a reaction that was to rebound across news syndicates globally. Rudd was appearing on Channel Nine's *Today* show the morning after the opening had been shut down. He had apparently not yet seen any of the controversial photos. *Today*'s presenter, Karl Stefanovic, displayed in quick slideshow succession five images of the girl identified only as "N," whose nude photograph graced the front cover of the exhibition invitation. Black bars veiled N's nipples and genital area, and below the slideshow was a news subtitle reading "Outrage over Child-Porn Art." Asked about what he thought of the images, Rudd said without hesitation, "I find them absolutely revolting. Kids deserve to have the innocence of their childhood protected. I have a very deep view of this. And, you know, for God's sake, let's just allow kids to be kids."[9] Several hours after Rudd's television appearance, about twenty police, armed with a warrant, seized up to twenty-one of the Henson photographs. Alan Sicard of the NSW police announced in a statement to the media that it "is likely that we will proceed to prosecution on the offense of publishing an indecent article under the Crimes Act."[10]

So began what journalist David Marr describes in his book on the case as "the biggest story in the country"[11] that year—a veritable moral, or sex, panic. Literally hundreds and hundreds of reports of the unfolding scandal were to be aired and published in Australia, and around the world, in the weeks and months that followed. What draws us to the Henson story? What makes it so controversial? I suspect that it is not all quite as it seems. Psychoanalytic theorist Tim Dean suggests that a "topic's volatility indicates its proximity to something psychically fundamental, something that gets to the heart of the matter."[12] Yet this is a heart, Dean is suggesting, that is fundamentally shrouded or misrecognized or defended against. The volatility of the Henson scandal was *ostensibly* about the sexualization and exploitation of childhood innocence and the unsettling emotions such treatment elicits. A great deal has already been said about this dimension of the controversy. This chapter is about what has been much less discussed, even tactically concealed (in the Foucauldian sense), in the way the scandal unfolded. My hypothesis is that what has been veiled, misrecognized, and avoided by the language of fear and anxiety is the question of child sexuality and agency, and this circumvention is as central, if not more so, to the issue's explosiveness as the widely announced accusations of sexualization, exploitation, and loss of innocence. I begin with this recent scandal because I think it has something to teach us about anglophone child sex panics of the last fifty years generally.

Shame and the Child Nude

"It's a tabloid page one of genius," declares Marr—"the heavy-set coppers heading up the stairs; N's fragile face turned away in shame."[13] Marr is here describing the front-page image in the *Daily Telegraph* newspaper of the police raid of the Henson exhibition. It featured an image of two policemen entering the Rosyln Oxley9 Gallery with the huge bold headline "CHILD PORN 'ART' RAID." At the bottom-right corner of the image, and underneath the exhibition title *Bill Henson*, is a small superimposed *Brady Bunch*–like headshot of N from the (bare) shoulders up. Taken from one of the full-body photographs from the exhibition, N is looking downward as much as to intimate that she is witnessing the furor but looking away embarrassed. Evocative of childhood vulnerability, the image of N's self-conscious pose was bound to inflame passions, Marr is suggesting. Inflame it did. Conservative journalist Andrew Bolt excoriated the art world, claiming shame "is dead in the arts." Only shamelessness persists, he said. "Henson should have been made long ago to feel too ashamed to show his face, let alone his pictures."[14] Hetty Johnston was equally enraged. "We are just handing our children on a bloody plate to paedophiles," she spat. "This is a disgrace for this country, absolutely shameful."[15] The distribution of the image on the internet was itself enough, numerous critics argued, to encourage and normalize pedophilia, and thus potentially lead to abuse of children. Celebrity radio announcer Derryn Hinch was among such vocal opposition, and he was outraged that the photos might be "drooled over by paedophiles."[16] Clive Hamilton, former Australia Institute executive director and sponsor of the *Corporate Paedophilia* and *Let Children Be Children* reports that helped galvanize the anti-child-sexualization-in-the-media movement, also echoed this fear of pedophilic desire, albeit in a more measured tone. Citing the testimony of criminologist Bill Glaser, Hamilton hit a notion of caution: "That paedophiles not only find stimulation in media images of eroticised children but take them as a justification for their own predatory urges inescapably casts a darkness over the Henson photographs."[17]

Henson responded rather cynically to these concerns about pedophilic titillation: "There'd be someone wanking over a shoe catalogue. There'd be someone wanking over choirboys. . . . There will be someone wanking over the Kmart catalogue."[18] In other words, images don't need to have nudity or any apparent sexual context for them to be incorporated into somebody's sexual fantasies. With this comment Henson is well aware of the mobility, pliability, and polymorphousness of sexual desire and fantasy, as well as what James Kincaid has famously described as Western culture's propensity to eroticize representations of childhood innocence.[19] However, inciting the desire of pedophiles was far from the only problem. For one thing, the extent to which the images themselves sexualized this so-called innocence of childhood was at the center of the issue of legality. Police were investigating the possibility of the images breaching child pornography and indecency laws, as Hetty Johnston had been arguing. Under the New South Wales Crimes Act 1900, child pornography at the time was defined as "depictions or descriptions of a child [under the age of sixteen] 'engaged in sexual activity' or 'in a sexual context'" in a manner that would cause offense to reasonable persons.[20]

After their investigations and in spite of Johnston's protestations, the NSW police ultimately decided not to lay charges against Henson or the gallery. This came as a result of advice from the Office of the Director of Public Prosecutions (DPP) and the national Classification Board. The board concluded that the image in question was "mild and justified by context . . . and . . . not sexualised to any degree."[21] Regarding the lesser charge of "publishing an indecent article," the DPP also expressed doubts about grounds for prosecution. "In my view," announced the director of the DPP, "mere nudity is not indecent in the legal sense. In the photographs under consideration, there is no quality in the poses, facial expressions, positioning or context that could reasonably be regarded as rendering them indecent."[22] Even some of those who argued the images should be censored (with the exception of Hetty Johnston) were not necessarily willing to claim that an image of an adolescent nude is automatically a sexual one. This was the claim of the DPP:

> Mere nudity is not sufficient to create a "sexual context." The context is the subject taken with what surrounds it and interacts with it. There is nothing in the photographs of the girl and her surroundings, in my view, that could be fairly described as providing a sexual context to her image.[23]

Many commentators, Clive Hamilton among them, reiterated this view. "Although not sexual images, they can be seen," wrote Hamilton, "as a commentary on the slow, halting and unsettling metamorphosis of child's body into an adult one."[24] Alison Groggon's letter of support signed by forty-three representatives of the prime minister's Australia 2020 Summit implied much of the same: "Henson's work shows the delicacy of the transition from childhood to adulthood, its troubledness and its beauty."[25] However, it was precisely on this point of depicting the supposedly "unsettling metamorphosis" of the adolescent body that struck such a resounding emotional chord with the public. This was, of course, just what Henson was seeking to capture. Asked why nude young people are a theme in his work, he replied that they are "the most effective vehicle for expressing ideas about humanity and vulnerability and our sense of ourselves living inside our bodies."[26]

Henson's comments only fueled the ire of his opponents, whose claims about child exploitation were themselves based squarely on notions of the vulnerability of children. Even so-called normal adults were apparently at risk of being complicit unwittingly in exploiting and harming vulnerable children merely by viewing the images. "Teenage children are developmentally fragile," argued Steve Biddulph, a psychologist with a high profile in Australian media. "They try on any number of selves, and have to be free to do so, without adult predation on their bodies and minds. What might seem cool and exciting one day to a teenager, they would regard with horror and embarrassment on another day and at another time."[27] Family psychologist Janet Hall pronounced similarly. Nude pictures "provoke judgement and possible humiliation," she said.[28] The standard refrain of anti-Henson and child-protectionist commentary was that the naked models have had their privacy taken from them, and thus also, according to this argument, their innocence. Said NSW opposition leader O'Farrell, "It is definitely not OK for naked children to have their privacy and their childhood stolen in the name of art."[29] Writing for the *Newcastle Herald*, Joanne McCarthy also raised the issue of privacy. "This debate shouldn't be about art alone but about the rights of children to be children, in private, in the buff sometimes as so many of them choose, doing inappropriate things, but safe and respected."[30] Or to quote Biddulph once more: "Photographing teenage children naked and exposed, while it could be innocent and beautiful in a different kind of world, takes their power away and their privacy away and lets the world in."[31]

Concerns about vulnerability and privacy were less about images of child nudes per se, than about the adult gaze—pedophilic or otherwise—witnessing the exposure of the nude child. A principal worry is that the repeated circulation and public display of the images might come back to bite unsuspecting and unaware children, resulting in future embarrassment, shame, and trauma. The presumption being made is that N is not of sufficient emotional and intellectual capacity yet to appreciate the fact that she has participated in an inappropriate form of social self-revelation that someday she might come to regret. N is assumed to have acted, in other words, as any "innocent" child might, *without* sufficient adult capacity for shame when it comes to public nudity. Not unlike a child parading with her clothes off on her family's home movies, she has innocently and *shamelessly* bared all in front of a much more invasive camera—or so the logic of these claims would suggest.

Other commentators, notably pro-Henson, worried that the fracas over whether the images are art or pornography might itself inadvertently shame the nude body of N, and other young bodies by association. Melbourne ethicist Leslie Cannold asked rhetorically: "Can we allow adolescents to feel proud of their bodies and sexuality, or will we—by condemning as pornographic the photographing of such bodies—forever insist on shame?"[32] The piece also concluded with a declaration to N aimed at redirecting the shame implicit in the anti-Henson position: "You are beautiful, darling. Be proud. Years from now you'll be admired. . . . Find it in your heart to forgive adults. It is we, not you, who are in the wrong."[33] Journalist for the *Herald Sun* Andrea Burns reiterated Cannold's view. "There is plenty of time to feel ashamed of the human body in adulthood," Burns stated. "Telling these children that their forms are offensive, dangerous and fodder for pedophiles is the sickness."[34] A number of letters to editors supported this view. Said one reader: "Anyone who has seen Bill Henson's work knows these images are poetic and in no way pornographic. Young people should be proud of their bodies, not ashamed of them."[35] Scores of pro-Henson media pundits seemed to concur with the tenor of these statements, which is evident in vociferous affirmations of the artistic merit and beauty of the photographs and the bodies photographed. As Terry Lane proclaimed in Melbourne's *The Age* newspaper: "Henson's work is chilly and austere. His pictures have a wintry, misty beauty that is the antithesis of pornography."[36]

Some attempted to counter this implicit shaming of children's bodies by situating Henson's work within a tradition of Western religious art history known for its nude images of children. "What, then, does [Prime Minister] Rudd make of the portraits of naked children created in the name of the Christian faith he espouses?" asked Christopher Kremmer rhetorically.[37] Drawing from Leo Steinberg's book *The Sexuality of Christ in Renaissance Art and in Modern Oblivion*, Kremmer highlights the historical association in Christianity of shame and nakedness via the story of Adam and Eve. He then makes an implicit comparison with the image of N: "'We may say that Michelangelo's naked Christ . . . [is] like the naked Christ child, not shameful, but literally and profoundly shameless.'"[38] Many agreed with this interpretation of Henson's main image as a representation of childhood innocence, vulnerability, and shamelessness.[39] "Henson's latest exhibition gave us the human condition poised between prelapsarian innocence and intimations of knowledge. His images were breathtakingly beautiful and without shame," commented one letter.[40] Just days after the story broke of the police seizure of Henson's works, a piece on the Australian website New Matilda poignantly broached the issue of shame. It was entitled "On Purity and Shame," and it was written anonymously by a man who declared that as a fourteen-year-old boy he had been abused by a male doctor. It was written as a response to the tactics and arguments of Hetty Johnston. "Hetty Johnston . . . was on TV tonight," began the article.

> She said that the one in five people who have been abused as a child were angry at the Bill Henson exhibition.
> I am one such person for whom she claims to speak. I was abused, but I am not angry at Bill Henson. I am saddened by those who would shut him up. . . .
> The message now being sent loud and clear during the controversy over Bill Henson's art is that their bodies are pornographic.

The author goes on to describe his experiences of abuse and the adolescent shame about his body that prevented him from telling his parents what the doctor had done to him. "Even now I cannot give voice to what led me to being so protective of my mother, to shield her from my body. For that is what I was doing. But now a lapsed Catholic, I know that a lot of it had to do with shame." And in the final sentence he declares, "I see no shame in Bill Henson's work."[41]

Shame as the Child Nude

The trope of shame everywhere saturated the public debate about the Henson images. Yet what seems to have united rather than divided pro- and anti-Henson commentary is a commitment to locating shame anywhere but with N in particular and nude children in general. Both sides register concern about the potentially debilitating effects of shame heaped onto N and vulnerable children, no matter what the source. Both agree that the sexualization of children—not to mention child pornography—is shameful and wrong, even if they differ as to what constitutes a sexual image and what constitutes the meaning and evidence of sexualization. Instead, it is with adults that the shame resides: shame for participating in N's sexualization, or shame for casting her image as pornographic, or shame for intruding on her private world.

I'd like to reorient this discussion of shame in order to bring more clearly into view an important dimension that seems to have been overlooked or uninterrogated—indeed, *shamed*—in and by the debate. Contrary to those who see no shame in the Henson image of N, I suggest that the photograph itself might instead be read as a quintessential representation of shame, and it is this that points in the direction of what is so troubling for many critics. David Marr perhaps unwittingly gestured at this, when he described in the front-page *Daily Telegraph* image "N's fragile face turned away in shame."[42] Marr does not elaborate on this comment. However, presumably he is referring to a sense of vulnerability and embarrassment about being at the center of a scandal that is evoked by her own visual depiction. That is, the representation of shame is symbolic of N's imaginary reaction to the social uproar about the exposure of her nude body. But I want to suggest that one of the things that might be so disquieting about the Henson depiction is precisely its *portrayal* of shame. It is not that Henson has exploited childhood and robbed it of its innocence. Rather, it is that he has captured an image that so resoundingly resonates with cultural narratives about the oft-referred loss or shattering of childhood innocence.

Although some critics referred to the connotations of shame associated with nakedness in the Christian tradition, none spoke of the representation of shame in the portrayal itself. This is not at all surprising given the almost uniform desire of most of the adult commentators, both pro- and anti-Henson, to recuperate the innocence (or at least vulnerability and nonculpability) of N and protect her from unnecessary scrutiny. However, the main image that so outraged Hetty Johnston, Rudd, and many others strikingly resonates with one of the most iconic Western images of shame. I am referring to Peter Paul Rubens's *Adam and Eve*, of the infamous couple. Like Eve, N's eyes are downcast and her genitals covered.[43] Unlike Kremmer, however, I see the Henson photograph as a characteristic expression of shame consciousness. To quote psychologist of affect Silvan Tomkins, shame is "literally an ambivalent turning of the eyes away from the object toward the face, toward the self."[44] Even the flushed, rosy cheeks of N perhaps might further evoke a sense of shyness, self-consciousness, or embarrassment.[45]

Of course, Eve's shame is made possible not by innocence, but by its loss or absence. She has eaten from the tree of knowledge and is aware that she is naked. She is catapulted into shame and must cover herself from the gaze of the other. Like the story of Adam and Eve, then, what the image of N indexes, I suggest, is the inevitable coming into being of a particular kind of shame consciousness or self-consciousness of the sexual body. I am not suggesting that N is ashamed in the photograph, only that it is an image of self-awareness intricately entangled with the knowledge of one's nakedness, the social strictures around the presentation of nude bodies, and an internalized understanding of privacy with regard to one's genitals. Tomkins and many other affect theorists consider the face to be a central site of affect and medium of affect transmission. "The face, particularly the eyes and muscles around them," he notes, "are the most important organs of expression and communication of affect."[46] Moreover, affect is notoriously contagious, as Tomkins emphasizes,[47] and this uneasiness about the display of adolescent affect has clearly reverberated with many audiences. With this idea in mind, perhaps it is not so much (or at least not only) the nudity of the Henson photograph of N by itself that so scandalized, but the facial display of adolescent self-consciousness, shyness, or shame consciousness in the context of nudity.[48]

Pivotal to the much-remarked issue of Henson capturing a moment in N's transition from childhood to adulthood is puberty. What makes N's image so powerful—and problematic for many, it would seem—is that this representation of shame consciousness is contextualized in relation to the budding pubertal body. Sally Munt suggests that shame "performs culturally to mark out certain groups."[49] When it comes to sexuality in particular, adolescents are prominent among these groups. Puberty, like nudity, has a palpable connection to shame in dominant cultural narratives and many experiences of adolescent development. Indeed, especially (although not only) for girls, puberty is often overdetermined with shame. Menstruation, breast development, and sexual objectification by others are often the source of shyness, embarrassment, vulnerability, and a newly emerging self-consciousness about their internally *sexualizing*, not just culturally sexualized, bodies.[50] Also like nudity, puberty is a metonym for sexuality. Puberty is discursively and experientially linked for many of us to the formation and consolidation of self-conscious sexual orientations. It is a time when young people usually first come to see themselves as even having a sexuality, sexual identity, or private sexual self.[51]

At its most basic, shame, as Donald Nathanson notes, is the result of an "exposure of something that we would have preferred kept hidden, of a private part of the self."[52] Nathanson reminds us, moreover, that there "is perhaps no aspect of adult life as securely linked to shame . . . as our relation to sex."[53] This is because shame is delicately woven with the positive affects and emotions most primarily constitutive of sexuality: interest-excitement and enjoyment-joy.[54] As Tomkins himself points out, shame "operates ordinarily only after interest or enjoyment has been activated," and is the result of the "incomplete reduction" of these affects.[55] Coupled with a naked pubescent body, therefore, it would likely be difficult in anglophone societies for the self-conscious, shame-like pose of N not to be evocative at some level of blossoming child sexuality, about which most anglophone societies are extremely taciturn. That is, N's expression of shyness or shame points to a sexualizing interiority and self-awareness of sexuality.

Drawing on Norbert Elias's account of shame in the civilizing process, Janice Irvine notes that shame has been "historically bound up with sex"; indeed, toward the end of the eighteenth century, shame became a mechanism for regulating sexuality.[56] To quote Elias, the "feeling of shame surrounding human sexual relations has changed and become noticeably stronger in the civilizing process."[57] Therefore, just as shame affect inhibits an individual's ongoing expression of sexual interest, so too do social scripts of shame regulate the appropriate norms of (sexual) expression and interaction. This is especially apparent in the almost universal socialization of children's sexual behavior and the taboos surrounding depictions of sexually developed (or developing) nude bodies. According to Elias, in modernity shame has exerted and extended its power at the same time our cultural awareness of it has diminished.

Precisely by referencing a shame-infused and naked pubertal child—the so-called loss or shattering of childhood—Henson is raising the specter of the child sexuality that ghosts, and indeed constitutes, the nascent sexual self.[58] This apparent shattering and loss are not therefore the effect of the adult gaze, the invasion of privacy, or the public circulation of the nude pictures. Rather, childhood and "innocence" are *transformed* by the subject's awareness of the embodied unfoldings of puberty intra-acting with an apprehension of cultural taboos around nudity and sexuality.[59] This is the assimilation of the knowledge and embodied experience that in Western cultures sexuality and nudity are tightly braided with privacy, interiority, and shame. Henson is inviting us to conjure the private world of nascent child sexuality and subjectivity. But shame and sexuality form a particularly potent and high-risk coupling in child-protection and sexual-abuse discourses, especially given the fact that, in Western societies, sex, as Michel Foucault reminds us, is "that secret which seems to underlie all that we are."[60] It is thus perhaps the bringing together of shame and sexuality so overtly within the same frame that has prompted both pro- and anti-Henson camps to describe the depictions as "unsettling," "haunting," "disturbing," and "confronting"—not to mention "revolting" and "disgusting."

Interestingly, many of these affective reactions to the Henson photographs resemble Freud's description of some of the effects of the uncanny. For Freud, the uncanny refers to "certain things which lie within the field of what is frightening," although fear does not exhaust the range of possible uncanny feelings; included also in this realm are feelings of repulsion, distress, dread, and horror.[61] Just as shame is often the result of an "exposure of something that we would have preferred kept hidden, of a private part of the self,"[62] so is the uncanny the effect of what "*ought to have remained . . . secret and hidden but has come to light.*"[63] The signifier of childhood sexuality is that which many believe Henson ought to have kept hidden, and whose exposure via the imaging of pubertal shame has perhaps prompted for many adult viewers forms of uncanny experience. Henson's image has dredged up some extremely disturbing feelings or ideas about the sexual child that some adults would prefer to have kept buried.[64]

A sense of uncanniness, according to Freud, can manifest in a wide range of situations: the unexpected intermingling of something at once familiar and unfamiliar; eerie coincidences; fears of losing one's body parts; the sight of madness or uncontrollable fits; a sense of helplessness; unintended repetition of the same situation; the appearance of ghosts; a feeling of magical powers or suspicion of someone else having them; and the phenomenon of liminality, such as an inanimate object becoming animate, a doll coming to life, or something turning into its opposite.[65] "The uncanny," says Freud, "is that class of the frightening which leads back to what is known of old and long familiar."[66] Why might such an image of the sexual child be so disturbing for some? At the most general level, witnessing the shame of another, especially when this is a public exposure, can, as Carl Schneider reminds us, inflame shame in us.[67] The reasons for this are many, but among them are the dynamics of identification, empathy, and facial affect transmission.[68]

For some, the Henson image might "lead back" to their own experience of blossoming sexuality about which they recall both excitement and shame. For others, the daring of N may trigger reminders of their own audacious sexual desires and omnipotent sexual thoughts and intentions that they have now renounced as naivety or even repressed through shame. An example here might be Steve Biddulph's certainty about impending shame for exhibitionistic teens ("What might seem cool and exciting one day to a teenager, they would regard with horror and embarrassment on another day and at another time"[69]). This apparent certainty may be derived from his own proximity to experiences of teenage exhibitionism or omnipotent thinking (his own or his children) about which he is now, or once was, embarrassed or ashamed. Or it might be derived from the norms of the master discourse of child sexual abuse that have rendered unspeakably shameful any notion of childhood sexuality in adult contexts. Or there are those, such as the politicians Rudd and Iemma, for whom the images may trace back to their own shameful proximity to—and thus interest in—that which disgusts them. Oftentimes revulsion and disgust indicate that, as Tomkins puts it, "one permitted the offending object into the closeness of taste and *then* rejected it."[70] This might also be compatible with Germaine Greer's

Freudian-inspired reading of Rudd's response: "Any man who calls Henson's pictures 'revolting' protests too much," she chided.[71] Alternatively, it might mean something else and different for each of them. And there is the class of contemptuous critic, such as Hetty Johnston, whose uncanny experience may be a reminder of her sense of shameful failure at preventing her daughter from being sexually abused.[72]

Then there are those experiences of uncanniness that are not immediately or necessarily associated with shame. Liminality and ghostliness are among these. One of the most widely discussed features of the Henson photograph is the capturing of N at the threshold, or liminal point, between childhood and adulthood. Indeed, this aspect of the image of nascent adolescence was described repeatedly as "haunting."[73] Transforming into her opposite, the adult, N's birth into the world of adulthood is haunted by the death or dying of (her) childhood. Overlaying this representation of liminality might also, for some, be fears or associations of the child falling from the grace of childhood innocence into the shameful world of adult sexuality that all too often exacts abuse on young people. From this to notions of the "bad seed," the seductive or overly sexualized child, or the masturbating child is anything but a very small leap, as the history of modern Western sexuality has made amply clear. Such fantasies might themselves prompt uncanny feelings, in somewhat similar fashion to when a person is suspected of having evil intentions or hidden motives out of sync with his or her social identity. I recall an experience of uncanniness as a teenager at a dinner party of friends of my parents when I was confronted with an eight-year-old girl confiding in me and recounting in great detail, and with great delight, her sexual exploits with a thirty-year-old man. "He sticks his udder into my udder," she said with a smile. The intermingling of childhood and adulthood in the realm of sexuality struck me as intensely disconcerting. For me this was perhaps "a crisis of the proper," to use Nicholas Royle's words for the disturbance at the heart of certain forms of the uncanny.[74] I thought I "knew" this female child as a Child, with all its Western connotations of innocence. Yet, in the course of our secret conversation, this certainty was completely unsettled, as was my own sense of self as an adolescent. I distinctly remember fearing this child and feeling ashamed at being privy to her inner world. Parents themselves, as Joanne Faulkner argues, also (and not occasionally) experience feelings of helplessness, anxiety, and loss of control in the face of the strivings of their adolescent child for autonomy, sexuality, and independence. What this reflects in the uproar over the Henson case, she suggests, is less adult disquiet about children's vulnerability than adults' *own* unsettling vulnerabilities:

For parents, for whom, especially, the transition from childhood to adolescence is too swift and who often feel ill-equipped for the challenges of adolescence, Henson's images evoke the myriad feelings we have for our children. . . . Teenage desire—and our inability to control it—heightens adults' sense of vulnerability and helplessness, and signals a loss of the sweet refuge from worry and work that childhood innocence is supposed to represent.[75]

What these examples also highlight is the cultural and epistemological dimension of the uncanny. Like shame, uncanniness is never simply an intrapsychic phenomenon; it is inextricably an interpersonal and cultural affair. Allan Lloyd Smith has written of the uncanny in broader cultural terms, arguing that it can issue from "unresolved contradictions, unadmitted fears and desires, and incompatible assertions of . . . culture."[76] When these hidden or repressed or taboo cultural meanings emerge, they can prompt crises of meaning and uncanny disturbances. Only several decades ago, ideas of precocious, seductive, and erotic children were commonplace, particularly in relation to adults. With the advent of the feminist anti–child sexual abuse movement, however, this representation of children has been discredited (as we will see in chapter 3). Any hint or suggestion of the precocious sexual child is often greeted in contemporary discourse with intense shame and horror. The scandal surrounding the Henson images is, at the very least, reflective of a cultural crisis of meaning vis-à-vis normative childhood and the place of sexuality within it.

Shaming the Sexual Child

The revelation of child sexuality is so troubling that it is scarcely articulable in the current climate of pedophilia and child sexual abuse panic. Indeed, commenting on the Henson scandal, Kylie Valentine noted that "there has been very little discussion about adolescent sexuality."[77] *Sydney Morning Herald* journalist Paul Sheehan went even further to claim that "hysteria and opportunism engulfed both Henson and the entire issue of pubescent sexuality."[78] Certainly many commentators mentioned the pubertal body of N, with some noting the image's registration of pubescent sexual awakening. Many others also established metonymic connections to the sexual child with descriptions of N's state of biological in-betweenness. However, for the most part it was left at that; or else the sexual impulses, desires, motives and intentions of the so-called sexually awakened adolescent were themselves rewritten as innocent: infantile, immature, protosexual, and *un*adult-like. Direct discussion of childhood sexuality was displaced and avoided. Debate instead was framed overwhelmingly around the following questions and sets of issues: Are the images art or pornography, and what is the line dividing the two? Are the "child" models sexualized? Do the images exploit childhood innocence? Is it possible for child models to consent to being photographed nude? And does the circulation of the images cause harm to the young people photographed? It has therefore largely been the figure of the *sexualized* rather than sexual child, swathed in emotive language of fear, loathing and loss, that has dominated public discussion. In Marr's summary of the suite of issues dominating the public debate, nowhere is adolescent sexuality mentioned:

> From coast to coast, papers were full of letters asserting the *real* issues at stake here: the truth of art; the lies of pornography; the armour of innocence; the fate of the model; the dereliction of her parents; the appetites of paedophiles; the duty of artists to live within the law; the obligation of art to confront; lines crossed and boundaries pushed; privacy; beauty; the perils of the internet; the dangers of advertising; the United Nations Convention on the Rights of the Child; Australia as an international laughing stock; Australia as the beacon of the world; society can't live without risk; any risk to children is unacceptable.[79]

Why has there been such a dearth of discussion around the question of child and adolescent sexuality? How can we be so glaringly confronted with an image redolent of nascent adolescent puberty and sexuality, or at very least sexual development, yet busy ourselves talking only about all these other adult preoccupations? If there had been any substantive degree of attention to issues of child and adolescent sexuality, we might be forgiven for thinking that in anglophone cultures the subject is less consequential or fraught than the apparently more critical issue of child exploitation by adults. However, this is clearly anything but the case. Even according to those few commentators who had serious reservations about the Henson representations but were nonetheless willing to broach the issue of child sexuality, the implied consensus seemed to be that adults should not be voyeuristically scrutinizing the emerging sexualities of young people, let alone talking and writing about them. Lindy Allen, chief executive of Regional Arts Victoria, asks: "Whose province is it to explore pre-teen sexuality?"

> Is it the province of people who are well into their middle-age to explore that or is that, given that [it] is really 40 years ago that Bill was at that age, is that something that is the province of teenagers themselves to explore, and shouldn't we leave them alone and let them get on with it?[80]

Paul Sheehan echoed these arguments against the sexual objectification of children for adult use, remarking rather cynically, "If you mine the terrain of adolescent sensual awakening for commercial gain, if you spend years living on the artistic edge while gaining public attention and financial reward, don't complain when your actions begin to carry the taint of exploitative voyeurism."[81] Or, as Michael Coulter pronounced in response to Henson's own claims that there has been a hysterical reaction to the photos, "It is not puritanism and 'pandemic fear' (his words) to ask: is there a moral issue with photos taken for adults that dwell so intently on the sexual awakening of children?"[82] Like Lindy Allen's, this question is rhetorical, and Coulter has already decided it is morally highly problematical. The underlying assumption of the anti-Henson and child-protection camp is that adults ought to avert their gaze because, as Coulter puts it, "images of nude girls might normalise the idea of children as sexual objects."[83] At most it seems we can only barely allude to the question of child sexuality. Interestingly, this call to avert the gaze mimics the very movement of shame itself.

But is objectification, and the harm thought to result from it, all that we are really trying to screen children, and ourselves, from? We have heard a great deal about children as sexual objects. But if we are to accept the consensus among commentators that the sexual objectification of children is wrong, then the "sexual awakening of children" being cited and simultaneously skirted in the public debate refers not to children as sexual objects, but indeed to children as sexual subjects. N's subjectivity was eclipsed entirely in the public debate, and she was stereotyped as the sexually awakening, vulnerable pubescent. Routinely reduced to the undifferentiated category of Child, she was robbed of any subjective complexity and became a screen for innumerable adult projections. According to the *Report of the APA Task Force on the Sexualization of Girls*, "A person is sexually objectified" when "made into a thing for others' sexual use, rather than seen as a person with the capacity for independent action and decision making."[84] If we are to accept this widely held understanding, it is difficult to avoid the conclusion that N was objectified by the very terms of the public debate and her representation in it. Even the DPP's conclusion unwittingly partook of N's objectification, or what Ann Cahill more usefully describes as "derivatization." This is a practice of "ontological reductionism" that fails to appreciate individual specificity and reduces someone "to the being of another."[85] In the case of N, she was reduced to the being of generic Child. When the DPP declared that there was "nothing in the photographs of the girl and her surroundings . . . that could be fairly described as providing a sexual context to her image"—where this context is "the subject taken with what surrounds it and interacts with it"—effectively they elided the sexual subjectivity of N and her role in cocreating the image. N was not consulted as part of these deliberations. She was merely pronounced upon. Her sexuality, or "sexual awakening," was appropriated by law enforcement officials and adult commentators for the purposes of advancing certain arguments about law, morality, art, pornography, sexualization, and childhood, and for advancing arguments about N herself (and every other thirteen-year-old, by implication), with no knowledge or experience of her as a unique person. Even much of the pro-Henson support misfired and (perhaps intentionally) dodged the thorny question of adolescent subjectivity. It did this by staking its defense of Henson on his artistic reputation, his artistic integrity, and the fact that the parents consented to the shoot.[86]

The figure of the child as a sexual subject, even sometimes a *resilient* one, is, I argue, the elephant in the corner (or center?) of the Henson scandal—and anglophone culture generally. To be sure, the master discourses of child protection and childhood innocence militate against its appearance. But by raising the specter of this ghostly subject—the child who volunteered to be photographed nude, agreed to have images of herself publicly exhibited, and may have the resilience and wherewithal to do so competently—Henson placed pressure on our cherished constructs of childhood innocence and infantilized subjectivity and agency.[87] I have a hunch that the Henson sex panic is as much—perhaps even more—about the discomfiting effects elicited in the face of this child sexual subject as it is about concerns over adults sexualizing and objectifying nude teens. So when Paul Sheehan and others lament that hysteria engulfed the entire issue of adolescent sexuality, I suggest this is precisely one of the strategies, in the Foucauldian sense, of the sex panic response.[88] For example, it is not necessarily the case that anti-Henson campaigners, such as Hetty Johnston, *intend* to deny and conceal the issue of adolescent sexuality. They may intend to counter the sexual objectification of children. However, the nonsubjective consequences of their interventions are that adolescent sexuality is eclipsed. As Foucault himself said, "People know what they do; they frequently know why they do what they do; but what they don't know is what they do does."[89]

The so-called hysteria is therefore performative. It serves not just to express adult anxieties and fears about the exploitation of children. Among other defensive strategies—whether intentional or unwitting—are the deflection of attention and diversion of the adult gaze from not just the figure of the child as sexual object, but from her as sexual *subject*.[90] Indeed, the former requires the latter. Observing the paucity of discussion of child and adolescent sexuality in the scandal, Kylie Valentine also noted the scant attention given to "the *agency* of children and young people in negotiating both sexuality and representation."[91] Again, I don't think this is incidental or accidental. The inattention to subjectivity and agency smacks of avoidance at best, denial at worst. And I think it gets at the heart of the matter, the heart of some of the powerful yet barely spoken adult investments in placing child sexuality under erasure.

Comments made by Hetty Johnston under attack perhaps offer a glimpse of this. Johnston has fiercely and repeatedly rebuked N's parents for allowing her to be photographed nude, claiming that it will scar her for life. Meanwhile, in her own child-abuse crusading, Johnston has for many years been publicly exposing the fact her daughter was abused by Johnston's father-in-law when she was seven. Marr recounts an incident when Johnston was pressed to defend the hypocrisy of her invasion of her own daughter's privacy by public exposure: "It's a very different scenario," she snapped. Johnston said her daughter was not "being exploited for commercial purposes," and that "she didn't strip off naked."[92] This last comment reeks of a backhanded Freudian swipe at N herself. Although perhaps an extreme example, there are, I submit, only several degrees of separation from Johnston's remarks to those of child psychologists such as Biddulph and numerous other media commentators cited earlier. Biddulph seems to be rather certain—and here he is directly addressing the issue of N posing nude—that teenage behavior considered "cool and exciting one day . . . they *would* regard with horror and embarrassment on another day."[93] Similarly, recall that journalist Joanne McCarthy declared that the "debate shouldn't be about art alone but about the rights of children to be children, in private, in the buff sometimes as so many of them choose, doing *inappropriate* things, but safe and respected."[94] The obvious inference is that N's nude modeling is one such example of inappropriate behavior. Either way, and whether or not consciously intentional, N's behavior is explicitly being placed under negative scrutiny, even if it is couched within a notion of childhood innocence. Such comments hover dangerously close to, if they are not already irrevocably entangled with, the suggestion that N ought someday to be ashamed of having posed nude, or she ought to be some day ashamed of thinking she knew what she was doing at age twelve or thirteen.

Herein lies one of the major bugbears of this scandal—and others that preoccupy this book—as I see it: What are we to do with the fact that the child sexual subject is not the passive recipient of the adult gaze or adult sexuality or adult sexual frameworks? Often he or she looks back, speaks back, touches back, and indeed initiates and colludes with adults, not to mention often strips for them or has sex with them voluntarily (with or without parental consent, with or without "informed" consent).[95] The emotive debate over whether or not twelve- or thirteen-year-olds are capable of making informed decisions to pose nude only deflects attention from this fact: irrespective of legal notions of consent, young people will participate voluntarily in representing and performing their sexual selves. Henson's work directly raises the phenomenon of an agentive teenage subjectivity that no amount of pontificating can ever fully know, control, or contain within the tropes of (childhood) innocence and (adult) exploitation.[96] Aside from trying to squeeze children into the catchalls of innocence and vulnerability, however, as a culture we don't seem to know what to do with the diversity of their autonomous, ebullient, resistant, and often dissident and sometimes competent and resilient sexual subjectivities. We seem to avoid, infantilize, homogenize, marginalize, trivialize, or ignore them, all in the process of circumscribing and regulating—ostensibly protecting—them. Only one child is legitimized (enforced) in these scenarios, and it is the innocent and vulnerable child. Not too far are we removed here from mid-twentieth-century characterizations of youth transgressive of narrow norms of childhood as delinquents—only today, delinquency is dressed up in the language of victimology. Wayward children are victims of poverty, upbringing, exploitation, abuse, sexualization, environmentally induced early puberty, pornography, and so on. Missing is a discourse on diversity, difference, and multiple (actual and possible) childhoods.

"We can also speak of a living person as uncanny," says Freud.[97] I propose that the agentive sexual child is just such an uncanny person that haunts many adults and challenges conventional epistemologies in contemporary anglophone societies. How we repeatedly turn away from a meaningful encounter with the uncanny sexual child when he or she makes so palpable an appearance is the subject of the chapters that follow.

TWO

Premarital Sex

National statistics tell part of the story. Venereal diseases among teenagers: over 80,000 cases reported in 1966. . . . Unwed teen-age mothers: about 90,000 a year, an increase of 100 percent in two decades. One out of every three brides under 20 goes to the altar pregnant. . . . Illegal abortions performed on adolescents run into the hundreds of thousands. One of the findings that decided New City's New Lincoln School to adopt sex education was a poll of its 11th-graders on their attitudes toward premarital intercourse: The majority saw nothing wrong with it. . . . Newspaper reports of dropouts and runaways, of drug-taking, sexual precocity and general delinquency intensify the worries of parents.

—John Kobler, "Sex Invades the Schoolhouse," *Saturday Evening Post*, 1968[1]

In the 1960s, a moral/sex panic erupted across the United States, Australia, and the United Kingdom around the issue of an apparent rapid rise in rates of premarital sex, promiscuity, illegitimate births, and venereal disease (or VD) among young people and adolescents. The widely publicized Schofield report, *The Sexual Behaviour of Young People*, noted that, within just four months between 1961 and 1962 in the United Kingdom alone, a minimum of 441 articles were published on aspects of adolescent sex.[2] A majority of these were condemnatory, in part or full, of sexual activities of teenagers. Notwithstanding the circulation of a range of moral or ethical positions at the time with regard to premarital adolescent sex, one theme seemed to predominate community responses. It was summed up by an editorial in one of Australia's leading newspapers, the *Sydney Morning Herald*. There it was declared that "sexual experiment among young people presents a social problem."[3] National medical associations and government departments lent weight to the sense of social disquiet. Urgent committees and task forces were set up in England, the United States, and Australia to inquire into the "problem" of teenage sex and to develop strategies for tackling it.[4]

A 1965 editorial in the *Journal of the American Medical Association* reported that, of the escalating venereal disease rates, the "rising incidence in young people is without parallel."[5] Complacency was warned against, and in the unlikely event that publics were not sufficiently alarmed by this trend, the editorial outlined the appointment of a venereal disease task force whose principal aim was first to "succeed in *dramatizing* venereal disease at the community level."[6] The British Medical Association (BMA) produced a 160-page report in 1964, *Venereal Disease and Young People*.[7] In it the promiscuous behavior of youth was blamed for the increases in venereal disease rates and illegitimate pregnancies, and, as noted by a reviewer at the time, a "*panic*-stricken search [was] made to find the reasons for this 'underlying malaise affecting the social and sexual life of our society.'"[8] The *Medical Journal of Australia* also endorsed a similar, albeit slightly more measured, report of the Child Welfare Advisory Council of New South Wales (CWAC). Entitled "Social Problems Arising in Relation to Premarital Intercourse," the 1967 report reiterated the findings of the British and American Medical Associations.[9] In fact, findings from Britain and the United States were regularly communicated in such Australian reports, as well as in the Australian press and in parliamentary debates and inquiries. International research was cited as evidence for making similar claims about the Australian experience, and for advancing arguments about broader Western trends. The trend—or rather, argument—common to the anglophone experience was that premarital teenage sexuality was on the rise and identified as a serious "social problem" to be counteracted.

Premarital sex and promiscuity were not the only pressing concerns about youth. The 1960s were also marked as a time of mounting unease about, among others things, the commodification of sex in the media—dubbed "spectator sex"[10]—youth subcultures and protest movements, challenges to "traditional morality" and adult power structures, and the transformation of the experience of youth itself. In this context, calls for universal sex education of children in schools were being made to avoid what many were forecasting as the rapid rise of hedonism and immorality, and the impending decline of civilization. This chapter examines an Australian response to this moral/sex panic as indicative of broader anglophone responses.[11] New South Wales, the most populous state incorporating the largest of the country's capital cities, was very quick to react (at the very least, rhetorically and publicly) to the exhortations to action. New South Wales was also one of the first states to propose a statewide school-based sex education program.

Of principal concern was the notion that an expansive education on sex and human relationships would only unleash and further encourage adolescent sexual behavior. The argument made here is that the mobilization of fear was a vehicle for advancing several interlinked social, discursive, and political strategies (in the Foucauldian sense).[12] It was a way of stimulating community action toward controlling the sexualities of young people, enforcing a series of social and moral norms of sexuality, reaffirming boundaries between children and adults, and buttressing adult power. It was also, importantly, a way of undermining young people's claims to sexual agency, autonomy, and knowledge by recasting the teenager as essentially immature and incompetent in matters of sex.

To describe this historical scenario as a moral/sex panic about adolescent sex is not meant to suggest there were not competing perspectives and other factors also driving the panic, or that there were not less emotive responses than the term panic may imply. My reason for splicing morality to sex panics is that, at the heart of the often fierce debates during the 1960s, regardless of particular perspectives, was indeed passionate dispute about questions of morality. To propose, as does this chapter, that the question of adolescent sexuality was placed under erasure in this moral/sex panic might seem somewhat counterintuitive. How are we to reconcile this idea with the explosion of concern and discussion on matters of adolescent sex? As we will see, however, understanding the sexual lives, experiences, and perspectives of teenagers was not high on the agenda of many of the stakeholders. Indeed, despite widespread agreement about the need to tackle head-on the problem of adolescent sex, an encounter with the sexual subjectivities of teenagers was persistently deferred. Notwithstanding the specificities of the Australian experience, this abiding evasion was a feature common to all anglophone countries throughout the 1960s and 1970s in their efforts to address the predicament of adolescent sex.

Moral and Sexual Revolutions

That a certain degree of conflict between young people's aspirations and adult norms is an inevitable part of psychosocial development was routinely acknowledged in the 1960s. A British report on the youth service summed up the prevailing view: "Adolescence is always a period in which the energies and growing needs of individuals conflict with the customs, the necessarily restricting adult customs, of society as a whole. This much is unavoidable."[13] There was also little doubt among many cultural commentators and sociologists as to the *social* factor responsible for this trend: the sexual revolution. Premature and irresponsible adolescent sex was the inevitable debris washed up by the "sea of permissiveness" and social and economic changes sweeping across Western countries.[14] Some doubt was certainly cast on alarmist claims of massive change in sexual behaviors wrought by the "permissive" culture.[15] Throughout the 1960s the major newspapers and magazines debated whether the sexual revolution reflected significant shifts in actual sexual practices or merely an increase in the discourse on sex and in sex's public and commercial visibility. However, what was rarely contested was the idea of a seismic shift in attitudes to and representations of sex. The mass media routinely pumped out articles throughout the 1960s and 1970s about the revolution in morals and mores rocking Western societies.[16]

Jeffrey Weeks refers to the 1960s as a period of "fragmentation of the moral consensus."[17] In their examination of the profound shifts in attitudes to sexual morality, cover stories in the international magazines *Time* and *Newsweek* in 1964 reflected this. The reports described the liberalization of attitudes to premarital sex as indicative of a "new morality" and, as *Time* put it, a "second sexual revolution."[18] The Australian news magazine *The Bulletin* echoed much of the same in its 1966 cover story entitled "Morals: The Sexual Revolution."[19] Religious newspapers employed particularly alarmist terminology and headlines. Phrases such as "moral collapse," "world catastrophe" of moral laxity, "on the edge of a smoking volcano," "new morality a threat to nation," and "moral pollution" were just a handful of the countless references to the morality revolution.[20] This new morality was made possible by a well-recognized set of social factors. The relaxation of obscenity laws, policies and attitudes, in conjunction with a period of relative postwar affluence, had produced a flourishing commercial market of sex. A sizeable proportion of this target market was the teenage consumer and youth subcultures, or the "bulge generation," whose numbers (and purses) had rapidly swelled as a result of the baby boom. Youth were also more mobile than ever before, and were staying at school longer and enjoying greater independence than previous generations. Student protest movements were in full swing. Religious and parental authority declined and availability and advances in contraception—most notably the pill—materially and symbolically detached sex from, and thus challenged, the reproductive imperative. Greater general wealth and leisure time contributed to a growing emphasis on the pursuit of individual pleasure. Cries of a mounting "cult of hedonism" and cultures of narcissism were frequently heard.[21]

The "new morality" of permissiveness and code of privacy was an avowed rejection of Victorian norms of reticence, modesty, guilt, and shame. "The new moralists," declared a 1964 *Newsweek* cover article, "The Morals

Revolution on the U.S. Campus," "argue that the guilt [of sex] does not come from anything inherent in sex itself but is, in fact, induced by the vestiges of Victorian Puritanism. . . . All this may be true."[22] The *Bulletin* magazine's 1966 cover story cited above made similar pronouncements: "After the long, cold, murky decades of frigidity, guilt, and perversion, it is probably inevitable that the social pendulum will swing."[23] Another way of understanding the revolution in morals and mores is to frame it in terms of a shifting shame threshold, or a historical transformation of cultural emotion control. The concerted effort to challenge norms of Victorian puritanism led to a considerable lowering of the cultural threshold of shame vis-à-vis sexuality. Shame began to lose its hold as a regulator of human conduct.

Adolescent behavior—routinely lamented at this time as uncouth, anarchic, and *shameless*—was often singled out by doomsayers as symptomatic of a culture with no morals, no shame. That adolescence was widely understood as a time of rapid developmental change only intensified social anxieties. For instance, much was made of the findings that adolescents were reaching puberty and achieving physical maturity at ever-younger ages each decade. The combination of the "storm and stress" of adolescence and early physical sexual development was thought to make young people particularly susceptible to the strains of social change and growing permissiveness.[24] As a report by the British Ministry of Education into the "problems of youth" in a rapidly changing society noted, "Adolescents are the litmus-paper of a society. Subject to continuous and considerable mental, emotional and physical changes, as yet unregulated by the formal demands in the daily life of the breadwinner or housewife, adolescents are unusually exposed to social changes."[25] Or, as one Sydney newspaper article put it, this "early maturing throws them [adolescents] open to adult stresses much earlier than usual."[26] Especially troubling was a broadly perceived and growing "generation gap," as well as the contradiction observed between the extension of youth—as a result, for example, of greater age stratification in society and increased time in formal education—and their premature sexualization. In other words, young people were being flooded with sexual solicitations by the market and mass media at the same time as they were being adjured, according to a *Sydney Morning Herald* report, "to remain celibate from the age of 13, or 14, when they mature, to the age of 26 when (on average) they marry."[27] One worrying upshot of all of this, it was bemoaned time and again, was the problem of "youth alienation." Youth were thought to be alienated as a result of the social instability and rapid change engendered by the morals revolution.[28]

Sex education was almost universally touted as the answer to the problems of adolescent sex and identity confusion, and of the upheaval in morals, although there was widespread disagreement about the content and approach it ought to take. Even those who questioned the severity of the problem and the tendency of societies to malign and scapegoat adolescents agreed that rapid social changes of the late 1950s and 1960s required a pedagogical response.[29] In the United Kingdom, the United States, and Australia, debate over sex education was polarized chiefly, as Jeffrey Moran and Janice Irvine note, in terms of liberal versus conservative positions. Liberals were not always secular in their moral beliefs, but often were; and conservatives were not always religious in their moral beliefs, but also often were.[30] For conservative and religious groups, this usually meant a return to the teachings of traditional morality and the values of marital and reproductive sex. But to secular and liberal humanist groups, the changing climate of the sexual revolution meant that existing forms of sex education were inadequate. Up until the 1960s, blanket moral prohibitions and tactics of scaremongering about venereal disease and illegitimate pregnancies stood in largely for sex education classes as a means of deterring adolescents from premarital sex. However, as the deputy commissioner of the West Australian Public Health Department pointed out in a 1964 report entitled "VD Upsurge in the West: Too Many Drive-Ins?," in contemporary society, "medicine has removed the first deterrent, tolerance the second."[31] Regarding the latter, it was increasingly acknowledged that, with the liberalization of attitudes to sex and the "fragmentation of moral consensus," many young people were rejecting absolutist moral codes.[32] Where in earlier decades reticence, modesty, and shame were seen to be appropriate checks on frank discussions of sexuality in front of children and premature sexual behavior of children, such checks began to be considered by many to be part of the problem of teenage sex.[33]

Liberalization was evidenced to some extent in a report in the *Sydney Morning Herald* on three academic studies of 1,600 teenagers and their attitudes to sex: "The striking result for an educator," the author and academic said, "though no surprise surely—was the fairly general acceptance of extramarital intercourse by all groups."[34] Weeks describes this as a move "towards the centrality of individual consent in place of imperatives of public morality."[35] Another significant development in this regard was the growth and popularity of discourses of scientific rationalism and humanism, with their emphasis on the notion of individual autonomy and private morality.[36] Privatizing morality—in consensual scenarios absent of harm—was, of course, the tenor of the British Wolfenden report, whose recommendations were influential in the development of legal and social policy in the United Kingdom and Australia. In the United States, a similar shift toward private morality was emerging, albeit in the American pragmatic liberal tradition, argues Weeks.[37] Indicative of this logic of private morality was the growing trend toward the acceptance of premarital sex in meaningful and loving relationships. *Time* magazine summarized this logic in its cover story on "The Second Sexual Revolution": "1) morals are a private affair; 2) being in love justifies pre-marital sex . . . ; 3) nothing really is wrong as long as nobody else 'gets hurt.'"[38]

The other major concern with approaches to sex education was the contentious issue of delivery: Who should teach it, where should it be taught, how should it be taught, and to what ages? Here the question of parental control and responsibility was fiercely debated. Up until the 1960s, sex education was widely touted to be the responsibility of parents. The Child Welfare Advisory Council noted this in its report, saying, "The concept of sex education at home appears to be almost universally accepted."[39] Yet parents were coming under attack from all angles for failing in this task, as the report also went on to highlight. Sex education "is often not carried out to the satisfaction of either parents or adolescent. There is a considerable gap between what is generally considered to be desirable and needed, and what is actually done."[40] Schofield found that parental advice was inclined to focus on "moral problems, and was unspecific and vague."[41] It was repeatedly lamented that not only were parents often unqualified to teach sex education, but also that far too many of them suffered from shame and nervousness to do so frankly and effectively. The journal *Medical Health in Australia* published a study of 609 parents and 951 high school students, wherein author and psychologist John Collins reported that one of the principal reasons for the "conspiracy of silence" maintained by many parents with regard to frank sex instruction was the issue of embarrassment.[42] Collins pointed out, "One of the most interesting findings of the survey was the number of times embarrassment dictated the answers of so many of the respondents to the questions asked of them."[43] In fact, the vast majority of parents supported school-based sex instruction, themselves citing embarrassment and lack of knowledge as a primary part of the rationale for this attitude.

In its 1967 reporting of the BMA's call for sex education as early as primary school, a *Sydney Morning Herald* editorial made a scathing critique of parents along these lines: "The policy of the [NSW Education] department, as far as an onlooker can determine, is to leave sex instruction to parents. This would be fair enough if all parents were capable of giving it, but many (perhaps the majority) are so uninformed or inhibited that they cannot do more for their children than their own parents did for them."[44] In another of its editorials published only five days later, the issue of an Education

Department pilot sex education program for high schools was discussed. The department was urged to broach the program in greater detail with parents because, "after all, the parents are in so many ways the problem."[45] In short, the revolution of morals and a broadly perceived and growing "generation gap" meant that conventional methods of sex instruction were considered anachronistic. Such methods ignored the realities of young people's sexual activity and their desire for more comprehensive knowledge beyond the facts of reproduction and venereal disease. This much was revealed in a number of studies of teenage attitudes on the subject. For instance, both Schofield's British study and Collins's Australian study found that, to quote the former, "teenagers were dissatisfied with the amount of sex education they received, and with its quality."[46] Shame, it was frequently complained, was obstructing young people from gaining appropriate knowledge about sexuality.

New South Wales Sex Education Debates

> It is time now for this whole question of sex education in schools, complicated as it is, to be *faced squarely* by the responsible authorities in the Departments of Health and Education.
>
> —"Sex Education," editorial, *Sydney Morning Herald*, 1967

When the *Sydney Morning Herald* urged the NSW state government to heed the BMA's call for holistic sex education in all schools, the first major social debate about the subject was launched. The rhetorical positions mirrored debates in the United Kingdom and the United States. School-based sex education was controversial enough, but the idea of comprehensive sex education beyond the facts of reproduction and adult moralizing was especially divisive. The NSW state government responded much more swiftly and directly to the urgency of the teenage sex "problem" than other state governments. In fact, at the time the *Sydney Morning Herald* editorial was printed, the Department of Education was already underway developing a pilot syllabus to trial in thirty schools that year. The term *sex education* would be substituted with *human growth and development*, ostensibly as a way of ensuring, as the BMA was reported to state, "that sex is seen in perspective and in relation to other parts of individual and family life."[47] If successful, the syllabus would be rolled out to all secondary schools.[48] But, asked one journalist, presaging what was to become one of the more discussed and contentious issues: "Just how frank will the lectures on boy-girl relationships and preparation for marriage" be?[49] The issue of reticence, and by association shame, saturated almost all discussion. Even imperatives of action, such as the one cited in the epigraph to this section, used (anti-)shame-inflected imagery to frame their demands: sex education was "to be *faced* squarely" or "faced head-on." This, as we saw in chapter 1, is the direct antithesis (and defeat) of the shame tendency to "look away."

A flurry of letters and articles debating the proposal for a government-led, school-based sex education program appeared in the *Sydney Morning Herald* and other newspapers. A radical departure from conventional sexual pedagogies, two fundamental principles lay at the controversial core of the proposal. The first was the move away from *withholding* sexual information from teenagers (other than the general facts of reproduction and disease), which had been the chief characteristic of deterrence-based sex education until (at least) the 1960s.[50] The second was the *removal of moral proscriptions* from sex instruction and their replacement with so-called "objective," scientific information on all aspects of sexuality and human relationships. The pedagogical logic behind withholding knowledge and replacing it with moral commandments was a performative one, as Irvine has pointed out.[51] Simply to talk of sex was to incite sexual curiosity in children, or so it was believed, just as to talk about morality was to produce moral behavior, or so it was hoped. While there was certainly a range of nuanced views expressed, stakeholders largely lined up as either proponents or detractors of these two new sex education principles. A virtually identical set of debates, positions, and logics also epitomized the British and American contexts at various times in the 1960s and 1970s.

The detractors—at least, the most publicly vocal—were religious groups and individuals or those subscribing to religious-like codes of morality. Over and over they reiterated a rhetoric of performativity. The "danger in studying sexual relations in a definite course," cautioned an editorial in Australia's leading multidenominational evangelical newspaper, "is that it would perhaps encourage and awaken an interest before the due time."[52] Even the *Sydney Morning Herald*, which had been arguing for school-based sex education, advanced similar reasoning. Calls by the government's Child Welfare Advisory Council to include "education in contraceptive techniques" to be part a school's approach to sex instruction were vehemently dismissed in an editorial:

> To carry sex education to the point of including "contraceptive techniques" in a secondary school counselling service on "preparation for marriage" would be both dishonest and unwise. Dishonest because it is plainly not primarily intended as a preparation for marriage, unwise because it would act as

a stimulus and encouragement to "premarital sexual intimacy" and would, in fact, be interpreted by immature minds as an endorsement of it. The one central point that the earnest ladies and gentlemen of the committee seem to have overlooked in their desire to be broadminded, understanding and "with it" is that a child is a highly suggestible creature.[53]

Two days prior the minister for child and social welfare had also affirmed this view and rejected the committee's recommendation as "completely unacceptable."[54] A front-page *Sydney Morning Herald* report quoted him as saying that not just the recommendation but indeed the report itself "could have the effect of encouraging immorality by 'further inflaming' young minds."[55] Detractors were appalled at the move both to do away with moral teachings and to introduce sex instruction at primary-school level. This was typified in one reader's angered response to the director of physical education's comment that school-based sex education "'is not a morality crusade or anything like that,' as if this approach must be shunned."[56] Another reader sarcastically likened the proposal to a recommendation to "advise our young people the best methods to be used in the [other] various anti-social actions [such as theft, vandalism, and violence] so that while indulging themselves they could do so with the minimum of fear of personal inconvenience to themselves."[57]

Churches of all denominations weighed in on the debate, as did doctors, community groups, and parents. Although various indications suggest that detractors constituted a minority of opinion in Australia (perhaps unlike in the United States), they were a sizeable and influential minority, and importantly, highly public and vocal in their denunciation.[58] As Alison Bashford and Carolyn Strange point out, the effectiveness of gaining support for a sex education message is affected by the marketing of that message as well as its form and content.[59] Activists against morally neutral, school-delivered sexual pedagogies did not rely simply on official reports or statements. Utilizing vast religious and church networks, detractors held public meetings and rallies and initiated letter-writing campaigns and pamphleteering in order to disseminate their messages and marshal support.[60] Emotive and dramatic rhetorical language of social catastrophe and child exploitation routinely accompanied these very effective forms of local and mass communication.[61] In this way they were quite successful in stirring up what Irvine dubs, in a parallel context in US sex education debates, collective "transient feelings"—feelings that are socially and dramaturgically produced, which often makes them contagious and prone to mobilization in the form of collective sex panics.[62] Thus, after detractors had successfully created a degree of palpable community uncertainty, disapproval, and negative emotion, the minister for child and social welfare was doubtless emboldened to declare publicly, "I propose to take no further action on the CWAC's controversial recommendations for sex education."[63]

There seemed little likelihood of returning to the model of marriage and chastity-based sex instruction, however. That approach had not been working, as was repeatedly made clear by the growing numbers of young people reportedly having premarital sex, or at the very least now willing to admit to and support the practice. The Presbyterian Church of Australia Church and Nation Committee in NSW that had inquired into the Child Welfare Advisory Council report conceded, "Certain basic realities remain which no measure of wishful thinking can dissolve or dissipate."[64] Ironically, it was the very attempt of detractors to insist on reaffirming a pre-1960s unified moral framework for sex education that ultimately undermined their arguments and strengthened those of the proponents of the comprehensive pedagogy. The latter seized on this intransigence to argue that precisely because there was not a moral consensus in society, uniform moral precepts could not be imposed. Exactly the same debates over morality versus moral neutrality in sex education were being played out in the United States between sexual liberals and fundamentalist religious groups opposed to secular pedagogies.[65] It is in this context that we can see how sex education debates dovetailed into, and gave weight to, the principle of private morality reorienting Western societies.[66]

The Council of Australian Humanist Societies, drawing directly on US, UK, and European counterparts, was a quintessential champion of this private "new morality." They were particularly active in engaging, debating, and promoting comprehensive sex education. With chapters in each of the states and territories bar Tasmania and the Northern Territory, the council was a member of the International Humanist and Ethical Union founded in 1952. After the atrocities of World War II, a revivified discourse of liberal humanism was promoted by the international humanist organizations disillusioned by the ineffectiveness of religion as the basis of morality and ethics. Among the tenets espoused in the international manifesto were the familiar liberal beliefs in scientific rationalism, equality, secular morality and ethics, "free inquiry," "open" societies, the interdependence of human beings, and progress as "progress in freedom."[67] Like religious organizations of the time, humanist groups fostered various forms of social activism and education. Group members fired off an offensive of letters to newspapers to counter the anti–sex education "moralists" who they felt were trying to railroad the NSW sex education debate. For example, here is Dr. I. S. Edwards, the chairman of the Humanist Society of NSW:

> The traditional Christian attitudes to sexual conduct have long been questioned by non-Christians. Today they are increasingly criticised by Christians. Now that this first timid move has been made towards adequate sex education in schools, it would be a disaster if the course were to become only a front for the propagation of traditional attitudes.[68]

As the term *disaster* suggests, the humanists were fiercely opposed to religious morality and wedded to the doctrine of rational humanism. It was this intense political conviction that often—in spite of their avowed belief in prioritizing reason and rationality over emotion when engaging in debate—resulted in humanists being equally as dramaturgical as their religious counterparts in the production of collective emotion and sex panic. This was strikingly revealed in a heated exchange of letters following Dr. Edwards's intervention cited above. When a B. Trump pushed the humanists to explain why "the feminine members of the Humanist Society [don't] write letters to the press about denying a 'moral and ethical basis' for High School sex education,"[69] a male humanist member fired back. "The Humanists will read B. Trump's letter with a smile," began Dr. John McCluskie sarcastically. "It will be a well-heeled, smooth-faced, well-tailored smile of well-disciplined, and, perhaps, condescending tolerance. If they reply it will be with charm."[70] By the end of the letter he unleashed: "The Humanists . . . have, largely speaking, one main problem, how to handle the misled and in some cases vile Christians in the arena like B. Trump and those of us who in humility stand with him."[71]

Humanists steadfastly refuted most moral panic ideas about teenage sex. "The so-called teen-age problems—illegitimacy, forced marriage and VD—are not limited to teen-agers," pronounced Beatrice Faust; indeed, "[there] is no conclusive evidence that VD is peculiarly a teen-age problem."[72] Humanists acknowledged nonetheless an urgent need for sex education. Criticism was directed at anxious and shame-prone parents and schools for biasing existing sex instruction "towards non-human reproduction or human reproduction without discussing intercourse," and for dispensing "moral admonition" instead of technical information and "moral advice."[73] Like religious groups and churches, humanist organizations in various states published articles in their magazines and ran seminars, lectures, and sex education classes. They also participated in international humanist networks, inviting speakers and publishing influential pieces from the United States, United Kingdom, and other countries. A book was published, controversially entitled *Sex for Modern Teenagers*.[74] In stark contrast to the morality and deterrence-based approach that predominated the country until this time, the humanists, following Mary Calderone and SIECUS (Sexuality Information and Education Council of the United States), insisted on the need to dispense frank, scientific, "objective," and rational facts and information to students in a nonemotive and shame-free environment. "Modesty, shame, or the fear of ridicule prevent many young people from asking for information about sex," boldly advertised the back cover of *Sex for Modern Teenagers*.

Just as it was for detractors, sex education was for the humanists inextricable from their broader political and philosophical agendas. The renunciation of Christianity and the church as well as reticence and shame, plus their substitution with frank rational humanism, was an important part of this. A *Sydney Morning Herald* story, "Sex and the Teenager," reflected this in its coverage of a sex-information session for teenagers held at Sydney's Humanist House. "I suppose you'd be happy if I could give you answers to the questions which concern teenagers," announced the speaker. "The trouble is that most of the questions for which we'd like clear answers are those we're only now getting around to asking." Blame was placed squarely on the churches for shying away from a face-to-face confrontation with sex, as he went to say:

> This is because the traditional Churches have denied that there are any fair questions at all. They all say sexual experience outside marriage is wrong and that's that. They have discouraged inquiry and as a result we don't have all the facts we should. Well, people are not accepting this attitude anymore and the foundations for the old codes for sexual conduct are collapsing. We are now trying to get on to a more rational basis.[75]

Humanists did not reject morality per se. Instead, it was recast as "the morality of responsible decision-making, not of preconceived notions for or against premarital sex."[76] It was widely accepted in Western countries that teenagers were already having sex, and were having it earlier and in greater numbers than peers of past decades. The humanists were keenly aware of the demand among teenagers for more information about sexual matters, just as they were cognizant of the desire of many young people for advice free of moral admonition. The Schofield report had earlier concluded from a survey of 1,873 teenagers that "there is a lively demand for information about sex, and there are indications that this demand is not being fulfilled."[77] The principal argument of the humanists—and one that was indicative of the thrust of the new private morality also in the United Kingdom and the United States—was that young people ought to be given all the information necessary in order to make their own decisions. "In being objective, and in refraining from telling young people what NOT to do," declared *Sex for Modern Teenagers*, "our efforts [are] to let the young readers come to their own conclusions."[78] Also indicative of the logic of the state government's moves, this seemed like a positive step toward the recognition of young people's experiences and sense of sexual agency and subjectivity.

"Crisis for Teenagers," or, The Problem of Teenage Sexual Subjectivity[79]

At the close of the decade, the pro-comprehensive sex education campaign was given a boost. In August 1969, a select committee of the NSW Legislative Council, set up a few months earlier to inquire into violent sex crime, reported its findings. Covered on the front page of the *Sydney Morning Herald*, a crisis for teenagers was announced with regard to sexual violence, such as "gang bangs" and "pack rape."[80] The line between consensual gang bangs and pack rape was somewhat blurred in the report, and the shadow of teenage promiscuity and uncontrollable delinquent behavior hovered over the inquiry. Parents were said to be unprepared and not sufficiently competent "to undertake sex education in its entirety."[81] They were taken to task for not exercising appropriate authority and power over their children. "Lack of parental control is regarded as an important factor, giving rise to delinquent behavior, 'gang bangs' and promiscuity of both boys and girls."[82] The committee recommended as a matter of urgency that sex education be made mandatory in both primary- and secondary-school curricula.

However, just as in the discussions and debates of the preceding years, there was a palpable tension between images of teenagers as ignorant *victims* of a rapidly changing sex-saturated society and as *perpetrators* of defiant and irresponsible (sexual) behavior. At the heart of this tension was a widely articulated bewilderment of adults about how to understand and come to terms with the emergence of multiple forms of assertive and vocal adolescent subjectivity. This was reflected in countless media stories on the "generation gap" and purportedly inexplicable teenager behaviors, such as: "Why Girls Leave Home," "Why Students Drop Out," "Anarchism: What Do the Students Want?," and "The Thinking of Modern Youth: 'Why You Can't Understand Your Teenager.'"[83] When it came to sex education, there was little doubt what teenagers themselves wanted: much more of it. Numerous studies in Britain and the United States had established this fact.[84] In Australia, John Collins published his second study on the attitudes of 1,426 teenagers with regard to sex education. Reported in the *Sydney Morning Herald*, it confirmed the British and American trends.[85] Teenagers wanted a great deal more sex education and wanted a much broader range of topics covered.

The significance of the issue of teenage sexual subjectivity was underlined by the fact that, of the later adolescent group (sixteen to eighteen years of age), between one-fifth and one-fourth of boys wanted discussion on the topics of intercourse, contraception, and dating, while nearly two-thirds of girls wanted to discuss dating. Young people wanted their voices heard, and their needs and interests recognized and addressed by adults.

With such a groundswell of concern over the imperative of sex education, the state government took decisive action in the early 1970s. An interdepartmental advisory committee was established to review policy regarding sex education in government schools. As part of this, the committee would also review the 1967 pilot program carried out in thirty schools in order to develop the most appropriate pedagogical solution to teenage sexuality. A shift toward a more interventionist policy by the Department of Education seemed inevitable. As the deputy premier and minister of education and science commented to the media, the "policy of the department has been that sex education is primarily a matter for parents. . . . [However,] it is felt that this is an area of education in which a greater degree of deliberate planning and policy is desirable to avoid the possibility of unco-ordinated, independent programs." The imperative of holistic and comprehensive sexual pedagogies was also foreshadowed by the minister, the idea being that sex ought not to be treated as an "isolated topic."[86]

Since there existed few, if any, positive or favorable significations of teenage sex, adult attention to the attitudes of young people was very narrowly focused. In fact, where adolescent perspectives were sought at all, usually this was confined to gaining confirmation of problem sexual behaviors and teenage immorality, immaturity, irresponsibility, and misinformation. The desires, pleasures, competencies, and emotional investments and issues of young people, and how they would like these to be addressed, were not usually part of these exchanges. Hence, the common finding of surveys that young people wanted to know more about sexual relationships. That the subject of adolescent sexual agency and knowledge aroused enormous opposition and exaggerated emotional rhetoric was typified, even if in rather extreme terms, by a principal of a prestigious Sydney high school after the subject of introducing broader sex education had been raised in a parents and citizens meeting. "School is no place for teaching boys how to fuck," he blasted.[87] Nonetheless, in a rather unprecedented move, the perspectives of students themselves were to be canvassed as part of the advisory committee's review of community responses.

In April 1972, the NSW Department of Health held a one-day seminar with two hundred students from 150 government and private schools. After reading sex education literature and hearing lectures by doctors, sociologists, counselors, and women's liberationists, the students were divided into groups of around fifteen. Each group nominated a representative who was responsible for collating the views of group members. According to media accounts and those involved at the time, a subcommittee of the student representatives drafted a final report for submission to the advisory committee. Recommendations were made as to the content, delivery, and presentation of sex education.[88] Indicative of the broader humanist shift to private morality, students stressed the importance of adolescent autonomy in values and decision-making. They were also in general agreement that they did not want moralizing from adult sex educators. "Sex education must be essentially factual," they were quoted in the press as saying,

> a course where moral and emotional overtones are discussed rather than taught. In this way each individual will develop his or her own set of morals and codes of behaviour. A school must have no part in forcing upon children particular philosophies and standards. In all schools, Government and non-Government, the young person should be encouraged to come to his or her own decisions about these important issues.[89]

The students called for frankness in sexual pedagogies rather than prevarication and euphemizing, reticence and shame, all of which they felt had characterized sex education to that point. "Teachers should be familiar with sexual slang and should beware of using polite terms that pupils do not know."[90] Their views generally mirrored those of comprehensive sex education advocates with regard to the breadth of topics to be covered, from (among others) contraception to abortion, petting to sadism and masochism, and prostitution to homosexuality.[91] However, the students argued for the commencement of sex education even earlier than most of the adult groups. "Children and adults disagree about what is the right age to begin sex lessons at school," began an article about the seminar in the *Sydney Morning Herald*. Said the student report:

> It should commence no later than in the earliest years of primary school. By the age of 10 all pupils should have a confident understanding of the basic facts of sex, namely puberty, masturbation, menstruation, intercourse, conception, development of foetus, care of mother and child during pregnancy, and childbirth. By no later than the first year of secondary school, all students should have been taught about contraception and the types of contraceptives that may be used. The teacher should provide the information objectively, taking care neither to advocate nor condemn the use of these items. The Roman Catholic and other viewpoints should be explained and discussed.[92]

The seminar, and its reporting in the media, was certainly an unprecedented step in the direction of acknowledgment and recognition of young people. Not long after the seminar, the state government's advisory committee on sex education released its interim report for public discussion and response. The report recommended a statewide, comprehensive program of sex education that would situate sexuality within the much broader context of "personal development"; this was an approach understood to be "attitude-centred and integrated as part of health and personal development programmes, into the total education of the pupil."[93] It should not be "an insurance against unwanted pregnancy, deviant behaviour, promiscuity or venereal infection," said the minister for education in commenting on the report, but as "a positive influence towards personal development of each pupil."[94] Five broadly conceived areas were proposed as a way of covering all aspects of sexuality: biological aspects, personal development, family life, social aspects, and health.[95] While there was much debate around morality, the topics to be included, and the readiness of students, the report appeared to receive "substantial" approval.[96] When the final report was released in April 1974, it seemed there was no turning back. Preparation for Australia's first statewide and secular sex education program that took account of the sexual subjectivities of adolescents was likely to begin in 1974. This was reflected especially in the first aim under the principle of "personal development": "To help the student acquire an understanding of the sexual component of his personality and an appreciation of the satisfying and creative part that sexuality, properly understood, can play in his life."[97]

However, consensus over a "statement of principles" for sex education is not enough to guarantee the successful delivery of a program in all schools. The state government did not go as far to make the introduction of comprehensive sex education mandatory in all schools. In fact, it would be left to the discretion of principals whether it were to be introduced in particular schools at all, and it would be up to the discretion of principals in conjunction with teachers and parents what might actually be taught in the programs.[98] In other words, the "statement of principles" was a set of guidelines with no binding power. What this meant, as critics of the Education Department's policy pointed out, was that the very same conflicts, debates, reticence, and emotionalism that had fueled the public discussion of sex education would likely only be displaced to schools and local communities.[99] That community groups, educationalists, and sociologists twenty-five years later would still be castigating governments and educational authorities for failing to make sex education mandatory and for continuing to frame sex education in narrowly medicalized terms and with inadequate attention to issues of sexual subjectivity, pleasure, and emotions, brings this into stark historical relief.[100]

Subjectivity Dispossessed

The views and strategies of *both* the opponents and advocates of comprehensive sex education leading up to the release of the government's statement of principles represented a decisive *turn away from*—if not, at times, denial of—adolescent sexual subjectivity. The figure of the sexual adolescent was everywhere yet nowhere. It was rhetorically deployed (repeatedly) only to be simultaneously divested of any subjective or experiential specificity. Attention was largely diverted from adolescent sexualities and subjectivities in the present tense and displaced onto other adult concerns. For example, focus was placed primarily on preventing prior causes of problem teenage sex and its troublesome after-effects. This was dramatically literalized in the government's handling of the student report on sex education produced from the Department of Health seminar. First, there was no indication in the final report that the advisory committee had even considered the views and the report of the students themselves. Second, and more insidiously, the government refused to release the student report or provide the National Library of Australia with a copy for its collection. When a written request was made from the National Library to the Department of Education, the director general of education, had this to say:

> The . . . document to which you refer is, I understand, the statement by a selected group of senior students prepared following a seminar conducted by the Department of Health and this Department in 1972. It was not a "survey" but an expression of *opinion* from seminar participants. This paper has not been released, nor is it proposed to release what is not a finished and representative report but a commentary intended to reflect pupils' reactions for the guidance of people organising the seminar and planning future action.[101]

However, in addition to the material and sociopolitical marginalization of adolescent voices, there were also various rhetorical and discursive strategies, common also to sex education debates in the United Kingdom and the United States, that effectively staved off both the actual and symbolic recognition of the sexual subjectivities of young people. The term *discursive strategies* is not intended to imply these were intentional and deliberate strategies, although it is not to rule these out either. Again following Foucault's description of power relations, strategies can have a "series of aims and objectives" that are not reducible to individual will.[102] As part of broader intersecting fields of discourse, therefore, discursive strategies can also be anonymous and unintentional.

The first of these strategies was the attempt, dramaturgically, to generate widespread fear and anxiety in the community about the purported problems of delinquent and immature adolescent sexuality in order to advance particular social and religious ideas. Those groups opposed to comprehensive sex education made no secret of their worldviews regarding morality and ethics. The second strategy was the long-standing notion, discussed earlier, that young minds were liable to premature sexualization as a result of a too-early exposure to adult sexual knowledge and sex-saturated culture. Far from recognizing adolescent sexual subjectivity, the discourse on premature sexualization disqualified its appearance by rendering it a pathological societal or familial implantation. The assumption of a temporal mismatch in adolescent development, whereby physical maturation outpaces emotional maturation, was a third discursive strategy. This is the idea, purportedly aggravated by the trend of earlier onset of puberty, that children are at the mercy of a powerful biological sexual urge the consequences and stresses of which they are as yet emotionally unprepared to deal with. Ordinarily this had been the rationale behind the insistence on premarital chastity as a way of reining in unruly sexual urges. Social surveys, academic and anecdotal research, and popular opinion typically (even if at times inadvertently) bolstered this logic with reports of young people lacking adequate knowledge of many aspects of sexuality.[103] The very notion of adolescent sexual subjectivity was swallowed up by the gulf between the rigid and mismatched poles of a mind/body dualism.

For those subscribing to these ideas, there were few if any acceptable or normative forms of active adolescent sexuality. One implication was that young people were often constructed as tabulae rasae until attaining majority or marriage, at which time they were to be educated with adult sexual knowledge. Another was a model of development in which sexual subjectivity is construed as the linear and incremental effect of biological maturation. The category of "promiscuity," routinely associated with "delinquent" girls, became a convenient rhetorical device for pathologizing most forms of premarital teen sex. For the Child Welfare Advisory Council, the promiscuous teens were those having sex not "in 'steady' relationships"; in their report they declared that the "promiscuous group of girls . . . are, by and large, a disturbed and/or deprived group."[104] Even the Schofield report, which had refuted among others the myth of widespread teenage promiscuity, ultimately had a very restrictive view of normative adolescent sex.

Promiscuity seems to be any "sexual intercourse not limited to only two individuals," and venereal diseases, it was concluded, "must be associated with promiscuity."[105] Combined with the widely circulating premature sexualization theory, the more or less universal agreement of promiscuity being a developmental anomaly meant that very few spaces were available for the articulation and legitimization of nonmonogamous adolescent sexuality.

A fourth discursive strategy that served to diminish adolescent sexuality was the overriding focus on personal development, maturation, and transitionality. Sex education discourses were overwhelmingly concerned, as the NSW government interdepartmental advisory final report put it, with "developing individual potential."[106] Almost every aspect of sex education was framed by the future perfect tense. Sexual pedagogy was thereby conceived as a process of guiding students on a path to realizing their ideal *future* selves. With adolescence constructed through the tropes of transitionality, becoming, plasticity, and potentiality, the adolescent, as Angus Gordon notes, has been constituted as "a subject in transit."[107] Caught in a temporary and indeterminate space between the more hardened dichotomous poles of child and adult, adolescents were figured less as human subjects in the here and now than, as the *Sydney Morning Herald* editorialized, as "future citizens."[108] In other words, teenagers were stuck in the neverland between past childhood and adult future. Nancy Lesko sums up the discourse of adolescent developmentalism: "The more that adolescent development-in-time is invoked, the harder it is to find the teenager in the present moment."[109] Already existent adolescent sexual subjectivity in the present tense was dispossessed in the hegemony of the future perfect and its accompanying discursive evasions.

Future Perfect Adolescence

The social and discursive strategies through which sexual subjectivities of teenagers were disenfranchised were not specific to Australia. The mobilization of fear and anxiety; the silencing of adolescent voices; the pathologizing of sexual agency ("promiscuity"); the prevailing tropes of premature sexualization, temporal developmental mismatch, transitionality, and the future perfect citizen, all were common features of a broader anglophone response to the "problem" of adolescent sex and sex education. This is not to suggest that the different national, temporal, and sociopolitical trajectories of sex education debates in the United States, Britain, and Australia during this time can be reduced to a common historical narrative. However, it is to suggest a number of important threads underpinning and uniting them all. Despite the advances of sexual liberals in challenging the hegemony of a morality-based mode of sex education in the United States, Britain, and Australia during the 1960s and 1970s, as Moran highlights, in all countries an "instrumentalist" paradigm still held sway. Not unlike contemporary harm-minimization approaches, this was an approach principally directed at "behavioral and social changes" and the minimization of damage *rather than the acceptance of adolescent sexuality*.[110] Endemic to this instrumentalism was a tendency "to conceive of sexuality and adolescence," as Moran notes, "primarily in terms of danger."[111] Fear was thus in close proximity with, if not constitutive of, the instrumentalist paradigm and its accompanying evasions. In other words, national, temporal, and sociopolitical specificities within the anglophone experience were in important ways subordinate to a similar set of logics, tropes, and master emotions (fear, anxiety, shame) surrounding the confrontation with child sexuality.

The instrumentalist paradigm was in part a defensive response, one aim and/or effect of which was to evade a face-to-face encounter with the agentive, and often dissident, sexual child. In so doing, dominant cultural reactions to sex education during this period mimicked one of the fundamental features of shame: a turning away from the object that is the very stimulus of shame. The instrumentalist paradigm and its evasive social and discursive strategies might themselves therefore be seen as an expression of, and response to, adult shame surrounding child sexuality. For, as we saw in the sex education debates, shame, embarrassment, and reticence were particularly salient features of the professed apprehension of adults when faced with the sexual teen. This is not to say that genuine care, concern, and acceptance of the sexualities of children and adolescents were absent during this time. Many sexual liberals and humanists publicly exhibited just these qualities, as we have also seen in this chapter.[112] However, the negative discursive and epistemological terms through which teenage sex and sex education debates were framed during this period meant that adolescent sexuality was mostly a site of conflict and ambivalence, and at worst a site of danger, fear, negativity, and shame. Thus, the turn away from adolescent sexual subjectivity and shame dynamics indicative of the sex education debates unfortunately redoubled *as a mode of shaming itself*.

The controversial nature of adults talking with children about sex and the predominance of the instrumentalist paradigm meant that even in the most liberal approaches—such as the humanists—it was recommended that only factual information be dispensed in an "objective" and nonemotional manner. Young people ought to make up their own minds free of adult bias or influence. However, within a discursive field dominated by tropes of temporal and developmental mismatch, immaturity, and incompetence, one of the glaring gaps even of this supposedly impartial and unemotional approach to adolescent sex education was any commitment to engaging adolescent's actual subjectivities, let alone their desires, pleasures, interests, and emotions pertaining to sexuality. Instead, it was encouraged to leave them to absorb the information being dispensed and to reach their own conclusions when sufficiently mature. Under the conservative morality-based approaches, of course, this question of adolescent sexual subjectivity was moot.

In the sex education debates of the 1960s and 1970s, shame was everywhere acknowledged as one of the primary bases of this trepidation. Confirming Foucault's observation of the ubiquity of the "repressive hypothesis," it was widely accepted that shame and embarrassment were merely the consequences of an enforced Victorian reticence, prudery, and silence on matters of sex. John Collins's 1972 study of 1,560 parents and children on the subject of sex education was exemplary of the repressive hypothesis: "The mystery, secrecy, shame and guilt that surround sex are a product of our past . . . the taboos and superstitions which were the products of the Victorian age." A "new enlightenment," he presumed (like most anti-shame champions), would rid individuals and societies of such apparently unnecessary timidity and negative emotion.[113] Yet what this obscures is the more insidious performative dimension: that the negative emotional tropes of fear, anxiety, and shame were not just aroused in some people in the face of child sexuality. They were *mobilized* strategically to thwart comprehensive sex education campaigners, advance political and moral agendas, divert attention from teenage sexual subjectivity, and dishonor and control young people.

That comprehensive sex education advocates have been lamenting for the last four decades—and continue to lament—the overemphasis on risk and danger and the failure of school-based sex education to integrate substantive discourses and discussions of desire, pleasure, emotion, and ethical relationships only attests to the enduring power of our mobilizations of anxiety and fear around child sexuality.[114] Abstinence-only education in the United States is obviously at the more extreme end of this fear-based approach. But sex education researchers and campaigners keep reminding us that young people across most anglophone countries are consistently critical, just as they were four decades ago, of school-based sex education programs for failing to address their needs, interests, and topics of concern. "These areas include," Louisa Allen and Moira Carmody observe, "avoidance of discussion of emotional aspects of sexuality, a focus on reproduction, absence of a discourse of desire and a concentration on the dangers of desire for women—pregnancy, abortion and sexually transmitted infections."[115] Much of this reflects the routine infantilization of young people and the way they continue to be positioned, just as they were in the 1960s and 1970s, "as reckless, easily pressured, unknowledgeable, or unwise."[116] As scholars and comprehensive sex education experts have been at pains to communicate, what is so critically needed are education programs and discussions that engage young people not primarily as passive or incompetent objects of sexual danger but as sexual *subjects* that often engage in sex and negotiate *complex* sexual relationships, emotions, desires, and pleasures. As Allen and Carmody (among others) propose, "Constructing sexuality education and intimacy on the basis of ethical sexual subjectivity" offers a much-needed "counter discourse" to fear-based and pathologizing approaches.[117]

Eschewing the rhetoric of fear and pathology is obviously alone not enough to promote a more sustained recognition and engagement with youth subjectivities. As we have seen in this chapter, there are a number of discursive strategies that undermined this goal in the 1960s and 1970s, and these same strategies remain palpably prevalent in various contexts today. One needs only to scour the media or burgeoning research in biomedicine on early pubertal development and the neurosciences on adolescent brains to notice how central are versions of these narratives of premature sexualization, temporal mismatch, and ontological transitionality and plasticity. In popular and medical accounts on the increasing prevalence of early-onset puberty among girls, for instance, concerns are still regularly raised about the physical maturation of girls outpacing their cognitive and emotional capacities to cope with such early development. Such an apparent temporal mismatch also exposes girls, it is feared, to sexual exploitation and predation by men and boys.[118] A version of this idea of temporal mismatch is popular as well within the recent neuroscience of adolescent risk-taking. Many neuroscientists argue that teenagers are more prone to risk-taking behaviors because of a "temporal disconnect . . . between the development of the reward centres of the brain and those responsible for executive function, including rational consideration and judgment."[119] What underpins both of these biomedical discourses of early puberty and teenage brains is the notion that adolescents are essentially transitional, developing, or becoming beings whose neuronal plasticity means they have not yet achieved optimal growth. Neuroscience has, of course, demonstrated that this neuroplasticity is not the child and adolescent's alone; neuroplasticity is a feature of adult brains as well. However, adolescence has been identified as a period of profound neuronal flexibility and brain transformation, and one that many worry needs to be protected. One of the problems with this research though, as Howard Sercombe importantly demonstrates, is that the adolescent brain tends to be viewed through a lens of deficit and dysfunction. Decades-old stereotypes of adolescent turmoil, vulnerability, incapacity, and developmental deficiency problematically permeate the epistemological architecture of current neuroscience. Yet there is no reason to assume, as Sercombe suggests, that the teenage brain's greater flexibility in creating new neuronal connections and greater capacity for risk-taking—or what he calls, less loadedly, "extension"—may not also serve critical evolutionary and adaptive functions: "As living systems, along with the stability and efficiency of older brains, communities may depend for their survival on the flexibility and capacity for extension of teenage brains."[120] An overemphasis on risk and danger occludes an appreciation of young people's strengths, potentialities, and capacities of adaptation, resilience, and agency; and impedes efforts, as Sarah Johnson, Robert Blum, and Jay Giedd argue, to develop "policies that help to reinforce and perpetuate opportunities for adolescents to thrive in this stage of development, not just survive."[121]

THREE

Child Sexual Abuse

> Historians do not usually like to speak of the "lessons of history," as if she were some objective, finally definitive schoolteacher. But in many years of work at the craft, I have never come across a story that so directly yields a moral. The moral is that the presence or absence of a strong feminist movement makes the difference between better or worse solutions to the social problem of child sexual abuse. . . . Without a feminist analysis, evidence of child sexual abuse means that danger lies in sex perverts, in public spaces, in unsupervised girls, in sexually assertive girls. . . . As with adult rape, child sexual abuse without feminist interpretation supplies evidence and arguments for constricting and disempowering children.
>
> —Linda Gordon, "The Politics of Child Sexual Abuse: Notes from American History," 1988[1]

In the 1970s and 1980s, the English-speaking world was in the grips of a revolution. Spearheaded by feminism and the child-protection lobby, this was a revolution to fight the problem of child sexual abuse. A critical objective was to generate a public discourse intent on challenging widespread ignorance, denial, and misinformation regarding the severity of the problem. Alarming statistics and highly emotional exposés of a hidden epidemic of incest and molestation were produced and disseminated at a staggering rate. The *Los Angeles Times* reported in 1985 on research indicating that "*at least* 22 percent of Americans have been victims of child sexual abuse."[2] Some estimates publicized in Australia were as high as 40% of girls and 30% of boys.[3] The child sexual abuse movement's success in bringing the issue out of the closet is partly registered by the extraordinary shift in reported cases. In the United States, for instance, there was an eighteenfold increase in reports of sexual abuse between 1976 and 1985.[4] This was a sex panic of epic proportions.

This "rediscovery" of child sexual abuse—perhaps more accurately defined by Linda Gordon as a "reinterpretation"—has been profoundly important for Western culture as a whole.[5] Few would dispute that patriarchal social structures, male sexuality and power relations between the sexes and between adults and children have been subject to much-needed critical scrutiny, and that our reexamination of the dynamics of child sexual abuse and its detrimental effects have generated valuable insights with regard to diagnosis, therapeutic intervention (for both offenders and victims), and management. The myth of stranger danger was unmasked as a patriarchal ruse, as feminists produced an array of statistics revealing fathers, male relatives, and male acquaintances to be the primary offenders in cases of child sexual assault. They were also vigorous in contesting legal definitions of abuse that ignored or downplayed nonpenetrative sexual acts. Drawing directly from the language and rhetoric of radical feminist antirape and antipornography movements, a new approach to abuse emerged that expanded the definitional terrain of sexual abuse as well as eroded distinctions between the various acts included under its rubric. Feminists were particularly influential in challenging notions that children subjected to sexual abuse were somehow complicit in the crime (by seducing adults, "asking for it," or fabricating charges), or that child prostitutes and children involved in child pornography or intergenerational sex could willingly consent to such sexual activities. Concepts of the innocent, powerless, blameless, and unconsenting "victim" and "survivor" of sexual abuse became key cultural terms.

These are certainly enormous achievements. However, significant gains are often accompanied by equally significant losses, and unfortunately the child sexual abuse movement is no exception in this regard. Despite admirable efforts to protect and empower children from the harmful consequences of abuse, this chapter suggests that children in one particularly notable way have been disarmed and disempowered by the child sexual abuse movement. It argues that the discourse of child sexual abuse has expanded at the expense of a discourse on child sexuality. Efforts to expose the reality and dynamics of child sexual abuse have been aided—if not in part made possible—by efforts (wittingly or otherwise) to conceal, repress, ignore, or evade the realities and dynamics of child sexualities and forms of sexual agency. This cloaking of child sexuality, I will suggest, has deleterious consequences at both the level of everyday practice and at the level of theory. First, and far from insignificant, the desexualization of childhood has potentially damaging psychological and psychotherapeutic consequences for child victims of sexual abuse. Second, with "child sexuality" figured largely as an oxymoron within the feminist discourse of child sexual abuse,[6] the categories of "child" and "adult" are kept apart at safe epistemological distance. For scholars trained to unpack the invariable entanglement and mutual constitution of binary poles, this is a highly problematic move. Third, as we will see in the following chapters, the socio-legal child sexual abuse frameworks developed in anglophone societies as outgrowths of the child sexual abuse movement have left us with a set of impoverished conceptual tools for grappling with issues of child sexuality, consent, and power.

Sigmund Freud and the Normalization of Child Sexuality

Although various cultures and societies may have always recognized in children what we might call sexual desires and behaviors, in the West the concept and hence the experience of child sexuality have a definite history. In a broad historical sketch of changing conceptualizations of child sexuality since the seventeenth century, Sterling Fishman offers the following rather crude periodization: (1) In the seventeenth century, little concern seemed to be paid to child sexuality; (2) in the eighteenth century, medical moralists began denouncing child sexuality (as it manifested in the form of masturbation) as sinful and physically injurious; (3) in the nineteenth century, this denunciation was intensified and projected outward to society, such that child sexuality was deemed a "social evil," the codification of which was essential to the well-being of both the individual and the broader society; and (4) in the twentieth century, under the leadership of Sigmund Freud, there was "a complete *volte face* and childhood sexuality is now seen as a normal and natural expression of the infant and child, the suppression of which creates both individual and social problems."[7] However much we may caution against such a loose and imprecise periodization of mentalities, I think it is nonetheless difficult to contest Fishman's general description of the Freudian revolution that took place in understandings of child sexuality in the twentieth century.

Backed by the influential Freudian theory of infantile sexuality, various sociological, psychological, anthropological, criminological, and legal discourses began explicitly acknowledging child sexuality as a normal and natural reality.[8] In fact, in all decades prior to the 1980s, representations of child sexuality were commonplace, particularly in the context of sexual encounters with adults.[9] For instance, notions of sexually flirtatious, precocious, and seductive children were typical in the psychiatric literature. The work of Bender and Blau is indicative of this tendency; in a study of prepubertal children who were admitted to a psychiatric facility for observation following sexual relations with adults, it was suggested, these children undoubtedly do not deserve completely the cloak of innocence with which they have been endowed by moralists, social reformers and legislators. The history of the relationship in our cases usually suggested at least some cooperation of the child in the activity, and some cases the child assumed an active role in initiating the relationship. . . . A most striking feature was that these children were distinguished as unusually charming and attractive in their outward personalities. Thus, it is not remarkable that frequently we considered the possibility that the child might have been the actual seducer rather than the one innocently seduced.[10]

As late as the mid-1970s, psychiatric theories continued to cite evidence that young children are capable of seduction and engaged in it. In canvassing psychiatric literature in his 1974 *Guide to Psychiatry*, Myre Sim found it "surprising" how "little *promiscuous* children are affected by their experiences [of sex with adults], and how most settle down to become demure housewives. It is of interest that [Sir Basil] Henriques lists two categories—the unaffected and the guilty—and that seems to put the matter in a nutshell."[11] Or consider this quotation from a 1970 sex education text, *The Facts of Sex*:

There is the incontrovertible fact, very hard for some of us to accept, that in certain cases it is not the man who inaugurates the trouble. The novel *Lolita* . . . describes what may well happen. A girl of twelve or so, is already endowed with a good deal of sexual desire and also can take pride in her "conquests." Perhaps, in all innocence, she is the temptress and not the man.[12]

In anthropological research, child sexuality was also the norm and not the exception. In Clelland Ford and Frank Beach's examination of 191 cultures in *Patterns of Sexual Behavior*, they concluded that, "as long as the adult members of a society permit them to do so, immature males and females engage in practically every type of sexual behavior found in grown men and women."[13] Alfred Kinsey's sociological study of orgasm in prepubertal boys was clear in its "substantiation of the Freudian view of sexuality as a component that is present in the human animal from earliest infancy."[14] Like many scholars of his time, he was also dismissive of the idea that intergenerational sexual interactions are in themselves harmful. For many researchers, this belief was based on the widespread assumption that not only is child sexuality normative but children can be sexually precocious. In *Sexual Behavior in the Human Male*, even Kinsey, a proponent of the cultural-conditioning model, implied this in his discussion of children who are brought to orgasm by adults. "The males in the present group become . . . hypersensitive before the arrival of actual orgasm, will fight away from the partner and may make violent attempts to avoid climax, although they derive definite pleasure from the situation," he noted; however, *"such individuals quickly return to complete the experience, or to have a second experience if the first was complete."*[15] Thus, he found it difficult to entertain the idea of intergenerational sex as harmful to children. Echoing Freud's disbelief at Dora's feelings of disgust when approached sexually by Herr K, Kinsey noted that it "is difficult to understand why a child, except for its cultural conditioning, should be disturbed at having its genitalia touched, or disturbed at seeing the genitalia of other persons, or disturbed at even more specific sexual contacts."[16] He proffered a common explanation of the times: "Some of the more experienced students of juvenile problems have come to believe that the emotional reactions of parents, police officers, and other adults who discover that the child has had such contact, may disturb the child more seriously than the sexual contacts themselves."[17]

A California state government–sponsored study of child sexual molestation in 1955 described the mostly female victims as seductive, flirtatious, and sexually precocious, claiming that in the majority of cases there was "evidence of participation," and indeed, evidence of pleasure on the part of the child.[18] Lindy Burton's analysis of around thirty studies of sexual assault against children between 1930 and 1960 reveals the popularity of this view.[19] The adult offender was often portrayed as a harmless victim of child seductiveness, and the usually female victims were often deemed aggressive delinquents acting out their sexual psychopathologies.[20] While these representations of child sexuality prior to the 1980s are far from unproblematic—indeed, they have been importantly and rigorously critiqued by feminists working in the area of child sexual abuse—the point I wish to underscore at this time is simply that child sexuality, however (poorly) conceived, was nonetheless widely accepted as normative. If not openly discussed, at the very least child sexuality was a structuring assumption in discussions of intergenerational sex.

Nowhere is the recognition of child sexuality more apparent than in the child emancipation and sexual liberation movements of the 1970s. The widespread assumption that modern society had inherited an attitude of repressive intolerance of sexuality led many reformers to argue for a lifting of repressive strictures and the creation of more open and positive attitudes toward sexuality.[21] These, it was claimed, would free society of unnecessary inhibitions, mandates, and guilt, which were themselves targeted as the causes of sexual perversions, sexual malaises, and marital troubles. Some reformers touted the benefits of family nudity,[22] while others advanced the idea that adult sexual activity in the presence of children might have beneficial pedagogical effects.[23] Hal M. Wells, infamous author of *The Sensuous Child*, argued that the traumatic effects on children of sex with adults have been exaggerated and that "children have the right to sexual pleasure."[24] Even the incest taboo was challenged.[25] In her book *Sex without Shame*, the psychiatrist Alayne Yates suggested that "some incestuous unions are less harmful than is generally supposed" and that there is "an important lesson to be learned from non-coercive father-and-daughter incest. It is not early erotic pleasure by itself that damages the child. It can produce sexually competent and notably erotic young women."[26] Such views were often framed by the belief, promoted powerfully by the discourse of psychiatry, in children's ability *and desire* to initiate sex with adults, or at least collude in it.[27] They were often justified as well by cross-species comparisons, which emphasized the naturalness of adult-child sex in other mammals. In *Sex Offenders*, Paul H. Gebhard and colleagues claimed that "sexual activity between adult and immature animals is common and appears to be biologically normal"; indeed, it is "precisely what we see in various animals, particularly monkeys."[28] This fact should lessen "the horror with which society views the adult who has sexual relations with young children."[29] Or, as Robert S. de Ropp summed up in a more matter-of-fact articulation of the variously underlying masculinist assumptions, "The craving of the elderly male for the young female is not necessarily confined to the human species. Old stags are always after little ones and the young does are always willing."[30]

At the same time, various interest groups in the United States, England, Australia, and Western Europe also advocated intergenerational sex and agitated for the lowering or abolition of the legal age of consent.[31] Edwin J. Haeberle, who argued that children were being refused their "right to sexual satisfaction," called for an end to laws prohibiting incest: "It would be a crime to force our children and adolescents into blind acceptance of a morality long overdue for reform."[32] As we will see in the next chapter, many pedophile groups employed the rhetoric of gay liberation and positioned themselves as the representatives of an oppressed minority akin to homosexuals. Not only was child sexuality a palpable conceptual figure for most of the twentieth century, but it had even become an overt political issue by the 1970s. Such a position is unthinkable in the climate of pedophilia panic of the late twentieth and early twenty-first centuries. I am not suggesting that throughout the twentieth century there was a near universal consensus regarding child sexuality or that there were not wildly competing claims concerning its existence and meaning. Of course there were multiple constructions of childhood. Many people still retained a belief in the notion of childhood asexuality or sexual innocence. Alongside the narrative of childhood sexual precocity ran that of childhood sexual purity.[33] Both themes were deployed by a range of social actors, depending on their theoretical, political, and social positionings. However, despite—or rather, because of—these competing conceptions of childhood, a signifier or discourse of child sexuality was writ large in twentieth-century Western cultures until the 1980s. In other words, the affirmation and the negation of child sexuality are two poles of the same dialectic. Even in negating child sexuality one cannot avoid reinscribing it. The advent of the child sexual abuse movement in the 1970s and 1980s, however, forced a significant change in this dynamic between the contradictory notions of child sexuality and child sexual innocence.

The Use of Power and the Evasion of Child Sexuality

Fishman's brief history of childhood sexuality concluded with only a gesture toward the 1970s and the rise of the movement against sexual repression, which as we have seen culminated in calls for child sexual liberation. I would like to update Fishman's historical analysis to demonstrate how in the late 1970s and 1980s a monumental shift occurred in the representation of child sexuality. With the advent of a hegemonic discourse of child sexual abuse, feminists, Linda Gordon notes, thought that they "were engaged in an unprecedented discovery."[34] However, bringing child sexual abuse "out of the closet" and correcting the "historical amnesia" of whole societies were not their only significant achievements.[35] Perhaps even more important, in that it directly contested decades of conventional wisdom, was the feminist "reinterpretation" of the meaning of adult-child sexual encounters and child sexual abuse. Feminists worked hard to reverse the tendency to blame the victims of child sexual molestation, and they did it by reinterpreting child sexual abuse "in terms of male power" and child powerlessness.[36] This move was an extension of radical feminist analyses of rape, which had been redefined not as a sexual act but as an act of violence and an assertion of power.[37] The standard argument was that, although "many children appear to consent passively or even to cooperate," children "are incapable of truly consenting to sex with adults."[38] David Finkelhor, influential child sexual abuse researcher, was at the vanguard of this feminist reinterpretation with his article "What's Wrong with Sex Between Adults and Children?," and his ideas are indicative of the standard (radical) feminist logic. "For true consent to occur," he argues, "two conditions must prevail. A person must know what it is that he or she is consenting to, and a person must be free to say yes or no" (694). Drawing on the ethics of human behavioral research, Finkelhor's notion of informed consent requires that "a person *really* understand" the meaning, social context, and consequences of his or her "decision"—in this case, the decision to participate in sexual activity with adults (694). Children are incapable of informed consent because they "lack the [relevant] information":

> They are ignorant about sex and sexual relationships. It is not only that they may be unfamiliar with the mechanics of sex and reproduction. More importantly, they are generally unaware of the social meanings of sexuality. For example, they are unlikely to be aware of the rules and regulations surrounding sexual intimacy, and what it is supposed to signify. They are probably uninformed and inexperienced about what criteria to use in judging the acceptability of a sexual partner. They probably do not know much about the "natural history" of sexual relationships, what course they will take. And, finally, they have little way of knowing how other people are likely to react to the experience they are about to undertake, what likely consequences it will have for them in the future. (694-95)

Moreover, Finkelhor contends, children ultimately lack the "freedom to say yes or no" (695). Drawing here on radical feminist analyses of power, he suggests that children "have a hard time saying no to adults" (695) because adults control the resources essential for children's survival and usually are stronger than children. Finkelhor is quick to point out that many sexual relationships between adults—for example, secretary-boss, prostitute-client, and some wife-husband relationships—would also fail both of his conditions. He concedes that "ignorance" is often present in sexual encounters between adults, although "at least they have accessibility to that knowledge" (696). He also suggests that "implicit coercion is present in many, if not most, sexual encounters in our society" (696). "What makes adult-child sex any different?" he asks. To distinguish between adult-adult and adult-child sex, Finkelhor makes a curious distinction between coercion and power. Subtle degrees of coercion are part of most sexual encounters, but subtle degrees of power apparently are not. Power, not coercion, is at issue for him, and the dynamics of power/powerlessness lie at the heart of objections to intergenerational sex. Adults possess power (and knowledge); children lack power (and knowledge). This ensures the "fundamental asymmetry of the relationship" (695), the "inherent power differential," between adults and children (695, 696).[39]

If there is an underlying logic to the feminist discourse of child sexual abuse, it rests on this question of power and powerlessness. Arguments about child powerlessness and the inability of children to give informed consent structured almost every influential analysis of the problem in the 1980s and 1990s. In her landmark book, *The Best Kept Secret*, Florence Rush relies on the radical feminist redefinition of child molestation as a "male abuse of sexual power."[40] Judith Lewis Herman and Lisa Hirschman's groundbreaking studies on father-daughter incest take it for granted that child incest victims were in a position of "utter helplessness" in the face of their father's "abuse of power and authority."[41] The differential of power between adults and children is "an immutable biological fact."[42] Using the analogy of "freeman and slaves," Herman and Hirschman conclude that children "are essentially a captive population, totally dependent upon their parents or other adults for their basic needs"; this asymmetry ensures that "there is no way that a child can be in control or exercise free choice."[43] Ann Wolbert Burgess and Nicholas Groth's study of sexual victimization of children begins with the assertion that only "through negotiation and consent can sexual relations properly be achieved."[44] It is also axiomatic to their analysis that "such consent is precluded in sexual encounters between a child and an adult."[45] For Burgess and Groth, as for Finkelhor, Rush, and Herman and Hirschman, the reason is the inherent power differential between adults and children; the adult, "by virtue of being mature, occupies a position of biopsychosocial authority and dominance in regard to the child."[46] In the context of sex with adults, therefore, children can therefore only ever be coerced victims. As Roland Summit declared in his landmark article, "The Child Sexual Abuse Accommodation Syndrome," "No matter what the circumstances, the child had no choice but to submit quietly."[47] To ignore the power imbalance between adults and children is to ignore "the basic subordination and helplessness of children within authoritarian relationships."[48]

Shifting the emphasis from a question of sexuality to power was an ingenious way for feminists to counter the belief that children were willing, desiring, culpable participants in sexual encounters with adults. The arguments put forth are simple and powerful, and on the surface make some intuitive sense. It is beyond the scope of this chapter to offer a thoroughgoing critique of these feminist arguments. Yet I would like to register briefly a number of objections to them.[49] First, the category of the "child" is only loosely defined in this body of work, and a child of five is rarely distinguished theoretically from a child of fifteen or sixteen. In this model, *all* adult-child sex is refigured as abuse. Second, while the feminist analysis of power was something of an advance over earlier analyses, which had largely ignored the question of power—and thus had implicitly construed the dynamic of power in intergenerational sex as a relation of equivalence—this analysis was far from unproblematic. As I have noted, the discourse of child sexual abuse has drawn and continues to draw on the radical feminist model of power. In Foucauldian terms, it is a "sovereign" or "juridical" model, construing power as something adults possess and children lack. It likens the child to a slave or prisoner, condemned to bondage to the adult and outside networks of power and knowledge.[50] As Finkelhor notes in his discussion of why adult-adult sex differs from adult-child sex, "The crucial difference in adult-child sex is the combination of children's lack of knowledge *and* lack of power."[51]

Whatever intuitive sense this kind of argument makes, however, normative arguments about intergenerational sex are sustainable only if they have as their implicit referent normative adult-adult sex. Crucially, when we take a closer look at the assumptions made of normative adult-adult sex, the limitations of this model of power for thinking about sexual relations in general become much clearer. The entire body of child sexual abuse research during the 1980s and 1990s leans on the presumption that normative, consensual sex between adults does not, or ought not, involve differential power relations; indeed, it is, or ought to be, virtually free of power dynamics. Normative adult-adult sex is seen as occurring between autonomous equals in relationships free of dominance and subordination.[52] For Burgess and Groth, the minimum conditions for informed consent are the adult "knowledge or wisdom or social skills to be able to negotiate such an encounter *on an equal basis with an adult.*"[53] Echoing their emphasis on equality and mutuality, Summit asserts "that no child has equal power to say no to a parental figure or to anticipate the consequences of sexual involvement with an adult caretaker."[54] From utopian statements about future nonpatriarchal societies one can also glean the radical feminist figuration of a normative sexuality free of power dynamics. Herman and Hirschman postulate that only when society has been restructured according to the liberal principle of equality will it be possible "for men and women, parents and children, to love one another without coercion or exploitation"[55]—in other words, to enjoy forms of love uncorrupted by power.

In my view, this radical feminist conceptualization of a sexuality uncorrupted by inequality and power differentials is not only a regulatory construction, but also a construction that profoundly misunderstands the dynamics of human sexual and intersubjective relations. While I would certainly claim that children and adults do not share a relation of equivalence, this is not to say that children are universally positioned outside of power. On the contrary, no non–physically forcible sexual relations (adult-adult or adult-child) and no parent-child relations can be disarticulated from power. Children exercise power in myriad and subtle ways in their relationships with parents and adults. As James Kincaid has argued, "All forms of human contact involve unequal power equations."[56] In fact, not only are both sexual relations and parent-child relations only ever constituted in and through unequal networks of power relations, they are also constituted in and through relations of power that cannot be compared. Both of these arguments seem to be rather straightforward Foucauldian and poststructuralist, even psychoanalytic, propositions: each subject is differentially marked and positioned in power and discourse structures. Yet this circumstance represents the complete inversion of the radical feminist argument concerning child sexual abuse.

I suggest that the radical feminist simplification of our understanding of power relations has had damaging ethical implications for social relations in general and child sexuality specifically. For if inequalities of power are thought only to corrupt sexual and parent-child relations, then there can be no ethical sexual and parent-child relations. As Rex Stainton Rogers and Wendy Stainton Rogers put it, "All childhoods are oppressive, if by that we mean power unequal."[57] After all, isn't the very field of unequal, indeed incommensurable, power relations precisely the very condition of possibility for the ethical? Clearly, this is a rhetorical question: I am not foreclosing the possibility of either ethical sexual or parent-child relations, only exposing the contradictions of radical feminist arguments, as well as their implications for understanding all forms of sexuality and intersubjective relations. Moreover, I am alluding to the fact that ethical relations are much more complex than the radical feminist discourse of child sexual abuse would have us believe. For if we are to use the inequality-of-power argument to disqualify all adult-child sex as unethical, then surely we ought to apply the same logical and ethical test to all other adult-child interactions. Alternatively, we are obliged, as Terry Leahy argues, to specify and rigorously defend sexuality's difference from other modes of human interaction.[58]

Within this radical feminist-inflected understanding of power, there appears to be a tension between the ontological register (what is) and the ethical register (what ought to be). On the one hand, there is a critique of current formations of sexuality as they have been constituted through unequal power relations; on the other, there is the implicit ethical ideal of how formations of sexuality ought to be constituted in a nonpatriarchal society. Margaret Jackson's analysis is typical of the kind of radical feminist position from which the discourse of child sexual abuse draws. Arguing that power differentials in sexual relations between men and women are culturally rather than biologically determined, Jackson shifts to the ethical register to speak of an ideal, egalitarian world free of such differentials, a world in which all power dynamics in sexual relations between equals would be eliminated. We "must challenge the assertion that the association between sex and power is inevitable or desirable," she implores, "and that dominance and submission are inherent in sexual activity and essential to pleasure."[59] With this I cannot agree. But my disagreement issues, as I have made clear, from a post-Foucauldian, nonjuridical conceptualization of power which assumes that where there is a power relationship between two people—and not a state of bondage or pure force—power is exercised and not possessed. I am not claiming that there is a biologically inevitable power differential between the sexes or between adults and children. I am claiming that, in the field of power relations, no two people are situated in a dynamic of equivalence. We are all positioned differentially within social and discursive networks of power. Dominance and submission are not fixed positions determined by the presence or absence of power. Unless he or she is in a state of complete bondage, it is incorrect to assume that the person purportedly in submission does not exercise varying degrees of power.[60] Thus in the domain of sexual relationships we are never situated outside of power; there is no position of equivalence with regard to its forces. As long as we think that a society of egalitarian power relations is possible, not only do we misunderstand power and sexuality, but we are also led to formulate simplistic, unhelpful political analyses and ethical agendas. It is highly unlikely that somehow the "child" at some arbitrary age—say, sixteen, seventeen, or eighteen—goes from a position of powerlessness to one of (adult) power, or from a position of sexual ignorance to a position of sexual knowledge. We ought to at least interrogate such assumptions by way of rigorous empirical and theoretical analysis. By and large, however, notions of child powerlessness and child sexual ignorance stand as unsubstantiated assumption, begging the question of their political and performative function. The metaphor and rhetoric of power sorely require, as Kincaid demonstrates, a systematic and exhaustive deconstruction.[61]

Too often it would seem that adult discourses of sexuality function primarily to reinforce certain relations of power and domination between adults and children. As we are all too aware in this post-Foucauldian climate, power is exercised through knowledge and discourse relations. Accordingly, children's apparent lack of knowledge cannot be disentangled from adult efforts to exercise power through these knowledge and discourse relations. Sex education, for instance, is routinely a question of adult attempts to control children's access to knowledge about sex and sexuality—that is, an attempt to ensure power *over* knowledge. It is far from self-evident, however, that all children lack the capacity to understand adult meanings of sexuality. Interestingly, the relations of domination inherent to this dynamic between adults and children seem to result from adult efforts to instate a kind of juridical form of power (the very notion of power that they decry when the topic is consensual intergenerational sex). Hence we continue to witness a near-hysterical outcry regarding children's access to "adult" material on the internet, for example. The internet, it is feared, threatens to undermine adult control of adult sexual knowledge, meanings, and practices. The discourse of child sexual abuse therefore has a great deal at stake in remaining bound to a juridical understanding of power. Put simply, the dual concept of child ignorance and powerlessness is that on which adult efforts to control child sexuality pivot. I am not suggesting that all forms of child sexuality should be made conceptually equivalent to adult sexualities; only that our blanket assumptions about the imprecise and homogeneous category of the child and its relationship to power and sexuality ought to be interrogated.

In the case of intergenerational sex, it may even be that a more complex account of power would be required than the Foucauldian theory of power and resistance or, indeed, any theory of power provides. The Foucauldian critique of juridical formulations of power certainly seems to be a good place to start, as it opens up the possibility that children can exercise power and that they may not be unable, necessarily, to "consent." However, it may be that a theory of power is in fact not the place to address questions raised by child sexuality and intergenerational sex.[62] For the purposes of this discussion, the important point I wish to make is that, although reinterpreting the issue of power and its relationship to knowledge was a critical way for feminists to challenge our society's tendency to blame the child victim, the question and discourse of child sexuality were rather unfortunate casualties of this process. In fact, *concepts* of power, consent, and ethics replaced the signifier of child sexuality in the feminist discourse of child sexual abuse. Assumed to be outside adult power and knowledge economies, children are excluded from the domain of (adult) sexuality. Shifting the focus away from child seduction or precocity and toward the question of adult abuses of power thus enabled feminists to avoid the thorny issues of child sexuality.

This is not to say that feminists working in the area of child sexual abuse rejected the concept of child sexuality. Indeed, many began in the late 1970s by acknowledging it. Finkelhor not only recognized the existence of child sexuality but approved of "sexual experimentation among adolescents . . .

[and] sex play between prepubescent children."[53] Herman and Hirschman were also quick to recognize child sexuality, but they were just as quick to shift the discussion to the question of adult power and responsibility:

> Children do have sexual feelings, and children do seek out affection and attention from adults. Out of these undeniable realities, the male fantasy of the Seductive Daughter is created. But . . . it is the adult, not the child, who determines the sexual nature of the encounter, and who bears the responsibility for it.[64]

This move is indicative of almost all the influential texts on child sexual abuse during the 1980s (and, indeed, indicative of many of those up until the present day). If the question of child sexuality is brought into the frame of reference at all, it is routinely displaced by a discussion of power and consent. It was primarily in the early years of "rediscovery" of child sexual abuse that child sexuality registered in feminist accounts.[65] Strikingly, in fact, many of these accounts relied on the Freudian model of infantile sexuality. However, with the expansion of the feminist discourse of child sexual abuse in the 1980s, there was less and less acknowledgment of—perhaps less need to acknowledge—child sexuality, which was increasingly being ignored as the focus turned to issues of power and consent. The feminist use of power has functioned to evade, discount, silence, and repress a signifier of child sexuality.

When brought into the feminist frame of reference under these political and epistemological imperatives, child sexuality is severely compromised. Either it ceases to be sexuality, or else the use of terms such as *sex play* or *sexual experimentation* work to disqualify it by suggesting that childhood sexual desire and agency are safely located outside power's reach and are only immature precursors to adult sexuality.[66] This trivialization of child sexuality is reflected in the fact that ideas of child *protosexuality* form the epistemological kernel of the concept, almost universally accepted in child sexual abuse discourse of the time, of "premature introduction into adult sexuality."[67] But an introduction into adult sexuality can be premature only if children are not deemed properly sexual beings. So although many feminist theorists recognized forms of childhood eroticism, and even grouped them under the rubric of "child sexuality," this approach was altogether different from their implicit construction of an adult sexuality that acted as the feminist referent. As immature and not yet adults, children's "sexuality" could be construed only as a pre-, or proto-, or latent simulacrum of adult sexuality; hence it was referred to as "play" or "experimentation." Post-1980s writings tended to collapse all forms and developmental stages of childhood eroticism into a form of childhood exploration that is seen to be distinct from, and to precede the onset of, "real" adult sexuality. Childhood and adulthood are thus separated by sexuality rather than bound together by it, and the (psychoanalytic) concept that child sexuality inextricably informs adult sexuality is repudiated.[68] This demarcation of childhood and adulthood is evident in the late-twentieth-century shift to a more identity-based construction of sexuality, from which children are generally excluded. It is also apparent in the late-1980s emergence of the categories of "child sexual abusers" and the "sexualized child."[69] As Paul Okami points out:

> The extremely narrow range of acceptable behaviors—and the fact that virtually any sexual behavior may be defined as abnormal or abusive under circumstances of the investigators choosing—leave the irresistible impression that childhood sexual activity itself is being condemned.[70]

Whereas the pre-1980s witnessed the coexistence of contradictory notions of childhood—as sexual *and* innocent—the post-1980s have been characterized by a conscientious effort to resolve this representational dynamic. The dominant post-1980s figuration of children in terms of asexual innocence differs significantly from that of earlier decades. One side of the contradiction has been repressed or disavowed as overt representations of child sexuality have been eliminated by the hegemonic discourse of child sexual abuse.

Historical Myths and Analytic Simplifications

When a new social movement or set of discourses mobilizes itself around a political or epistemological identity, that identity usually authorizes itself by way of a historical-origins story. For those working in the field of child sexual abuse, that story almost always begins with Freud's supposed rejection of the seduction theory. Freud is routinely positioned as the forerunner in the suppression of the truth of child sexual abuse, and feminists and child care professionals are the "pioneers" or revolutionary "pathfinders" who uncovered this hidden truth.[71] In his early work on psychoneurosis, Freud had identified seduction, assault, and premature childhood sexual experiences as the root causes of hysteria.[72] By 1924, however, this thesis had been "corrected," as Freud began to appreciate the importance of infantile sexual fantasies. Freud explains this alteration to his seduction theory of hysteria by pointing out that, when he first formulated it, "I was not yet able to distinguish between my patient's phantasies about their childhood years and their real recollections"; he also points out, "I attributed to the aetiological factor of seduction a significance and universality which it does not possess."[73] Feminists working in the area of child sexual abuse have pounced on this shift in theoretical emphasis, considering it a disingenuous attempt to conceal not only the prevalence of sexual abuse but also the evidence, which Freud infamously tried to subvert, that fathers and not uncles were the primary perpetrators. Feminists have also argued that Freud's shift is the basis of the twentieth-century tendency to blame the victims.[74] These events are read together to suggest that, because the "discovery" of incest committed by fathers was far too great a "challenge to patriarchal values,"[75] Freud was forced to abandon it. Herman and Hirschman assert that "though Freud had gone to such great lengths to avoid publicly inculpating fathers, he remained so distressed by his seduction theory that within a year he repudiated it entirely. He concluded that his patients' numerous reports of sexual abuse were untrue."[76]

As many commentators have demonstrated, however, Freud never repudiated the seduction theory. Nor did he consider it "erroneous," as Rush has claimed.[77] In fact, he maintained for his whole life the reality of seduction as a pathogenic force in neurosis.[78] What is more, Freud did not withdraw the claim that the sexual seduction of children was "not a rare abuse."[79] Instead, he affirmed it, arguing in "Female Sexuality" that, alongside infantile fantasy, "actual seduction, too, is common enough."[80] In *Three Essays on the Theory of Sexuality*, he clarified:

> I cannot admit that in my paper on "The Aetiology of Hysteria" (1896) I exaggerated the frequency or importance of that influence [seduction], though I did not then know that persons who remain normal may have had the same experiences in their childhood.[81]

Freud repudiated not the seduction theory as a whole but the part of the theory that had assumed hysteria was universally caused by actual sexual abuse. His reasoning was not that abuse was rare, but on the contrary, that so many children were sexually abused without becoming hysterics that abusive encounters themselves had no *necessary* etiological significance. As Freud pointed out even in the 1896 paper, "*Hysterical symptoms can only arise with the co-operation of memories.*"[82] Here we glimpse an early formulation of Freud's notion of deferred action, which is pivotal to his theorization of neurosis:

Our view then is that infantile sexual experiences are the fundamental precondition for hysteria, are, as it were, the *disposition* for it and that it is they which create the hysterical symptoms, but that they do not do so immediately, but remain without effect to begin with and only exercise a pathogenic action later, when they have been aroused after puberty in the form of unconscious memories.[83]

As Freud came to understand the complexity and implications of deferred action in relation to the sexual etiology of neurosis, it became clear to him that, because hysteria emerges only in concert with the "co-operation of memories," a subjective reconstruction of the original event happens later. This enables us to grasp more fully what Freud and Josef Breuer meant by the phrase *"hysterics suffer mainly from reminiscences."*[84] Many child sexual abuse feminists imply—erroneously, in my view—that Freud's discovery of infantile sexuality resulted from a disingenuous denial of the widespread reality of sexual abuse and from an attempt to conceal the fact that fathers were the primary perpetrators. Further, they mistakenly assume that Freud considered all patients' claims of sexual seduction to be nothing more than fantasies. Instead, however, Freud remained so committed to a belief in the reality of widespread child sexual abuse that he was driven to seek an explanation for why most people are not hysterical. This search, in conjunction with his gradual discovery of infantile sexuality and the Oedipus complex, must be viewed in this context. It is certainly true that Freud began exploring—indeed, emphasizing—the dynamics of sexual fantasy in analyses of neurosis and unfortunately favoring oedipal interpretations. This shift is somewhat easier to understand, though, when we bear in mind the importance of deferred action, for fantasy plays an integral and inextricable part of symptom formation. It is fantasy that works over the original scene of seduction and provides it, retroactively, with its neurotic force. So it is not enough to identify an act of sexual assault or seduction as the pathogenic cause, because it is the retroactive reinterpretation of this event in the context of later events that yields the clue to neurotic symptomatology. Freud himself was quick to remind his audience as early as 1896, *"No hysterical symptom can arise from a real experience alone, but that in every case the memory of earlier experiences awakened in association to it plays a part in causing the symptom."*[85]

The typical narrative in the discourse of child sexual abuse is that Freud de-emphasized the reality of sexual trauma and so led later analysts to disregard its importance in understanding and treating trauma. Herman and

Hirschman argue that, rather "than investigate further into the question of fact, Freud's followers chose to continue the presumption of fantasy and made the child's desire and fantasy the focus of psychological inquiry."[86] Notwithstanding the compelling critique of Freud's overreliance on oedipal fantasy, one of the shortcomings with this account is that it simplifies and misrepresents the psychoanalytic notion of trauma by attempting to impute a traumatic essence to a single sexual act. As I have demonstrated, psychological trauma is for psychoanalysis a dynamic process. It is not based on a single sexual act (e.g., a sexual assault), as this alone would tell us nothing about the psychical processes that assign meaning to that act and thereafter give rise to neurotic symptoms. Symptoms emerge only in association with later acts or events, as memories are reworked and revised and the original assault is given its meaning and sexual definition for the child. Child sexual abuse feminists such as Herman and Hirschman, Rush, and Olafson who cast doubt on the prevailing pre-1980s assumption that the sexual seduction of children is not necessarily inherently traumatic, and that children often participate in or desire such seductions, do so on the basis of an oversimplified notion of trauma: all childhood sexual acts are deemed inherently traumatic. This theoretical move is yet another means by which childhood is desexualized in the discourse of child sexual abuse.

The point to underscore here is that the feminist assumption of Freud's notion of infantile sexuality as a smoke screen for his discovery of the prevalence of male abusers functions rhetorically to devalue—even to evade—the notion of child sexuality. This revisionist narrative provides those working in the area of child sexual abuse not only with some discursive consistency and a founding point of identification but also with a call to action to reverse the Freudian-led overemphasis on child sexuality and fantasy. Thus the discourse of child sexual abuse has insistently refocused on the reality of sexual abuse. However, as we will see, the resulting neglect of, if not the utter disregard for, for child sexuality (and fantasy and agency) may be as damaging to a child's social and psychological well-being as the discounting of the reality of sexual abuse.

Child Sexual Abuse and Child Sexual Neglect

According to the discourse of child sexual abuse, the traumatic kernel of a child's sexual experience with an adult is formed, at least in part, by the child's premature introduction into adult sexuality. This conceptualization depends on the installation of sexuality as the dividing line between childhood and adulthood. Child sexuality is conceived of as premature (play, experimentation, imitation), whereas adult sexuality is conceived of as mature (developed, fully realized, authentic). Therefore it is no longer socially acceptable to view forms of childhood behavior through the lens of adult sexual meanings. Although we may recognize childhood behavioral erotics in adult-child interactions, it is no longer appropriate to take these erotics as evidence of either a child's desire to have sex with an adult or a child's capacity to understand adult sexuality. A child's ability to consent to sex or to be held in part responsible for a sexual encounter with an adult is no longer at issue. In short, hegemonic norms ensure that childhood erotics are not read as a sign of (adult) sexuality or (adult) sexual capacity. I want to suggest that to trivialize child sexuality as premature, as play, and as imitative of adult reality is socially irresponsible. I do not wish to deny that there are important differences between child and adult forms of sexual expression, or that adults must be accountable for their behavior toward children. But along with any psychological and developmental differences, there are important similarities and continuities between "child" and "adult" sexualities that only psychoanalysis has analyzed rigorously, and these similarities and continuities give the lie to simple oppositions between premature and mature sexualities, between childhood and adulthood. Far from protecting and empowering children, the feminist evasion of child sexuality may have disempowered some children and made some abused children more vulnerable to psychological trauma.

One of the most consistent findings of research into child sexual abuse is the child's self-blame. In fact, self-blame is a typical means by which victims accommodate the abuse.[87] Therapists and psychologists routinely refer to instances of self-blame as "cognitive distortions" and see this as a root cause of the overwhelming feelings of shame and guilt that an abused child often experiences and that frequently lead to anxiety and depression in later life. The therapist generally aims to change the child's perceptions (i.e., distortions) of reality in order to help him or her work through the shame and guilt (and thus avert anxiety and depression). As John Pearce and Terry Pezzot-Pearce put it, therapists "must correct some of the cognitive distortions children have about their victimization experiences for them to be able to reformulate the meaning of the abuse."[88] Children need to be convinced that they did not cause the abuse and that they were not responsible for their victimization. Or, as Sandra Wieland advises, it "is important to explain to the older child or adolescent that seeing oneself as causing events is a result of the limited breadth of a young child's thinking (egocentric) and is not from the reality of the situation."[89]

But the problem with these approaches is that they attempt to impose a meaning that often directly contradicts the child's own perception and experience. While this kind of therapy may well lead the child to reinterpret the event, often it does not, and many children firmly believe in their own power and control in sexual encounters with adults. This is especially true of children who may have contributed to the continuation of the abuse by returning to the perpetrator's home or by seeking gifts or rewards by engaging in sexual activities. "Saying 'it's not your fault' is not helpful," psychologist Sharon Lamb says, because

> sexually abused children may feel that in the abusive situation they made some choices, however small, that led to the continuation of the abuse. With a greater intuition than many adults, children seem to conceptualize the situation as an interaction between two people. And, no matter how unequal the power in terms of physical strength, status, or mental capacity, from a systems point of view and the views of both the abuser and the abused it remains an interaction.[90]

Lamb's important cautionary note has been positively cited by Pearce and Pezzot-Pearce, who in fact encourage therapists to tell abused children that they may have made mistakes or uninformed decisions; for instance, the decision to return to the perpetrator's home. Despite their appreciation of the need to avoid casting the child purely as victim, Pearce and Pezzot-Pearce's overarching aim is still to "help children *change* their belief that they were responsible for the maltreatment."[91] Attempting to do so, however, only reinforces in children the idea that they lack power and control in encounters with adults. In other words, Pearce and Pezzot-Pearce merely confer on children the blameless-victim attribution that they caution against. Reliance on the therapeutic goal of correcting reality distortions brings into relief the problematic residue of debates about Freud's supposed abandonment of the seduction theory and his overemphasis on childhood fantasy. Rather than view the child's perception of the sexual encounter as constituted through the complex interaction between reality and fantasy, as Freud did, therapists working in a child sexual abuse framework try to alter the child's perception of reality in the hope that a change in fantasized memory reconstruction will follow. This approach is akin to simplistic notions of brainwashing. It relies on a linear understanding of causation, at the center of which is the omnipotent, all-controlling adult and the powerless, passive child. It also assumes—erroneously, in my view—that reality and fantasy can be definitively disentangled.

However, the attempt to replace a child's "reality" with an adult's fosters more than a misrecognition of psychological dynamics. It also ensures, at best, the trivialization or evasion of child sexuality and, at worst, its complete eradication. Yet another of the common research findings is that, in addition to a sense of sexual power over the adult abuser, children often experience excitation and pleasure in the encounter. Herman and Hirschman found that most of the women in their study had experienced sexual pleasure in their incestuous relationships and that the "daughters seemed almost uniformly to believe that they had seduced their fathers and therefore could seduce any man."[92] Typically, these feelings lead to massive shame and guilt, which, if not worked through, can cause chronic anxiety and depression. However, when a therapist attempts to "correct" a child's cognitive distortions and convince him or her that they stem from an unrealistic, childish egocentrism,[93] the unresolved shame and guilt over child sexuality might only be compounded and left untreated.[94] However much we may consider their perceptions to be immature, a child's sexual desires and experiences of power and pleasure must be acknowledged and normalized. Unfortunately, however, these feelings are stripped of any power or force for the child when they are rendered mere "infatuation" or "curiosity."[95] As Wieland explains:

> Sexual curiosity and, as the child gets older, a wish to experience sexual feelings are part of normal sexual development. When curiosity and feelings are explored with a peer in a nonthreatening manner, these experiences are at a level that can be absorbed within the child's understanding and are part of normal growing up. When the demands of someone older or in a threatening position are *imposed*, the sexual experiencing is shifted from the child's level to an older level, and the experience becomes abuse. It is not the child's curiosity or wish to experience something sexual that created the abuse, but the exploitation of this by someone older or threatening. Discussion along these lines with the therapist can help the child realize that her own increasing sexual awareness was normal and did not cause the abuse.[96]

Here we see a clear attempt to not truly recognize and engage the child's sexuality and sense of power but to impose the regulatory norm of sexuality as the marker dividing childhood and adulthood. Once again we are back at the juridical formulation of power, in which the therapist tries to convince the child that the abuse "resulted from a decision made by the older or more powerful person."[97] This represents a clear failure to take the question of children's sexual subjectivities seriously. Moreover, as Lamb has compellingly demonstrated, child victims of abuse are not well served by therapists who assume child powerlessness and "emphasize the adult's responsibility to the child."[98] To avoid encouraging the amplification of shame and guilt, and thus anxiety and depression, it is imperative not to impose an adult perception (fantasy) but to engage and take seriously the child's perception (fantasy). In other words, we must take child sexuality and children's subjective sense of power seriously. As long as we evade these issues or dispossess them of their force by way of "correcting" "cognitive distortions," or of reducing a child's sexual feelings to a form of passive "curiosity" or effect of adult manipulation, we constrain children from venting, symbolizing, and working through the shame and guilt that compound the trauma.

Sexual abuse therapists often go even further and completely minimize the significance of child sexual arousal. In her discussion of children's inability to disclose an abusive encounter because of shame, the renowned clinical psychologist of child sexual abuse Anna Salter renders a child's sexual arousal during an encounter with an adult a mere mechanical, biological response to genital manipulation.[99] "The issue of physical responsiveness is particularly shame-based for victims," writes Salter in her sexual abuse manual *Transforming Trauma*:

> Because the grooming offender is trying to justify his behavior by blaming the victim, it is important to him that the child respond physically. He will often stroke the child's clitoris or penis in order to induce arousal, while telling the child that she or he wants him to do this.
>
> The child is faced with a conflict that, however he resolves it, is likely to leave sequelae. If his body responds to the abuse, he will find it difficult to resist the offender's interpretation of that response: that he wants the abuse to occur, that he is enjoying it, and that his "wanting it" was the reason it occurred in the first place.[100]

Salter is here suggesting that children are not really experiencing their own subjective sexual feelings but merely exhibiting an inevitable biological reaction to having their genitals fondled by the clever and powerful older person. Instating a Cartesian split, Salter assumes the child's subjective sense of self is divided from his or her physical self. In neither the mental nor psychical self does the child appear to have any degree of control or agency. Instead, he or she figures largely as the passive recipient of adult sexual practice and meaning. At least with regard to sexual encounters with adults, the child merely internalizes the offender's projection of the meaning of his or her physical arousal. By trivializing and flattening out child sexual subjectivity, such approaches may leave some children *more* vulnerable to psychological harm.

Although springing (perhaps in part) from a protective concern with alleviating shame for abused children, the minimization and negation of child sexual subjectivity and agency within therapeutic discourse and practice effectively circumvents rather than grapples with the psychical dynamics of shame. Displaced by juridical power, the child's shame is in certain respects decoupled from the dynamics of his or her own desire, excitation, pleasure, and sense of self. Shame is construed, like sexual arousal, as something produced by the adult, as something infecting the child from the outside in. This represents a defensive and, as I have argued, potentially damaging turn away from the agentive sexual child and from the intrapsychic (and intersubjective) machinations of subjectivity. Shame, in this approach, is worked through by emphasizing adult power and responsibility. The adult perpetrator is shamed instead and held entirely responsible for causing the child's sexual desire, pleasure, and shame. Conceivable though it is that some children may experience a shame-inflected conflict as a result of physical manipulation and identification with the adult aggressor, evidently this is only one kind of scenario. Yet even in such scenarios, highlighting the child's passivity at the hands of an adult is still imprudent. As Lamb points out:

> although most therapists will deal these feelings [of sexual arousal] by insisting that the body has a mind of its own and that these were merely physiological reactions, such a response would seem to encourage the symptoms of dissociation while the victim herself is trying to feel connected (if ashamed) to her body and its reactions.[101]

Even Lamb does not extend her analysis to a consideration of child sexual subjectivity as a substantive psychobiological agency. Indeed, she sidesteps this issue somewhat by diverting to the prevailing assumption that "the overstimulation of sexual excitation before a child's body is prepared for it can be overwhelming."[102] However, equally as probable as such scenarios, if not more—particularly in those not uncommon instances where children voluntarily and without threat of harm return to perpetrators whom they know after an abusive encounter—are the encounters where children's sexual arousal springs not merely from adult's manipulation of their bodies, but from the children's own desire, curiosity, and interest. Notably, the dominant paradigm of child sexual abuse of which Salter is an exemplary proponent largely disavows or at best avoids this second class of cases. In these contexts, even a minimalist psychological understanding of shame requires us to consider the specific intrapsychic qualities of the self and intersubjective dimensions of relationships. It is not enough to reduce shame to the child's mistaken identification with adult meaning, or to frame the intersubjective relations as a one-way relay of adult power imposed on the child. Nor is it enough to render the shame-conflict as arising simply from the adult's manipulation and the child's identification with the aggressor. By misrecognizing the intrapsychic and intersubjective dynamics and the child's agentive subjectivity, this model of trauma risks misfiring and threatens to redouble the debilitating shame (and guilt) affect therapists seek to resolve for the child, particularly for the child who retains a sense of agentive involvement.

Within this second class of cases—that is, where there is desire, interest, pleasure, and excitement springing from the child—the model of shame proposed by Silvan Tomkins is especially instructive. For Tomkins, shame "operates ordinarily only after interest or enjoyment has been activated."[103] At first blush, this might appear to support the Salter model of trauma and shame in which the adult activates the sexual enjoyment and pleasure of the child, which in turn creates the conflict of shame and guilt. However, something cannot be activated out of nothing and activation is not a one-way process, no matter what age. Nor can interest simply be implanted in a child. There is another critical component of Tomkins's theory of shame: that shame is the result of the "incomplete reduction of interest or joy."[104] What this entails is that shame is bound up with the *remainder* of interest and/or the *ongoing* experience of excitation or enjoyment. Each of these—interest-excitement, enjoyment-joy—is a decisively agentive, active, and mobile phenomenon. Interestingly, in her discussion of the incapacitating nature of sexual overstimulation for children, Lamb footnotes Tomkins in a discussion of shame but does not refer to shame's correlates (interest-excitement, enjoyment-joy).[105] Yet these directly encompass sexuality. She discusses the gender differences in experiences of shame, where girls tend to experience greater shame than boys. The implications of this are especially troubling for child sexual abuse discourse that is intent on circumventing attributions of victim blaming and avoiding a direct confrontation with child sexual subjectivity. For if we stick with Tomkins's baseline definition of shame for a moment, one possibility may be that the degree of shame experienced by victims after the abuse might in some cases be proportionate to the degree of interest, excitation, and pleasure experienced during the encounter or the relationship.

Tomkins's account of shame does more than leave open the question of childhood (sexual) interest and enjoyment. It makes child sexual interest, desire, enjoyment, and agency central to any understanding of shame.

Where there is shame, there is sexuality; and where there is sexuality, there is shame; the two go hand in hand. Thus when we figure shame only as a pathological imposition on sexuality or sexual development, as that which healthy sexuality or development ought to be free from, we may well misrecognize—often to detrimental effect—the routine interlacing of shame and sexuality in the constitution of subjectivity. Effectively targeting and treating shame therefore obliges serious consideration of child sexual subjectivity as a substantive and dynamic agency. The problem is, however, that in Western societies child sexuality is overdetermined by negative emotions (fear, shame, contempt, disgust). Often we *fear a confrontation with shame* and repel or avoid those objects and subjects, the sexual child exemplary among them, that so palpably raise the specter of this encounter. Precisely because shame is so intimately interwoven with interest-excitement and enjoyment-joy—some of the main affects constitutive of sexual desire and pleasure—the fear of shame sometimes encourages, even if unknowingly, an avoidance of the sexual child.

Beyond the Homogenous Child

Displacing agentive child sexuality is, however, not the only troublesome effect of a protectionist paradigm. Correlatively, juridical power is conflated with sexuality, and this sexualized power operates as a strict division demarcating the power*ful* sexual adult from the power*less* protosexual child. The result, at least concerning adult-child sex, is a conceptually undifferentiated category of the child and a rigid child/adult opposition. Consequences flow from this. With no gradations of power, a child of six merges inappreciably into an adolescent of sixteen or seventeen. The juridical model of power also has ramifications concerning the recognition of gender differences within the category of the child—among many other differences such as race, class, ethnicity, religion, ability—and the ways these differences uniquely shape intersubjective power relations and subjectivity. It has, of course, become commonplace for those working in the field of child sexual abuse to highlight that girls *and* boys are victims of child sexual abuse, notwithstanding the fact that statistics reveal that many more girls are victimized than boys. Also highlighted is the fact that women also sometimes commit sexual offenses against children, even though as a group they are in the minority in terms of offender cohorts. The recognition of these facts, once historically overlooked or downplayed, has led to important changes in definitions and assumptions about child sexual offenses, victims, and perpetrators. Consequently, gender neutrality has become the standard socio-legal principle in child sexual abuse discourse. However, the historical transformation from a gender-specific sexual abuse formula (perpetrator = male, victim = female) to a gender-neutral one is not as clear-cut as it might seem. Residual gendered assumptions, as we will see specifically in the chapters on teacher-student sex scandals, inflect the discourse of gender neutrality and its conceptual apparatus.

Let us return to Lamb's remarks cited above to explore this briefly. When discussing the issue of shame and dissociation, Lamb refers to the generic victim with female pronouns. She says that therapists who frame child sexual arousal in abusive encounters as mere physiological reaction "seem to encourage the symptoms of dissociation while the victim herself is trying to feel connected (if ashamed) to her body and its reactions."[106] This use of female pronouns is something of a standard convention with the feminist discourse of child sexual abuse. Lamb is fully cognizant of the fact that girls are in the vast majority of victims, just as she is acutely aware of the fact that boys are also sexually victimized. Presumably her use of female pronouns is an acknowledgment of the overrepresentation of girls as victims, as well as perhaps an implicit registration of the fact that historically the predominant focus of the feminist sexual abuse movement was initially on women and female children. However, I think the use of the female pronoun to reference the generic victim is illustrative of one of the shortcomings of the homogenization of the category of the child within discourses of (intergenerational) sexuality and sexual abuse. It is also illustrative, as I will argue more fully in chapter 6, of the epistemological and socio-legal messiness created by the transformation from a gender-specific to a gender-neutral discourse. For now, I want only to note that the use of the female pronoun by Lamb (and others in the field) unwittingly, it seems to me, registers the fact that the conceptual referent of child sexual abuse discourse is not gender-neutral. Despite gender-neutral sexual-offense laws and the widespread recognition of boys as victims of sexual abuse, the discourse of child sexual abuse—and the concepts of power, consent, adult perpetrator, and child victim at its core—has been historically and politically constituted around a presumed female victim. Gendered assumptions have infused the conceptual framework of child sexual abuse discourse. Serious social consequences follow from this conceptual foundation, as we will see in chapters to follow. The gender-neutral socio-legal framework developed in anglophone societies as an outgrowth of the child sexual abuse paradigm has left us with a set of limited conceptual tools for grappling with issues of child sexual subjectivity, agency, consent, power, and, indeed, criminal prosecutions and their ramifications. These frameworks and tools have been designed to protect children from abuse, but they also operate in part as (at times unwitting) defenses against specific (and not generic and neutral) agentive children and childhoods.

The moral of this history of child sexual abuse is not that feminism is an automatic guarantee that "makes the difference between better or worse solutions to the social problem of child sexual abuse," as the quote from Linda Gordon cited at the beginning of this chapter would have us believe.[107] The moral is a more modest one. Child sexual abuse feminism has undeniably led to enormous improvements in tackling the problem of child molestation. However, it also has its limitations—specifically around frameworks for thinking through power relations and the intricacies of agentive sexual children. In seeking to acknowledge multiple child sexualities and differing forms of agency, though, I have no interest in imputing to children some positive and distinctive ontological content. In fact, I would actively resist such a move, recognizing as I do the specificity of each and every individual assemblage of child sexuality and agency. Nor am I arguing for a return to simplistic, pre-1980s ideas of child precocity, flirtatiousness, and seductiveness. Far from it. But we ought not let the history of these discursive formulations prevent us from engaging the differential realities and complexities of child sexualities. At a minimum, we need not shy away from theorizing the constitution of children's subjectivity through those dynamics routinely encapsulated under the general rubric of adult sexuality, such as desire, agency, identification, unconscious fantasy, affect, pleasure, and so on. Neither do we need to install some unbridgeable spatial, temporal, and epistemological gulf between childhood and adulthood and between child and adult sexualities. Better understanding the inevitable relationality and entanglement of childhoods and adulthoods does not have to undermine our efforts at protecting children from abuse.[108]

FOUR

Homosexual Pedophilia

In the winter of 1978/79, the editorial collective of the British gay socialist journal *Gay Left* observed what to them appeared to be a worrying trend in Western societies. They were referring to a conspicuous displacement of cultural anxiety concerning the visibility of dissident, or nonnormative, sexualities. "It is striking," began the editorial, "that over the past two or three years conservative moral anxiety throughout the advanced capitalist countries has switched from homosexuality in general to sexual relationships between adults and young people." The reason proffered for this shift was that because the "moral conservatives" had in some countries already lost (and in others were losing) the battle to retain private, consensual homosexuality as a criminal offense, there was a concerted effort to rebuild a new conservative "moral consensus." "Realistically," in other words, "the moral right wing cannot get much support out of campaigning against homosexuality as such. . . . Moral reactionaries can serve their cause better by building alliances on easy issues such as the protection of childhood." The conclusion reached by the collective was that "'child molesters' and 'exploiters of children' were the new social monsters."[1]

Homosexuals and homosexuality were not as a result emancipated from the anxious and scrutinizing gaze of the so-called moral majority. As the collective suggested, there was also an increasing concern over the interconnections between a visible and public homosexual identity and pedophilia. It "is not so much private, consensual adult homosexual behavior which is of primary concern" to the moral majority, they argued, "but so-called *public* decency, and the related question of 'corruption of minors.'"[2] The collective did not go on to elaborate on this statement. However, the point they appear to be making is that in the public imagination a normalized, publicly visible homosexuality in the late 1970s seems to have invoked a fear of pedophilia and child seduction. Whether indicative of homophobic political rhetoric or genuine concern, or both, this fear appears to have been attached to the idea that if a publicly visible homosexuality is accepted as valid and equal to heterosexuality, then children might be encouraged—not to mention *seduced* and *corrupted*—into experimenting with and adopting homosexual practices, identities, or lifestyles. In this way homosexuality and pedophilia are imagined as inextricably linked, with homosexuality imagined as a kind of pedophilic seduction or corruption.[3]

Although the collective generalized about advanced capitalist societies, they did not make mention of Australia. Perhaps this was due in part to the fact that, at the time the editorial was written, homosexuality was still illegal in six of eight Australian states and territories, and thus in a temporal sense a "switch" of concern from homosexuality to pedophilia and childhood was not yet possible to discern. Or perhaps it was because no similar high-profile scandals about homosexual pedophile organizations, publications, and child pornography had occurred in Australia as they had in the United Kingdom and North America. For instance, the collective made specific mention of the furor over the pedophile support and activist organizations Paedophile Action for Liberation and the Paedophile Information Exchange (PIE) in the United Kingdom, and the police raid of the Canadian gay liberation magazine *Body Politic* after the publication of an issue on pedophilia. The group also mentioned the Anita Bryant anti-homosexual-equality campaign in the United States, which had gained momentum by mobilizing fears about a fantasized close relationship between homosexuality, pedophilia, and child seduction. Historians have since documented just this rhetorical entanglement of homosexuality with pedophilia and child sexual abuse in these and other moral panics in the late 1970s and early 1980s.[4] However, exactly as the collective observed of the United Kingdom and North America, the time was also ripe in Australia for just such an entanglement, if not at times conflation, of the distinct issues of homosexuality, pedophilia, and child seduction. In fact, the Australian experience was fundamentally influenced by developments and key figures in these countries.

This chapter offers a case study from Australia in the early 1980s of a scandal surrounding the police raid of the Melbourne chapter of the international Pedophile Support Group. It traces the public and political debates that ensued when the group was defended by a gay activist organization. My aim is not so much to contextualize the Australian experience as an instance almost identical to those of the earlier North American and British pedophile panics beginning in the late 1970s—although this is certainly the case at least in terms of the mobilization of fear and the typical logics, debates, and rhetoric framing them.[5] Rather, my aim is to offer a close reading of the Australian scandal in order to advance a slightly different historical take on the forces shaping anglophone scandals usually described as "pedophile" panics. Numerous scholars (including myself) have argued that homosexuals and those labeled as pedophiles were scapegoated for the problems of child sexual abuse (in the home) and murder, child pornography, teenage homosexual prostitution, child poverty, and missing children.[6]

This chapter draws our attention not just to the role of the scapegoat but to that of the sexual child. I argue that protection of children from exploitation, abuse, and harm at the hands of homosexual pedophiles is the *manifest* or publicly avowed driver of the pedophilia panic, and the negation of youth sexuality the *latent* and often disavowed underside. That is, this is as much a child-sexuality panic as it is a pedophile panic, even though a focus on the latter routinely serves to occlude the former. Another way of saying this is that the signifier of child sexuality has as important a role to play—sometimes perhaps a bigger one—in the historical evolution of pedophile panics as do anxieties about child sexual abuse. The closer we get to this sexual child, as we seem to especially with regard to homosexual pedophilia, the greater the fear mobilized (and perhaps for some actually generated) and the greater the avoidance strategies employed.

Operation Delta: From Street Kids to Homosexual Pedophiles

"Operation Delta," a task force of the Victoria Police, is said to have begun its campaign in October 1982. Comprising eleven members, the group was reportedly set up after eight top ranking members of the Victoria Police Force viewed the documentary *Street Kids* a month earlier. The documentary is a rather grim real-life portrait of alienated and homeless youth in the Melbourne suburb of St. Kilda, an area notorious in the 1980s for drug addiction, homelessness, and prostitution. About the documentary, Rob Scott, one of the filmmakers, said: "The intention was to look at real kids in real situations . . . and to get their perspective of the world around them, the sorts of things they had to go through to survive." The sorts of things Scott is referring to—and which are glaringly and depressingly depicted in the film—are drug taking, heroin addiction, child prostitution, poverty, broken families, and homelessness. Most who previewed the film, including the eight police officials, responded with horror and disbelief. "Their response once they had absorbed the shock," recalls Scott, "was 'what can we do?'" Similarly, he recalls the horrified responses of two social workers: "They just freaked out. One initially reacted by bursting into tears. The initial reaction was one of revelation. But the considered opinion was 'this film should not be screened.'" Not long after previewing the film, Victoria Police launched "Operation Delta" in order to tackle the interlocking issues of homelessness, poverty, drugs, prostitution, and juvenile delinquency.[7]

The following year, the operations of the Delta task force hit the headlines. On March 30, 1983, the Melbourne newspaper the *Sun* published a front-page report. With a full-page image of Senior Sergeant Neil Comrie looking disturbed while checking files on child vice in St. Kilda, the report, entitled "'Delta' Probe Shock," contained further capitalized attention-grabbing headlines: "THE KIDS ON OUR STREETS."[8] It went on to detail not the multiple issues that were highlighted in the film *Street Kids* and that formed Delta's original brief, but rather only the issues of child prostitution and child pornography. Delta, the report told, "has discovered sexual use of children by adults which has disgusted police"; and that "police believe as many as 150 boys and girls aged between nine and 16 are involved in prostitution in the area. . . . The head of the Delta task force . . . said police feared one of the boys might be murdered by a sexual deviant."[9] As Danny Vadasz pointed out at the time, in a scathing critique in the gay magazine *Outrage*, conveniently the "media, abetted by the police force, had redefined the problem."[10] Vadasz went on to argue that *Outrage* had interviewed the *Street Kids* filmmakers, who had not come across anything like the scale of the problem outlined in the *Sun* article and trumpeted by police. They had also conducted their own research with sex workers and self-identified pedophiles and found that the youths involved in prostitution were invariably between ages fifteen and twenty and, far from totaling around 150 workers, constituted roughly only a "floating population of about 30–40."[11]

The *Sun* "story spread like wildfire."[12] A string of articles appeared in local and interstate newspapers, and the issue received extensive coverage on television news and radio programs. Even a public meeting attended by around one thousand people was held at the St. Kilda Town Hall. Notwithstanding the accuracy of either Comrie's or Vadasz's account regarding the extent of child prostitution in St. Kilda, the one thing that is clear is that the front-page report did much more than raise alarm bells and incite widespread community and media concern. The whole media campaign— and Delta's involvement in it—effectively shifted attention away from the interlocking issues of poverty, youth homelessness, drug addition, broken families, and prostitution and refocused it not just toward child prostitution and pornography but, more insidious, toward a purported problem of homosexual pedophiles. Although the *Sun* report mentioned the involvement of young girls in both brothels and street prostitution, the accent was placed squarely on homosexuality. After it opened with a general statement about child prostitution and pornography, we are then told in only the second sentence that "police have found boys as young as nine working 'the beat' as homosexual prostitutes in a St. Kilda street."[13] If the tenor of the report is not suggestive enough of a rhetorical association of homosexuality and pedophilia, and of this shift in direction of Delta, the actions of the task force later that year leave little doubt of this.

On November 5, 1983, following half a decade of widespread concern in North America and the United Kingdom surrounding child pornography— and of innumerable raids of suspected child pornographers and pedophile groups, such as the North American Man/Boy Love Association (NAMBLA) and PIE in the United Kingdom—the Delta task force of the Victoria Police raided the Australian Pedophile Support Group (PSG).[14] "All the hard work has paid off—it has worked out as well as we could have hoped for," Comrie told a newspaper reporter from the *Sun* after arresting the nine Australian PSG members.[15] With a thirty-strong police contingent, Delta simultaneously stormed a house in Melbourne, arresting seven men, and apprehended one man at his place of work in Melbourne and a ninth man at his home in Sydney. All nine men were gay, and police alleged that the group was part of an international child pornography ring and the largest group of child exploiters in Australia. The men were charged with "conspiring to corrupt public morals." Never before used in Australia, "conspiracy to corrupt public morals" was a British common-law charge. It had been used in very similar circumstances in Britain only two or three months earlier that year against members of PIE.[16] Far from specific to an Australian peculiarity, this was part of a broader anglophone pedophilia panic. Two of the PSG men were also charged with a number of other offenses, including the use of premises for the sexual penetration of a child, the actual sexual penetration of a child, the possession of prohibited imports, child stealing, the manufacturing of child pornography, and gross indecency.[17]

In both Sydney and Melbourne, crisis talks among gay-and-lesbian-rights campaigners were held. Fully cognizant and wary of the familiar rhetorical association of homosexuality with child seduction and molestation, activists agreed that, in spite of competing views in the gay community regarding the issue of pedophilia, the groups would nonetheless denounce both the police tactics employed by Delta and the use of antiquated and draconian conspiracy charges.[18] Alison Thorne, spokesperson for the Gay Legal Rights Coalition, gave an interview to Mike Edmonds of Melbourne's 3AW radio later that week. In the interview she condemned the arrests of the PSG members, foregrounding the fact that most of the men were charged not with actually organizing, photographing, or engaging in the sexual penetration of children but merely with talking about issues relating to pedophilia. Thorne argued that this was an infringement of an individual's civil liberties and right to freedom of speech. At this stage the predominant focus was on child sexual abuse allegations; however, the figure of the sexual child, as we are about to see, was a ghostly presence.

The raid of the PSG, code-named "Rockspider," headlined in the media and was heralded as not only the "biggest of its type in Australia"[19] but also "the most successful police offensive ever launched against the sexual exploitation of children."[20] In what was proclaimed as both a national and international coup, newspapers reported that the PSG was the Australian satellite of the international organizations PIE and NAMBLA. This provided the Victorian police force, as one *Age* newspaper report noted in an article the following year, with "tremendous kudos" for its success in tackling the problem of child sexual abuse.[21] Philip Jenkins notes of the UK pedophile panic only a few years earlier how similarly inflated claims exaggerated "both [the] scale and structure [of pedophile rings], in order to depict a more threatening enemy whose removal could be depicted as a substantial achievement."[22] However, that same *Age* report was in fact an exposé of the operations of Delta leading up to the PSG raid. The raid was the culmination of a one-man Delta infiltration of the PSG, brought about after Delta observed an advertisement for the group in the gay press. It read: "Australian Pedophile Support Group. A NSW-based organization set up to provide a supportive mechanism for gay men and women, throughout Australia, attracted to or in relations with children. More information, in confidence, from the Gayline."[23]

Delta had employed Stephen John Mayne, a South Melbourne public servant, to infiltrate the group as a self-identified pedophile named Greg Daniels. After writing and arranging to visit the Australian Lesbian and Gay Archives for information on pedophilia, Mayne was given the phone number of a PSG member in Sydney, whom he subsequently visited. He discussed the possibility of setting up a Melbourne support group and was put in touch with a Melbourne man who had already been planning to do this. Wired with a microphone and radio transmitter, Mayne attended the inaugural twelve-strong meeting of the Melbourne group, and four more meetings after that. According to the *Age* report, it was clear from the transcripts that Mayne had been attempting to entrap the PSG members. During a discussion of age-of-consent laws, he asked, "In Sydney, do you sort of introduce other peds to kids and this sort of thing, or is it strictly just a meeting type?" One member responded in no uncertain terms: "Introducing people to kids and so on, I personally think that that's out, as far as we're concerned. I think as far as people with like interests and so on, I think that's the whole purpose, but I think once we start to act as sort of a recruiting centre for kids, I think we would really be up shit creek." While one of the members did offer tips on how to acquire a boyfriend by "flashing," as he had done, that same member responded impatiently at the same meeting to another of Mayne's comments: "Look, let's get this quite straight. This organization, the PSG, does not supply boys."[24]

At the November 5 meeting, Mayne opened the front door and in entered about eighteen policemen. All attendees were charged with "conspiring to support and actively encourage one another to participate in acts of sexual penetration with persons under the age of 16 with intent to debauch and corrupt public morals and create in their minds inordinate and lustful desires."[25] It was apparent that the police had very little in the way of evidence, and the untried charges of conspiracy to corrupt public morals were most likely invoked as a politically expedient means to legitimate Delta's actions and to further their own reputation and homophobic antipedophile agenda. The charges also perhaps served to assuage community concerns about an adequate police response to the problem of child sexual abuse. The legal case against the PSG never made it to trial; it was thrown out of court at a committal hearing due to insufficient evidence. A defense barrister himself later suggested that the police and prosecution had more than likely "banked on having the case committed for trial by jury"[26] in order to exploit shifts in community attitudes. "If it had gone to trial," he said, "I think it would have been very hard to defend a charge of this nature, given current community attitudes towards child molestation and towards pedophilia."[27] The gay press reported this as "the first success in the Melbourne gay community's campaign to have the self-appointed morality squad, officially known as the Delta task force, disbanded."[28] However, as we will see, the Delta operations—like those against PIE in the United Kingdom, *Body Politic* in Canada, and NAMBLA in the United States—index a significant turning point in Australian, as well as British and North American, societies regarding questions of intergenerational sexuality generally and child sexuality in particular.

Manhood under Fire

The police and prosecution had hoped to exploit mounting community intolerance and fear about child sexual abuse and pedophilia. Notably, as we saw in the last chapter, this was a time of enormous public concern and discussion of child sexual abuse across the entire Western world. The child-protection lobby and feminist child sexual abuse movements had been incredibly successful in bringing the problem of child sexual exploitation to public and government attention. They had successfully challenged the twentieth-century tendency to blame victims of sexual assault for being complicit in their victimization. By reframing issues of sexuality through the lens of power, they had also renounced the view that children were capable of providing meaningful consent in relationships of unequal power with adults. What this meant was that there was little if any social, political, or discursive space left for entertaining the notion of childhood sexual agency in the context of intergenerational relationships. There was even less opportunity for gaining any support for the kind of pro-pedophilia position some radical gay liberationists had espoused in the 1970s. Yet insisting on a distinction between pedophilia and child sexual abuse was precisely the ongoing concern of groups like NAMBLA, PIE, and the PSG. At the heart of this distinction were questions of consensual sex and the sexual agency of young people in intergenerational encounters. However, the grounding axiom of the feminist child sexual abuse movement was that inherent adult-child power inequalities placed these questions and finer distinctions between voluntary and exploitive sex out of reach.

Feminism had, of course, begun challenging the expression of male power through sexuality. By way of campaigns not only against child sexual abuse but also rape, sexual harassment, and pornography, the unequal and oppressive relations of power that structured society and organized genders and generations had been exposed. Along with the passing of sex discrimination and equal opportunity legislation, feminists initiated a serious critique of scripts of normative masculinity and male sexuality.[29] Child sexual abuse was exposed as a problem endemic to the patriarchal nuclear family and to hegemonic rather than marginal or deviant versions of masculinity and male sexuality. The critical spotlight, in other words, was placed squarely on the roles, behaviors, and beliefs of men in general rather than those of isolated groups of aberrant male deviates, as it had been earlier in the century. The patriarchal assumption of male sexual access to women and children was no longer tenable. Women and children were not only seen to be oppressed by men as a group but were considered to be in far greater danger from men they knew than from strangers they did not know. If 1970s antirape feminism hit at the heart of gender relations and normative masculinity with images of every man as a potential rapist, 1980s child sexual abuse feminism delivered a second severe blow as it honed its "doctrine of intimate danger."[30] This was the idea that children are at greater risk of being sexually abused by fathers, male relatives, and male family friends—in short, men they are intimate or acquainted with—than by "mythical strangers."[31] As the Alliance of Revolting Feminists (ARF) put it in their manifesto, "Just as all men are potential rapists, so are all men potential paedophiles."[32] The social construction of hegemonic masculinity was identified as one of the key factors responsible for structures and norms of gender and sexual oppression. As Diana Russell declared in her acclaimed work on incest, violent sex crime "points to a critical problem in the collective male psyche that is proving lethal to women and to men alike. . . . This culture's notion of masculinity—particularly as it is applied to male sexuality—predisposes men to violence, to rape, to sexually harass, and to sexually abuse children."[33] Or, to quote the ARF once more, men are potential pedophiles precisely because they "are in control of both women and children and thus have the social, political and physical power to impose their sexuality on them."[34] The National Organization for Women condemned "pederasty," and Russell, like many child sexual abuse feminists, also publicly declared her opposition to pedophile groups. Labeling groups such as NAMBLA "blatantly pro–child sexual abuse," she joined forces with a powerful feminist and lesbian feminist lobby opposing intergenerational sex.[35]

This was a serious condemnation of normative manhood. Indeed, such a refiguring of both the boundaries of childhood and adulthood and the relations of power structuring adult-child interactions was nothing short of a paradigm shift. Employing antirape arguments about women as victims of male power, child sexual abuse campaigners highlighted children's powerlessness at the hands of adult-male sexual abuses. As observed last chapter, almost every influential child sexual abuse theorist rejected outright the possibility that children could exercise power, and thus consent, in any sexual encounter with an adult. Instead, children could only be in positions of "utter helplessness" in the face of the inherent power imbalances.[36] This revolution in understanding the sexual and power dynamics of intergenerational sexual interactions and child molestation is reflected in changing social categorizations. By the mid-1980s victim-blaming narratives had been almost entirely overturned. The ambiguous categories of "carnal knowledge," "moral neglect," and "moral danger"—categories that had often variously implicated both the children and the parents as culpable in acts of intergenerational sex—were being replaced by the terms *sexual abuse, sexual exploitation*, and *sexual assault*.[37]

Mirroring developments in the United States, where the issue of child molestation had been politicized nationally a few years earlier, Australia witnessed an explosion of public and media concern regarding child sexual abuse in the early to mid-1980s. Media and government accounts reported "astonishing" and "staggering" rises in reported cases of abuse.[38] This said nothing of unreported cases, which were assumed to be much higher. One *Sydney Morning Herald* article detailed these increases and estimates, claiming that, in NSW alone, there was a rise from 45 reported cases in 1980 to 2,519 in 1985. Estimating that "only about 10 per cent of child sexual assaults are reported," the article went on to suggest that "there could be 25,000 cases in NSW at present."[39] Reported overall prevalence figures, in both the media and in government publications, were sometimes as high as 40% of girls and 30% of boys.[40] Readers were left in no doubt that this was a growing problem confined mostly to the male offender population: "Ninety per cent of child sexual abuse offenders are male."[41] Even television ad campaigns, such as "Child sexual assault—it's often closer to home than you think," were launched to highlight the threat of intimate *male* danger.[42]

According to newspaper reports of claims in Britain and the United States of a Western epidemic of child sexual abuse, men were feeling the impact of this feminist challenge to norms of masculinity: "Many fathers of the 1980s, who have just learned the importance of displays of affection to their children, are becoming afraid that they will be accused of sexual abuse."[43] A related report on the same page highlighted the unease with the advancing feminist child sexual abuse movement, suggesting that the claims of epidemic proportions of incest and child sexual abuse might be something of a "feminist plot."[44] *Sydney Morning Herald* columnist Richard Coleman was of this view. In a scathing critique of a Channel Nine television documentary on child abuse and "sex abuse zealots," he declared in an overwhelmingly disparaging tone that "child abuse, like its older sisters anti-discrimination and equal opportunity, shows every sign of becoming a growth industry."[45] Male discomfort with feminist claims of endemic child molestation was certainly perceptible.

The child sexual abuse paradigm shift arguably triggered something of a "crisis" of normative manhood. This need not imply a kind of universal psychical trauma for individual men or some wholesale psychosocial epidemic of male anxiety—although, as we will see, neither does it rule out particular manifestations of individual and collective disquiet. What I am pointing to in a more general sense is a profound social and discursive challenge to the legitimation of male-subject positions wrought by the feminist exposure of male privilege, power, and abuse. This challenge, as Susan Faludi and Michael Kimmel, among others, have demonstrated, often provoked extremely vehement responses by many men and male social commentators.[46] For

Faludi, the reactions were nothing short of a "backlash" against feminism in the 1980s, and for Kimmel they were definite signs of male beleaguerment with feminist images of men as sexual oppressors and abusers. In the *New York Times*, for instance, Lloyd Cohen referred to a "fear of flirting" that had besieged many men as result of the sexual harassment and date-rape campaigns of the 1980s[47]; and *Playboy* columnist Asa Barber argued that men were the real victims of "antimale sexism."[48] Feminism had ushered in a "sexual inquisition" that not only had men "walking on eggshells" but also made them "vulnerable in the extreme to false charges of sexual harassment," Baber complained. "All it takes to lynch a man these days is the accusation of rape."[49] Disquiet over feminist critiques of masculinity and male sexuality was similarly palpable in Australia.[50] Indeed, an article in Australia's national newspaper, *The Australian*, reportedly referred to a "national male identity crisis."[51] However much male responses were merely the rhetorical flourishes of a bunch of sexist men is in the final analysis less important than the new politico-discursive climate in which male behavior was being critically scrutinized like never before. It is this dynamic of interrogation and defensive response—whether rhetorical or anxious, or both—to which I am referring when I speak of a "crisis" of normative manhood (or of male-subject positions). This is less an actual crisis—whatever that might mean—than it is a performative and theatrical spectacle and appropriation of crisis rhetoric for advancing particular social agendas.

In Kimmel's account of men's dissatisfaction with feminist critiques of masculinity, he suggests that American men became confused due to a loss of positive male role models. With normative manhood under attack, men instead "sought out negative models to attack."[52] Kimmel identifies the emergence of the "wimp" and representations of "soft masculinity" as negative models that served to reinforce a besieged masculinity.[53] Such models of manhood also made their appearance in Australia.[54] Whether or not the phenomenon of "male confusion" was widespread is debatable, in my view; however, Kimmel does identify an important dimension of the profound challenge feminism posed to social norms of masculinity across the entire Western world. Extending Kimmel's historical account, I suggest that the category of the pedophile emerged alongside the wimp in the United States, Britain, and Australia as another, more sinister and negative model of masculinity, and one that served in part as a scapegoat for the problems of child sexual abuse.[55] Homosexual pedophilia, and the PSG particularly, occupied this site of negative masculinity. Far from suggesting this to be a case of heterosexual men *consciously* scapegoating homosexuals as primary child molesters, I am simply foregrounding the ways in which the rhetorical association of homosexuality with child sexual abuse and pedophilia in popular discourses often became inextricable from a defensive male (and/or masculinist) response to manhood's trial-by-feminism.

The rhetorical association of homosexuality and pedophilia is reflected in dominant psychomedical research, where the tendency at this time became one of grouping pedophilic offenders into two categories: "regressed" versus "fixated" types.[56] Fixated offenders were thought to be those who exhibit an exclusive sexual preference for young boys, while regressed offenders were those exhibiting "normal" sexual preference but who have been "situationally induced" to have sex with children. Neil McConaghy, known in the late 1960s and 1970s as an expert in aversion therapy as a cure for homosexuality, summed up the general rule of thumb: "Men who have a history of offending against girl children could all be considered as regressed, and homosexual pedophiles and hebephiles are fixated."[57] "True" pedophiles, in other words, were homosexual men, while "regressed" offenders were the more harmless, somewhat normative, heterosexual men suffering from stressful life circumstances such as unemployment or marriage breakdown.[58] Curiously, however, contemporaneous research on child sexual abuse statistics and offenses also clearly revealed that heterosexual men were in the vast majority of perpetrators. In one authoritative and widely circulating North American study, the authors concluded that "the heterosexual adult constitutes a higher risk of sexual victimization to the underage child than does the homosexual adult."[59] The reason for this, they claimed, was that homosexual men tend to be sexually attracted to pubertal and postpubertal masculine qualities (hebephilia and ephebophilia), which the prepubescent child is said generally not to exhibit. According to claims made by many gay pedophile groups such as the PSG, this finding correlated with many members' sexual desires and identities.[60] Yet, in spite of this, the sex panic about pedophiles focused largely on cases of hebephilia. (Obviously many group members did themselves no favor by misnaming their category as pedophile.) This is tellingly evinced in the media coverage of the NSW state government's pedophilia crackdown. On the same day the *Sydney Morning Herald* published Coleman's piece about "sex abuse zealots," the newspaper also carried a report on the pedophilia blitz. The latter began by outlining the government's strategy to combat child sexual assault, only to contort into a discussion *not* of the most statistically common forms of such abuse—that is, incest or intrafamilial abuse—but of the rarest: "consensual" homosexual hebephilic relationships. It even ended with quotations from a self-identified PSG pedophile highlighting this point: "People who are pedophiles—who call themselves pedophiles, like myself—are people who are attracted to teenage boys or perhaps younger. The people being got by this stranger-danger campaign are not child-abusers, but gay men having relationships with teenage boys."[61]

This contortion or displacement was clearly at work in the PSG scandal in remarkably similar fashion to North American and British pedophile scandals, as the work of Philip Jenkins has shown. But this displacement was not merely a case of scapegoating homosexuals and pedophiles for the broader problems of normative male sexuality, child sexual abuse, child murder, child pornography, teenage homosexual prostitution, and child poverty. I argue that the sex panic about homosexual pedophilia was indeed much more than a defensive response to the problem of child molestation and exploitation, and feminist critiques of male sexualities. It was also, as Pat Califia noted of the US child pornography and pedophile panic of the late 1970s, significantly a response to the legitimacy and recognition of the sexual child.[62] The boundaries of acceptable public discussion of intergenerational sex had been radically redrawn as a result of the child sexual abuse paradigm shift. Distinctions between pedophilia and hebephilia, children and adolescents, and child molestation and consensual sex were being dissolved or downplayed in order to cast all kinds of adult-child and adult-teen sex as intrinsically abusive. Downplaying child sexuality was a central maneuver (witting or otherwise) of the child sexual abuse paradigm and its redrawing of boundaries of age and sexuality. As we saw in the last chapter, the disavowal of child sexuality that this represented was, in part, the result of an understandable effort to protect children from those who would blame them for their victimization. However, it also resulted in child sexuality being overdetermined, as James Kincaid has cogently shown, by adult anxieties, preoccupations, and politics.[63] So when gay and pedophile groups like the PSG, NAMBLA, and PIE tried to make visible the sexually agentive child or teenager—and thus to differentiate between voluntary and coercive adult-child sex—as we are about to see, they struck an especially troublesome discursive and emotional chord.

Defending Child Sexual Innocence, Denying the Sexual Child

The raid of the PSG and the mobilization of pedophilia hysteria to which it contributed intersected with a number of other controversial social and political issues preoccupying anglophone countries during the 1970s and 1980s. In addition to concerns about child sexual abuse were homosexual decriminalization and equality campaigns, child pornography, calls for lowering the homosexual age of consent, and, as we will see shortly, a further round of sex panics about secular and comprehensive sex education for secondary-school students. The figure of the sexual child ghosted these debates—indeed, it yoked them together. As Califia argued in relation to the anglophone child pornography and pedophile panics at the time, the motivations of moral crusaders were as much to keep children asexual as they were to prevent sexual violence against them.[64] During the 1970s, campaigns for decriminalizing and equalizing homosexuality (and sodomy) were gaining momentum in Australia and the United States.[65] With the passing of the bill to decriminalize homosexuality in Victoria in December 1980 and the debating of similar bills in New South Wales until decriminalization in 1984, the issue of homosexual equality with regard to age-of-consent provisions and the effect these might have on sex education programs and on children generally had been fiercely and widely debated. Community and government concern was sparked by the idea that, if homosexuality were to be treated as a valid, alternative lifestyle—as gay teachers and activists had been demanding—then impressionable youth might be exploited and recruited into that lifestyle by pedophiles and homosexual teachers (and their supporters) at a critical time of adolescent sexual ambivalence.[66] Anita Bryant spearheaded this conflation of homosexual equality and pedophilia in the United States with her Save Our Children and Protect America's Children campaigns. Bryant exemplified the predominant anglophone Christian logic with her widely disseminated statement, "Homosexuals can't reproduce, so they have to recruit."[67] And it was on the back of this broader concern about the effects of homosexual equality on children that the Thatcher government introduced the infamous Section 28 of the Local Government Act 1988. As a response to claims that councils were promoting gay relationships in schools, the act decreed that a local authority shall not "intentionally promote homosexuality or publish material with the intention of promoting homosexuality . . . [or] promote the teaching in any maintained school of the acceptability of homosexuality as a pretended family relationship."[68]

Australian parliamentary petitions railed against the idea of homosexual decriminalization and equality. The standard argument against the move reflected Bryant's popular slogan: that "legalization or decriminalization . . . would imply community approval and acceptance of these unnatural acts, and would encourage public solicitation of adults and particularly children in leisure and recreational areas as well as schools and other educational institutions."[69] Infamous antihomosexual religious activist Reverend Fred Nile proffered a similar argument. The "youth of society," he argued, "are particularly vulnerable to exploitation and undue influence," and thus measures "of public protection afforded by the present law should be reinforced by amendments to the law to prevent all forms of promotion of and recruitment into the homosexual lifestyle."[70] The idea of recruitment implied not just a notion of unnatural, homosexual corruption but, more specifically, one of homosexual pedophilic seduction. Even some of those in support of decriminalization found it difficult to accept equality in terms of the age of consent, and the underlying logic of these arguments reinforced the equation of homosexuality with pedophilic seduction or recruitment. For example, even though NSW member of Parliament Deirdre Grusovin stated categorically, "I strongly support the [Unsworth decriminalization] bill," she nonetheless argued for unequal ages of consent for heterosexual and homosexual sex. "In setting 18 as the minimum age of consent"—rather than 16, as it was for heterosexual sex— "the bill provides protection for our young people in their impressionable years."[71] These arguments were the mirror image of those advanced in the United States and the United Kingdom around various campaigns for homosexual equality. Indeed, Australian anti-homosexual-equality campaigners drew inspiration and support from leading campaigners in these countries, such as morals crusaders Bryant and Mary Whitehouse (and their followers).

The logic at the heart of the opposition movements against homosexuality was a feared slippery slope from decriminalization to homosexual sex education to the seduction of children. Opposition had already been mounting against moves to depathologize homosexuality in sex education booklets for young people. *The Little Red School Book* was one such infamous publication. Written by two Danish schoolteachers and first published in English in 1971, the book dispensed frank and nonmoralizing information and advice for young people on matters of sex, homosexuality, alcohol, drugs, and the school system. Emerging out of student protest movements of the 1960s, the booklet was widely seen to be promoting the development of student power and antiauthoritarian attitudes among young people. It was controversially disseminated in many countries, including Australia, where innumerable calls were made for its prohibition; it was banned in England, France, and Italy.[72] Inspired by *The Little Red School Book*, the Melbourne Gay Teachers and Students Group, of which Alison Thorne was a member, also wrote a sex education booklet of their own, but focused exclusively on homosexuality. Entitled *Young, Gay, and Proud*, the central message of the booklet reiterated the approach of the Danish booklet, arguing that homosexuality is an equally valid form of expression to heterosexuality.[73] Even more contentiously, however, the booklet had ardently championed not only teenage sexual agency, but teenage homosexual agency. Actual practical pointers were offered to adolescents who might be exploring or wishing to explore lesbian and gay male sexual activities. Enter the agentive sexual child—as well as a small number of actual young people who were part of the group.[74]

In the chapters "Doing It—Lesbians" and "Doing It—Gay Men," young people with homosexual desires were encouraged to explore the erogenous zones of their bodies and to masturbate in order to prepare them for sex with other individuals of the same sex. Quite explicit sex instruction examples were also given. Among them were the following:

> First, fingers. Using your fingers, try caressing the *labia*, running them around the whole area, inside the vagina, out again and up to the clitoris until sexual excitation or orgasm happens. You can do this to each other at the same time or take it in turns.
>
> You can use your tongue. You could trace the edges of her labia, kiss and push at her clitoris with your tongue, and you can both do this at the same time, too.
>
> Another way of making love is to just lie together, one on top of the other and use the friction of one body on another. (36–37)

> Because mouths are soft and warm, having your penis sucked feels really good. If you are doing the sucking, hold the other person's penis with one hand, and put it gently into your mouth. It feels nice and smooth. Run your tongue up and down it towards the tip, and try and watch out your teeth don't get in the way too much . . . they're hard. Don't worry about swallowing the semen. It just tastes salty. And it's perfectly harmless.
>
> Anal intercourse is just one way of having sex. . . . Just experiment and do what you like. . . . It's good taking it in turns to play the "active" part with each other. . . . Your anus is not only an organ to remove waste. It can be sexually exciting, just like your penis, because it has a lot of nerve-endings around the outside and also inside it. . . . When these nerve-endings are being touched or stroked it can really turn you on. . . . Try using your fingers to begin with. . . . It is a good idea to use something slippery when having sex this way, such as baby oil or Vaseline. You can use spit when there is nothing else around. (40–41)

These are extremely direct exhortations to young people. Yet no sooner does the figure of the agentive sexual child make its most conspicuous appearance than it is immediately displaced by sex panic rhetoric about corruption and abuse. Political opposition was staked on the need to protect the innocent and protoheterosexual child. Member of Parliament Jeff Kennett (later Victorian state premier) sounded the common community refrain: "I am not opposed to homosexuality between consenting adults in private. . . . I am certainly opposed to such people trying to convert others to their own lifestyles."[75] The "others" Kennett was referring to were, of course, children. Kennett was merely tapping into concerns already made much more explicit by a number of media reports, members of Parliament, and parent groups opposed to homosexual equality and its teaching. The *Geelong News* ran the headline "Homosexual Education—No Says [Victorian State Premier] Hamer." Other local newspapers ran articles attacking the booklet. The Concerned Parents Association (CPA) and the Committee to Raise Education Standards (CRES) were two community groups that emerged to take up the fight. Each attempted to whip up hysteria by exploiting the rhetorical association of homosexuality and pedophilia. The CPA had disseminated a pamphlet entitled *They've Got Your Kids*, in which they dramatized the indoctrination of children into homosexuality as the aim and likely result of the movement geared toward homosexual equality and its teaching in schools. So divisive was the issue that the Victorian Education Department issued an edict to secondary-school principals "to ensure that copies of books seeking to foster homosexual behaviour are not available to children with[in] the school library."[76] What the department meant here was that views espousing homosexuality as a valid and equal lifestyle are one and the same as cultivating homosexual behavior. In NSW, the Department of Education banned the *Young, Gay, and Proud* booklet from all state schools.[77]

The CRES also began a campaign to warn the public about the homosexual slippery slope. Distributing a pamphlet called *The Continuing Homosexual Offensive. Next Target: Anti-discrimination*, they made dire predictions about burgeoning homosexual families, homosexual education, and homosexual adoption being the end result of decriminalization. Under the subtitle "Exposing Children to Risk," CRES put forth the claim that

> clearly, the intent of the recommendation for homosexual books in school libraries, and the introduction of non-judgmental material on homosexuality into courses on sex education, is to introduce children with homosexual ideology during the period of sexual ambivalence. Primary school children would be indoctrinated and taught homosexual practices before reaching puberty.[78]

Returning to the PSG raid, when Alison Thorne, spokesperson for the Gay Legal Rights Coalition and member of the Melbourne Gay Teachers and Students Group, weighed in on the debate about the Delta raid of the PSG in her radio interview on 3AW, the media frenzy and parliamentary debate that ensued immediately dovetailed into this fear of predatory homosexual pedophiles. The panic escalated rapidly, and it was irrevocably inflamed by the subject of child sexuality.

During the interview, Mike Edmonds asked Thorne, "Alison, can you understand the feelings of, I would suggest, the large majority in the community who have children, the feelings that they would bear towards pedophiles?" In her response, Thorne attempted to hint at a distinction between sexual exploitation or harassment and pedophilia: "I can understand people's feelings from the point of view that they have a lot of misconceptions and I don't think that a lot of the things that the media are doing really helps terribly much. Because pedophiles really care for children. Pedophiles would absolutely abhor . . . abuse of children, are really concerned about consent."[79]

On the issue of consent, Edmonds inquired, "Does a child know about consent?" Thorne responded, "I believe children are in a position to consent and it depends on the definition of the child," responded Thorne. "What the media has been talking about is people aged between 10 and 16 and I believe that those people are capable of consenting." In response to a further question about whether she would like to see the age of consent lowered or dropped altogether, Thorne said, "I believe that age of consent laws in themselves are reactionary things."[80]

On this point, Thorne was reiterating the gay liberationist position articulated by the Gay Left Collective that a "legal age of consent is arbitrary fiction."[81] In fact, PIE in Britain had similarly caused significant controversy over precisely this cut-off point in the age of consent. In a submission made to the Home Office Criminal Law Review Committee on the age of consent in 1975, they argued that children between the ages of ten and seventeen ought to be able to consent to sex with an adult.[82] However, the mere suggestion of child sexual agency provoked extraordinarily hostile and emotional responses.

The interview with Thorne ended when the recess bell went off at the school at which she was teaching. Thorne had been speaking from a public phone that teachers were instructed to use to make personal calls. Appalled by the fact that a secondary-school teacher could hold such views—not to mention disseminate them on radio from a phone in the school—and determined to incite community rage, polemical 3AW radio presenter Derryn Hinch (now an independent senator in the Australian Parliament) then edited and replayed parts of the original interview on his radio program the next day. "I was appalled to hear yesterday just after I came off air," he said, "appalled to hear an interview with Mike Edmonds . . . an interview with one Alison Thorne from the Gay Legal Rights Committee. She was blaming the media, can you believe it, for pedophiles' bad public image."[83] At the end of Hinch's broadcast, in a performance of amazement and disgust, he said: "Well there, you heard the recess bell. The woman expressing those views about the rights of kids to have sex with adults, the woman expressing those views, Alison Thorne from the Gay Legal Rights Committee, is a schoolteacher. In fact she is a teacher at Glenroy Technical School and I tell you I would not want, I would not let that woman teach my child."[84]

Other members of the media pounced on Thorne's comments. A front-page *Sun* article appeared with massive headlines: "'SEX-AT-10' TEACHER OUTRAGE."[85] Sufficiently distorting the content and intent of Thorne's discussion, the article began by saying that "parents and MPs yesterday reacted angrily to a woman teacher's call to lower the age of consent for sex to 10."[86] The article went on to outline the appalled responses of the minister for education Robert Fordham, opposition spokesperson for education Walter Jona, and parents. "No person who blatantly advocates that it is acceptable for children to be the subjects of sexual acts with adults should be entrusted with the legal responsibility of educating children," Jona declared in Parliament.[87] The education minister himself found the comments "tactless and repugnant," as did a concerned parent who was quoted as saying they were "revolting" and that "all the parents feel the same."[88] Outside Parliament, Jona told reporters he would be shocked if the government refused or was unable to guarantee moral protection for schoolchildren or safeguard them from unacceptable sexual influences such as Thorne's: "If departmental regulations do not empower the minister to act as the community would expect him to act, the minister should change the regulations."[89] Whether or not the minister of education had legal sanction to act in the manner implicitly suggested by Jona was—at this stage in the controversy, at least—not a matter of concern. On November 12, 1983, the director general of education, Dr. Norman Curry, in collaboration with Fordham, removed Thorne from her teaching position and transferred her to an administrative one. *The Age* ran another article on page 3, "Sex Talk Teacher Taken from Class," in which Fordham defended the move on the grounds of parental reaction to media reports. "This step is necessary," he said,

> because of the importance of maintaining the trust and confidence that are such vital elements of the parent-teacher-student relationship. Ms Thorne's

reported public statements, her use of a school telephone number as a contact point for statements and the subsequent strong reaction from parents at the school have all placed her in an extremely difficult position.[90]

What ensued was an extremely lengthy battle for Thorne to get reinstated. Despite a favorable decision by the Education Department's Committee of Classifiers to post her to Tottenham Technical School for the 1985 school year, Thorne again found herself at the mercy of an intractable education minister. After the announcement of Thorne's appointment was reported in the *Sun*, Fordham himself announced that she would "not be taking up the appointment."[91] He was backed by, in cahoots with, or perhaps at the behest of Premier John Cain, who himself told a press conference that because of her views Thorne was "not an appropriate person to be put before a classroom."[92] Thorne then lodged a complaint with the Victorian Equal Opportunity Board. On November 6, 1986, the board ruled that Thorne had indeed been discriminated against and ordered not only her reinstatement to a classroom, but to a classroom in a technical school from a list of ten schools that Thorne herself would provide.[93] The board noted in its report that

> one of the most unfortunate aspects of this case is the media reporting of Ms Thorne's views and the Board has found that the acts in respect of which Ms Thorne has lodged complaints would be highly unlikely to have taken place if the press and radio reports of the Gay Legal Rights Coalition's Press Release and Ms Thorne's interview with Mike Edmonds had been full and accurate. Some member of the press and certain radio "personalities" appear to have seen the press release and interview as an appropriate occasion for indulging in sensationalist reporting of the worst kind.[94]

Just when the matter seemed to have been resolved, an even more extraordinary turn of events took place. The government vowed to do more than simply appeal the decision in the Supreme Court. Not satisfied with awaiting a decision on the appeal and unwavering in their belief that Thorne's views made her an unacceptable educational influence on children, Premier Cain declared that he was prepared to legislate to keep her and others with views like hers out of the classroom. A government spokesperson told the press that the wording of the legislation would refer to "public disquiet on sexual matters relating to children."[95] All the major political parties backed the government's proposed legislation. The Liberal Party spokesperson on education summed up the almost uniformly held view, when he told the media that Thorne's views on the age of consent and pedophilia made her unacceptable for a direct teaching role with children.[96] The thrust of the proposed legislation, the Teaching Service (Amendment) Bill, was to enable the forcible transfer of any teacher—in particular, those responsible for sex education programs—espousing views on children and sexuality that could be deemed "unacceptable" to community standards.[97] This move was considered all the more urgent when gay teachers were involved, as many felt they might recruit impressionable schoolchildren to the "homosexual worldview or lifestyle." That the Melbourne Gay Teachers and Students Group had been such an influential and controversial force in the Victorian Teachers' Union in the late 1970s only added weight to the apparent necessity of the Teaching Service (Amendment) Bill.[98] Informing the concerns of members of Parliament and parents was the putative homosexual and pedophile equation and the underlying discomfort with the sexual child. It had been unequivocally articulated in the ongoing sex education debates that were animating many Australian (and American) states as a result of the various equalization and decriminalization of homosexuality (and sodomy) campaigns. However, arguably the unsaid in this rhetoric is the issue of what made seduction possible: children's sexual willingness and adventure. In a community context where the only publicly acceptable view was that no child of any age could consent to sex with an adult, what this meant was that one of the underlying functions of the legislation was to deflect attention away from the figure of agentive sexual child. As we saw in chapters 2 and 3, this was made possible by notions of premature sexualization, the implantation of sexuality into the immature child, the premature introduction into sexuality, and protosexuality.[99]

Only a matter of hours before the second reading of the Teaching Service (Amendment) Bill in the Victoria Parliament, a deal was struck between the Victorian government and Thorne. The government agreed to withdraw its appeal to the Equal Opportunity Board ruling and remove the certification that prevented Thorne from teaching in exchange for the replacement of the clause requesting Thorne to provide a list of ten secondary schools from which the Education Department was to find one to accept her. While remaining a member of the teaching service, Thorne was to be seconded to the tertiary Technical and Further Education sector. As well as being granted her choice of college and teaching area, there was an additional proviso that she may return to secondary teaching sometime in the future; however, in order to do so she must first obtain the approval of the chief executive of the Education Department.[100] While Thorne claimed that the agreement meant "the government has conceded they discriminated against me," due to having "withdrawn their challenge to the [Equal Opportunity Board] decision" and agreeing "to pay my $3,000 court costs," it is clear that the government was also successful in its homophobic goal of removing Thorne from the secondary teaching classroom and, importantly, foreclosing the issue of teenage consent in matters of intergenerational sex.[101]

The Extension of Childhood

When the Gay Left's editorial that I began this chapter discussing was summarized in the Australian *Newsletter of the 5th Homosexual Conference* in August 1979, Australian gay activists appeared to be poised to engage in a rigorous discussion of complex issues with regard to pedophilia and child sexuality. Many gay activists and scholars influenced by North American and British liberationist rhetoric of the 1970s felt that such an interrogation of the issues was socially and politically imperative. Informal debates had been bubbling away in gay circles for some time. From the perspective of gay activists, the time certainly seemed ripe for the advancement of efforts at disentangling the oft-conflated issues of pedophilia, ephebophilia, homosexuality, child sexuality, child seduction, and abuse. It was not to be, however. Just as in the United States and the United Kingdom—and, indeed, significantly shaped by those trajectories and responses—by the mid-1980s analyses of pedophilia within the gay community largely ceased. In a climate of rapidly growing concern over both child sexual abuse and a slippery slope of homosexual equality, any discussion that did not reject intergenerational sex tout court had little hope of gaining support, but great prospects for being socially and politically censured. Viewed through a homophobic and heteronormative politics of "reproductive futurism," to use Lee Edelman's term,[102] homosexuals and pedophiles together were thought to threaten the futures of children, that is, their progress toward heterosexual development. This is because, as Edelman argues, the field of the political is secured through an investment in the "unquestioned value" of a forward-looking agenda (futurism) in which the innocent, protoheterosexual child is its principal "emblem."[103] By seeking to open up discussion of child and adolescent sexuality and agency, gay liberationist and pedophile groups were striking a direct challenge to the logic of reproductive futurism and its evasion of child sexuality in the present tense.

The effects of homosexual decriminalization and equality campaigns in this volatile climate of pedophile panic were double-edged. Homosexuality may well have been decriminalized in a number of Australian states (and sodomy in a number of US states), but homosexuality was also in certain respects pathologized in its relationship to children and childhood. Homosexual equality was considered a potential threat to a child's sexual development and education. To those opposed to same-sex equality, homosexuals and pedophiles were united in their corrupting effects on children. The setting of higher ages of consent for homosexual sex and accompanying legislative preambles stating either Parliament's disapproval of homosexual relationships or its unwillingness to condone such relationships are indicative of this attitude.[104] In the United Kingdom, Section 28 of the British Local Government Act 1988 was a similar response. Of the four Australian states and one territory that decriminalized male homosexuality between 1980 and 1990, all but Victoria included higher age-of-consent provisions for homosexual sex.[105] However, even the Victorian legislation—which was much more progressive than campaigners had expected—incorporated a new positions-of-authority offense. This stipulated that it is an offense for anyone involved in the supervision or care of children under the age of eighteen to solicit or encourage them from engaging in any form of sex, even if the young person is otherwise over the age of consent.[106] According to one report at the time, the attorney general's office had confirmed that the positions-of-authority legislation was intended to hit at sex educators who, as we have seen, were rendered a threat to children by promoting homosexual equality and the idea of child sexual agency.[107]

Jenkins identifies the category of the (homosexual) pedophile in this historical period as a "folk devil" or scapegoat for broader problems of child sexual abuse and murder, child pornography, teenage homosexual prostitution, child poverty, and missing children.[108] In my own earlier work, I argued something similar, that pedophilia panic was "a defensive projection of a homophobic and heteronormative discourse that served, on the one hand, to deflect attention from the fact that child sexual abuse had been exposed as a problem inherent to dominant and not marginal forms of masculinity and male sexuality and, on the other, to halt the advancing campaigns for homosexual equality."[109] However, when we foreground a scapegoat model of the sexual predator in order to narrativize history or historicize this period via homosexual and pedophile social movements, we risk in very subtle ways taking sex panic rhetoric about a fear of child sexual abuse and pedophilia at its word. The rhetorical accent, to put this in terms used in the preface, is again placed on the problem of the *sexualized* rather than *sexual* child. The result is something of an unsuspecting historiographical complicity in the discursive processes that led sex panic discourses to turn away from child sexuality in the first place.[110] In some respects this narrows our understanding of the forces of historical change, and attention is redirected from the powerful role of the signifier of the sexual child in shaping panic formation and history.

This chapter has recast this account with a slight shift in focus. At this historical juncture, anglophone homosexual pedophile panics were more than a defensive response to the problem of child molestation and exploitation, feminist critiques of male sexualities, and movements for homosexual equality. That these are important dimensions to many articulations of fear is not in dispute. What I have emphasized instead is that pedophile panics, and the ways they unfolded, were in significant respects shaped by the mobilization of highly emotive responses to the legitimacy and recognition of the sexual child. Intergenerational sexual desires *of* young people themselves, explicitly conjured by homosexual pedophile campaigns, were as troubling as adult pedophilic desires—at times, even more so. At critical moments in the escalation of panic, it was the ghostly appearance of the image or mere suggestion of the sexual child (usually a teenager) that contributed to the public reaction. Indeed, fear and panic were strategically deployed (in the Foucauldian sense) to switch the focus from forms of agentive child sexuality. On this critical point, feminist child sexual abuse advocates and conservative anti-homosexual-pedophile campaigners became bedfellows. The political and discursive positions of both groups were made possible by bracketing out questions of child sexuality, agency, and consent. The sexual child was not to be countenanced; or if it was, it was to be downplayed or minimized simultaneously. Concerned with more than child protection from abuse, this was also a means of regulating acceptable norms and practices of childhood.

The public critique and shaming of pedophilia was in part an indirect or implicit—even if this means unwitting—critique and shaming of child sexuality. If this were not the case, one would perhaps expect to have witnessed comparable witch hunts about the most statistically common and grievous of child sex offenses: intrafamilial abuse. These did not eventuate in anything like the fashion they did in relation to homosexuals and pedophiles. Instead, raids and arrests of homosexual individuals, groups, and organizations that were engaged in, or accused of, sex with (agentive) adolescent boys were the primary targets across North America, Britain, and Australia. There was the Boston sex scandal of 1977, in which twenty-four men were arrested for allegedly being part of a pedophile sex ring. The reality, according to John Mitzel and Philip Jenkins, is that the defendants were part of a loose group of men obtaining sex from teenage male sex workers.[111] NAMBLA formed in response to the scandal, and they too were subject to a number of raids and arrests.

These usually resulted in charges being dropped. There were the raids and arrests of the members of the Canadian gay liberationist newspaper the *Body Politic*, which had published articles on pedophilia, and there was a public and legal campaign mounted against PIE in the United Kingdom. Roger Lancaster has noted of the 1980s in the United States that, in a "culture of hypervigilant child protection, the denial of childhood sexuality and the perpetual hunt for the predatory pervert are opposite sides of the same coin."[112]

At the height of the homosexual pedophile panic, Daniel Tsang argued that "the age taboo is much more a proscription against gay behaviour than against heterosexual behaviour."[113] When we foreground the signifier of child sexuality, we can perhaps better understand why homosexual pedophiles became "scapegoats" for child sexual abuse and not intrafamilial offenders. Unlike groups such as the PSG, PIE, and NAMBLA, intrafamilial offenders were not agitating for child sexual rights and for the decriminalization of certain classes of intergenerational sex. Thus, one of the issues arousing the most controversy was, as Ken Plummer has observed of Britain and the United States, that pedophile organizations were seeking to challenge age-of-consent laws.[114] By explicitly raising the question of the possibility of children's sexual consent, desire, and pleasure, pedophile groups—in stark contrast to intrafamilial offenders—were holding up to society an image of the sexually agentive child.

The prevailing social reaction to pedophilia mirrored reactions to the sex panics canvassed in previous chapters. There was a decisive turn away from the figure of the sexual child. The strengthening child sexual abuse paradigm's exploitation model of harm based on inherent power differentials between adults and children effectively displaced the sexual child with tropes of innocence, powerlessness, victimization, and abuse. The displacement did not escape the attention of pedophiles and gay liberationists themselves. Three days after the announcement of the NSW government's pedophilia crackdown, an article appeared entitled "Pedophiles: We Love Children." In it a self-identified homosexual pedophile argued for the right of children to consent to sex with adults. "The government doesn't talk to the children. Why are people not interested in a child's point of view? As soon as a child says they consented, no-one will listen."[115] Perhaps one of the things that so troubled society about self-identified pedophiles (or, specifically, hebephiles and ephebophiles), in addition to genuine concerns for children's welfare, was their dogged exposure of the fact that children sometimes themselves embark on—indeed, initiate and enjoy—sex with adults. In any case, dodging the sexually agentive child was as critical to the evolution of pedophile panics and the politics of child protection as the imperative to apprehend and punish perpetrators of sexual abuse.

FIVE

Power

> The seeming U.S. epidemic of cases involving female teachers raping or molesting their students has been exported Down Under, as Australia is experiencing a similar rash of cases.
>
> —Joe Kovacs, "U.S. Teacher Sexpidemic Spreading across the Planet," WorldNetDaily, 2005[1]

> Move over, Mrs. Robinson. The new public enemy is the bespectacled babe who teaches our kids math in the classroom and sex in the parking lot.
>
> —William Saletan, "Teachers' Pets?" *Slate*, 2006[2]

The last two decades in North America, Australia, and the United Kingdom have seen a spate—some say a growing "epidemic"—of criminal cases of female secondary-school teachers in sexual relationships with male pupils.[3] The most famous of these, and the one that piqued media interest, is that of former elementary schoolteacher Mary Kay Letourneau, who in 1997 at the age of thirty-four was arrested for an affair with Vili Fualaau, one of her twelve-year-old pupils. Letourneau spent seven and a half years in prison and gave birth to two children fathered by Fualaau. After her release in July 2004, the pair was married. Although this situation occupies the extreme end of the spectrum of recent criminal cases, the media has since been awash with similar scandalous stories involving teachers. What is curious about the reportage is that the overwhelming focus has been on women. Yet female teacher offenders—like female sex offenders generally—constitute a very small fraction of the total number of offenders.[4] The WorldNetDaily news website cited above provides one striking example of this skewed interest. As an exercise in public shaming, the article "U.S. Teacher Sexpidemic

Spreading across the Planet" featured a list of teacher sex offenders.[5] Over sixty women were at one time listed, with many of their names accompanied by photographs. Remarkably, however, there have been no male teacher offenders on the list. In her book on sex scandals involving students and female teachers in North America and the United Kingdom, Sheila Cavanagh argues that we have witnessed not so much a "sexpidemic" but a sex panic about female teachers. Not only is there a disproportionate focus on female offenders, she says, but curiously, these women, in stark contrast to men, are committing misdemeanors of lesser concern and fewer sexual misdemeanors.[6]

This chapter examines one of the central preoccupying or manifest concerns of these female-teacher sex scandals: the widespread disquiet over the shameful abuse of trust and power these relationships are thought to involve. The US Department of Education became so concerned about the issue of sexual abuse in schools that it commissioned a report, *Educator Sexual Misconduct*, to examine the problem.[7] The report had this to say:

> Sexual abuse of students occurs within the context of schools, where students are taught to trust teachers. Schools are also a place where teachers are more often believed than are students and in which there is a power and status differential that privileges teachers and other educators. . . . Like sexual predators everywhere—sexual abusers in schools use various strategies to trap students. They lie to them, isolate them, make them feel complicit, and manipulate them into sexual contact. Often teachers target vulnerable or marginal students who are grateful for the attention.[8]

One of the issues highlighted in the report is that, in contrast to the Letourneau case, a specific category of relationship falls outside standard child-rape and sexual-offense statutes in some US states. These are for the most part voluntary relationships in which the pupil is under the age of majority but over the general age of consent. In many anglophone jurisdictions, what is now often referred to generically as "relations of authority" legislation,[9] or what I will call positions-of-authority legislation, has been introduced to cover these cases. This is a modern incarnation of statutory-rape laws. Specific statutory definitions differ from country to country and, in Australia and the United States, from state to state. The British legislation is defined as "abuse of position of trust," and Canadian legislation as sexual exploitation from a "position of trust or authority." And to take one example each from Australia and the United States, the Victorian state legislation defines the crime as "sexual penetration of a child . . . under care, supervision or authority," while Colorado's legislation defines it as "sexual assault on a child by one in a position of trust."[10]

Although the term *power* is not explicitly instated in these legislative rubrics, what unifies or underwrites the various statutory definitions, and the legal reasoning propping them up, is a particular concept or epistemology of power. This is an epistemology of power inherited from the child sexual abuse paradigm canvassed in chapter 3; recall that this is a linear and, as we will see in this chapter, one-dimensional model in which power is seen as something developmentally, experientially, or positionally possessed, acquired, or appropriated. It is what Foucault has called a "sovereign" or juridical model of power.[11] Positions-of-authority laws operate on the assumption that unequal relations of power are intrinsic to the adult-child dynamic in specific contexts of authority, and that this power asymmetry compromises the capacity even of mature minors (those over the general age of consent but under the age of majority) to give informed consent, leaving them vulnerable to potential harm.

This chapter relates an Australian criminal case as a way of interrogating anglophone positions-of-authority legislation and the socio-legal epistemology of power informing it. It tracks the construction, and fate, of child sexual subjectivity and modes of agency within this juridical paradigm. Suggesting that the application of positions-of-authority laws, and the model of power enshrined, is often less about protecting young people from potential harm, I argue that such legislation aims to legislate adolescent sexuality and instill generational axioms of age, sexuality, capacity, and power. Positions-of-authority legislation, moreover, simplifies the complexity of power relations often to devastating effect. Not only the sexual subjectivities of adolescents, but also the intersubjective dynamics between teacher and student are disregarded in laws that take the mere fact of a sexual act as evidence of criminal abuse. Yet it is precisely the nature of these intersubjective dynamics that is at issue when determining whether an *abuse* has been perpetrated. This model of power is far from benign, I argue, and its foreclosure of teenage agency often inflicts greater damage than the sexual relationships on trial. The chapter concludes with a discussion of the negative socio-legal and pedagogical ramifications of this model of power, and offers a new framework to advance the evaluation and recognition of adult-child power relations and adolescent agency.

Crimes of Power?

Positions-of-authority legislation places primary emphasis on institutional and positional meanings of power. Adults occupying certain social and institutional positions—such as teachers, priests, sporting coaches, counselors, child care workers, and doctors—are believed to be in roles of particular influence, responsibility, trust, authority, control and thus *power* in relation to youth. Often referred to as the institutional—or, as Greetje Timmerman describes it, "organizational power"—model, the logic is that, "within organizations, people have different levels of access to power positions. The power hierarchy puts supervisors in a position to misuse their authority. Within schools, teachers and other members of the school staff *have power over students.*"[12] The institutional context and positional location purportedly confer forms of power to the teacher in a linear schema of cause and effect. Power resides in the school, the school bestows power to its teachers, and teachers then possess a power that is wielded (intentionally or not) over students. Until reaching seventeen or eighteen years of age—when individuals are deemed developmentally to have accrued the capacities necessary for the exercise of autonomous power—students in "relationships of authority" are viewed as particularly defenseless and vulnerable. They are defenseless and vulnerable to manipulation, defenseless and vulnerable to power's seductive appeal, defenseless and vulnerable due to incomplete competencies, defenseless and vulnerable to the powers of their own body, and defenseless and vulnerable by virtue of occupying positions of subordination vis-à-vis the dominating and controlling power of adults. Power leaves young people particularly vulnerable to exploitation and harm, so the argument goes.

Some variants of positions-of-authority legislation take an even harder line on questions of age and institutional power. Consider an amendment to Texas law, which removed the age provision—originally set at seventeen years of age—from the statutes. The amendment decreed that a teacher is prohibited from having sex with a student of *any* age, and if convicted faces a penalty of up to twenty years. This echoes one of the recommendations of the Department of Education's *Educator Sexual Misconduct* report, which called for the standardization of state laws to protect "any student, no matter what age, in an educational institution."[13] On May 25, 2006, the new Texas law was enforced, when twenty-five-year-old high school teacher Amy McElhenney was arrested for allegedly having sex with an eighteen-year-old male student. The representative who put forward the amendment had this to say: "If they're a student, I just think they're off bounds regardless of their age. I felt like if we didn't do that, we just virtually made it open season on students that are 18-year-olds."[14] In discussing the new law, high-profile American legal scholar and rape-law specialist Susan Estrich highlighted the operative logic of sovereign power. "Power trumps age," she said, and "abuse of power is about power, not age."

> Most teachers don't need a criminal law to tell us that it's wrong to have sex with our students no matter how old they are (mine are in their 20s and 30s, and it's still wrong). Teachers have power over students, which undercuts the notion that consent can be given freely; we control their lives, which means it's not fair to the individual student, or to the other students in the class; it's an abuse of a teacher's power.[15]

Discussions of teacher power are tightly bound with notions of care, supervision, and trust, even though the relationships between these concepts are rarely unpacked.[16] As noted, in many jurisdictions with positions-of-authority legislation, the term *power* is nowhere mentioned in the statutes. Might then the principal issue in sexual transgressions by teachers revolve not necessarily around questions of power, but rather the question of duty of care or breach of trust? For a teacher who transgresses the law is said to have breached a duty of care to the pupil and duty of trust to the parents, schools, other students, and communities. Consider this proposition in relation to the Victorian and British legislation, as the term *power* is indeed nowhere mentioned in the statutes. In Victoria, the age of consent for heterosexual and homosexual sex is sixteen years of age. Teacher-student sex is prohibited under the offense of "sexual penetration of a child age 16 or 17 *under* care, supervision or authority."[17] Although the "or" in the terminology of "care, supervision or authority" seems to suggest three distinct areas of criminal infraction, it is clear that each of the terms is intimately connected, indeed inseparable, with regard to the logic of sovereign power. For instance, it is not possible for an adult to be given permission to care for or supervise children without first having been granted the authority, or power, to do so. At an epistemological level, the notion of a duty of care, supervision, or authority is secondary or subsidiary to prior considerations of power.

The British law definition of "abuse of position of trust" similarly pivots on assumptions about institutional and positional power. Even if it were conceivable to define "positions of trust" without reference to prior power differentials, the very term *abuse* metonymically instates power as the defining feature of the offense. However, even notwithstanding this direct association, the rationale behind the definition of "positions of trust" already rests on prior presumptions about power. This was exemplified in the UK government's policy advice for schools: "A relationship of trust . . . [is] one where a member of staff or volunteer is in a position of power or influence *over* a pupil or student by virtue of the work or nature of the activity being undertaken."[18] Any account of "abuse of position of trust" or "abuse of care, supervision or authority" is predicated on the idea that adolescents are not sufficiently *empowered* to take care of themselves. As teachers, carers, and supervisors are acting in loco parentis, they have had handed over to them forms of surrogate parental *power*: the *power* to supervise, the *power* to protect, the *power* to control, and the *power* to care for the children who are *entrusted* to them.[19] No matter the legislative terminology used, the logic of a betrayal or abuse of one's duty, trust, care, or responsibility always refers back to a model of power as institutional or positional possession. With some notable exceptions in a number of European countries—which will be discussed below—it is clear that sovereign power is the epistemological nucleus of all legislation of this kind. Indeed, as we will see in the following case study, sovereign power is one of the primary conceptual instruments used to regulate the child/adult opposition and teenage sexuality.

The law is by no means out of step with public and academic opinion on this matter. Popular media representations and cultural commentary routinely reaffirm the notion that teacher-student liaisons inherently are violations of an adult's duty of care and trust, and abuses of power. Such has become the hegemonic and normative position, as Pat Sikes has argued.[20] In her survey of the literature, she notes that even many feminists and antihomophobic educationalists engaged with queer studies—and who foreground the importance of sexuality as a positive force in pedagogical relations—accept as axiomatic the notion of inherent power differences between teachers and students. Take Debbie Epstein and Richard Johnson's text *Schooling Sexualities*. "Teachers," they argue, "are not supposed to engage in sexual relationships with their students (quite rightly, in our view, given the power relations involved and the potential for abuse)."[21] Kate Myers employs a similar argument. Despite acknowledging a difference between the sexual abuse of a child and a consensual relationship between an adult and a seventeen-year-old, the self-evidence of the institutional and positional-power model is uncritically accepted: "However slight the age gap and regardless of who is the initiator, in a teacher/pupil relationship there is an important power relationship and a professional responsibility not to be involved in such liaisons."[22] Due to the hegemony of a sovereign reading of power, there is no need even to specify what an "important power relationship" means. It has an immediate transparency, or so we are invited to believe, and readers are expected to know and agree with the implied terms of this formulation. Aside from Sikes's critique of the standard line that power is always weighted in favor of teachers in sexual relationships with students, and aside from my own earlier work, I am aware of no recent sustained academic critiques of this legislation and the model of power informing it. Sikes has importantly challenged the normative reading of teacher-student sexual relationships by presenting a number of examples of actual relationships that defy this reading; however, her focus is not a theorization of power and power relations. Even queer theorists—perhaps surprisingly—have been silent on this issue. In her book *Sexing the Teacher*, Cavanagh offers a number of compelling queer readings of teacher-student sex scandals involving female teachers. While this work represents "an invitation to ponder the pedagogical possibilities of scandal and to unearth queer desires, which are otherwise masked by the master narratives of danger and professionalism that govern school life," unearthing a queer relation to, or understanding of, power is not among its concerns.[23]

However, I am far from convinced that an epistemology of sovereign or juridical power is either accurate or helpful; quite the contrary, in fact. Although the laudable imperative of the protection of children from abuses of power provides the rationale for a reliance on a model of sovereignty, as this and the following chapter will demonstrate, not only does this model not always serve the best interests of children, it can sometimes work to their detriment. The sovereign model of power also contains unacknowledged performative, punitive, and defensive functions.

Let us now turn to our case study in order to complicate this reading of sovereign teacher power and begin building an alternative multidimensional model of intersubjective power relations. From there we will consider some potentially deleterious legal, social, intrapsychic, intersubjective, and pedagogical effects of the institutionalization of sovereign power via positions-of-authority legislation.

Adolescence, Agency, and Sexual Subjectivity

In April 2005, thirty-six-year-old Australian schoolteacher Natalina D'Addario was employed at Roxborough Park Secondary College in Melbourne. Within only a few weeks, D'Addario had performed oral sex on a student—let's call him B—who was, on the first of three occasions, five days shy of his sixteenth birthday and the general age of consent. B was sixteen at the time of the second and third encounters. On July 25, 2006, D'Addario was sentenced to four months of prison for three statutory offenses, one count of sexual penetration of a child under the age of sixteen, and two of sexual penetration of a sixteen- or seventeen-year-old child. The total sentence given was eighteen months, but fourteen of these were suspended. In line with the mandatory provisions of the Sex Offenders Registration Act 2004, the Class 1 offenses she perpetrated also resulted in her registration as a serious sexual offender.[24]

According to the Crown prosecutor, it appears that "upon commencing as Form Care teacher, the male students in the class began calling Ms D'Addario 'sexy' and in the terms of the statement of the complainant, generally mucked around with her."[25] From all accounts it is clear that this was a distinctly working-class, "rough and tumble, largely male school."[26] To quote detail from the transcript of court proceedings for *The Queen v. Natalina D'Addario*:

> Some two weeks later, on or about 4 May 2005, Ms D'Addario attempted to contact the complainant at his home and left a message for him. The next day the complainant spoke to Ms D'Addario and asked why she'd called. She replied that she wanted to speak to him about work experience and asked for his mobile telephone number. She asked the complainant not to call her sexy in front of other students, but to reserve it for one on one occasions.
>
> When the complainant left the room, he turned and asked her whether she thought that he was sexy, to which she replied, "the feeling is mutual." He asked what that meant and she said "yes" meaning yes, I find you sexy. (2–3)

From this point on a series of text messages were exchanged. The two also spoke numerous times on the phone and, according to D'Addario, "she could detect, or became aware, that he was sexually excited and that he apparently would masturbate while talking" with her (11). B informed his friends of what was being exchanged and discussed, and they encouraged him to "go for it" (4)—which he did. He and D'Addario met, and in the first of the three incidents in her car, B initiated oral sex by unzipping his pants and telling D'Addario to go down on him. (In fact, apparently he pushed her head down.) Far from being unsure of himself—and by all accounts, he was sexually experienced—B said that "while she was doing this I asked her if she spat or swallowed."[27] He also requested they "go the whole way" and have sexual intercourse, but D'Addario refused. The text messages continued, and D'Addario appealed to B not to tell anyone about what was occurring or of the text messages being exchanged. Ignoring her request, he instead told "quite a number of students" and kept all the messages she'd sent (9). Meanwhile, B asked her for money to put toward a school social—a social that didn't exist. Interpreting this as a form of manipulation or bribe, D'Addario informed the vice principal of the school, but omitted the details of their sexual interactions. Then, in a kind of preemptive strike, B himself revealed to the school authorities the details of their sexual relationship. "I think she went to speak to the Vice Principal after this about me, so I decided if she was going to start trouble, I would tell someone about what she had been doing *with* me," he said in a victim impact statement (24; emphasis added). While at first glance it may appear trivial, it is far from insignificant that through a kind of Freudian slip, B referred to what D'Addario had been doing not "to" him, but "with" him. This is not a student incapable of effectively consenting and participating in relations of power, or at the very least *perceiving* himself as capable, which is inextricably entangled with "being" capable.

D'Addario was depicted in court as a rather sad, lonely, naive, vulnerable, sheltered, and sexually immature Italian woman who had lived her whole life with her parents. She was also, it was claimed, struggling to come to terms with life in a school she described to her psychiatrist as like "a jungle, like the Bronx" (16). Questioning D'Addario's emotional maturity is indeed tempting when one reads the accounts presented in court. For example, in one—possibly even the first—text message she sent to B, D'Addario remarked, "Hey sweetie, just wanted to let you know that you have gorgeous eyes, looking forward to seeing you tomorrow, love and kisses, XOXOX, Natalie. Don't tell anyone about our messages" (3). We must always, of course, be cognizant of the historical tendency of courts to construct female sexual offenders as vulnerable, pathological, and at the mercy of uncontrollable emotions, and we ought ourselves try to avoid too hastily imputing particular emotional states, authorial intentions, or cognitive capacities onto particular speech acts or behaviors in the absence of more detailed psychological and interpersonal information. Additionally, as Eve Sedgwick cautions, it would be "foolhardy to embrace" the category of ignorance—which in such contexts of sexuality often is used interchangeably with immaturity—as an explanation for D'Addario's speech acts or behavior, precisely because "ignorance [like immaturity] is as potent and as multiple a thing . . . as is knowledge."[28] In other words, for D'Addario there are any number of possible subjective motivations and interpersonal factors that may have shaped what appears like rather puerile behavior, but may be considered and strategic, as well as unintentional and unconscious, actions. However, while it might certainly be imprudent for us to reach conclusions about D'Addario's emotional states and cognitive abilities in the absence of more detailed information, I think the "narrative bites," as presented in court, while rather tragic, enable us to conclude at a bare minimum that they are indicative of a more complicated series of power relations than the law presumes.[29]

Yet in spite of allusions to a more complicated set of power relations and his concession that B was a willing participant, even the judge, constrained by law, merely reiterated a juridical interpretation of exploitation embedded in the statutes:

> You were his teacher and you were 35 or 36 years of age, some 20 years older than him, and he was under your care, supervision and authority and you, therefore, owed him a duty to protect him and his welfare and his well-being and you owed his parents a duty to look after their child when he was at school under your care and indeed, all members of the community are entitled to expect that when they send their kids to school that the teachers at the school are going to exercise their duty to take care of the pupils and to look after them and certainly not *exploit them*.[30]

Even from this very brief account it seems painfully obvious that the sovereign model of power enshrined in positions-of-authority legislation—and that constitutes D'Addario as a serious sexual offender and B a child victim in advance of any evaluation of the relationship dynamics—is of little use in helping us understand, and ethically and legally adjudicate upon, such a case. Sovereign power here functions performatively to produce that which it has already statutorily named at the same time as it defends against adolescent sexuality, agency, and power. In my view, D'Addario could not have been further from occupying a position of control, authority, and power as conventionally conceived. And in this respect, the case is not especially unique but indicative of a large number of North American and Australian cases involving a female teacher and a male student in which the boys assert their agency.[31] There are many possible ways to read the power dynamics structuring this particular case but that are foreclosed by sovereign power. Let us consider a possible alternative reading.

As it is likely to be for many teachers new to any school—even highly disciplined private, middle-class schools—D'Addario's arrival at the male-dominated, rough, working-class Roxborough Park Secondary College must have been immensely emotionally and psychologically challenging, if not anxiety inducing. To her psychiatrist she described it as a "particularly difficult school, [with a] poor academic level, [and] serious discipline problems." "Every student was a problem child," she said.[32]

A new teacher in this classroom situation is often anything but authoritative and powerful and has quite a task ahead of them to garner the respect of students—respect that is surely crucial for the maintenance of order and control. Teachers, even new ones, certainly have the institutional prerogative to send students to the principal's office or mark them down on their assignments, but this privilege is of little consequence in the context of volatile and challenging classroom interactions absent of serious transgressions of school rules, or in situations where students have no respect for the teacher, no concern about grades, and no fear of a confrontation with the principal. Moreover, confronted with boisterous and cocksure adolescent boys of fifteen and sixteen years of age, who were likely mobilizing together against or at least in relation to the lone teacher by "mucking around with her," taunting her, and calling her "sexy," the collective and relational pressures of such a situation are far from innocuous. As Kate Myers has pointed out, students often attempt to exert influence sexually and in an intimidating fashion in relation to female teachers.[33]

Perhaps D'Addario, in a partial attempt at attenuating what she perceived as the collective and intimidating power of the boys, enlisted one of them to her side by returning the force of the collective sexual gaze to B. Actual sexual desire for B is not mutually exclusive from a strategic (and perhaps unconscious) move of this kind, but it may very well enhance the strategy's effectiveness. By reciprocating B's sexual desire, D'Addario likely bestowed him with a sense of recognition as an adult sexual subject in his own right. In a culture such as ours, within which adolescent sexuality is placed under suspicion—that is, acknowledged and yet simultaneously infantilized—this is plausibly a psychically empowering situation for B.[34] In return, D'Addario may have consciously or unconsciously sought recognition by way of being exalted or at least accepted in B's heterosocial circle, and thus perhaps the classroom. It is this sexual recognition, often perceived as necessary for respect, that feminists have long known and lamented as a not-atypical strategy of some women attempting to achieve at least a baseline position of exiguous power and some semblance of control in a male-dominated environment.

When we turn to the interpersonal dynamics of the private sexual encounters between D'Addario and B, these too are far from indicative of an imbalance of power weighted in favor of the teacher. B was, apparently, sexually experienced. At the very least, he had enough self-assurance to initiate receptive oral sex—indeed, to direct D'Addario to do it: "I told her to go down . . . to put her head towards my penis."[35] He also, on each occasion, ejaculated. And if the sequence of events from the first encounter were repeated, B had announced prior to ejaculating that this was forthcoming, presumably to give her the option of swallowing or not. This does not sound like a young man following the teacher's lead, submitting to her requests, or in fact uncontrollably ejaculating—a clichéd sign of youth sexual immaturity. (Interestingly, in her statement to police, D'Addario claimed—rather dubiously, it would seem—that she had been coerced into performing oral sex.[36]) The actual sex acts were clearly carried out on B's terms, and he initiated many of the significant moments of the encounter. Indeed, while performing oral sex D'Addario asked B to touch her, and he went only so far as to touch her legs (6).

The final striking aspect of the power dynamics is the way B managed some of the extrasexual elements. For one thing, he did not exactly rush headlong into sex with D'Addario, but first sought advice from his friends before making his move. Additionally, not only did he retain all the text messages D'Addario sent him—and showed them to his friends—but he also, as noted, made a preemptive strike against D'Addario by informing the vice principal of their relationship after she had ratted on him over the false request for money. As the presiding judge noted, B "had enough maturity and nous" to have manipulated this situation to his advantage. It is safe to conclude (inarguably, I think) that a form of sovereign teacher or adult power most certainly did not dictate the terms of the D'Addario-B relationship. What we have here is the distinct *lack* of a one-dimensional, uniform relay of sovereign power.

From Sovereign Power to Multidimensional, Intersubjective Power Relations

If a sovereign model is unable to illuminate the complexity of power's operations, how might we better capture the multiple and nonlinear circuits of power structuring the D'Addario-B scenario in order to bring the agentive adolescent subject into clearer view? Here I must acknowledge the groundbreaking work of Wendy Hollway, who—also recently in collaboration with Tony Jefferson—has to my knowledge done more to theorize power at the nexus of the social and the psychic than any scholar I am aware of to date.[37] In concert with Hollway as well as Hollway and Jefferson, I would like to foreground a number of insights in order to deconstruct sovereign power and build a methodological framework for analyzing power relations and bringing the sexual child into view. First is the post-Foucauldian reworking of relational power as an intrinsically intersubjective phenomenon animated by the dynamics of recognition.[38] Under this model, power is not to be conceived as a substance or entity that an individual possesses, wields, and controls, as Foucault argued. Instead—and this is where Hollway and Jefferson importantly extend Foucault to engage the question of subjectivity—power is always only a relational phenomenon referring to struggles to control the giving and receiving of recognition. Second is an emphasis not so much on multiple "types" or "forms" of power, but on what I will call multiple *dimensions* through which power relations materialize. It is commonplace in the humanities and social sciences to refer to "types" or "forms" of power, such as gendered or structural or political power. However, this terminology usually returns us to a nonrelational, substantive notion of power, and one that gives the impression that power is located somewhere (such as in an institution or in adults). The terms *type* and *form* detract from the Foucauldian insights that power exists only in a relational sense—that is, as a strategic relationship between subjects—and, therefore, that the term ought only to be used in the phrase *power relations*.[39] They also detract from what I take to be a key implication of Hollway and Jefferson's post-Foucauldian analyses: that what go by the names of "types" and "forms" of power are really the intersubjective *effects* or experiences of power relations, of the conferral (or not) of recognition.[40] For instance, having a sense of personal power from, say, being viewed competently in the workplace is an affective and subjective experience that is not a sign of the existence of power as some substance or entity contained within an individual. A subjective sense of power is only ever an "intersubjective accomplishment," to use symbolic interactionist Robert Prus's wording.[41] It is the effect of the intersubjective dynamics of recognition within a network of multiple dimensions.

Let us return to the D'Addario-B scenario to explore some of these dimensions. My alternative reading, to date, has referred to at least four possible dimensions of power relations, none of which are mutually exclusive. They are, instead, invariably mutually constitutive and "intra-active." The concept of "intra-action," taken from Karen Barad, replaces that of "interaction." As she explains:

> "Intra-action" *signifies the mutual constitution of entangled agencies*. That is, in contrast to the usual "interaction," which assumes that there are separate individual agencies that precede their interaction, the notion of intra-action recognizes that distinct agencies do not precede, but rather emerge through, their intra-action. It is important to note that the "distinct" agencies are only distinct in a relational, not absolute, sense, that *agencies are only distinct in relation to their mutual entanglement; they don't exist as individual elements.*[42]

Barad's groundbreaking reworking of conventional notions of causality supports and offers a new dimension to relational (psychoanalytic) theories and my attempt to theorize the invariably mutually constitutive relationship among dimensions of power (in a relative and not absolute sense). In order to better grasp the complexity of power relations and their subjective experience, however, we need to specify these dimensions by keeping them at least analytically distinct. I make no claim to have offered an exhaustive list of possible dimensions that can provide answers to the question of who "has" greater or less power in an interpersonal scenario; this would only return us to sovereign power. Nor do I suggest that these dimensions are the only or even the best way to conceptualize the spheres to which they refer. This is merely an attempt to loosely formalize a framework or methodology for analyzing some of the critical aspects of this network of power relations that often get collapsed and conflated when researchers and lawmakers aim to find where the "balance of (sovereign) power" lies in any given situation. It is also a way of exposing the various levels, or dimensions, of avoidance the socio-legal discourse of child sexual abuse engages in concerning adolescent sexuality. The intention to "loosely formalize" these dimensions of power is deliberate. As will become clear, the dimensions identified—drawing in part on Hollway and on decades of feminist theorizing on multiple contexts of power—are expansive enough to incorporate a wide array of individual, interpersonal, and collective aspects of life. They are also expansive enough to be employed using a range of methodologies, psychoanalytically inflected or otherwise.

The first dimension I have implicitly referred to pertains to the sphere of the classroom and the relations of power between teacher and student body. We might call this the institutional dimension. Even in this dimension—which is usually the one that colonizes all discussions of teacher-student sex—the subject (D'Addario)-power relation is most clearly not conditioned by some uniform relay of power from institution to teacher. That is, it is not conditioned, let alone dominated by, a form of power *over* students, as I noted earlier with regard to the precariousness of many a teacher's position in the classroom and as is evident from the D'Addario example.

The second dimension concerns the sphere of private, interpersonal relations between B and D'Addario. Let us call this the intersubjective dimension. Again, here exists no one-way flow of power, nor any *inherent* asymmetry that invariably leads to the subordination of the student (let alone any predetermined material or psychological outcomes). This is because power relations are the contingent cause *and* effect of relational dynamics of intra-activity and recognition.

The third dimension relates to the sphere of collective or peer relations among B, his friends, his classmates, and any others making an impact on the lives of all participants. Let us call this the heterosocial dimension. Recall that B had confided in his friends and they had encouraged him "to go for it." After one of the encounters, he also revealed the details of what went on in the car and, as noted in his victim impact statement, his friends thought he was "a bit of a legend."[43] Similarly, his older brother reacted with what Kate Legge describes as "a mix of envious amazement." "I was shocked and . . . a bit rapt for him," said the brother.[44] Not only did B likely attain a sense of recognition as an adult sexual subject from D'Addario, but he also had this reinforced by his friends and brother. This resonates with Karin Martin's research on puberty and early sexual experiences, which has demonstrated compellingly how the achievement of socially valued sex usually makes adolescent boys, often in stark contrast to girls, "feel more agentic, masculine, adult, and bonded with other men."[45] In other words, sexual experiences that have been validated by peers and family, such as B's, often *empower* young men.[46] The other noteworthy feature of this heterosocial dimension of power relations is the weight of the collective engagement in the situation by some of B's peers/friends—both in the classroom through the use of "sexy" taunts, and when they later challenged D'Addario upon learning of the sexual relationship: D'Addario reported to police that "the complainant had got his friends to harass her, by confronting her and telling her to her face that she should be ashamed of herself."[47]

A fourth dimension of power relations, which I have only so far hinted at, is what I call the intrapsychic dimension. By intrapsychic dimension I mean broadly *one's relations with oneself*, however we might conceptualize these dynamics. Intrapsychic power relations might thus be thought of as encompassing emotional, biological, and cognitive development, experience, and maturation, and the capacity of individuals to manage their desires and feelings in order to make decisions and "to regulate one's own life and affairs with appropriate attention to both external reality and internal needs."[48] An individual's self-esteem and embodied sense of self and sexual subjectivity are pivotal here. Of course, like all analyses of psychical dynamics, this dimension is the most difficult to track—especially without access to detailed interviews, as in criminal cases involving minors such as the one examined here—as well as the most difficult to substantiate, due to its seemingly more speculative nature and its inevitable incorporation of unconscious dynamics. But this is certainly no good reason for ignoring it; quite the reverse, in fact. In line with relational psychoanalysis, I consider the intrapsychic dimension to be inextricable from the intersubjective. However, this does not mean we ought to then do away with an analytic distinction between them. On the contrary, such an analytic distinction enables us to highlight the inevitable and mutually constitutive relational "intra-actions" among and between the intersubjective and the intrapsychic. It also helps us apprehend individual sexual subjectivity—and subjectivity generally—not as the bounded, interior property of an individual but as something more akin to *subject-act-ivity*: the material knot of performatively enacted bodies, processes, practices, relations, and experiences at the nexus of these dimensions.

With regard to the intrapsychic dimension and this chapter's case study, one of the significant findings to emerge from the growing body of nonclinical research on sexual interactions between male adolescents and female adults is that boys tend to experience these as consensual, positive, and status-enhancing.[49] This finding also squares with the research of Martin mentioned above, notable as one of the few scholars to rigorously theorize the question of adolescent subjectivity. Martin found that commonly "puberty facilitates the development of sexual subjectivity in boys"—whereas for girls puberty often lowers their self-esteem.[50] Boys generally look forward to adulthood and emerge from puberty with an enhanced sense of agency and control. They tend to take pride and pleasure in their maturing bodies, have an increased sense of self-worth due to male puberty's associations with culturally valued meanings of male sexuality, and gain a greater form of subjective bodily knowledge through masturbation, an experience they find largely positive. Boys are also usually granted social and interpersonal recognition, independence, and a degree of freedom when they reach puberty and look older and more mature. Within working-class families, as Martin found, this recognition is often even more pronounced.[51]

What all of this suggests is that, when it comes to sexuality, many young men such as B are often robustly situated within the intrapsychic dimension.[52] It also highlights important gendered dynamics and patterns that need to be considered when assessing adult-adolescent relationships. A gendered dimension is frequently a critical factor in how young people experience sexual relations with adults as well as with peers (although it is not singularly, universally, and uniformly determinative). However, these often important gender differences are being obfuscated or downplayed in many recent criminal cases of teacher-student sex, including the one discussed here, because of a gender-neutral model of sovereign power. As explored in detail in the following chapter, in recent years there has been a push toward gender-neutral interpretations of sexual offenses and gender-neutral sentencing practices with regard to teacher offenders. Here the operative assumption of courts is that gender dynamics ought to make no difference to prosecution and sentencing, as we ought to treat offenses, offenders, and victims as though gender did not matter. However, gendered power relations are not necessarily the same in cases with male teachers and female students, or in homosexual intergenerational encounters. The aim of this chapter is to avoid a one-size-fits-all approach to power and sexuality, by making visible a multidimensional framework that is suitably calibrated to incorporate the recognition of any relevant social dynamics and differences, such as gender, class, race, and ability that are part of and shape relations of power.

The alternative reading of multidimensional power relations through the D'Addario-B affair is not offered as a definitive account. Yet no matter how speculative, it is profoundly more feasible than the scenario implied by the law—namely, that D'Addario is a "serious sex offender" (who abused her position of power) and B is a "child victim." However, the point to emphasize is not so much whether we can construct a more accurate reading of the relationship. Of course, due to legal constraints on identifying minors in sexual-offense cases and the near impossibility of recruiting research participants and gaining ethics approval in such volatile criminal contexts, any detailed information on such relationships is almost completely foreclosed.[53] These constraints notwithstanding, the critical issue is that we cannot even begin to understand the relational dynamics between D'Addario and B until we deconstruct the model of sovereign power embedded in the law. For this is a model that predetermines the subject positions of "adult perpetrator" and "child victim" in advance of an analysis of actual intersubjective power relations and relations of intra-activity. As I have argued in this chapter, however, it is only possible to ascertain a student's capabilities and whether an abuse has taken place precisely by attending to the multiple dimensions of power and the intersubjective and intra-active dynamics constituting each case. Due to the current statutory prohibition of all sexual relationships between teachers and mature minors, this remains the responsibility of the judicial system alone. But it is a responsibility that cannot be—and that is at present inadequately—dispatched due to the simplification of the dynamics of subjectivity and power.

There are glaring contradictions in the way the law simultaneously recognizes and denies adolescent sexual competencies and abilities to exercise power in various legal contexts.[54] To continue the example of the Victorian legislation—which applies to many anglophone positions-of-authority laws—youth between the ages of consent and majority are deemed capable of consenting to sex and participating in sexual power relations with *any* adults outside relationships of authority, even those commonly thought to command positions of immense social and economic power and influence, such as multimillion-dollar-earning sports or pop stars, politicians, or businesspeople. Adolescents as young as twelve years of age can also legally prove their competency to receive contraceptive information, devices, or prescriptions, not to mention prove their competency to receive an abortion without the approval of their parents—an explicit recognition if ever there were one of the sexual maturity, sexual power, and competency of some adolescents under the age of consent. Even if we were to grant—and I do not—that power is intrinsic to certain social and institutional positions of so-called authority, it does not follow that those positions necessarily disqualify adolescent capacities for effective consent and participation in relations of power. How an adolescent's—or anyone's—abilities and capacities are mobilized and the effects these produce depend on how an individual negotiates his or her encounters with others in the context of networks of multiple, mutually constituting dimensions and dynamics of recognition. The notions of positional or institutional power are given weight they cannot carry, as we have seen in the D'Addario-B scenario. While it might be argued that power and authority are conferred to a teacher by an institution, obviously this does not guarantee that all individuals will thereafter recognize this so-called power and authority. That recognition of power and authority is context-specific and contingent on interpersonal and collective dynamics of "intra-action" is evidenced by the rather banal fact that one student may experience a teacher as commanding, scary, and controlling, while another may experience the same teacher as unimposing, meek, and ineffectual.[55] In the absence of providing mature minors with full legal personhood—which I think we should provide—a multidimensional model of intersubjective power relations might assist in ameliorating their inconsistent and contradictory positioning within the law by offering much greater recognition of adolescent subjectivity, diversity, and agency.

In my mind, this is where Australia, the United Kingdom, and the United States could learn a great deal from European countries that have had positions-of-authority legislation but have not always defined sex acts between a teacher and student *automatically* as abusive and criminal. In a number of European jurisdictions, it has not always been the fact of sex within a relationship of authority that constitutes a crime, but whether that authority has been misused in attempting to gain the minor's consent.[56] Where mature minors are stripped of their capacity and right to give informed consent in relationships of authority in Australia, the United Kingdom, and the United States, in many European countries judicial spaces have been provided at various times in the recent past for the recognition of the adolescent capacity for consent and sexual agency, the recognition of nonsovereign relations of power between adults and youth, and thus the recognition of adolescent subjectivity and intersubjective dynamics even within so-called relationships of authority. This makes good sense, given that the archive of research on the effects of intergenerational sex and child sexual abuse establishes clearly that it is not necessarily the sex act in itself that produces damaging consequences. Rather, it is the network of intrapsychic, intersubjective, contextual, and heterosocial dynamics of sexual encounters and their reception and ongoing intersubjective assimilation that account for negative, neutral, or positive outcomes.[57] Indeed, it is this multidimensional network that produces anew what go by the names of agency and power relations.

With its reliance on a sovereign model of one-dimensional, one-way power, and its assumption of inevitable abuse, current positions-of-authority legislation is made possible by the occlusion of these very dynamics. While premised on an ostensible and laudable concern to circumvent the abuse of children, the reductionist and paternalist logic of such legislation has a profound impact beyond prevention and protection that directly implicates the youth involved. This is brought into stark relief in recent criminal cases, with their accompanying high-profile media publicity, prison sentences, sex offender registrations, and delicate psychological dynamics of responsibility and blame. Protectionist legislation very often backfires, itself often producing more negative outcomes and harm than what existed in the first place. The automatic application in law of the default categories of "perpetrator" and "victim"—even in cases where it is plain that they are a poor fit with individuals involved—is, I will suggest, socially irresponsible and psychologically detrimental.

Responsible Sexual Citizenship

Many supporters of laws against teacher-student sex may well agree with a critique of the model of sovereign power inherent to positions-of-authority legislation, but remain committed to such laws in the interests of protecting young people from harm. Better to protect the many vulnerable children than frustrate the few competent ones—who surely can wait a year or so—as the argument goes. The problem with this argument is that it assumes protectionist logic is self-evident. Recall that adolescents like B are legally permitted to have sex with any adult not in a position of authority. What this indicates is that the law indeed recognizes his ability to make mature and informed decisions—positive sexual rights—but it does so only in certain sexual scenarios and not others. In the state of Victoria, as in many Western jurisdictions, recognition of the positive sexual rights of adolescents in-between the ages of consent and majority is thus partial and depends on context. The law also recognizes the negative sexual rights of adolescents: the right to be free from coercion, abuse, and harm. However, unlike adults, for whom sexual citizenship seems to entail an equal balance between positive and negative sexual rights, for adolescents the law prioritizes the negative right to be free from sexual coercion and harm. In addition to other inconsistent discursive-legal framings of adolescence as simultaneously adult *and* child, empowered *and* powerless, this has resulted in adolescent sexuality being constructed as a site of contradiction in law. The law emerges not only from judicial cognizance of internal contradictions and inconsistencies in its construction of the adolescent as *both* adult and child. The law is in fact predicated on such contradictory and inconsistent framings. It seems to me that in conjunction with the sovereign epistemology of power, these contradictions and inconsistencies provide the very leverage for adults to regulate the boundaries both of the adult/child binary and of adult-child power relations. They also, wittingly or not, provide the basis for the marginalization and neglect of child and adolescent sexualities in particular discursive contexts. Adolescents can be constructed as children in certain settings and for certain social and political purposes (such as regulating their sexualities), and as adults for others (such as prosecuting them as adults for certain crimes). What are the ramifications of this messiness with regard to adolescence? Does the contradictory framing of adolescence fulfill the protectionist mandate of child-abuse legislation? One way of considering these questions is to switch our angle of vision to the other side, or correlate, of sexual rights: sexual responsibilities.[58]

Even under current laws, adolescents are not immune from considerations of sexual responsibility. Consider a hypothetical scenario involving B and D'Addario. Imagine that D'Addario did indeed feel coerced into performing oral sex on B, as she had actually claimed to police upon or after being charged. Recall that B had also actually suggested they "go the whole way." Imagine, in response to D'Addario's refusal, that B decided to force her into having penetrative sex. Imagine that B confessed to committing the rape. Would he be held accountable for the crime? You bet he would. How irrelevant is the question of subjectivity, agency, and power here? How well does partial and contradictory recognition of sexual subjectivity and agency stand up when we consider these two scenarios together? How is it that B could be deemed responsible in the context of rape and devoid of *any responsibility for his actions whatsoever* in the context of consensual sex? Inarguably, this contradictory treatment of adolescents is problematic, if not untenable. The comparison between the consensual and the forced scenarios also confounds the sovereign formulation of power constitutive of positions-of-authority laws. For even if we were to accept their terms (and obviously I do not), when rerouted through the rape scenario, sovereign power cannot be conceived of as the reserve of teachers alone. An adolescent who were to commit rape would be held responsible for perpetrating sexual assault, for abusing a form of sovereign power. Yet that adolescent is stripped of any responsibility for exercising power in a voluntary sexual encounter in a relationship of authority. If an ethics of sexual responsibility is always already implicated in an ethics of sexual rights, and if adolescents are partial bearers of these rights, is it not incumbent upon us to recognize adolescents also as bearers—even if only partially—of certain responsibilities? How can we in good faith facilitate adolescents to engage in responsible and ethical sexual behavior and relationships when we fail to hold them at least partially accountable for their actions? How can we assist adolescents to participate in social and interpersonal power relations more responsibly when we simultaneously recognize them in very polarized terms as participants and nonparticipants, empowered subjects and powerless victims? How might we more effectively and ethically facilitate the development of responsible sexual citizenship for adolescents?[59]

Let us return for one last time to the D'Addario-B encounter to consider some of the possible destructive effects of this contradictory and ambiguous scenario. B initially engaged in sexual relations with D'Addario consensually in good faith, or so it seems. However, it appears that this is where his honorable intentions ceased. B publicized to a not-insubstantial number of friends the clandestine affair, undoubtedly disregarding a secret pact between D'Addario and himself. He also tried to benefit from his position in an attempt to extort money. With what seems to be a much more profound awareness than the judiciary affords itself of the ability of an adolescent to participate—advantageously, in some regards—in sexual relations of power, B was able to leverage on the default legal categories of adult perpetrator/child victim and manipulate, attempt to bribe, and entrap D'Addario. Astonishingly, however, he was not held in even the slightest way responsible or culpable for *any or any part* of his actions. B was thus empowered—and his actions in many respects vindicated—to participate in relations of power with ignoble intentions and effects. This is, in my view, a distasteful pedagogical and ethical scenario indeed.

I am not suggesting that B ought to be held *wholly* responsible for the "crime" committed by D'Addario. What I am suggesting is that, if we are genuinely committed to facilitating in adolescents responsible citizenship and responsible participation in social relations of power, then we must *empower* them—especially, although certainly not only, when they have reached the general age of consent—*to be responsible*, and thus at some level accountable, for their actions and their roles in relationships, sexual or not. I think it is ethically, sociopolitically, judicially, and pedagogically irresponsible for a society to do otherwise. Yet this does not even seem to be registered in terms of current pedagogical imperatives and discussions. Even in the suite of recommendations in the US Department of Education's *Educator Sexual Misconduct* report there is no sign of any recognition of student agency or responsibility. One recommendation that deals with the education of students makes this glaringly apparent:

> **12.8 Educate Students.** Like staff, students need to understand the boundaries that *educators* should not cross. This is important both for students who might be targeted and for students who observe such behaviors. Both sets of students need to know that such behavior is prohibited and that there is a person to whom they can and should report such incidents. Materials and programs that have been developed to protect students from sexual abuse rarely include examples of predators who are educators. Students need to know that *educators* might cross boundaries and what to do if this happens.[60]

Influential researcher David Finkelhor echoes this one-sided approach to pedagogy and responsibility. Reciting the standard axiom trumpeted in the media and academic discourse, he decrees: "The bottom line is that it's the educator's responsibility to put a stop to it. They are the grown-ups."[61]

In her excellent book *The Trouble with Blame: Victims, Perpetrators, and Responsibility*, psychologist and child sexual abuse specialist Sharon Lamb reflects on two decades of work in the area of child sexual abuse prevention and treatment. In spite of all the positive effects of this work, she observes a worrying development:

> Those of us who have seen and fought against the absurd blaming of victims have, at times, gone too far in the other direction, thereby denying victims any responsibility for their behavior and for their reactions to their abuse, which often include depression, anxiety, anger, and other post-traumatic stress symptoms. Although we have created a context in which victims' rights and injuries are now acknowledged, we have also cost victims some modicum of respect and personhood.[62]

The failure to tease out appropriate degrees of responsibility can, as Lamb notes, *compound* rather than alleviate these debilitating symptoms of sexual abuse. If "we choose a road that emphasizes the victimization and does not deal directly with issues of self, character, and responsibility, then we risk," she argues, "turning victims into victims for life."[63] In chapter 3 I went further than Lamb to suggest that the failure to take seriously young people's sense of sexual agency, power, and responsibility in cases of sexual abuse can also produce some of these symptoms in the first place. The point to emphasize here is that, for Lamb, labeling and objectifying children as "victims" can pose serious problems, even for those who have been victimized. It strips them of their subjective complexity and robs them of agency and the acceptance of some degree of responsibility essential for recovery. Lamb is, of course, referring to children who *actually* have been abused. She is not thinking about students like B, who has clearly not been abused in the act of sex and who, like many other boys at the center of recent similar criminal cases, has reached the general age of consent and has either instigated or had an agentive role in sexual relations with his teacher. Taking this important insight of Lamb's, let us finally consider the inverse scenario: the denial of his sexual agency and the impact of assigning to boys like B the label of "victim" where they have clearly not been victimized.

The depreciation of sexual subjectivity and denial of agency and power of nonvictim participants is also, I submit, potentially psychologically detrimental. In the case of B, while the judge surmised from his victim impact statement that it was unlikely he suffered any emotional damage from the incidents[64] and, indeed, that he was just "embarrassed by it,"[65] he will nonetheless have to contend with the ongoing knowledge that his actions *contributed* to a woman going to prison and having her life catastrophically ruined. Embarrassment is part of the shame family of emotions and ought to by no means be trivialized. It may be an expression of, or co-assemble with, more virulent and debilitating forms of guilt and shame. Even if B were to convince himself that D'Addario committed a crime and not he, that she was wholly responsible and not he, it will always be registered psychically for B—even if only unconsciously—that the power relations were not self-evident, that he was not intrinsically sexually abused, and that he was not a victim in the manner assumed by law. This is doubtless an extremely difficult emotional challenge for him to endure and to integrate into his subjectivity. Profound shame and guilt—debilitating enough for child sexual abuse *victims* to endure, let alone when it revolves around someone going to prison in relation to your voluntary actions—might be only the beginning of psychological conflicts and difficulties for B.

Power as Intra-activity

The purpose of my rereading of the D'Addario-B case has not been to invert the standard narrative of positions-of-authority legislation by locating power and responsibility solely at the hands of B. This would be merely to remain squarely within the model of sovereignty being problematized. Among this chapter's aims have been to open up these laws to long overdue deconstruction and to provide an example of a practical analytic framework without which it is impossible *even to begin* the tasks, which ought to be central to legal proceedings in the first instance, of analyzing networks of sexual (power) relations and determining whether consent has in fact been compromised and abuses taken place. I have sought also to expose the unacknowledged work and the performative foreclosures around teenage sexual agency being advanced with sovereign applications of power. At present, when analyzing power dynamics there is a tendency to privilege or prioritize certain dimensions of power (such as the institutional, in the case of positions-of-authority legislation)—and ignore or downplay others. What I have attempted to do is sustain a focus on a network of multiple dimensions of power—specifically in this case the institutional, heterosocial, intrapsychic, and intersubjective—that simultaneously and mutually constitute *any* encounter, relationship, practice, phenomenon, or intersubjective moment. We cannot begin to understand these phenomena in the absence of an account of *all* of the dimensions of power, of their co-constitution. Nor can we understand subjects and subjectivities without attention to multidimensional relations of intra-activity. These dimensions must be teased out within each contextual frame of analysis, phenomenon, or moment if we are to do justice to the complexity of intersubjective dynamics and if we are to understand all subjects—including young people—not as preexisting relations of power and practice but as emerging through their multidimensional intra-action. Without adequate recognition of the specificity of sexuality, intersubjective dynamics, and the multidimensionality of power relations and ontological practices, the application of positions-of-authority legislation risks improperly incarcerating some teachers, homogenizing and disempowering adolescents—or empowering them to absolve themselves of responsibility—and creating far more harm than good.

That the kind of legislation examined here dismisses adolescent enactments of consent and sexual agency and participation in relations of power, and potentially leaves young people at risk of harm where there may have been none in relation to the sexual encounters, brings into stark relief the legislation's punitive, defensive, and performative, rather than simply protective, functions. Adults and agentive young people are punished for transgressing the intergenerational prohibition, and young people's sexuality agency, and power are infantilized. The legal prohibition also therefore functions as a form of disciplinary power that performatively produces a set of normative categories that it has statutorily already assumed: power*ful* adult perpetrators and power*less* child victims. If youth sexuality were not being punished and disavowed and if dominant socio-legal discourse were not concerned with imposing a singular model of childhood or adolescence, then standard child-rape and child-sexual-offense laws would satisfy child-protection imperatives. Or, alternatively, North American, British, and Australia jurisdictions might adopt, or consider adopting, legislative provisions such as those that have been adopted at various times by some European jurisdictions that have recognized mature minors.

The blanket refusal of the law and popular discourses to countenance the sexual agency and exercise of power of some boys (and some girls and other young people) is underscored by the increasing willingness of judicial systems to prosecute adolescents as adults for serious crimes. A contradiction emerges here, and it concerns the uneven recognition of adolescent capacities for the exercise of power and agency. Courts are more than willing to recognize the agency and power of adolescents in voluntarily perpetrating crimes against adults, but not so when adolescents voluntarily engage in sex with adults. Judicial systems thus seek to support victims (as we would hope), but sometimes unfortunately punish empowered adolescents or else absolve them of any responsibility for their voluntary actions in sex with adults. "Pretending that children possess nothing like sexuality or sexual agency makes a poignant kind of sense," suggests Peter Coviello, "since that pretense assures that children are within the reach of our control until we decide they are not. It is a way of pretending that parenting [and we might add state paternalism] is an exercise in sovereignty."[66] What Coviello is suggesting is that child and adolescent sexual agency is often troubling for adults, as it directly challenges intergenerational power relations. I wonder whether this perhaps goes some way to explaining the contradictory recognition of agency within these respective scenarios. When young people are convicted for crimes perpetrated against adults, they remain within the control of adults. However, granting them the power to consent to sex with adults entails a relinquishing of adult control.

The implications of this legal imbroglio extend well beyond the domain of law and positions-of-authority legislation. They pertain to any attempt to trade in notions of childhood and adolescence (and adulthood), any attempt to understand intersubjective power relations, and social and legal efforts to regulate young people's behavior. Young people of all ages are not positioned outside networks of power, only to become bestowed with "its force" as they age incrementally. Like all subjects they are inextricably and ceaselessly constituted and reconstituted within networks of power. Barad puts it this way: "Subjects and objects do not preexist as such but are constituted through, within, and as part of particular practices . . . [and] through the intra-action of multiple apparatuses"[67]—and within, I would highlight, multiple material-discursive dimensions. If we recast power *as* intra-activity, individual "capacities" such as agency and sexuality can be rethought by seeing them not as properties of individuals but as assemblages that are sustained and reformed through material-discursive dimensions and alliances, some of which I have outlined. This might, of course, entail that some people are better equipped in various ways in various contexts. As I show in this chapter, boys such as B are often, through specific assemblages and networks, very well positioned to be active, empowered, and resilient. The effects of such relations of multidimensional intra-activity are necessarily uneven and individual. And they cannot always be captured by generic ontological and developmental categories, or the master discourse of child sexual abuse. Ontology is not fixed and pre-given according to crude biological and developmental categories. As Annemarie Mol states, "If practice becomes our entrance into the world, ontology is no longer a monist whole. Ontology-in-practice is multiple."[68] Ontologies are enacted in particular relations, practices, histories of intra-activity, and at every moment. It is a mighty feat of arrogance that presumes knowledge of the individual capacity and potentiality of all of those within a given set (childhood, adolescence) now and into the future. Yet such is the assumption implicit within any attempt to circumscribe fixed boundaries around age-based ontologies. Assumptions of this kind, wherever they are made—within law or the classroom—are not benign descriptions but politically motivated drives to intra-act in the world to performatively produce young people according to preconceived specifications. It is time to throw away the blueprint, or at least muddy its inscriptions. Fixed, biologically deterministic notions of childhood and adolescence ought to give way to multiple bodies, multiple ontologies, and multiple potentialities. It is up to us to recognize and nurture these multiple realities. Not all sexual interactions between young people and adults are harmful or abusive, even if they challenge prevailing social and moral views of acceptable behavior.

The literalization of the legal presumption of inherent power differentials and its limitations are brought into ever starker focus by the increasing introduction in US universities of policies banning all professor-student sexual relationships, whether a relationship of direct supervision exists or not.[69]

There have been calls by some Australian academics for Australian universities to follow suit.[70] If, as I have argued, the notion of inherent positional power fails in the domain of adult-teen relations, its extension to adult-adult relationships brings even further into relief its misleading and universalizing assumptions. It also seems rather absurd in the current context of consumer-driven education, or what Wendy Brown has recently described as the model of universities as businesses and "students as indebted self-investors."[71] The power exercised by students through course evaluations, complaints, litigation over grades or harassment, and other mechanisms of consumer demand are hardly indicative of student powerlessness. This is a model of power disingenuous in its application, and one that is driven by the performative politics of blame, victimhood, and overzealous protectionism. And I argue, along with a number of other feminist scholars such as Laura Kipnis and Janet Halley, that such a model of power, when applied in blanket fashion encourages vulnerability, weakness, and irresponsibility, as well as the potential for misuse and manipulation—as a number of scholars have highlighted in relation to the growing number of questionable sexual harassment accusations in American universities.[72]

While perhaps understandable from a protectionist standpoint, it seems to me that the drive to define simple, clear divisions of power only works to paper over the inherent instability, difficulty, fluidity, unknowability, discomfort, and murkiness of sexuality. Telling stories about so-called inherent asymmetries of power is in part a way of defending against the complexity of power *relations*. It also firms up the child/adult opposition, or so it is hoped. But I think this is a naive attempt at neutralizing power,[73] if not in part a disingenuous attempt at reproducing egotistical fantasies of professorial power and influence. Because power does not settle straightforwardly into classes or categories such as man, adult, teacher, professor, and so on—especially, it has to be said, in consensual sexual relations.[74] Sexuality is being problematically reconstituted as a site of especial and inherent vulnerability in relation to other dimensions of life at the same time as childhood is being extended into the adult world of university and workplace. It doesn't matter if some young people or some young adults articulate a sense of powerlessness at the hands of teachers and professors (or other "authority" figures in the workplace). If not *all* are so disempowered—as is glaringly apparent in the face of so many empirical realities (including my own experience as a teenager and university student[75])—then the model of positional power ought never to be applied *universally*, either in law or institutional policy. It might be one analytic lens to consider in the quest to understand and adjudicate specific cases, but it cannot and does not reflect or predict universal ontological or ethical truths.

SIX

Gender

> Female sex offenders are a new breed in a criminal caste monopolised by men. Prosecutions are on the rise here and overseas, as public awareness breeds vigilance and a campaign to make women as accountable as men creates a class of abusers previously overlooked.
>
> —Kate Legge, "Teachers' Pets," *The Australian*, 2006[1]

> Dozens of female teachers have been caught with male students in recent years, and the airwaves are full of outrage that we're letting them off the hook.
>
> —William Saletan, "Teachers' Pets?" *Slate*, 2006[2]

In 2004 a scandal erupted in Australia over the issue of gender bias in the judicial treatment of sexual offenders and victims. It was sparked by the sentencing of Karen Ellis, then a thirty-seven-year-old physical education teacher, who pleaded guilty to the "sexual penetration of a child under the age of 16 years." The "child," one of her students—Ben Dunbar—was three months shy of his sixteenth birthday and the general age of consent at the time of the offenses.[3] Ellis, initially receiving a wholly suspended sentence, was immediately compared to Gavin Hopper, the famous international tennis coach who, only three months earlier, had been sentenced to a minimum prison term of two years and three months for a sexual relationship with a fourteen-year-old student in the mid-1980s.[4] Ellis's sentence aroused widespread public outrage from victims of crimes groups and parents and child-abuse support groups, among others. Indeed, the case has been held up as an example of the judicial system's more lenient treatment of female offenders, and of the need for gender-neutral interpretations of sexual offenses.

Australia is far from unique in its preoccupation with this issue. Precisely the same politics of indignation about female teacher offenders and their sentences has been shaping public discussions in North America. In fact, Australian debates have been heavily influenced by those in the United States. At the heart of this controversy is the allegation that women receive lesser sentences than men for similar crimes for two reasons. First, courts view women as less culpable offenders, and second, they view encounters between women and boys as less harmful due to the lingering patriarchal myth of the "lucky bastard."[5] This is the idea that it is every heterosexual boy's ultimate fantasy to have sex with a hot female teacher. The chapter takes the high-profile Ellis case as a window onto this broader anglophone sex panic over gender and justice. Less important are any peculiarities of the Australian judicial system than the transpacific similarity in narrative and debates. Variants of the Ellis-Dunbar affair have taken place in a number of jurisdictions in North America. Here we explore the question as to what difference gender makes, and ought to make, to our social and legal understanding and treatment of this category of sex crime. I argue against prevailing wisdom to suggest that cases such as this highlight the need not for gender neutrality—or, at least, not the way it is being conceived—but for the recognition of gender difference. This is part of a broader claim that there are serious problems with the principle of gender neutrality as it is often applied in this recent incarnation of statutory-rape-like cases. On one hand, its application is premised on a singular model of the powerless female victim. On another, derived from scenarios of abuse within which notions of sovereign-like power prevail, the conceptualization of gender neutrality is extended improperly to adjudicate voluntary and nonabusive interactions in which power is much more complex and relational. Both of these moves are intimately entangled with an even more profound social and political shift in which young people are increasingly being *delimited* as almost inherently homogenous, vulnerable, immature, and inept with respect to sexuality.

The Seduction of Karen Ellis

"In the way that it happened, you could say I was a predator," Dunbar asserted confidently to Liz Hayes in a *60 Minutes* interview two years after the offenses.[6] "I mean, I went after her . . . I took my chances. And I just went for it." But Hayes wouldn't have a bar of any inversion of the standard adult-perpetrator/child-victim formula. "But you know that's impossible," she responded. "You can never be the predator. You know that, don't you?"

Despite the arrogant and didactic tone, Hayes's rhetorical question highlights how a narrative of inevitable child sexual abuse often functions to determine the normative boundaries of adolescent subjectivity at the same time as censor the experiences of actual adolescents. Dunbar was at pains to stress the misfit between the legal categories subsuming him (child, victim) and his experience: "Well, apparently I'm the victim. You know that's . . ." But before he could even finish, Hayes cut him off. "But you are. Not 'apparently.' You are." Still emphasizing a distinction ignored by Hayes between legal definition and what it seeks to describe, Dunbar replied, "By the law, yeah, yep." *60 Minutes* then provided him with a rare moment to articulate his position—albeit in an aggressively infantilizing context, and one reflecting his experience at the hands of the law. "You don't see yourself as a victim?" "Definitely not, no," he said with conviction. Prior to the interview, in his letter to the court in support of Ellis, Dunbar preempted the question of potential harm and victim status, saying: "The only way this will affect me is if she was to go to prison or was harshly sentenced. I would feel guilty because I know that she is a good person. . . . At all times I knew what I was doing and wanted to do it."[7]

According to the court transcripts for *R v. Ellis*, in October 2003 Ellis and Dunbar began a sexual relationship while Ellis's husband was traveling interstate (71). She was having marriage difficulties, and her husband was frequently away on work trips. Presumably these facts led the forensic psychologist treating Ellis to conclude that she was "vulnerable to . . . flirtation and succumbed to it" (71). In his statement, Dunbar said he initiated the relationship and Ellis had "displayed reluctance" but eventually agreed (69). "Everyone at the school thought she was a bit of all right, and so did I," he explained. "I found her attractive . . . so when you find someone attractive you go after them."[8] Describing the affair, he said, "I thought it was pretty good, but, I mean . . . I wasn't hoping for any long-term relationship."[9] Around the time of the sixth offense, however, Dunbar's mother saw them getting into Ellis's car "looking like husband and wife"[10] and became suspicious, as she had "noticed a change in her son's behaviour" (66). She then notified the school and the police. Upon pleading guilty, Ellis was given a twenty-two-month wholly suspended sentence and placed on the sex offender registry.

Judge John Smallwood justified the sentence by saying the circumstances in the case were unique and exceptional, among them: Ellis pleaded guilty "at the earliest opportunity . . . displayed remorse . . . [and had] no prior convictions" (64). He also noted that "whilst consent is not a defence it is a mitigating factor," and "I have no reason to doubt that he [Dunbar] was a mature teenager" (70). He went on to say there was no evidence contradicting the fact Dunbar had initiated the relationship, had previously been in a sexual relationship, and said he had not suffered any "psychological damage or trauma" (70). In his decision to wholly suspend, Smallwood made reference to the Hopper case—which itself had achieved notoriety—due to the fact the counsel for the Crown had also used *Hopper* "as an indication of the general principles which relate to offending of this nature" (67). Smallwood made clear that comparisons with *Hopper* were inappropriate in sentencing Ellis, given the significant differences in each case. For instance, the victim in *Hopper* testified to having had a crush on the offender, but to feeling threatened by his behavior. She felt coerced by his pressurizing and predatory overtures, and became dependent on him in a relationship in which she described Hopper as like a "father and husband in one" (*R v. Hopper*, 4). The result, she said, was a feeling of being out of her depth and pressured to please him sexually. As Smallwood explained in *R v. Ellis*:

> The circumstances in relation to Mr Hopper . . . are greatly different. That relationship occurred over a period of two years. The victim was 14; not going on 16. Mr Hopper denied it from the outset. He conducted a trial. The victim was cross-examined and as I understand it called either a liar, or mad, or both . . . [and] Mr Hopper showed absolutely no remorse. In that particular crime His Honour found that the victim had suffered very considerably. Those factors do not exist in this particular situation to anything like the extent they occurred in *Hopper*. (68)

This reckoning did nothing to mollify public disquiet. Despite Smallwood's efforts to discount the relevance of *Hopper*, a slew of media articles and public statements insisted on a comparison with his jail term of two years and three months. The crux of the outcry was around the issue of gender and the law, and the idea that the same penalty should fit the same crime. For example, Elaine Crowle from Parents Victoria worried that the "main problem is the example that it could show to the community, and it does seem to show, perhaps, that a female teacher having a relationship with a male student isn't as bad as the opposite situation." Noel McNamara from the Crime Victims Support Association opined, "I just think it's disgusting. It's . . . clearly a travesty of justice when Hopper gets a jail sentence and Ellis gets a non-custodial sentence. . . . And . . . to draw a line in the sand and make it a gender issue, which has obviously been done [by] Smallwood, it's disgraceful."[11] Similarly, Hetty Johnston, founder of the Bravehearts organization for the prevention of child sexual assault, said: "It's the same offence, it matters not by gender. . . . That woman is as guilty as Gavin Hopper and she should be sentenced likewise."[12] And Steve Medcraft, president of People Against Lenient Sentencing, remarked with disbelief: "I thought the days of giving them ([female] sexual offenders) suspended sentences and taking these offences lightly were over. But they are obviously still alive and kicking."[13]

Such was the outcry that the director of public prosecutions for Victoria appealed it on grounds it was "manifestly inadequate."[14] While ten particulars were offered as rationale, for the presiding judges the case turned principally on the issue of gender equality before the law. As Justice Frank Callaway summarized:

> A sentence of 22 months' imprisonment, wholly suspended, for six counts of sexual penetration in the circumstances of this case is so lenient that it can be explained only by an unconscious sympathy with a female offender or a belief that no real harm had been done to the victim. The sentence unintentionally violated the rule of equality before the law, including equality of concern for male and female victims and equality in the sentencing of male and female offenders.[15]

The appeal was upheld, and Ellis was resentenced to six months in prison.[16]

(En)Gendering Victims

What can we make of this decision? On the surface it might appear reasonable to refuse—as the appeal judges have done here—to uphold an apparent gender bias. However, I argue that the *interpretation* of the principle of equality (or, neutrality) of treatment of offenders and victims obscured important considerations regarding the specificity of gender that ought to be registered in sentencing in this case and others like it, a specificity that adds an important dimension to the meaning, experience, and effect of the offenses and gender relations in question.

Judges usually have considerable discretion with regard to sentencing. The reason is that there are maximum and minimum penalties laid out for such crimes, and thus a spectrum of sentencing possibilities. The spectrum is designed with a degree of flexibility in order to account for the specificity of circumstances constituting each case. Variability in sentences for offenses is, moreover, the result of courts having to weigh the various factors they are instructed to take into consideration, including "the presence of any aggravating or mitigating factor concerning the offender or of any other relevant circumstances."[17] When Smallwood handed down the suspended sentence, it was precisely the "very exceptional" nature of the context-dependent circumstances, rather than some notion of inherent and universal meaning of particular (gender-neutral) sexual offenses and their associated penalties, that informed his decision.[18] This is standard sentencing practice, whereby courts at the stage of determining how a sentence is to be served consider "more heavily" the "individual characteristics of the offending and the offender."[19] Smallwood refracted his analysis of these individual characteristics through each of the sentencing criteria. As noted, for instance, he took into account Ellis's good character, admission of guilt, and remorse, as well as Dunbar's prior sexual experience, initiation, willingness, and lack of psychological damage.

In the appeal decision, Callaway and colleagues effectively reversed this exceptional-circumstances reasoning. Importantly, this was underpinned by a comparison with the prison sentence handed down in *Hopper*. What Callaway compared was not so much the length of sentence but the fact that one received a prison sentence and the other did not. Irrespective of particularities, he attempted to treat male and female offenders and victims equally by treating seemingly similar offenses or sex acts "objectively" and gender-neutrally. As he noted, when quoting from and upholding the prosecution's argument in *R v. Ellis*, the "fact that in this case the offences involved heterosexual intercourse between a mature female and a young male does not make the offending less serious than that between a mature male and a young female."[20] This statement is inextricable from one of the fundamental criteria governing the suite of sentencing principles: "the nature and gravity of the offence."[21] Of course, in ascertaining "the nature and gravity of the offence," focus is not restricted to the child victim. Courts are instructed to consider broader forms of impact—namely, "the impact of the offence on any victim of the offence."[22] Judges in both cases considered the impact on other victims—namely, Dunbar's mother, the school, and the broader community. The "nature and gravity of the offence" is also not the only basis for sentencing. Other factors include protecting the community from the offender, as well as general "deterrence, just punishment and the denunciation of . . . conduct."[23] Callaway stressed the importance of the latter over the former, due to the expectation that "it is very unlikely . . . the respondent will re-offend."[24] However, he made it clear the decisive issue was the objective seriousness or gravity of the offense—an objective gravity unmitigated by gender.[25] In short, the issue of gender equality/neutrality trumped other sentencing factors.

In reaching this conclusion, Callaway and colleagues upheld the prosecution's claim that Smallwood failed to give sufficient weight to the nature and gravity of the offense in so far as "the statutory regime is designed to protect persons in the position of victim."[26] But what if Dunbar is not a "victim" in the sense of the female victim to whom he is compared (i.e., the *Hopper* victim)? What if he did not suffer any, or suffered less, physical and psychological harm? What if gender-specific dynamics are important factors shaping the "nature and gravity of the offence"? Would this undermine the gender comparison justifying the prison sentence for Ellis?

In his letter to the court and in various media interviews, Dunbar vociferously and repeatedly rejected the moniker of "victim" and its associations of harm or negative consequences. "At no stage has this affected my life. If anything I've gained," he said on one occasion, "from not knowing where I was heading in school to doing a pre-apprenticeship course and will come out a second year electrician. I work as a part-time tiler on my free days. I won the best and fairest for cricket which shows that my concentration hasn't changed and this hasn't affected me at all."[27] Although we must be cautious of taking such statements at face value, I suggest that Dunbar's experience might usefully be situated within research on adolescent sexuality, which demonstrates clearly how a gendered dimension is an important aspect of the development of sexual subjectivity and of how young people experience sexual relations. In a study of gender dynamics and intergenerational sex, feminist researchers Andrea Nelson and Pam Oliver argue that, despite "laws that treat adult-child sexual contact in gender-neutral terms, the data show that the gender of the participants is always central to the experience."[28] The conclusion of their research is that gender dynamics often result in sexual encounters of a *qualitatively* different kind. I argue it is this gendered dimension that has been insufficiently accommodated in the Ellis appeal ruling.

Dunbar's claims of a positive outcome were sustained some years after the offenses, as well as after reaching the age of majority. His positive experience is also reflected in existing research. Summarizing nonclinical data of the last twenty years with regard to sex between male adolescents and adults, Bruce Rind reiterates that it reveals "overwhelmingly that such relations are characterized mostly by positive reactions based on consent if not initiative on the part of the minor, with perceived benefit rather than harm as a correlate."[29] Indeed, some boys report a sense of achievement from their encounters with women that "later gives them confidence about their sexuality."[30] The issue of *legally effective* consent—a capacity the law does not recognize in minors in offenses of this kind—is not the decisive issue regarding the question of positive, negative, harmful, beneficial, or indifferent outcomes. This is because it is not the law's definition of this capacity that determines psychical outcomes for the minor, but the minor's negotiation, understanding, integration, and experience of this capacity himself in the context of his encounters. Nelson and Oliver offer a sustained gender comparison in cross-generational sex. Their sample showed significant differences in male and female experiences that reproduced findings of earlier research detailed by Rind, Tromovitch, and Bauserman.[31] The results revealed that, while girls and boys tend to experience encounters with men as negative, abusive, and coercive, boys tend to experience encounters with women as positive and noncoercive. These findings are supported by Rind, Tromovitch, and Bauserman's meta-analysis of child sexual abuse using college students, as well as the observations of a number of earlier researchers.[32] Moreover, in a comparison between two gender-specific samples, Donald James West and T. P. Woodhouse noted that responses of women recalling experiences of child sexual abuse were "predominantly of fear, unpleasant confusion, and embarrassment . . . [while men's] remembered reactions were mostly either indifference, tinged perhaps with slight anxiety, or of positive pleasure, the latter being particularly evident in contacts with the opposite sex."[33] Although not a universal formula, this gendered algorithm is borne out in the comparison between the Ellis and Hopper cases. Dunbar insisted his relationship was positive and noncoercive, while the young woman involved with Hopper felt manipulated, coerced, and abused by him.

The other important feature contributing to a negative impact—an important factor shaping the "nature and gravity of the offence"—is the attitude and behavior of the offender. As Nelson and Oliver argue, "It matters to children what is done, how it is done, and who does it."[34] Once again, gender is significant here; they found that men routinely "took" from the children in their attempts to secure sexual contact, whereas women generally "asked" for sex.[35] This accords with research summarized by Rind, and Denise Hines and David Finkelhor, which revealed that a feeling of coercion is associated with negative reactions and perceptions of harm.[36] Worth highlighting is that Ellis neither "took" nor "asked," but was *asked by* Dunbar for sex—something differentiating this case even further from those of Nelson and Oliver's, in which boys still experienced sex with women as positive even when they did not initiate the encounter. There is compelling evidence that Dunbar was sexually experienced, that he pursued and initiated sex with Ellis, and that he does not appear to have been harmed—indeed, he claims to have benefited from the experience. These facts alone make him a very different "victim" than the victim in *Hopper*, who was sexually inexperienced; felt predatorily pursued, threatened, and manipulated by Hopper's behavior; and claims to have suffered substantial psychological problems.[37]

If we take a broader view of adolescent sexuality, this gendered algorithm is not surprising. Indeed, it resonates with research demonstrating a gendered pattern with regard to the impact of puberty and early adolescent sex on the development of sexual subjectivity. As noted in the previous chapter, Karin Martin's *Puberty, Sexuality, and the Self: Boys and Girls at Adolescence* found that frequently "puberty facilitates the development of sexual subjectivity in boys" (46).[38] Puberty for girls, in contrast, commonly lowers their self-esteem and is "characterized by ambivalence about leaving childhood and anxiety about their new bodies" (19). Typically boys are eager to embrace adulthood and leave puberty with a strengthened sense of agency and control. They often experience pride and pleasure in their maturing bodies, have enhanced self-assurance by virtue of male puberty's associations with culturally valorized meanings of "adult masculinity, agency, and male sexuality" (46), and achieve a more robust subjective bodily knowledge through masturbation, which is something overwhelmingly experienced as positive. Girls, in contrast, commonly leave puberty with ambivalence and uncertainty about their changing bodies. Menarche—often associated with dirtiness and shame—the growth of breasts, and the sexualization and objectification of their bodies often result in girls feeling self-conscious, confused, out of control, and alienated from their bodies (23, 40–41). They seem to masturbate later and less than boys—or, if they don't, often feel far more anxious about it (49)—have far less subjective bodily knowledge, and take less pleasure in their bodies (79).[39] Boys are also usually bestowed with "more independence and more recognition of their selves, decisions, and accomplishments," whereas for girls, "looking older means looking sexual and parents' response is toward greater restriction rather than independence" (51).

In support of results of earlier research by Sorensen, Martin also found that first and early sexual experiences for adolescents often amplify these gender patterns. "In sum . . . early experiences of sex, like puberty, make girls feel less sexually subjective and boys more" (91).[40] While we must be cautious of simplistic extrapolations from this data to the experiences of all boys and girls, it is often illuminating to situate case studies within the context of broader social patterns. Dunbar was at pains to demonstrate to the court and the public that he exhibited just this sense of maturity, agency, and sexual subjectivity that Martin found in the majority of boys in her study. And there are no indications that contradict this. As he said in his letter of support:

> I would like to say that I feel that although the law states I am underage, I am very capable of making my own decisions and I am very mature for my age.... My father left six years ago and I've had to grow up and mature quicker than your average 15- to 16-year-old. At all times I knew what I was doing and wanted to do it.[41]

Martin makes the important point that agency—"the feeling like one can do and act"—is critical in developing a "positive sense of self" and self-esteem (10). The example of Dunbar is not, it seems, of a young man with low self-esteem or a sense of being unable to act assertively and in accordance with his desires and intentions. Dunbar felt recognized by Ellis for his maturity, as he made clear in his interviews. He felt treated like an equal, like a peer. Ellis herself claimed that Dunbar often exhibited the maturity of a thirty-six-year-old. Martin goes on to point out that "sexual subjectivity is a necessary component of agency and thus of self-esteem.... One's sexuality affects her/his ability to act in the world" (10). Moreover, the development of sexual subjectivity requires "a link between agency and the body/sexuality" (10). Dunbar appears to have developed a robust sexual subjectivity prior to meeting Ellis. This is evidenced to a large extent by the fact that not only did he have prior sexual experience, but he also, as we have seen, had the self-assurance to actively pursue Ellis and initiate sex. It is conceivable that his sexual subjectivity was strengthened in the course of his relationship with Ellis.

Extending Jessica Benjamin's theory of the centrality of self/other recognition to the development of agency and desire in the child, Martin also stresses how critical it is for the solidification and ongoing activity of agency and sexual subjectivity in adolescents for them to *feel recognized* by others as autonomous sexual subjects.[42] Dunbar instigated a sexual relationship with a woman he found sexually attractive. They had sex numerous times over the course of six weeks. In what was clearly a restrained response in a hostile *60 Minutes* interview to the question of how he felt at the time about his relationship with Ellis, he still managed to avow his positively perceived experience, saying with a smile, "I thought it was pretty good."[43] Ellis herself spoke of the mutual recognition and respect each had for the other. It is not unlikely that, in his encounters with Ellis, with whom he developed a reciprocal, respectful friendship, there was no shortage of recognition for

Dunbar as an adult sexual subject.[44] As noted earlier, they were, according to Dunbar's own mother, "looking like husband and wife."[45] Not only is there nothing to suggest that Dunbar was coerced—the absence of which is correlated with a positive experience—there is also nothing to suggest any appreciable ambivalence with regard to the sex he had with Ellis. The interpersonal conditions in this scenario might conceivably provide Dunbar with greater self-recognition than those within a relationship with an inexperienced adolescent for whom he may well have less respect and whose very adolescence might preclude the bestowal of adult recognition. This is not a case of a young man objectifying Ellis as a mere sexual conquest, as their ongoing friendship suggests. Just as Ellis did for him, Dunbar recognized her as an autonomous sexual subject. Indeed, so close have the two remained since Ellis was released from prison, and two years after the affair, that they risked further scrutiny by appearing on *60 Minutes* in order to publicly avow this friendship and their support for each other.

Wither "Lucky Bastard"

One of the effects of the shift to a discourse of gender neutrality and power inequality in framing intergenerational sex offenses has been, as we have already seen, a minimization or disregard of adolescent sexual agency. Given that boys have been initiators and co-conspirators of sexual encounters in many of the high-profile female teacher cases,[46] and that they much more palpably challenge assumptions about juridical power, it is perhaps hardly surprising that child-protectionist discourses have focused on them. For instance, an extraordinary amount of media attention and discussion in Australia and North America has gone into fervently repudiating the idea of the "lucky bastard," and scarcely any defending it. Thanks to the hegemony of the (feminist) child sexual abuse paradigm, the narrative of the "lucky bastard" is overwhelmingly demurred—if not shamed—as it is no longer ideologically acceptable to claim that some boys fantasize, enjoy, and might be unharmed by encounters with women. But there appears to be something of a protesting-too-much quality to this ardent repudiation of the "lucky bastard." And I think it has much to do with both the exposure of a regulatory child sexual abuse paradigm and the discomfort with agentive adolescent sexuality. The media incitement around the "lucky bastard" has taken the form of a kind of public policing of what may legitimately be said about these cases and the boys involved.

High-profile child sexual abuse researchers and experts have commented on this recent shift in cultural attitudes. David Finkelhor says that "'there's been a decline in the double standard. That's why you're seeing more of these cases' . . . As more women enter law enforcement, he said the older attitude that boys are willing, even lucky, participants has changed."[47] Robert Shoop, author of *Sexual Exploitation in Schools: How to Spot It and Stop It*, agrees: "Many people in society feel boys should want sex and it's not harmful, and girls should not want sex and it is harmful. . . . The reality is, in both cases it's illegal, it's harmful and it's wrong."[48] In the media coverage of the Ellis case—which almost uniformly supported a custodial sentence—the narrative of the "lucky bastard" was predominantly dismissed. This is reflected in the *60 Minutes* interviewed cited earlier. Liz Hayes staged a contest between current thinking and the supposedly anachronistic notion of the "lucky bastard." This took place in her discussion with adolescent psychologist Professor Michael Carr-Gregg. "So when you hear people say, 'Good on him, no harm done,' what do you think," she asked disingenuously. "I think *taurus excretus*," he replied. "*Taurus excretus?*" inquired Hayes in a performance of bewilderment. "Bulldust," declared Carr-Gregg. "It's absolute nonsense. I don't know who they think they're kidding. This is a child."[49]

Australian and North American media have been awash with articles and reports detailing the cultural remnants of the "lucky bastard" narrative. In her article "Teachers' Pets" in Australia's national newspaper, *The Australian*, Kate Legge commented that the court's resentencing of Ellis "sought to drive a stake through the fantasy of older women deflowering young men." "Adolescent boys who once were heroes are now cast as victims," writes Legge, "ripe for counselling, not bragging rights."[50] Ian Munro's "The Harm When Women Prey on Boys," in Melbourne's *The Age* newspaper, offered something similar. The article begins with the following apparent axiom: "Being seduced by an older woman is seen as a young man's fantasy, but it is sexual abuse."[51] Munro quotes social worker Patrick Leary, who proclaims that the "idea that it's some sort of fantasy or that it will be a rite of passage is a myth."[52] Aimed not only at boys but also at anyone wishing to raise an objection, these statements clearly have a pedagogical and regulatory function: to preach the doctrine that a boy's fantasy of sex with a teacher is a falsehood, which if acted on will result in abuse. Academic and psychomedical commentators followed suit. As glossed by Legge, forensic psychologist Rebecca Deering suggested that "boys tend not to dob [i.e., tell authorities] because masculinity teaches them independence and strength, and society portrays early sexual contact with women as a positive initiation into manhood, an occasion to celebrate." But, she argues, "male victims mask their hurt and confusion."[53] Or, as clinical psychologist Paul Grech notes in a similar vein, "Bravado and the superficial perceptions of a heroic deed are not necessarily the reality."[54]

What is so troubling about acknowledging lucky bastards? What have we got to lose—or, rather, what are we forced to face—by acknowledging the documented possibility that some boys may enjoy and even benefit from sexual encounters with older women? In order to address these questions, I want to return to the work of Nelson and Oliver, "Gender and the Construction of Consent."[55] Although their work is now over twenty years old, it is exemplary in a more theoretically explicit way, it seems to me, of the set of predominant logics that continue to inform the broader socio-legal paradigm of child sexual abuse on which the mainstream media's repudiation of the "lucky bastard" is based.

I have suggested that the teacher-student sex panic about judicial gender bias and the findings of Nelson and Oliver's research bring into stark relief a tension between the ethical and legal principle of gender equality/neutrality in the treatment of offenders and victims and the gendered specificity of sexual experience. This is precisely because, as noted above, the bulk of research on intergenerational sex (including Nelson and Oliver's) has shown a gendered differential in young people's experiences of sex with adults. Boys predominantly report positive experiences and girls report negative or ambivalent ones. Given that victim harm is critical in determining the gravity of an offense and an appropriate sentence, this poses a challenge to the principle of equality/neutrality in terms of the way this principle is currently being conceived in the media and in the courts. It is this challenge that Nelson and Oliver refer to when they say that "the gender neutrality of the law belies the reality of gendered social constructions of sexuality that are very real in their consequences" (573, 576).

Despite imploring researchers to recognize the centrality of gender in adult-child sexual experiences and meanings, Nelson and Oliver appear to be extremely uncomfortable with their findings and the implications for feminist and legal analyses of adult-child sex. This was hinted at early on when, in the abstract for the article, after citing the gender-divergent findings, they comment that "extensions of feminist gender analysis are required to explain these patterns" (554). The reasons given for this necessary "extension" are that the patterns contradict some of the initial feminist presuppositions of the authors. Among these are: (1) "boys' experiences could be as traumatic as girls'"; (2) "the special problems of sexual identity and lack of social support might even make boys' experiences worse" (555); and (3) "most of the perpetrators of abuse on boys would be men" (555). Although Nelson and Oliver acknowledge "the tremendous variety of childhood sexual experiences and of the reality that children sometimes interpret their experiences in positive or ambiguous terms" (555–56), their study—informed by "the clinical literature on male incest survivors" (555)—presumes that all sexual episodes between adults four years or more older than minors are manipulative, coercive, and at the very least potentially abusive.

This standpoint is clarified when they explain the unexpected results. The following is offered for why boys might be able to experience and interpret sex with adult women as positive, even in "unequal relationships," and even where the women were the initiators:

> Girls and boys defined the majority of their encounters with men as abusive, even if they had not been overtly forced, while boys who were over 10 defined their encounters with women as consensual and desirable. Every encounter with women described by the boys in our interviews had clearly been initiated by the women (all of whom were at least four years older than the boy), and in most cases *the boy had obviously been manipulated or dominated by the woman*. That is, at an *objective* level, the boys' encounters with women were fairly equivalent to some of the girls' nonincestuous non-violent encounters with men and to some of the boys' encounters with men. Nevertheless, the *subjective* experiences were very different. Even though the boys' interviews revealed somewhat more ambivalence than the boys expressed in the questionnaires, their overall reactions were generally positive. *The boys could have felt manipulated and abused, but they usually did not.* Instead, the positive-status enhancement of having "sex with a woman" seemed to predominate. Even if they had been manipulated, their sense of masculine potency had been enhanced in the encounter. (572–73; emphases added)

This supposed "extension of feminist gender analysis" is deeply problematic. Nelson and Oliver provide no evidence that the boys had "obviously been manipulated or dominated" by the women. In fact, 82% of boys from the questionnaire data who had sex with women said their encounters were consensual (566) and that they had *not* been manipulated. The authors instate a highly dubious distinction between the objective and subjective aspects of the encounters and then insert their own subjective interpretation of the events under the guise of objective description. This substitution is made in direct contradistinction to the interpretations offered by the consenting boys. Notably, the same kind of distinction between objective circumstances of the sex acts and subjective experiences of the "victim" is employed in the appeal ruling in *D. P. P. v. Ellis* in order to privilege the former over the latter. Notably, the subjective interpretations reported by the girls and boys in Nelson and Oliver's study who felt manipulated, coerced, and forced into sex with adult men require no further interpretation.

Regardless of their claim to have "constructed a study that would seek out the experiences of women and men in an evenhanded and nonjudgmental way" (556), Nelson and Oliver's assumption (value judgment) that "consent cannot be wholly free in an unequal [child-adult] relationship" (573) effectively undermined this objective. It preemptively dismissed the specificity of the subjectivities of the 82% of boys claiming to have consented to sex with older women and to have felt positive about their experiences. The self-perceptions of these boys have been simply assimilated to those of the girls in the study who defined their encounters as manipulative, coercive, or forced. As Mark Cowling and Paul Reynolds emphasize, however, the meanings and experiences of consent are idiosyncratic and context-dependent, and thus depend on interpersonal relations, "the personal histories of the participants, [and] their experience and . . . understanding of the meaning of sexual consent."[56]

Nelson and Oliver are in powerful company with this reading—such is the standard framework in the master discourse of (feminist) child sexual abuse. The cultural valorization of sex with older women makes it difficult, Hines and Finkelhor claim, for "teenage boys and adult males to admit to any negative repercussions."[57] Hines and Finkelhor acknowledge that the obverse may also be true: "Because society tends to condemn . . . [adolescent female/adult male relationships], teenage girls may more readily describe harms done."[58] Indeed, there is evidence suggesting that some girls are not disinclined to reinterpret experiences they thought at the time were entered into voluntarily but at a later date describe as manipulative and/or coercive.[59] This certainly appears to be what occurred in the Hopper case. Yet the ramifications of this possibility are not considered. What is striking is that many feminist researchers (including Hines and Finkelhor) and judges appear to accept more readily the veracity of self-reports of those describing their encounters as negative and harmful. Presumably this is because these reports accord with the predominant definition of this as illegal, abusive sex. Self-reports of those describing their encounters in positive, beneficial, or harmless terms are, by contrast, much more vigorously problematized or discounted, even though there is abundant research documenting the lack of negative outcomes for many young people involved in cross-generational sex.[60]

Reflecting this feminist and legal tendency, legal scholar Kay Levine plainly advocates a much more skeptical interrogation of the claims of boys. In her article "No Penis, No Problem," she tacitly supports the views of clinicians who "believe that male victims who insist that their experience was positive have actually brainwashed themselves as a way to rationalize their victimization. In other words, the positive attitude they [the men] express toward early sex is nothing more than false consciousness."[61] Like Nelson and Oliver, Levine draws from scripting theory in order to infer that boys' positive perceptions are likely to be a form of self-denial by virtue of misrecognized identification with dominant social scripts of macho invulnerability. Presupposing that statutory rape perpetrated by an adult female is per se abuse, she diagnoses such cognitive distortions as an "inability (or *unwillingness*) of men to recognize or to define these interactions as abusive."[62] Levine implicitly advocates the correction of the so-called cognitive distortions of boys.

Aside from tendentious claims about scientific data that are contradicted by studies cited above, Levine is, in short, asking us to persuade boys that their perceptions are mistaken. She is imploring us to deny adolescent sexual agency and subjectivity and, like Nelson and Oliver, lays blame on faulty social "scripts" of masculine sexuality for boys' deluded perceptions of their sexual experiences. It is highly probable that some boys do find the social pressure to conform to scripts of masculine sexual prowess and invulnerability extremely difficult to negotiate and live up to. Equally likely, however, is that not *all* do. Indeed, for some boys such "scripts" of male sexuality resemble, or constitute, their experience and sense of self. Sexual encounters with adult women—and early sexual experiences generally—can also actually enhance the self-esteem, sexual identity, and agency of some boys in their future sex lives. Levine herself inadvertently acknowledges this when she suggests that the gendered social scripts of the passive female victim and the male sexual aggressor "tend to be self-fulfilling prophecies."[63]

These loose deployments of scripting theory are a dominant theme in both feminist sexuality and child sexual abuse research. However, as Hannah Frith and Celia Kitzinger note, although the concept of sexual scripts and its associated terms (stereotypes, social roles, socialization, norms) are widely used in feminist sexuality scholarship, "its underlying theory is often rather less apparent."[64] A popular rendition of scripting theory in the form of associated notions of socialization and stereotypes also predominates the "lucky bastard" media and legal discussions. The problem is that this explanatory paradigm simplifies and misconstrues the complexities of social constructionist scripting theory, and the relationships and experiences under examination. John Gagnon and William Simon are often credited as the forerunners of scripting theory within sexuality research.[65] Unlike the vague usage of scripting terminology in child sexual abuse research, however, Gagnon and Simon pay careful attention to an individual's agentive negotiation of sexual scripts, as this is entangled with relationship interactions and social contexts. They theorize scripting on three levels, none of which determines, or operates in complete isolation from, the others. These levels are cultural scenarios, interpersonal scripts, and intrapsychic scripts. For Gagnon and Simon, social scripts and subjectivity are inseparable, but not homologous. The three levels of scripting are mutually constitutive and produce highly idiosyncratic outcomes for individuals. This does not mean we cannot identify gender patterns in human behavior and meaning-making. However, it does suggest we ought to be extremely careful about our extrapolations about an individual's subjective reality from these patterns. A script alone does not tell us enough about the specificity of the embodied and agentive subject and how he or she lives and engages with these scripts. Each individual brings a whole repertoire of capacities and an ensemble of psychical and historical dynamics, attributes, feelings and emotions to bear on his or her experiences, and in so doing psychically negotiates, assesses the relevance of, gives meaning to, and often transforms these social scripts in the process of personal meaning-making.[66]

The script theory assumed by Nelson and Oliver, Levine, and other child sex abuse researchers who refute the "lucky bastard" narrative is stripped of this complexity. Instead, the script or stereotype is construed as external to individuals, an outside cultural imposition that is passively internalized as cognition. If a supposedly faulty script ("lucky bastard") is internalized, therefore, an individual is deemed to have a poor grasp on reality. Effectively he is under false consciousness. This approach is indicative of what Frith and Kitzinger diagnose as a problematic tendency within feminist script theory to "ignore social relationships and emphasize [individualistic] mental processes."[67] This is a reductive and deterministic rendition of social constructionism; indeed, Frith and Kitzinger point out that this is *"a-social"* rather than social constructionism.[68]

What is particularly puzzling about this repudiation of the "lucky bastard" is that, on one hand, it is assumed that social scripts produce the subjectivities of these boys; yet on the other, the very reality of that social production is rendered false, fragile, and delusional. According to Nelson and Oliver, the boys have escaped a negative self-interpretation of their sexual experiences as a result of the "ability to call on alternate [social] constructions of one's experiences."[69] The assumption made here is that the boys *misrecognized* an abusive scenario for a socially constructed, status-enhancing one. The alternate status-enhancing script is apparently of questionable veracity and belies what Nelson and Oliver see as the objective reality of manipulation, coercion, and sexual abuse. But might not this status-enhancing script reflect or intra-actively constitute the experience of some boys and, indeed, empower them? It seems to me that this approach confuses and conflates "ideology, or political templates for *changing* reality, with the concept of worldview or metaphysical templates for *describing* reality."[70] In this case the political template is a radical feminist–inflected call to recognize all cross-generational sex as abuse, and the metaphysical template is a theory of social construction in which the boys are dupes of patriarchal sexuality scripts that need to be changed.[71] Continuing in the vein of the discussion of sexuality and power from chapter 3, we might also view this conflation of political and metaphysical templates as a conflation of ontological and ethical imperatives. Thus, at the same time as they seek to interpret the sexual scripts of young boys, feminist detractors of the "lucky bastard" script are simultaneously advancing a performative political commitment to the unlearning and abolition of this script. Advisable though it might be to query claims of some teenage boys, it is imprudent simply to reject them—especially in Dunbar's case, where there is compelling evidence to support his account. The issue is surely not unpacking whether scripts are objectively "real" or superficial, but rather, *how an individual lives his or her script*. The greater one's capacity to live nondefensively within a cultural script or subject position, the greater the prospect of robust agency.[72] This must be carefully ascertained in each specific case, not presumed in advance according to presumptions embedded in law. However much a minor's capacity to consent is rendered irrelevant by law, and however much we view dominant scripts of male sexuality as coercive with regard to their influence in shaping *some* adolescent boys' experiences, it is also the case that for other boys these same scripts reflect their experiences and capacities for exercising power and agency.

There is a further problem with this feminist research. Not only are the subjectivities of these boys diminished in the present tense of their sexual experiences, but they are also placed under erasure into an unspecified future. For an implication embedded in this paradigm of inevitable sexual abuse is that these boys might forever be at risk of traumatization if the effects of the encounter are deferred, or if they are to reinterpret their experiences as abusive at a later period in their life—as was the case with the girl involved with Hopper. Nelson and Oliver seem to valorize this possibility, both in their discussion of girls in their sample who had reinterpreted past experiences as abusive, and also in their discussion of "empirical patterns in the sexual abuse of boys and girls."[73] Citing the "best U.S. national probability sample of adults," they reported the finding that "27 percent of women and 16 percent of men experienced behavior at some point in their lives (not limited to child-adult experiences) that they 'would now consider sexual abuse.'"[74]

The fact that Nelson and Oliver have subsumed the experiences of boys who consented to sex with women and felt positive about it to the category of "abuse"[75] already reveals a prioritization of the idea of deferred trauma. Impossible to substantiate and impossible to refute in the present tense, this prioritization serves the regulatory function of invalidating certain experiences and holding in abeyance the subjectivities of those who feel or are unharmed. To be sure, the specter of deferred trauma is invariably raised as a way of registering the very real possibility of long-term deleterious impact. However, in addition to this, it effectively deauthorizes or forecloses the possibilities of adolescent agency and consent in the past, present, and future much more than it represents a genuine effort to understand the specificity of gendered sexual experiences and the gendering of agency and consent. Instantiating the possibility, however probable or improbable, of future harm in cases of consensual sex also serves to valorize and privilege the discourse of child sexual abuse—and its prioritization of harm—by closing down or restricting any spaces for contesting its claims and for recognizing (and perhaps producing) alternative experiences and outcomes. This form of discursive and temporal colonization is reinforced by the correlative assumption of false consciousness, which is implicitly projected into the future and imposed even on those adult men whose retrospective self-reports have remained consistent from adolescence to adulthood.[76] Here we can see how such feminist interventions partake in the performative crafting of adolescent subjects and the production of future trauma.

I wish not to downplay the consequences of sexual abuse on those young people who have been harmed by it; thus it is important to register that there needs to be a way of distinguishing between the damaging effects of nonconsensual sexual abuse and the effects of consensual intergenerational sex, damaging or otherwise. The idea of deferred trauma appears to stem if not from the analysis of cases of nonconsensual sex, then at the least from the analysis of cases of ambivalently or negatively experienced sex. When this idea is used to evaluate cases of consensual intergenerational sex, I argue its aims are often more reactive, defensive, and prohibitive than they are inquisitive and interrogative. They might also, as I have said, be dangerously performative. In one particularly dubious example of this multitemporal erasure of male adolescent subjectivity that resonates with Nelson and Oliver's handling of the boys in their study, Australian forensic psychologist Rebecca Deering has been glossed as arguing that "young males must be encouraged to report behaviour they may not yet regard as abuse."[77] In some cases, such as Dunbar's, this suggestion would amount to a simplistic attempt at brainwashing: a forcible attempt at rewriting his experiences and encouraging trauma.

Nelson and Oliver, like most feminists, are understandably committed to gender-neutral laws about child sexual abuse. However, what is significant, they quite rightly point out, is that these laws "have been shaped by feminist discourses about rape."[78] Indebted to a radical feminist idiom, these discourses and laws are built on the presumption that where there are generational age and power differences, there is only ever exploitation, abuse, and the likelihood of harm. This model of nonconsent, power, and abuse is also gendered, insofar as its epistemological framework turns on the historical residue of a male offender and a powerless female, or feminized-child, victim. Yet what is often forgotten is that the presumption of age and power differentials undermining the possibility of consent has emerged out of analyses of the domain of nonconsensual sex (i.e., rape). Our conceptual tools for understanding this domain of coerced or forced sex have thus been imported as the basis for understanding the domain of voluntary or consensual sex. However, these two domains of consensual and nonconsensual, or voluntary and forced, sex are not symmetrical,[79] even when the participants under examination are minors, and even if in *some* cases there is a degree of overlap or entanglement with regard to consent and nonconsent. When we employ the same analytic categories—and the same model of power—to understand these respective domains, we are at serious risk of ignoring the important differences between them, just as we are at serious risk of ignoring other crucial axes of social difference uniquely shaping individual child and adolescent ontologies and sexual subjectivities such as gender, ethnicity, race, class, sexuality, religion, ability, and so on.

Collapsing the domain of voluntary sex into that of coerced or forced sex also disregards the very intra- and intersubjective, institutional, and heterosocial dynamics that constitute any sexual encounter (as we saw in chapter 5), and make it a negative or positive, enjoyable or unpleasant, beneficial or harmful, ambivalent or neutral experience. As Nelson and Oliver themselves highlight with regard to positive and negative perceptions of sexual episodes, it "matters what is done, how it is done, and who does it."[80] How an individual experiences, understands, and integrates an encounter into their enactment of self is critical in whether that encounter is harmful, traumatic, ambivalent, benign, or neutral. This depends on a whole range of contextual, subjective, and interpersonal factors, such as the adolescent's intellectual and emotional capacities and sense of self, whether they entered into the relationship voluntarily or felt coerced, whether they initiated the encounter, how their peers, parents, authorities reacted, how they affectively experienced the sex and the relationship, what forms of knowledge they have at their disposal to interpret and integrate their experience, and so on. Gender difference (among many other indices of social difference) is very often salient here. The principle of gender equality/neutrality in the treatment of offenders and victims may be applicable in the comparison of some cases within the categories of rape and sexual coercion. However, when the issue turns to voluntary and consensual encounters, this principle is often confounded by the very category and specificity of gender it was originally designed to respect.

Injurious Misrecognition

Current sexual-offense laws presuppose gender-neutral categories of adult offender and child victim. I am not suggesting that statutory definitions of offenses and sentencing guidelines ought to be redrafted in gender-specific terms. However, I am suggesting that, in the absence both of amending positions-of-authority laws and providing young people with what Roger Levesque calls a "juridical personality" of their own[81]—overdue and urgent tasks—gender dynamics (among a range of other dynamics), where relevant, ought to factor into criminal charges and the evaluation of sentences.

In calculating a sentence, questions of impact on and harm to victims are, as we have seen, critical in ascertaining the gravity of a crime. This has clearly been stated in the *Rules of Procedure and Evidence* of the International Criminal Court: in sentencing, courts shall have regard to "the extent of damage caused, in particular the harm caused to the victims and their families."[82] Or, as outlined in the Victorian Sentencing (Further Amendment) Act relevant to this chapter's court case, courts shall have regard to "the impact of the offence on any victim."[83] I have argued that gender was a critical factor in shaping the nature of the offense as well as the meanings and experiences of victim impact and harm. However, in the Ellis appeal decision, the categories of "victim" and "impact" were conflated with *harm* when Callaway and colleagues insisted on a gender-neutral reading of the case. Recall his claim that Smallwood's sentence had violated an equality of concern for male and female victims, as the likely result of "a belief that no real harm had been done to the victim."[84] If Callaway was making a comparison with the female victim in *Hopper*, it is clear from the evidence that the degree of harm was infinitely less or nonexistent for Dunbar; and if he was making a comparison with female victims generally, then the expected harm also was less, as the research discussed above in the context of the generic offending characteristics demonstrates. Despite the concession that

Dunbar "was not sexually inexperienced and that, in important respects, he took the initiative," Callaway rejected the gendered damage differential that figured in Smallwood's sentence.[85] Some legal scholars have argued that "evidence in a particular case that the offence causes less harm than 'normal' should generally mitigate sentence, but sentencers do not necessarily appear to appreciate this."[86] Callaway and colleagues failed to appreciate this, or overlooked it in prioritizing their rendition of gender equality.

If, as Sharon Marcus and Nicola Gavey each argue, we have to resist an automatic conflation even of rape and inevitable harm, or sexual coercion and victimization, we ought to be even more careful of resisting this where there is no demonstrable degree of coercion or ambivalence at all, as the Dunbar example indicates.[87] To gauge impact and harm, it is necessary to consider the subjectivities of, and intersubjective dynamics between, the "offender" and the "victim." Regarding Dunbar, however, his subjectivity was disqualified in the appeal case by being assimilated to the category of victim, irrespective of compelling evidence to the contrary and his own perception. As reflected in the research discussed above, Dunbar was arguably a minor who had emerged from puberty and whose early sexual experiences (prior to sleeping with Ellis) made him more sexually subjective and agentive, rather than less, as was the case of the female victim who lost her virginity with Hopper. While important differences among children between the ages of ten and sixteen are not taken into account in definitions of offenses, in the absence of providing adolescents with full legal personhood—and in the absence of changes to sexual-offense laws—these differences ought to be important considerations in judicial proceedings and sentencing. Dunbar was at pains to have his subjectivity, competency, agency, and lack of harm recognized, only to have these assimilated repeatedly to the generic subject position of child victim. As he said in frustration in an interview in response to an attempt to discount his subjectivity:

> You're saying I was seduced and I've got no mind of my own and I didn't know what I was doing. That's totally wrong. . . . Of course she had a responsibility and she's done the wrong thing but it takes two to tango. Obviously, it [the affair] was against the law but I'm telling you I'm not affected by it and I wasn't seduced. I got along fine for the past year and I'll get along fine for the rest of my life.[88]

Even after reaching the age of majority and after Ellis served her jail term, Dunbar adamantly maintained this stance. Without due regard to the specificity of gender and sexual subjectivity, each case is not judged on its own terms and penalties for the crimes, and in fact categories of "adult offender" and "child victim" are merely predetermined effects of statutory definitions—or the political pressure to ensure a certain kind of gender parity in the judicial process. What this means is that intra- and intersubjective dynamics, meanings, and effects of the encounter between Ellis and Dunbar are primarily preordained, and indeed misrecognized, by this legal idiom. Dunbar's comments indicate an awareness of this. As the lawyer representing Ellis declared: "The victim wants to give evidence. He wants to give evidence saying 'I am not the victim, she is.'"[89]

To argue that in some circumstances there are good reasons—at the very least, at the level of sentencing[90]—to treat male and female offenders and victims differently is not to advocate a rigid gender rule in this regard. It is simply to highlight that the specificities of gender are often (among a range of) crucial considerations in the meanings and effects of cross-generational sex. Such a proposition does not signify a violation of gender neutrality or equality before the law. As argued, the problem with the application of this principle in the Ellis appeal is that it was narrowly construed to gender-neutrally frame sex acts/offenses. The judges attempted to treat male and female offenders equally by rendering *alike* or the *same* the sex acts/offenses committed. The term *equality* was thus operating in the sense of *identical*. Treating offenders and victims *equally* in this way, however, requires a comparison of identical circumstances and identical profiles (subjectivities) of offenders and victims. These never exist. Sex acts and offenses acquire meaning only by virtue of *specific* contexts within which they are enacted. It seems that the spirit of the principle of equality before the law is less about equal treatment in the sense of identical treatment, as Callaway and colleagues assumed, and more about equality in the *mode or manner* in which we treat victims, offenders, and their respective and particular circumstances. This is indeed reflected in the preamble to the earlier Crimes (Sexual Offences) Act 1980, where it was stated that "it is desirable for the law to protect and otherwise treat men and women so far as possible *in the same manner*."[91]

Joan Scott long ago highlighted the deconstructive insight that equality and difference are not binary opposites but interdependent terms; equality of treatment, that is, is not the antithesis of differential treatment. Furthermore, "equality is not the elimination of difference, and difference does not preclude equality."[92] Rather, legal, or indeed political, "equality requires the recognition and inclusion of differences."[93] Equality in the *manner* in which we treat male and female offenders and victims therefore requires not identical treatment but equal recognition of the individual particulars and intersubjective dynamics of each case. "'Equal justice,' as Justice Mary

Gaudron puts it, "is justice that is blind to differences that don't matter but is appropriately adapted to those that do."[94] Feminist theorists have long been wary of the ways the *application* of the principle of equality sometimes functions in specific settings as a masculinist ruse.[95] This is most apparent when recognition of the particularities (differences) of cases or groups being compared in any call for equal treatment is suppressed in the name of an illusory sameness. A form of masculinism of this kind was evident in the Ellis appeal ruling. Ellis was measured against the norm of a male offender (Hopper). Interestingly, however, in an equally dubious reversal (or appropriation?) of this logic, Dunbar was measured against the norm of the female victim (Hopper's victim). Whereas in *R v. Ellis* discretionary sentencing was employed to respect gender specificity and sexual subjectivity, in *D. P. P. v. Ellis*, gender specificity and sexual subjectivity were subordinated, indeed sacrificed, to a rigidly gender-neutral interpretation of offenses. Just as gender stereotypes of the harmless female offender and the unharmed, agentive adolescent boy—the "lucky bastard"—may function as cloaks for abuse and masculine bravado (or anxiety) respectively, as child-protection advocates routinely suggest, so too, as research indicates, might these stereotypes *resemble* the dynamics of many sexual encounters and the subjectivities of those involved.

One wonders whether Callaway and colleagues' application of gender neutrality or *blindness* risks inflicting greater and needless damage and harm on Dunbar than the sex he desired, instigated, and enjoyed with Ellis. It is widely accepted that sometimes the "legal procedure may do more harm to the child than the original offence, and in some cases it may be the only cause of serious upset."[96] If this is possible for the sexually abused child, then it is also possible for the willing minor such as Dunbar. Indeed, as a result of Ellis's imprisonment, Dunbar's relationship with his mother had been severely damaged. At the time of the *60 Minutes* interview, two years after his mother informed the school and the police about the affair, Dunbar had not spoken to her for "at least, probably, 18 months." "Basically," he said, "I just can't bring myself to even be in the same room."[97] No matter how much the courts, or anyone, tries to convince him it was not his fault, that Ellis was culpable for abusing her position of care and trust, he will forever know that, as he himself said, "it takes two to tango," and he was an agentive player in that dance. He has been the center of a media and legal scandal, and for the rest of his life he must shoulder a good deal of responsibility for initiating an affair that has sent someone he knows "is a good person" to prison and has catastrophically ruined her life.[98] What an enormous burden for anyone to bear. Contrary to prevailing public sentiment, I think this is a case whereby the application of laws designed to protect young people from harm has actually misfired to produce greater harm.

Ever since the Ellis case there has been increasing pressure in Australia and the rest of the anglophone world for courts to place greater emphasis on victim impact and restrict the use of suspended sentences. To this end, two amendments to the Victorian Sentencing Act 1991 were made shortly after the Ellis case. The first was the Sentencing (Further Amendment) Act 2005, the primary purpose being to "promote the recognition of victims in court processes."[99] One of the principal means of achieving this was to require sentencing courts to consider the impact of the offense on any victim. The second amendment was the Sentencing (Suspended Sentences) Act 2006. The evolution of this act is implicated in the controversy over the Ellis scandal. As the Victorian attorney general said:

> The public viewed suspended sentences in too many cases as not much more than "a slap on the wrist or a get-out-of-jail-free card"—and that perception was understandable. The advisory council has recommended that the Government abolish suspended sentences for all serious crimes by 2009, believing that the courts' view of them as jail terms is undermining public confidence in the system.[100]

The offense of "sexual penetration of a child under 16 years" is included under serious crimes, alongside "murder, manslaughter, rape, . . . incest, causing serious injury intentionally, threat to kill and armed robbery."[101] Although the Sentencing (Suspended Sentences) Act 2006 retained an exceptional-circumstances clause providing some scope for issuing suspended sentences, one of its primary aims was "to create a presumption against a wholly suspended sentence of imprisonment being imposed for a serious offence."[102] Notably, suspended sentences have since been abolished in the state of Victoria altogether.[103]

These developments pivot in important ways on the objective of giving due weight to "the impact of an offence on any victim" and "the personal circumstances of any victim of the offence."[104] This is an important move. However, the abolition of suspended sentences only further enacts a prejudicial conflation of impact and harm, making it impossible for courts to recognize the subjective experiences of minors who are legally subsumed within but reject the appellation of victim. As we have seen with Dunbar, this leads to the imposition of a hierarchy of victims, with the court privileging the best interests and needs of one group over others. Competent and unharmed boys (and girls and others) are at a serious disadvantage here. Best interests and needs are narrowly circumscribed in terms of protection of children from offenders and from harmful procedural and evidentiary practices in the criminal justice system that might redouble the experience of victimization. However, what about forms of judicial victimization engendered by the creation of unvictimized victims? Genuine recognition of those labeled victims in judicial processes requires genuine recognition of individual needs and subjectivity and any differing forms of impact, some of which are positive and beneficial or neutral and indifferent. There is nothing in the original Sentencing Act 1991 that necessitated the interpretation of *impact* only in terms of negative and harmful outcomes. Sentencing principles ought to provide enough flexibility to accommodate non-universalizing understandings and responses to adult-child sex. In the absence of legislative change and a more substantive endowment of adolescent citizenship, the Ellis case offers an important illustration of the need for such flexibility, and for the recognition of a diversity of child and adolescent subjectivities.

Beyond Neutrality

When Western governments began amending sexual-offense laws in the latter part of the twentieth century to make them gender-neutral, part of the reasoning behind this move was to ensure that these laws protected male victims and prosecuted female perpetrators. Prior to this, the prevailing socio-legal assumption was that men were perpetrators of sexual abuse and women and girls the primary victims. All of this is well and good when we are dealing with actual sexual abuse, victims, and perpetrators. But when we are handling victims and perpetrators defined only *statutorily* as such, and when these labels misrepresent those involved, child-sexual-offense laws and judicial systems backfire, as I argue they have in the Ellis case and many other similar cases involving agentive boys.

Even if the so-called victim declares he has suffered no damage, he cannot escape the hegemonic insistence that what he was involved in was wrong and that he may suffer damage sometime in the future. The logic underpinning the latter claim is that children may later reinterpret their experiences of intergenerational sex as abusive. Of course, this reinterpretation requires cultural scripts to provide the child with a new framework for enacting their experiences. It is also made possible, presumably, by an unsupportive social milieu. It has long been acknowledged by numerous psychotherapeutic and legal specialists that societal reactions are often the cause of (greater) upset for young people involved in intergenerational encounters.

I am not suggesting that boys who are deemed victims of sex crimes do not receive social and psychological support. What I am suggesting, though, is that such support is almost always exceedingly partial and one-sided. As we have seen, within the hegemonic framework of child sexual abuse, children are encouraged to adopt scripts of wrongfulness, abuse, and harm. In this way we are partaking in the performative production of victims. There is virtually no social support of the kind that would reinforce in them that their experiences may not be wrong and damaging, let alone that those experiences were enjoyable and positive, and may even build competence, resilience, and character. Notwithstanding the fact that wrongfulness is attributed solely to the adult offender, the young participant, adamant about his agency and consent, is forced to bear some of the burden of this shame. What is particularly troubling about this scenario is that within the child sexual abuse paradigm, it is precisely shame and guilt that are seen to be almost intrinsic to an intergenerational encounter. Shame and guilt are at the causative core of psychological damage. However, lodged within the script of inevitable wrongfulness, harm, and abuse, this simplified paradigm encourages—perhaps sometimes performatively produces—the very shame and guilt that current taboos on intergenerational-sex and child-sexual-offense laws seek to protect against. Given the effects of the social stigmatization of intergenerational sex are themselves sometimes responsible for any damage caused (where there may have been none to begin with), this is as much an exploitation of shame and guilt—an insidious form of shaming and punishing of child sexuality under the guise of protection and justice. It must be said that the peculiarities of the Australian judicial system are not the issue here. These are broader lessons to be gleaned for all anglophone societies that refuse to grant the minor a judicial personality of his or her own in matters of sexual decision-making.[105]

There is another point to be made about the shift to a model of gender neutrality in the discourse of child sex offenses. Far from being limited to the issue of gender difference, the principle of gender neutrality (or equality) has ramifications for the recognition of other modalities of difference and for the reconstitution of the neoliberal subject. For if gender difference is being denied as a legitimate basis for the mitigation of harm and for the affirmation of unique forms of sexual citizenship and sovereignty, so too are differences of, for example, class, race, culture, ability, and religion (to name only some of the most obvious). These are rendered insufficient grounds for harm minimization or a defense of individual autonomy or difference. On this model, age trumps—indeed, neutralizes—other vectors of difference and becomes the defining marker of an individual's capacity.

In other words, in the realm of intergenerational sexuality, the principle of gender neutrality represents an affirmation of a conventional liberal notion of the generic, unmarked human, and one that continues to exclude (among others) minors. The figure of the agentive male adolescent is a particularly palpable reminder at present of the possibilities foreclosed for all young people. This is perhaps one reason that female teachers have come under scrutiny in spite of the fact that men commit the vast majority of intergenerational sex crimes. The "lucky bastard" is the unacknowledged target that is publicly sacrificed in order to bring all young people (and adults who dare to liaise sexually with them) into line with the child sexual abuse paradigm.[106]

Building on the discussion from chapter 5, my argument here is again much more general than an analysis of child sexual offenses. It is an argument against singularity and for the recognition of (childhood) difference more broadly. Twenty-five years ago, Eve Sedgwick lamented "how few respectable tools" we have for grappling with the "self-evident fact" that "people are different from each other."[107] Singular identity categories (man, woman, child) and crude axes of analysis (gender, race, class) cannot adequately capture the irreducibility and inevitability of difference. While we have come some way in the last several decades to develop analytical tools to wrestle with this fact of difference in adult populations, when it comes to our frameworks for dealing with young people, routinely we remain wedded to a universalizing paradigm of ontological singularity. The hegemonic expression of this paradigm is, of course, age-stratified developmentalism. It is part of what science and technology studies scholar John Law would, I assume, call a "one-world metaphysics."[108] Unified categories of the "child" and "adolescent" are mapped and imposed arbitrarily onto young people, and with these categories come a bundle of deterministic assumptions about ontology, capability, and vulnerability that have no *necessary* connection—aside from an imagined correlation—to the lived and multiple realities of youngsters.

Compare this, to take only one example, to the category of "woman." Decades of feminist intervention have ensured that no longer is it tenable in the anglophone West to deploy and defend a generic, singular ontological category of "woman" as a catchall or spokesperson or representative for *all women*. And no longer is it defensible to restrict or control the actions and behavior of living women (the once-called weaker sex) by making universalizing claims of fixed ontological capacity or incapacity. Performative and regulatory gestures of this kind are political strategies masquerading as ontological facts. Yet this is precisely what is routinely accepted and enshrined into law when it comes to young people. In matters of sexuality—although not only in this area—the imposition of singular categories of childhood and adolescence perpetrates forms of violence and misrecognition deemed unacceptable when they occur to adults, as though these categories can ever do justice to all the subjective, biological, and experiential complexity and multiplicity of young people.[109]

Extending earlier Foucauldian and Butlerian work on subject formation and difference, new materialist scholars such as Karen Barad, John Law, and Annemarie Mol indeed provide critical new "respectable tools" for dealing with Sedgwick's axiom of inherent difference. As Barad notes, "Individuals do not preexist their interactions" in the world; "rather, individuals emerge through and as part of their entangled intra-relating."[110] What this means is that, just like adults, young people do not share a fixed set of ontological and biological properties and capacities by virtue of the age bracket within which they are socially grouped. Individuals are constituted through the particular practices and apparatuses within which their lives unfold. *Individuals are different.* Young people are also different. Indeed, to redeploy Mol's terms, the individual is multiple; and so, as Law reminds us, is reality.[111] This does not mean there are no age-shaped constraints on action and ability, biological or otherwise. But it does mean we ought not to assume in advance of any rigorous analysis either what these constraints might be in any given context for any particular individual, or their consequences. Biologies and realities are fluid, not fixed; supple, not static.[112] The upshot of this is the failure of any generic notion of ontology and the failure of definitive and age-stratified categories of the child, adolescent, or adult. Invoking such definitive categories to authorize regulatory practices is to attempt to impose an "ontological politics" of singularity.[113] It is to participate in efforts to fashion young people in a narrowly idealized image. This ought to be resisted. There may certainly be times when singular categories serve useful descriptive purposes. And there may certainly be young people for whom our assumptions about childhood and adolescent capacities sometimes resemble their situations. But one situation cannot stand for all, and we ought to recognize uniqueness and difference. There is no singular species of child or adolescent that can serve as the ground for universalizing political and epistemological claims.

SEVEN

Sexting

In October 2008, school district officials in Tunkhannock, Pennsylvania, confiscated a number of student cell phones and discovered on them "photographs of 'scantily clad, semi-nude and nude teenage girls.'"[1] Many of the girls depicted were enrolled in Tunkhannock High School and the surrounding district. One image showed two girls "from the waist up wearing white, opaque bras," with one talking on her cell phone and the other making a peace sign. Another was a photograph of a third girl in a "white, opaque towel, just below her breasts, appearing as if she just had emerged from the shower."[2] The phones were turned over to the police, and in November 2008, George Skumanick Jr., then district attorney of Wyoming County, began a criminal investigation. That month Skumanick pronounced publicly to local newspaper reporters and an assembly at Tunkhannock High School that students with "inappropriate images of minors" could be prosecuted for "possessing or distributing child pornography," and that felony conviction could result in lengthy prison sentences, a permanent criminal record, and sex offender registration.[3] Then, on February 5, 2009, he sent letters to the parents of between sixteen and twenty Tunkhannock students whose phones held the offending pictures, including the three girls depicted in the photos.[4] An ultimatum was issued:

> [Child's name] has been identified in a police investigation involving the possession and/or dissemination of child pornography. In consultation with the Victims Resource Center and the Juvenile Probation Department, we have developed a six to nine month program which focuses on education and counseling. If you[r] son/daughter successfully completes this program no charges will be filed and no record of his/her involvement will be maintained.

We have scheduled a meeting with all of the identified juveniles and their parents to discuss the program in more detail and to answer your questions. Following the meeting you will be asked to participate in the program. Participation in the program is voluntary. Please note, however, charges will be filed against those that do not participate or those that do not successfully complete the program.[5]

Except for the three girls depicted and their parents, all the other parents and students complied with the conditions. The dissenting parents, however, filed a motion for a temporary restraining order to stop Skumanick from initiating criminal charges against them. The motion was granted and was affirmed later on appeal.

The Tunkhannock scandal catapulted teen sexting into the international media spotlight. Sexting stories had been appearing sporadically in various media prior to this event, but alarmist reports multiplied massively after the case became public in 2009.[6] Skumanick's efforts were unsuccessful, of course, but the incident signaled the very real possibility of criminal charges under various child pornography laws. Indeed, in 2008 and 2009 alone, "U.S. law enforcement agencies handled an estimated 3,477" sexting-related cases, and in the state of Victoria, Australia, it was reported in two of the country's leading newspapers that thirty-two teenagers had been charged with child pornography offenses stemming from sexting in 2007–2008.[7] By the end of 2009, at least twenty US states had introduced sexting legislation (with many more considering legislation at the time and subsequently), and a Victorian parliamentary inquiry was set up in Australia.[8]

Since Tunkhannock, a raft of criminal charges and convictions has come to light in the media. Consequently, fear, anxiety, and consternation about the dangers of sexting have been widely articulated across many anglophone countries. "Who could have predicted," began a *USA Today* report, "that the future danger of cell phones would be what kids are able to do and send with them visually?"[9] According to scores of major newspapers and television news programs in the United States and Australia, the problem of sexting was reaching epidemic proportions.[10] The *New York Times*, the *Washington Post*, and the *Wall Street Journal* each featured stories about how law enforcement agencies and educators were struggling to tackle the growing problem, with the latter announcing that sexting "has alarmed parents, school officials and prosecutors nationwide."[11] In the state of Virginia, Spotsylvania County's commonwealth attorney general declared that sexting was "growing in numbers and growing out of control."[12] Australia's *Sydney Morning Herald* earlier had been warning similarly, remarking that an "explosion of teenage sex texting is alarming teachers, police and youth counsellors."[13] Even *Law and Order: Special Victims Unit* featured an episode on sexting in 2009.[14] Massive education campaigns to warn young people and parents of the perils of sexting were launched (and continue unabated), with scores of brochures, kits, and videos on the dangers of sexting distributed to schools and families. School and community forums were held to broach the problem, the severity of which was taken for granted. For example, the *Washington Post* reported that in Fairfax, Virginia, police organized a community meeting and circulated a flyer announcing, "Sexting: It is here. It is destroying lives. It is your teen sending racy photos using their cell phone."[15]

However wary we might be of some of the alarmism surrounding sexting, clearly this is no superficial state of affairs about naughty teenagers. There is an enormous amount at stake when the law steps in to regulate and punish voluntary interpersonal interactions, for adults or young people. Some of these felonies—even when involving the consensual exchange of self-images to a friend or sexual partner—have resulted in adolescents being mandated to register as sex offenders. This chapter is about what is at stake in the socio-legal response to the practice of *consensual* teenage sexting. My interest is not so much in debating points of law and statutory definitions, even though there are myriad problems with the way criminal justice systems are handling them. Instead, the chapter examines some of the broader performative functions of the politics of emotion surrounding the judicialization of teenage sexting.[16] It offers an analysis of some of the representational and rhetorical maneuvers and performative strategies of criminal justice systems, community groups, the media, and educational campaigns in publicizing and grappling with the issue. As with previous chapters, the following discussion suggests that there is much more driving the sexting panic than the purported objectives of sounding alarm bells for teenagers, protecting them from harm, and having an appropriate legal or social policy response. It is not that such motivations are necessarily disingenuous, or that they are not part of the broader performative strategies of the sex panic. Rather, it is that alongside these are some rather less-than-explicit drives and motivations that go largely unacknowledged, but that in my view shape our protective postures *and* impact detrimentally on how we think about, interact with, educate, and nurture young people. I make two broad arguments. The first is that this sexting panic, like each panic studied in this book, is in significant respects a displaced conversation about teenage sexual agency with explicit and less explicit strategies.[17] On the one hand is the manifest objective of regulating adolescent agency, and on the other are the latent strategies of *avoiding* the complex realities of teenage agency and enacting a normative and homogenous figure of the immature and inept adolescent. The second argument is that the emotional or affective tropes of fear and shame have been mobilized in the service of these performative strategies. It is difficult to escape the conclusion that the adult drive to constitute or reconstitute the image of the normative teenager is occurring at precisely the historical moment when young people themselves, through new technologies, are palpably challenging norms of adolescence.

Signs of a Sex(t) Panic

The sociology of moral panic has been both a productive and contentious enterprise. Sociologists have nonetheless identified a range of concepts as well as rhetorical and discursive tactics some of which have become useful explanatory concepts for interrogating discursive outbreaks of public sentiment. Among these tactics and concepts are the branding of folk devils, scapegoating, the displacement (or misplacement) of fears, exaggeration, distortion (and even fabrication), and the repetition of provocative scripts.[18] Eschewing a rehearsal of the various debates around these explanatory concepts, I follow Janice Irvine's lead in rethinking them through theories of performativity. In so doing, I set aside any question of the reality or proportionality of fears, anxieties, and other emotions publicly articulated. I consider instead the work being performed when these tactics are deployed with, and in the broader social context of, certain emotional scripts.

Media reporting, information kits, and educational videos have been strikingly alarmist, fear-based, and negative in tone and content. Sexting has been framed almost exclusively as a dangerous activity and a serious social problem. Two well-known examples from the New South Wales government in Australia and the National Crime Prevention Council (NCPC) in the United States that were circulating widely in 2013 epitomize the overarching themes. Indeed, the framing of the NSW government information sheet neatly captures the tenor of popular community responses to teen sexting. In bold is the heading "Safe Sexting: No Such Thing."[19] The NCPC fact sheet has a more measured heading, "Sexting: How Teens Can Stay Safe," but the content is also alarmist.[20] In both brochures the central narrative concern is with safety and the protection of young people from harm. Like the NSW government example, the NCPC fact sheet also suggests that the *only* way teens can remain wholly safe is if they "never send or post sexually provocative pictures." Setting aside the affective dimension for the moment, the absolutist, categorical, and universalizing nature of these statements ought to give us pause. The claim that there is no form of safe sexting is dubious at best. A number of surveys were conducted early in the sexting panic in an attempt to determine the prevalence of the practice. The infamous *CosmoGirl* Sex and Tech survey of 1,280 teenagers, which Podlas argues is the basis of claims of a teen sexting epidemic, asserted that almost 20% of teens are sexting.[21] Other surveys reported similar findings (between 19% and 24%);[22] however, some have challenged these statistics. A report by Pew Research Center found that 4% of twelve- to seventeen-year-olds have sexted imagery of themselves and 15% have received such imagery.[23] The Crimes Against Children Research Center national study proffered even lower figures: of 1,560 ten- to seventeen-year-olds surveyed, 9.6% reported having created or received sexually suggestive (though not explicit) images, but only 1% reported having created nude or nearly nude images of themselves that showed "naked breasts, genitals, or bottoms."[24] Part of a twenty-five-country study, the EU Kids Online project found that 12% of eleven- to sixteen-year-olds in the United Kingdom have seen or received online sexual messages. However, only 4% of eleven- to sixteen-year-olds had posted or sent sexual messages within the prior year.[25] Accuracy and incomparability of surveys notwithstanding, even if only 5% of fourteen- to seventeen-year-olds are sexting (and doubtless the numbers shift and change according to social context), this is an enormous number in the United States, let alone across anglophone countries generally. It is scarcely conceivable—and there is no evidence to suggest—that *all* such incidences have been (or are) unsafe or have resulted in harm. If the categorical, absolutist, and universalizing imperative of "Safe sexting: no such thing" is not properly descriptive of any reality, it would appear that it serves other performative strategies, which I will take up shortly.

In his examination of sex crime panics, Philip Jenkins notes how "claims tend to be exaggerated and distorted."[26] To claim "safe sexting" as a contradiction in terms is doubtless a form of exaggeration and distortion. However, other forms of exaggeration and distortion inflect prevailing media stories as well as educational and informational texts, and these have as among their aims the generation of fear and bolstering of the categorical imperative of "no sexting is safe sexting." This is especially noticeable in representations of the potential consequences of sexting. Catastrophic and damaging consequences are almost the only things stressed, such as criminal prosecution, sexual assault, humiliation, psychic trauma, cyberbullying, or serious damage to university and job prospects. Even suicide has been widely cited in media reports as a potential risk. What "can seem an innocent joke or flirtatious fun [can turn] into a potentially devastating experience."[27] This is followed by the standard list of devastating consequences. "Sexting between minors is a felony and can have serious legal consequences. You could be charged with a crime," declares the NCPC. "If convicted you could be labeled as a sex offender for the rest of your life."[28] Yet, as the authors of one study of around 3,477 cases of sexting handled by US law enforcement agencies concluded, "it appears that most youth who simply produce or transmit images are not being treated as offenders" and child pornographers.[29] Sex offender registration is rare, and usually has been the result of a serious aggravated (i.e., nonconsensual) sexting offense, not private consensual sexting. Dire warnings of these extreme and uncommon consequences, and the conflation of nonconsensual and consensual sexting, are then repeated over and again in media and pedagogical texts.[30] As Irvine notes, sex "panics depend on repetition for their power."[31]

Another element of hyperbole and distortion concerns the apparent likelihood of damaging reputational consequences. That sexing might compromise job or university entrance prospects is endlessly offered to teens as a reason not to sext, as the brochures pictured above highlight. "Once the picture is out there, it will never go away," warns the NCPC brochure. "Don't risk your future college or employment hopes." Let us consider a scenario of this kind. Consider the first Australian sexting court case involving thirteen-year-old D. S., who sent a full-frontal nude picture of herself to a male friend. What are the chances of an unnamed sext of a nude thirteen-year-old landing on the desk of an employer or university committee, let alone being identifiable as D. S. when the child has reached university or the job market? In the Australian context, damage to university prospects is ever more unlikely, given that many admissions are based on written scores (rather than in-person interviews) from the final year of secondary school. Yet educational material from Australia continues to advance this potential consequence. In *Megan's Story*, a widely used education video designed for teachers and students that appeared on YouTube in 2010, teachers are encouraged to get students to reflect on the potential damage sexting might cause to their university entrance prospects.[32] It must be said that in the course of researching the media and social science material published on sexting, I have not found any evidence of actual cases in which a teenage sexter has been refused employment or entrance to university. In their national sample of police cases, Wolak, Finkelhor, and Mitchell found that nearly two-thirds of all sexts were distributed only via mobile phone. "Pediatricians may be able to use this finding," they suggest, "to reassure youth and parents that images in sexting incidents usually do not become generally available online."[33] Doubtless, such risks to career are infinitely greater if consensual teenage sexters are criminalized, which is a very good reason, as many have argued, for not bringing private, consensual sexting within the orbit of the law.[34]

A feature common to moral panics is that the social fear is not only exaggerated, but also "wrongly directed."[35] Or, as Stanley Cohen argues, the predominant societal reaction is "*misplaced* or *displaced* (that is, aimed— whether deliberately or thoughtlessly—at a target which was not the 'real' problem.)"[36] Notwithstanding critiques of Cohen's assumption of a hierarchy of real-versus-apparent problems, there is in specific cases some explanatory value in the notion of displacement. Displacements of various kinds are very much evident in prevailing responses to sexting. Consider the much-publicized and tragic suicide of Jessica Logan. Logan's story became a cause célèbre of the teenage sexting panic. After breaking up with her, Logan's former boyfriend Ryan Salyers forwarded a nude picture she had sexted only to him to others at her school, and these students in turn circulated the image to a large number of others in Logan's school and other schools. Logan was then subject to a vicious offensive of harassment and bullying. She went to a school peer counselor, to a professional counselor of the school, and to the school resources officer, police officer Paul Payne, in order to address the bullying.[37] "She was being attacked and tortured," said her mother. Lauren Taylor, one of Logan's friends, told *NBC News* that "she would come to school, she would always hear, 'Oh, that's the girl who sent the picture. She's just a whore.'"[38] As recounted in the civil complaint and jury demand, Logan's parents filed against the school for failing to respond appropriately to the bullying:

> The students of Sycamore and Loveland High Schools would chastise Jessica with epithets and derogatory remarks, such as "whore," "slut," and "skank." She also received phone calls, text messages, and internet messages while at school from . . . students [known and] unknown to her, using similar slurs and epithets. Some peers went beyond verbal torment and threw things at her while she was at school and school-sponsored events. This severe and pervasive harassment continued when Jessica would leave the school building, allowing her no reprieve from her tormenters. This continued through the end of the school year.[39]

Aside from ordering the offending students to delete the photo from their phones, Payne allegedly advised Logan there was nothing else that could be done. "The school conducted no investigation into Jessica's complaint."[40] At Payne's recommendation, Logan gave an interview to a local Cincinnati television station, warning young people of the dangers of sexting and weeping as she described the humiliation she was enduring. Although appearing only as a silhouette and with her voice altered, the interview was "widely seen by Sycamore school students, faculty, and administrators," and it was generally known that it was Logan.[41] The harassment and bullying, according to Logan and her parents, only worsened. Then, on July 3, 2008, after returning from the funeral of a close friend, she hanged herself.

Like the circulation of the image among Logan's peers, the story of the suicide went viral on the internet and in newspapers around the world. "Sexting suicide" became the governing trope for framing this event and the potential risks seen to accompany the practice of sending sexually explicit photographs among teens. As Kimberlianne Podlas notes, "Logan became a cautionary tale about sexting and proof of the threat that sexting posed to adolescents."[42] While most media reports articulate clearly the connection of the suicide to bullying and harassment, the overall framing of the apparent risks of sexting effect something of a displacement (or, distortion) of causal dynamics. In the *Sunday Times* report "Sexting Youths Dial Up a Storm" in Britain, the opening line establishes the connection between sexting and suicide: "'Sexting' is the latest teenage craze. Sending by text or e-mail scantily clad photos of yourself to a friend may seem harmless enough, but in America it has apparently already driven one Ohio girl to suicide."[43] A linear causal chain is established from the sext to humiliation/harassment to psychic trauma and, in this case, to suicide. The act of private, consensual sexting is rhetorically constructed to embody the risks of bullying, harassment, and psychic trauma, and the overarching narrative in the media and educational campaigns becomes one of the *problem* and *danger* of sexting. Yet by all accounts it was bullying and harassment that were at the heart of the devastating trauma. In order to illuminate this point, let us imagine an alternative scenario. An underage woman goes out one night to a bar wearing a miniskirt and revealing top. She is confronted by a group of girls and boys at her school, who start calling her a "slut" and verbally abusing her because of what she is wearing. She goes to the bathroom to escape the harassment. The group follow her and the boys gang-rape her while the girls keep watch. This is the stuff of decades of feminist campaigning of violence against women. That the rape victim was wearing such clothes is certainly a component of this event, and entangled in the group's reasons for harassing her. However, it would be ludicrous to construct a public and educational campaign aimed at warning women of the dangers of wearing miniskirts and revealing tops and advising them never to do so. The suggestion in any anglophone country today that wearing miniskirts and revealing tops leads to rape—irrespective of whether the victim illegally enters an adult bar or not—is no longer culturally acceptable. This is to displace and distort the causal dynamics and levels of responsibility. Just like this rape example, then, campaigns that attribute the risk of social humiliation and psychic trauma to consensual, private sexting shift the focus from component to cause. Although well intentioned, current campaigns framed by warnings of the dangers of sexting contribute to the deflection of attention from a more direct interrogation and exposure of the problems with unauthorized dissemination of sexts and the attendant invasion of privacy, defamation, bullying, and harassment.

Evidence of this misplaced focus can be found in educational materials designed for teens and parents. Take the NSW government information sheet for parents cited above. Below the heading ("Safe Sexting: No Such Thing") and the pictorial image of teens using mobile phones is the lead introductory line highlighted in pink: "Parents are urged to warn children about the dangers of 'sexting': the growing trend for young people to send provocative images *of themselves* to their friends via mobile phones."[44] Teens are also warned not to forward pictures of others; but the privileged subject of address is the teen (often a girl) who may be at risk of sending sexually explicit pictures of herself to friends. What is being problematized, in other words, is less the unauthorized dissemination of images of another person than the consensual practice of sexting self-images.

Problematizing also often slides into pathologizing. The Australian educational film resource *Megan's Story* provides an example of this. Designed for secondary-school teachers and students, it depicts a story of a girl's private sext gone viral in the classroom. The boyfriend forwards the photo, which is then circulated widely to students in the class. One boy responds with salacious flirtation, a girl looks at Megan with revulsion, and we are invited to think about Megan being subject to peer judgment and ridicule. Even the teacher is sent a copy of the image and looks concerned. However, the framing of the video itself and the narrative structure of the lesson plan first and foremost problematize and pathologize Megan's action. The promotional summary of the video describes "a teenage girl who sends an *inappropriate* image of herself and 'sexts' it to a boy."[45] Although it is important to note that teachers are encouraged to have students think not only about the actions of the boy and other classmates in forwarding the image, judging her, and not respecting her, nevertheless Megan's actions foreground the video and lesson plans and are the first to be scrutinized: "Why do you think Megan took that photo and sent it on her mobile phone?" Megan's actions are situated as the source of the "problem": "How did Megan's classmates *contribute* to the *problem?*" Students are encouraged to see Megan's classmates only as complicit to the "problem," as secondary to it, whereas Megan is presumed to have caused it. When the students are asked to consider the inverse gendered scenario ("Would things have been different if a boy had sent an image of himself?"), the first sample answer is "It shouldn't be different but it may have been; he's still done *the wrong thing.*"[46] That is, *Megan* has done *the wrong thing*. The video is not presented as a story of a young boy's foolish action of forwarding a private sext to classmates and the *intended* consequence of an invasion of Megan's privacy. Instead, the victim is blamed. Megan is cast as agent of principal responsibility and represented as having sexually expressed herself inappropriately and wrongly. A form of misplaced sexism inflects this narrative, as a number of feminist scholars have highlighted.[47] I am not suggesting that young people ought not to be made aware of some unwise decisions made, given the reality of unscrupulous practices of some individuals in disseminating unauthorized sexts. However, this could be done without making unnecessary and tendentious judgments and implicitly and explicitly casting the consensual sexter as the bad object.

One of the more insidious displacements in the teen sexting panic and educational literature occurs around the issue of child pornography. Not only are teen sexters criticized for the unauthorized dissemination of private, consensual sexts, but they are also in part scapegoated for contributing to the problem of child pornography.[48] Pedagogical texts almost uniformly warn young people that, in sending sexually provocative images of themselves, they could be held to be producing and distributing child pornography. It is a cruel irony—and one widely noted by critics of the criminalization of consensual sexting—that the very child pornography laws designed to protect young people from abuse are in some jurisdictions being used to charge teens with sending private images of themselves. In jurisdictions where the age of consent is lower (sixteen) than the definition of "child" within child pornography statutes (eighteen), this is especially disturbing. Wielding warnings of child pornography convictions—not to mention actually charging teens under those statutes—is an objectionable distortion of the spirit of these statutes and another means of displacing criminal responsibility. Returning to the resource guide to *Megan's Story*, teachers and students are encouraged to understand how "her image may contribute to the problem of child pornography." Echoes of blaming rape victims for wearing short skirts are hard not to hear. The information brochures cited above—like many fact sheets I have come across—similarly trade in the threat of child pornography. "Tell children that sending or possessing child pornography is illegal," pleads the NSW government.[49] "Sexting is a felony and can have serious legal consequences. You could be charged with a crime," warns the NCPC fact sheet for teens.[50] While child pornography is not explicitly mentioned in the latter fact sheet, the intertextual connection to it is obvious, and child pornography *is* mentioned on the accompanying fact sheet for parents. Moreover, the threat of serious crime is accentuated in the fact sheet for teens, on the one hand by not naming it explicitly and leaving open the possibility of legal infractions in addition to child pornography, and on the other by suggesting that teens might be at one with pedophiles: "If convicted you could be labeled as a sex offender for the rest of your life."[51] The paradigm of adult sexual offenses for behaviors of an altogether different order (i.e., intergenerational sex crimes) is hereby displaced onto teens and used as a framework to interpret their very different and *consensual* interpersonal interactions.

Stanley Cohen famously refers to the branding of folk devils that social anxieties can be projected onto as an emblematic feature of moral panics. Sex offenders and cyberbullies are, to be sure, routinely enlisted as secondary folk devils in the depiction of sexting's dangers. But what is particularly interesting is that unsuspecting and nonmalicious teens are the principal targets of sexting campaigns. They are targeted simultaneously as folk devils, or perpetrators, and as their victims. Indeed, as the judgment in a recent Florida court case ruled, this includes minors being victims of themselves. In 2005, a sixteen-year-old Florida teenage girl (A. H.) and her seventeen-year-old boyfriend (J. G. W.) were charged as juveniles under child pornography laws after taking digital photos of themselves naked and engaged in sex, and then emailing the photos to the boy's personal account.[52] A local court upheld the charges, and the two were adjudicated as delinquents. A. H. challenged the ruling on the basis that, because she did not email the photos to a third party, the charges were a violation of her privacy rights and thus unconstitutional. There is indeed precedent in Florida for the recognition of privacy rights for consensual sexual activity among teenagers (two sixteen-year-olds, *B. B. v. State*). While the age of consent in Florida is eighteen, there is a close-in-age exemption that allows for sixteen- or seventeen-year-old minors to have sex with someone between the ages of sixteen and twenty-three.[53] In spite of this, however, the court ruled that privacy rights do not extend to circumstances in which the "minor memorializes the act through picture or video."[54] Remarkably, the reason given for this is that neither of the two minors had a reasonable expectation that "the other would not show the photos to a third party" or that the photos will not be disseminated *unintentionally*. That is, they had, to quote the court transcripts, "no reasonable expectation of privacy." The defendants also, the court concluded, had "no reasonable expectation that their relationship [would] continue," apparently "unlike adults who may be involved in a mature committed relationship." Underpinning all these arguments was one of the foundational principles that the state has a compelling interest in ensuring that any "videotape or picture including 'sexual conduct by a child of less than 18 years of age' is never produced."[55] (Paradoxically, of course, this means that the consensual sex lives of teens as they are forcibly pulled within the orbit of the law in such cases are matters for public display—itself contrary to the state's compelling interest.) A. H. also challenged this ruling with the claim that criminal prosecution is not the least intrusive means of furthering the state's compelling interest.[56] The District Court of Appeal also rejected this argument, reiterating the child pornography statutes that "the State had a compelling interest 'to protect minors from exploitation by anyone who induces them to appear in a sexual performance and shows that performance to other people'"[57]—anyone, including themselves.

Increased surveillance by law enforcement agencies is a common response to the identification of folk devils and suspects, observe Erich Goode and Nachman Ben-Yehuda of moral panics.[58] The constant rhetorical threat, and actuality, of criminal charges and prosecutions arguably are signs of this. Broader forms of surveillance are also operative in the sexting panic, with parents routinely recommended to scrutinize their children's mobile phone and internet usage. "It's important for you to monitor your child's online activities," implores a tip sheet for parents from the NSW government, "including websites they visit, who they are communicating with, their online 'friends' and the information they are publishing."[59] Ever-increasing efforts to survey teens in order to ascertain sexting prevalence rates may also form part of this web of surveillance. The ruling against A. H. provides a striking manifestation and literalization in law of the imperative of surveillance, as do all convictions for nonaggravated sexting. Teens such as A. H. are deemed to have "no reasonable expectation of privacy" with regard to their private, consensual online activities.[60] In such cases, where the rationale for criminal sanctions is the protection of children from harm, prosecution and punishment are judged to be in the best interests of young people and society.

Agency and the Performativity of Emotion

Janice Irvine importantly cautions against taking the rhetoric of fear in sex and moral panics at face value, as though it is evidence of genuine emotion. That some individuals and groups might experience fear in the face of their children sexting is certainly possible, it seems to me. Equally possible for others, however, is the scenario in which expressions of fear are mere rhetorical and tactical flourishes. Setting aside the question of the truth or falsity of affect, what Irvine calls for, drawing on theories of performativity and social theories of emotion, is attention to the "role of emotions in politics."[61] Accounts of moral and sex panics are enhanced, she argues, when they attend to the "emotional dimensions" and the ways in which "collective emotion, evoked discursively, can bring publics into being, organize diffuse, sometimes inchoate beliefs and moralities into political action."[62] Emotions are performative in other words. They often do not, or do not only, *reflect* actual embodied affect, but *perform* particular social meanings, customs, and strategies. If someone expresses anger at another's belief that Muslim women ought to wear the hijab, that emotional expression is likely conveying alternative beliefs and expectations. Not unmediated embodied reactions, emotions are indissociable from social scripts, rules, beliefs, values, practices, and behavioral norms. The same is true—and often more palpably so—when it comes to carefully scripted media reports and pedagogical texts. Such texts highlight the performativity of emotion, and the way particular affects and emotions are deployed for a range of political purposes. As Irvine demonstrates, emotional language is used in sex panics to generate emotion in the reader or viewer, to mobilize a collective and gain support, and to advance certain political strategies, ideas, and practices. This is perhaps because, as psychologist and affect theorist Silvan Tomkins observes, "reason without affect would be impotent, [and] affect without reason would be blind."[63] Tomkins is here discussing the distinct combination of affect and analytical capacity that gives human beings freedom from deterministic instinct. However, a broader and perhaps simpler point is also being made, and it is one that resonates with performativity theories and social theories of emotion. Because the affect system is, for Tomkins, the primary motivational system for human behavior, affects give discursive meanings their impetus, depth, social influence, and urgency. Affects and emotions enable thoughts and ideas to be communicated, to be felt, to matter, and to be acted on.

Following Irvine, this book has viewed sex panics such as the sexting panic not as the simple *reflection* of social fears and anxiety—although these emotions might well be felt by some people—but as the performative and "dramaturgical" production of fear and other negative affects for various social and political ends.[64] Affective hues or hints often reveal as much, and sometimes more, about social scripts, rules, beliefs, values, practices, and behavioral norms as the textual or verbal messages explicitly accompanying them. And they bolster textual and verbal messages. Scripts, rules, beliefs, values, practices, and norms are among the sub- or paratextual performative strategies advanced in responses to sexting. Emotional postures and tones clearly imbue the rhetorical tactics in the sexting panic, as we have seen so far. Fear and shame—and, indeed, the *fear of shame*—are the main affective tropes framing public responses to teen sexting.[65] Fear is conveyed (communicated and transported) repeatedly through ideas about the danger to befall teens from sexting gone wrong. Such is the framework of virtually all media and educational texts. It is avowedly employed in something of a Freudian sense, as a warning signal of impending danger. Shame is another affect shaping media and pedagogical texts—which is not surprising, given that criminal charges and psychically damaging peer harassment and invasion of privacy are proffered as the main serious consequences. Fear and shame are marshalled supposedly to *reflect* or *describe* existing and possible consequences for sexters, families, and communities. However, much more is at play in these mobilizations of emotion. Operating not just as a passive representation of reality, these warnings are also performatives, in that they are active attempts at enacting certain realities, such as regulating teenage behavior, reinstating the division between adolescents and adults, and reinscribing public and private boundaries. However, when we take a closer look at the affective dimensions of responses to sexting in some of the texts considered so far, it is not difficult to see another, far less explicit performative strategy that arguably underpins all of these but that is rarely remarked on. It is the enactment of a particularly one-dimensional, homogenous, and exclusionary model of teenage agency. In this respect, the sexting panic is less unique than continuous with all the child sex panics studied in this book.

Attempting to reign in and control teenage agency by diminishing the practice of sexting and regulating the online activity of teenagers is among the more obvious performative strategies underpinning the delivery of sexting warnings.[66] Strategies are entangled with power relations that have aims and objectives, and in this way they are intentional; but these intentions are located in discourse and are not necessarily consciously present. But there are also less explicit strategies of power. I argue that fear and shame are deployed as a way of *enacting* certain norms of adolescence. "A young teenage girl takes a naked photograph of herself and sends it to her boyfriend," begins a front-page *Herald Sun* report in the United Kingdom. Citing the threat of pedophiles and child pornography, fear of danger is the article's unmistakable mise-en-scène. "When they break up, the image is circulated by phone, email and social-networking sites. Suddenly, what was intended to be a *foolish* flirtatious message has become social death and shame."[67] At first glance this is simply a description of the possible experience of shame that has certainly resulted after some young girls' acts of sexting. Yet a lot more is being advanced here with regard to constructions of agency and social values and norms. The boy's actions that initiated the unauthorized social circulation of the images after the breakup are hidden within the passively phrased statement "the image is circulated." Agency and causality, and thus responsibility and culpability, are not located directly with him—or, at least, they are backgrounded. The girl's decision, in stark contrast, is identified as the active causal agency, and it is an agency that is disparaged as "foolish," and elsewhere in the report "inappropriate." (Earlier in the discussion of *Megan's Story* we saw how the video also framed her actions as "inappropriate.") The girl's agency is seen as a capacity so compromised as to not constitute competent agency at all. Next to consider, shame is not merely something that might result from sexting but is a performative social script, norm, or value projected onto the girl's action via the terms *foolish* and *inappropriate*. Effectively, the mobilization (and misplacement) of shame displaces any substantive consideration of positive and competent forms of teenage sexual agency.

Fear and shame are also the primary affects framing Megan's experience in the video—notably in her expressions of anxiety, shame, and humiliation. As this is a pedagogical text, the representation of these negative affects performs a certain kind of work. Just as in the information brochures and media reports, the affective tropes also do more than function as constative or descriptive statements. In part, they function as "feeling and expression rules," to use Irvine's terms.[68] For Irvine, drawing on the sociology of emotion, feeling and expression norms denote social scripts for how individuals and groups are invited, and in some senses expected, to respond and make sense of the event. For example, viewers are summoned to identify with Megan's fear and shame, and fear of shame. Yet, the shame experienced by Megan then merges imperceptibly (and perhaps even unwittingly) into an implicit social attribution of shamefulness. We are summoned to witness contempt and disgust as normative reactions of peers, as shown by some of Megan's classmates. Although the lesson plans encourage students to think about how others in the class *contributed* to "the problem" by judging and not supporting Megan, no attempts are made in the video to challenge the place of contempt and disgust in this scenario. Viewers are solicited to interpret Megan's actions as inappropriate, foolish, and shameful, and she is positioned as reaping what she sowed, even if inadvertently and naively.

It "is important to deliver a message to a generation raised on technology and surrounded by sexually charged media," declared Florida's *St. Petersburg*

Times, "that the most damning consequence of sexting is the permanent invasion of a youth's privacy and the lasting embarrassment."[69] Or, as a US National Center for Missing and Exploited Children (NCMEC) tip sheet for preventing sexting puts it, sexting may "profoundly affect the emotional and psychological development of a child." Youth "who engage in sexting risk reoccurring embarrassment and victimization," and this "can be psychologically devastating."[70] These kinds of shame scripts are repetitively used in media and pedagogical texts as cautionary tales of the dangers of sexting. But when continually employed unaccompanied by any substantive effort to critique attributions of shamefulness, these scripts begin to perform more than their professed warning function. This is the dimension of performative affect. By uncritically trading in shame (and fear), media and pedagogical texts recruit affective tropes and performatively produce that which they are only purportedly describing. The shame experience borders on, if not becomes, the shameful act.

Media reports often make this connection more explicit. In the *Daily Mail* article "Generation Sexting: What Teenage Girls Really Get up to on the Internet Should Chill Every Parent," Penny Marshall describes the way "girls flaunt themselves shamelessly, apeing the adult behaviour they see around them on TV and in magazines."[71] Similarly, in the absence of a critique of the use of child pornography statutes against young people, the endless warnings to teenagers about possible criminal convictions veer dangerously close, if not already perform, threats of adult hostility and aggression. Child pornography charges, court cases, sex offender registrations, and even diversionary programs for *consensual*, nonaggravated teen sexting are the dramatic literalization of this.[72] However, as Kath Albury and Kate Crawford argue, educational and policy responses "should do more than threaten young people with legal penalties or sexual shame." They should challenge sexual bullying, promote sexual ethics, acknowledge young people's agency, and provide young people with "a sexual citizenship that includes mediated self-representation."[73]

Yet even media reports and pedagogical texts that refrain from explicit shaming language ("inappropriate," "foolish"), but that cite shame as a psychological consequence of sexting, nonetheless contribute to the shaming of unaggravated teenage sexting and the demonization of teenage sexual agency. This is because, in the broader social context of ubiquitous warnings about child pornography charges, the incessant trading in shame scripts is done *without any corresponding critique of assumptions about shamefulness*. So when issuing warnings about the potentially catastrophic consequences of the unauthorized dissemination of sexts, media and pedagogical texts rarely if ever reassure teenagers that there is nothing shameful per se about sending a private, consensual sext to a willing recipient. Whether or not directly connected to child pornography charges, uncritical representations of shame only enact and reinforce assumptions of shamefulness and ignorant agency. The South Eastern Centre against Sexual Assault in Australia outlines the "consequences of 'sexting'" in its two-page brochure: "Psychological impacts can lead to depression, isolation, anxiety, suicidal thoughts and suicide attempts."[74] These are then immediately followed by a long list of legal consequences:

> What many teenagers and parents don't know is that sexting is ILLEGAL!
>
> Australian Federal Law states that:
> - Anyone under 18 who is involved in sexting can be criminally charged under the same child pornography laws used to charge adults.
> - Sexting among minors is illegal under Commonwealth Criminal Law, State and Territory Criminal Law and Commonwealth Civil Law.
>
> Sexts between teenagers are considered to be child pornography because:
> - the sexts involve minors—children under the age of 18
> - the sexts depict or describe content or acts that are classified as sexually-offensive or sexually explicit.
>
> Teenagers can be arrested, charged and convicted if they
> - take/create a sexy image or clip = creation of child pornography even if they take a sexy photo of THEMSELVES and send it to someone whom they wanted to send it to or forward on a sexy image or clip = transmission of child pornography
> - receive a sexy image or clip (whether you asked for it or not) = possession of child pornography
> - ask for a sexy photo or video from another teenager = procurement of a minor.
>
> The legal consequences for teenagers involved in sexting could include:
> - jail-time
> - fines of up to $1000
> - a listing on the sexual offender register.[75]

Like shame, the stain of criminality, *left unchallenged*, operates in more than a descriptive sense. Not only does it reinforce notions of shamefulness, but it also functions as a punitive threat. Nowhere in brochures such as these is there any effort to acknowledge and educate young people about the ambiguities and contradictions in the law vis-à-vis teenagers, and the fact that in many anglophone jurisdictions the age of consent is lower than definitions of the child in child pornography statutes. Nor is there any effort to contextualize current legal debates about sexting. Numerous jurisdictions across the United Kingdom, Australia, and North America for several years have been debating how best to approach consensual sexting, with many concluding that charging teenagers with child pornography statutes designed to protect children *from* adult offenders contradicts the spirit of such laws and is unnecessarily punitive. Most of the educational brochures include sections on "What you can do to protect your children." The protection tips are about warning children about the legal and emotional consequences of sexting, monitoring their online activity, reminding them to think before they act, and so on. Given the highly contentious nature of criminal charges for consensual sexting, and the widely held view that prosecuting teens may be more harmful than beneficial, it is striking that there are no appeals to parents to lobby authorities and governments to challenge the judicialization of consensual teenage sexting. This only highlights the prevailing discursive investment in issuing threats and regulating teenagers.

The predominant legal, policy, and pedagogical response to sexting functions as something of a displaced conversation about the complexities of teenage sexual agency. Agency certainly features prominently in sexting stories. Media reports are responding directly to claims of an outbreak of online teenage sexual agency. Pedagogical texts are also premised on the assumption of teenage agency and seek to shape its development and exercise. However, these representations typically present a singularly compromised and deficient notion of teenage agency. Megan and her fellow sexters are portrayed as having exercised a transgressive and immature agency, often seen to be the result of the childish mimicry of adult behavior, coercion by peers, or stupidity. "They may be pressured by friends or trying to impress a crush," says the NCMEC. "Some are responding to a sexual text message they've received and others willingly send nude photos of themselves to boyfriend or girlfriend."[76] Despite the concession to voluntary sexting, teenage willingness is problematized in the sentence immediately following: "Youth make these decisions without thinking about how their futures may be affected. It's important for parents and guardians to understand that as technically savvy as their children are, they often don't think about the implications of how quickly digital information can spread via cell phone and the Internet."[77] Trading in popular, long-standing narratives of teenagers as foolish, rash, hormone-driven, and psychologically and emotionally immature, teenage sexters are represented as lacking the wherewithal both to engage in the practice maturely and to deal with any unforeseen consequences. "Remind children to think before they act" is the standard exhortation. Couched within a pedagogical literature uniformly and ominously warning teens *never* to sext, these kinds of texts only underline the fact that *all* sexting is deemed the expression of a defective, naive, and undeveloped form of agency. As a *USA Today* report put it, for "a disturbingly large minority of teenagers, the combination of technology, hormones and stupidity has led to a practice called 'sexting.'"[78] And so we return to the shaming of teenagers. Notably, this contrasts sharply with the world of adult sexting, which can recognize both negative and positive forms of sexting. According to *Cosmopolitan* magazine's article "The Sex Toy Hiding in Your Purse," sexting can spice up the sex and love lives of women.[79]

Just as with all the sex panics studied in this book, narratives of immature, rash, and hormone-driven teenagers go essentially uncontested, in spite of the voluminous research that cogently challenges such universalizing notions.[80] Again, these are not merely descriptive, but generative of norms of adolescence, social policies, laws, and adolescents themselves. Returning to the criminal case of A. H., the District Court of Appeal in Florida refused to grant the young teenage couple privacy protection on the grounds of such narratives. Majority opinion declared that "a number of teenagers want to let their friends know of their sexual prowess. . . . A reasonably prudent person would believe that if you put this type of material in a teenager's hands that, at some point either for profit or bragging rights, the material will be disseminated to other members of the public."[81] With no evidence whatsoever that either of them intended to show the photographs to anyone else (as the one dissenting judge highlighted), A. H. was declared delinquent on the basis of generalized notions of the normative adolescent as both immature and sinister. A. H. was assumed to be "without either foresight or maturity . . . too young to make an intelligent decision about engaging in sexual conduct and memorializing it."[82] No tests of the young woman's intelligence were even considered; she was merely reduced to the unified category of immature, unintelligent teenager. Any possibility of competent agency was disregarded and foreclosed. With the stroke of a stereotype, A. H.—and indeed, all teenagers—was deemed to have such a compromised capacity for agency that not only was the privacy afforded her to engage in sex with her boyfriend offline not also protected online, but she was in fact *punished* for this apparently deficient agency.[83]

My point is not that sexting is never risky and dangerous business. Criminal charges have been laid, some teenagers have been registered as sex offenders, and a number of young people have committed suicide in sexting-related incidents. Nor is my point that the excoriation and infantilization of teenage agency is disrespectful and discriminatory, although I certainly think it is. What I have aimed to highlight, instead, is that the affective politics of sexting (i.e., the sex panic) serves a number of functions beyond raising alarm bells and protecting children. The affective politics of sexting is also a battle over social norms. Not only does the mobilization of fear and shame work to bring communities to action to tackle the "problem," to warn young people about damaging consequences of sexting and scare them off it, to educate parents and young people about the issue, and to regulate teenage behavior. The mobilization of fear and shame also works performatively to enact a normative figure of the incompetent adolescent by displacing consideration of forms of affirmative, positive, and competent teenage agency. When pedagogical texts declare that there is "no such thing as safe sexting," what they are implicitly doing is directing attention from, or silencing, what are strictly excluded from this categorical imperative: safe, neutral, and positive forms of sexting. To include these examples, these realities, however, would be to contradict the categorical imperative and weaken its rhetorical and affective force. It would open up the question of noninfantilized forms of teenage sexual agency—something to which, as we seen throughout the book, Western societies are rarely willing to give due weight.

Unfortunately, current responses to sexting framed by the admonition of "no such thing as safe sexting" tend to work in concert with punitive and prohibitionist-like logics and simplistic notions of adolescence. The normative adolescent is also routinely gendered female. Cast as naive dupes of (largely male) peer pressure, girls are implicitly blamed as perpetrators and identified as victims most at risk. What do we have to lose by acknowledging and examining the complexities and competencies of different forms of (gendered) teenage agency, not to mention fostering these competencies? If we are so concerned about the protection of children, why are we not able even to consider protecting both victims of abuse and those young people with less developed capacities *and* teenagers exercising competent forms of agency? Why are we so quick to pigeonhole young people into some unified category of the "adolescent" that erases the uniqueness and specificity of a dizzying diversity of actual teenagers? How does the judicialization and punishment of consensual sexting—a practice permissible the minute one hits the arbitrary age of 18—advance principles of protection and minimization of harm? In my view, there ought to be moral panics about the discriminatory and punitive treatment of adolescents, the nonrecognition of multiple adolescences and agencies, and the damaging consequences often unnecessarily wrought by sex panics and fear-based pedagogies.

Ending this book on a contemporary sex panic about teen-teen behavior is a deliberate choice. For, in contrast to "intergenerational" cases, where it is all too easy to recruit statutory or conventional definitions of childhood to deflect and displace entirely the issues of teenage agency, responsibility, and culpability, in teen-teen cases this is much more difficult—at least, with any vaguely coherent and defensible rationale. Teen-teen sexting brings into stark relief some of the tensions, contradictions, anxieties, and negative attitudes enfolding the question of young people's sexual agency that this book has been arguing are routinely among the driving forces of the fear of child sexuality. The sexting panic, it seems to me, is masking the centrality of the issue of agency at the same time it functions to contain and control young people's freedom to exercise it. Our response to teenage sexting also exemplifies in particularly blatant fashion a rather pervasive, enduring, and pejorative sentiment and affective orientation toward teenage sexuality. This is a much darker and more disingenuous side to our protective postures and attitudes that we hear much less about but that cries out for our acknowledgment and attention. It is a dark side that manifests in the embarrassment, shame, hostility, and contempt for some manifestations of child and teenage sexuality that not infrequently rears its judgmental and ugly head.

ACKNOWLEDGMENTS

This book has been a long time becoming. It began unknowingly way back in 2002, during an Australian Research Council fellowship at the Australian National University, as a side effect of a project on the history of the psycho-medical category of pedophilia. In 2004 this side effect—an earlier version of this book's chapter 3 on the psychotherapy of child sexual abuse—was published in the journal *GLQ* as "Feminism, Child Sexual Abuse, and the Erasure of Child Sexuality." The essay received the Modern Language Association of America's Crompton-Noll Award that same year, although it has also been the subject of controversy, mainly among some Christian groups. In light of subsequent Australian government interventions vetoing peer-reviewed humanities and sexuality projects recommended for funding by the Australian Research Council's College of Experts, I have since realized how especially fortunate I was to have received the funding that sowed the seeds of this book. The book has also been made possible by a research fellowship in the Australian Centre at the University of Melbourne, as well as a five-year Monash Fellowship in the Centre for Women's Studies and Gender Research at Monash University. I am most appreciative of the generous research opportunities made possible by these institutions and fellowships and the key people who were instrumental in supporting them: Kate Darian-Smith, Barbara Caine, Pauline Nestor, and Maryanne Dever.

However, this fellowship fortune and academic recognition have been a double-edged sword. Publishing variously on the historical emergence of the modern pedophile, on child sexual abuse, on queer theory, and on child and adolescent sexuality has done me no favors in some respects. In a way that gets to the very heart of this book's fundamental concerns about child sex panics, my work across these areas has sometimes been maliciously misrepresented by people who are opposed to almost any examination of young people's sexualities and who have a range of political axes to grind. One of the unfortunate outcomes has been vicious online harassment and abuse by those who have sought to discredit me by either misquoting my words or quoting them so wildly out of context that they appear to suggest the very opposite of their original meaning. Merely writing on these topics has been enough for some people unwilling to properly read my work to presume falsely that I am an apologist for pedophilia. Nothing could be further from the truth. From my very early involvement in the emergence of queer theory in Australia, I am on the published record denouncing any attempt to normalize pedophilia by way of transgressive queer theories. It ought to be possible to ask important intellectual questions about the historical, biopsychosocial, and political realities of childhood sexuality without accusations of perversion.

Versions of most of the chapters have been presented in early forms at a number of universities, which were made possible by various colleagues: Nikki Sullivan and the Somatechnics Research Centre, Macquarie University; Jill Matthews and the School of Social Sciences, Australian National University; the Department of History, University of New South Wales; Kate Darian-Smith and the Australian Centre, University of Melbourne; Robert Reynolds and the National Centre in HIV Social Research, University of New South Wales; Po King Choi and Gender Studies, Chinese University of Hong Kong; Peter Cunich and the Department of History, University of Hong Kong; Murray Couch and the Australian Research Centre in Sex, Health and Society, La Trobe University; JaneMaree Maher and Sociology and the Centre for Women's Studies and Gender Research, Monash University; the late Barbara DeGenevieve and the School of the Art Institute of Chicago; David Murray and Sexuality Studies, York University; Robyn Wiegman and Gender, Sexuality, and Feminist Studies, Duke University; Barbara Baird and Women's Studies, Flinders University; and Catherine Driscoll and the Department of Gender and Cultural Studies, University of Sydney. I have been immensely fortunate to have had these opportunities to present my work and gain thoughtful feedback in supportive and engaging environments.

Numerous friends and colleagues have helped, encouraged, invited, excited, or inspired me in many and varied ways—intellectual, professional, and personal—over the years: Henry Abelove, Elizabeth Agostino, Barbara Baird, Leigh Boucher, Marion Campbell, Margaret Collins, Pauline Crameri, Joy Damousi, Duane Duncan, Danielle Egan, Jacinthe Flore, Suzanne Fraser, Gail Hawkes, Sally Hussey, Annemarie Jagose, Joe Rae Latham, JaneMaree Maher, Daniel Marshall, Narelle Miragliotta, David Murray, Kiran Pienaar, Sarah Pinto, Robert Reynolds, Kate Seear, Dave Sharry, Andrea Waling,

Shermal Wijewardene, Elizabeth Wilson, Jennifer Power, and Lynne Wrout. I want especially to acknowledge Nicole Vitellone for her enduring care, concern, and intellectual stimulation.

In Dublin I would like to thank Michael O'Rourke, Anne Mulhall, and Deirdre Daly for collaborating on the wonderful conference The Age of Sex: A Two-Day International, Interdisciplinary Conference on Child and Adolescent Sexualities, held in Prato, Italy.

Thanks to Marion Pitts, Gary Dowsett, Anne Mitchell, and Paul Twomey at the Australian Research Centre in Sex, Health and Society, who made my transition away from a standard academic role possible; and to Marina Carman and Jayne Lucke for providing the conditions and support for my current role and for making it rewarding.

I would like to acknowledge Phil Bloeman, Sally Hussey, and Sarah Pinto for conducting some of the research that went into the book. A very special thanks is owed to Duane Duncan, who came to my rescue with the book's subtitle, at a time when I was ardently resistant to having one at all. At the University of Chicago Press, I am privileged to have had the charming Doug Mitchell's belief in my second Chicago book and his guidance and backing along the way to publication. I am also thankful to the whole publication team: Tamara Ghattas, Kyle Wagner, Tyler McGaughey, Priya Nelson, and Dylan Montanari, along with freelance copy editor Johanna Rosenbohm.

I am eternally indebted to Jane Connell for showing me a better way through extremely difficult times, and for helping me to understand and harness agency. To Andrew Voya, thank you for continually challenging my habits of thought and enabling me, in exhilarating fashion, to think and feel otherwise. Finally, to Anhtuan Nguyen, there from the beginning and the bearer of all that comes with the highs and lows of being my confidant. I am forever grateful for your unwavering and continued support, belief, wit, energy, and enthusiasm.

Most of the chapters of the book are revised and expanded versions of previously published articles. I am grateful to the publishers for permission to reproduce them. An earlier, abridged version of chapter 1 was published as "What's behind Child Sex Panics?" *Lambda Nordica* 2–3 (2011): 102–25. An earlier, abridged version of chapter 2 was published as "The 'Second Sexual Revolution,' Moral Panic, and the Evasion of Teenage Sexual Subjectivity," *Women's History Review* 21, no. 5 (2012): 831–47. Chapter 3 was first published as "Feminism, Child Sexual Abuse, and the Erasure of Child Sexuality," *GLQ* 10, no. 2 (2004): 141–77. Parts of chapter 4 were published in "The Homosexualization of Pedophilia: The Case of Alison Thorne and the Australian Pedophile Support Group," in *Homophobias: Lust and Loathing across Time and Space*, ed. David A. B. Murray (Durham, NC: Duke University Press, 2009), 64–81, and "The Emergence of the Paedophile in the Late Twentieth Century," *Australian Historical Studies* 37, no. 126 (October 2005): 272–95. An earlier version of chapter 5 was published as "Inter/subjectivity, Power, and Teacher-Student Sex Crime," *Subjectivity* 26, no. 1 (2009): 87–108. An earlier, abridged version of chapter 6 was first published as "Sexual Offences against 'Children' and the Question of Judicial Gender Bias," *Australian Feminist Studies* 23, no. 57 (2008): 359–73. Parts of chapter 6 were also published in "Subjectivity under Erasure: Adolescence, Gender Equality, and Teacher-Student Sex," *Journal of Men's Studies* 15, no. 3 (2007): 347–60. Chapter 7 was originally published as "'Technology, Hormones, and Stupidity': The Affective Politics of Sexting," *Sexualities* 16, nos. 5–6 (2013): 665–89.

NOTES

PREFACE

1. Land of Giants, "Cannibal Dolls," in *Cannibal Dolls/Seven Men*, MP3, CD Baby, 2008 (originally released on vinyl by AV Records, Canada, 1982).
2. Kathryn Bond Stockton, *The Queer Child, or Growing Sideways in the Twentieth Century* (Durham, NC: Duke University Press, 2009), 126.
3. Rebecca Sullivan, "Miu Miu Ad Banned in UK for 'Inappropriately Sexualising Young Women,'" news.com.au, May 8, 2015, http://www.news.com.au/lifestyle/fashion/miu-miu-ad-banned-in-uk-for-inappropriately-sexualising-young-women/story-fnjev30n-1227346978810.
4. Quoted in Sullivan, "Miu Miu Ad Banned."
5. Quoted in Sullivan, "Miu Miu Ad Banned."
6. On the United States, see American Psychological Association, *Report of the APA Task Force on the Sexualization of Girls* (Washington, DC: American Psychological Association, 2007). On Canada, see Canadian Women's Foundation, *Fact Sheet: Moving Girls into Confidence*, updated January 2014, http://canadianwomen.org/sites/canadianwomen.org/files//FactSheet-Girls-ACTIVE_2.pdf; and Susan Delacourt, "It's the Girl's Fault?," *Toronto Star*, July 16, 2009, http://www.thestar.com/news/politics_blog/2009/07/its-the-girls-fault-.html. On the United Kingdom, see David Buckingham, Rebekah Willett, Sara Bragg, and Rachel Russell, *Sexualised Goods Aimed at Children: A Report to the Scottish Parliament Equal Opportunities Committee* (Edinburgh: Scottish Parliament Equal Opportunities Committee, 2010); Linda Papadopoulos, *Sexualisation of Young People Review* (London: Home Office, 2010); and Reg Bailey, *Letting Children Be Children: Report of an Independent Review of the Commercialisation and Sexualisation of Childhood* (London: Department for Education, 2011). On Australia, see Commonwealth of Australia, Senate Standing Committee on Environment, Communications and the Arts, *Sexualisation of Children in the Contemporary Media* (Canberra: Parliament of Australia, 2008); Emma Rush and Andrea La Nauze, *Letting Children Be Children: Stopping the Sexualisation of Children in Australia*, Australia Institute, Discussion Paper No. 93 (December 2006); Rush and La Nauze, *Corporate Paedophilia: Sexualisation of Children in Australia*, Australia Institute, Discussion Paper No. 90 (October 2006).
7. Quoted in Sullivan, "Miu Miu Ad Banned."
8. Stevi Jackson, *Childhood and Sexuality* (Oxford: Blackwell, 1982); Stevi Jackson and Sue Scott, "Risk Anxiety and the Social Construction of Childhood," in *Risk and*

184 / Notes to Pages x–xii

Sociocultural Theory: New Directions and Perspectives, ed. Deborah Lupton (Cambridge: Cambridge University Press, 1999): 86–107.
9. While British sociologists and cultural studies scholars in the 1970s such as Jock Young, Stanley Cohen, and Stuart Hall spearheaded the popularization of the concept of moral panic, American and British historians and sexuality scholars such as Carole Vance, Gayle Rubin, Estelle Freedman, Jeffrey Weeks, Simon Watney, and Lisa Duggan were pioneers in the 1980s of applying the concept to sexuality conflict. See Jock Young, *The Drugtakers: The Social Meaning of Drug Use* (London: Paladin, 1971); Stanley Cohen, *Folk Devils and Moral Panics: The Creation of the Mods and Rockers* (London: MacGibbon & Kee, 1972); Stuart M. Hall, *Policing the Crisis: Mugging, the State, and Law and Order* (London: Macmillan, 1978); Carole S. Vance, ed., *Pleasure and Danger: Exploring Female Sexuality* (Boston: Routledge and Kegan Paul, 1984); Gayle Rubin, "Thinking Sex: Notes for a Radical Theory of the Politics of Sexuality," in Vance, *Pleasure and Danger*; Estelle B. Freedman, "'Uncontrolled Desires': The Response to the Sexual Psychopath, 1920–1960," *Journal of American History* 74 (1987): 83–106; Jeffrey Weeks, *Sex, Politics, and Society: The Regulation of Sexuality Since 1800* (London: Longman, 1981); Weeks, *Sexuality and Its Discontents: Meanings, Myths, and Modern Sexualities* (London: Routledge and Kegan Paul, 1985); Simon Watney, *Policing Desire: Pornography, AIDS and the Media* (Minneapolis: University of Minnesota Press, 1987); and Lisa Duggan and Nan D. Hunter, *Sex Wars: Sexual Dissent and Political Culture* (New York: Routledge, 1995).
10. Frank DiCataldo, *The Perversion of Youth: Controversies in the Assessment and Treatment of Juvenile Sex Offenders* (New York: New York University Press, 2009), 1. See also James R. Kincaid, *Erotic Innocence: The Culture of Child Molesting* (Durham, NC: Duke University Press, 1998); Kincaid, *Child-Loving: The Erotic Child and Victorian Culture* (New York: Routledge, 1992); Judith Levine, *Harmful to Minors: The Perils of Protecting Children from Sex* (Minneapolis: University of Minnesota Press, 2002); Steven Bruhm and Natasha Hurley, eds., *Curiouser: On the Queerness of Children* (Minneapolis: University of Minnesota Press, 2004); and Nancy Lesko, *Act Your Age! A Cultural Construction of Adolescence*, 2nd ed. (New York: Routledge, 2012).
11. Kevin Ohi, "Molestation 101: Child Abuse, Homophobia, and *The Boys of St. Vincent*," *GLQ* 6, no. 2 (2000): 196.
12. Ohi, "Molestation 101," 196. On childhood innocence and moral panics, see also Kerry H. Robinson, *Innocence, Knowledge, and the Construction of Childhood: The Contradictory Nature of Sexuality and Censorship in Children's Contemporary Lives* (London: Routledge, 2013), 42–63.
13. Stockton, *The Queer Child*, 12.
14. I first made this argument about child sexuality being placed under erasure beginning from the 1970s and 1980s in Steven Angelides, "Feminism, Child Sexual Abuse, and the Erasure of Child Sexuality," *GLQ* 10, no. 2 (2004): 141–77. My use of the phrase *under erasure* is not to be confused with either Martin Heidegger's or Jacques Derrida's practice of *sous rature*, or writing "under erasure," even if there might be points of overlap. See Gayatri Chakravorty Spivak, "Translator's Preface," in *Of Grammatology*, by Jacques Derrida, trans. Spivak, 40th anniv. ed. (Baltimore: Johns Hopkins University Press, 2016).
15. R. Danielle Egan, *Becoming Sexual: A Critical Appraisal of the Sexualization of Girls* (Malden, MA: Polity, 2013), 10.

Notes to Pages xii–xiv / 185

16. DiCataldo, in *The Perversion of Youth*, 118, says something similar: "There has been limited interest in mapping the wondrous diversity of childhood sexuality and how a child's unique expression of sexuality informs one about the unique idiom of that person."
17. Emma Renold, Jessica Ringrose, and R. Danielle Egan, eds., *Children, Sexuality and Sexualization* (Houndmills: Palgrave Macmillan, 2015): 1.
18. Michelle Fine and Sara I. McClelland, "Sexuality Education and Desire: Still Missing after All These Years," *Harvard Educational Review* 76, no. 3 (2006): 297–338. By "thick desire," Fine and McClelland refer to young people's entitlement "to a broad range of desires for meaningful intellectual, political, and social engagement, the possibility of financial independence, sexual and reproductive freedom, protection from racialized and sexualized violence, and a way to imagine living in the future tense" (300). Fine and McClelland, along with a host of scholars of girlhood, paint something of a pessimistic picture of the constraints on young women that hinder the development of "thick desire" and what we might call robust agency.
19. For instance, the manifestation of "problem" sexual behaviors in prepubescent children is frequently read as a sign of prior child sexual abuse. See Paul Okami, "'Child Perpetrators of Sexual Abuse': The Emergence of a Problematic Deviant Category," *Journal of Sex Research* 29 (1992): 109–30; and DiCataldo, *The Perversion of Youth*, 117.
20. R. Danielle Egan and Gail Hawkes, *Theorizing the Sexual Child in Modernity* (New York: Palgrave Macmillan, 2010), 154.
21. Michael Warner, "Introduction: Fear of a Queer Planet," *Social Text* 29 (1991): 16; Stockton, *The Queer Child*.
22. Steven Bruhm and Natasha Hurley, "Curiouser: On the Queerness of Children," in Bruhm and Hurley, *Curiouser*, xviii, xxx.
23. Janice M. Irvine, "Transient Feelings: Sex Panics of the Politics of Emotion," *GLQ* 14, no. 1 (2008): 3. Rather than assume panic reactions are authentic emotion, Irvine uses the term *dramaturgical* to emphasize the social, political, and discursive performance of emotion ("transient feelings").
24. This argument was made in Steven Angelides, "What's Behind Child Sex Panics? The Bill Henson Scandal," *Lambda Nordica* 2–3 (2011): 117. Egan, in *Becoming Sexual*, 114, also suggests something similar: with regard to the sexualization of girls panic, she says that our "'obsessive focus on protection' may also have its origins in moments when we come into contact with a child who is autoerotic, unashamed, omnipotent, and curious."
25. "What is surprising," laments Ohi (and I agree), "is the uniform tedium of the response to pedophilia and child sexual abuse almost, one is all but brave enough to generalize, worldwide." Ohi, "Molestation 101," 196.
26. Michel Foucault, *The History of Sexuality, Volume 1: An Introduction* (London: Penguin, 1990), 94–95.
27. As Foucault himself said, "People know what they do; they frequently know why they do what they do; but what they don't know is what they do does." Quoted in Margaret A. McLaren, "Foucault and Feminism: Power, Resistance, Freedom," in *Feminism and the Final Foucault*, ed. Dianna Taylor and Karen Vintges (Urbana: University of Illinois Press, 2004), 231n13.
28. My own work has focused on adolescent boys as well as child sexual abuse generally. See Steven Angelides, "Feminism, Child Sexual Abuse, and the Erasure of Child Sexuality," *GLQ* 10, no. 2 (2004): 141–77; Angelides, "Subjectivity under Erasure: Adolescent Sexuality, Gender, and Teacher-Student Sex," *Journal of Men's Studies* 15, no. 3 (2007): 347–60; Angelides, "Sexual Offences against 'Children' and the

Question of Judicial Gender Bias," *Australian Feminist Studies* 23, no. 57 (2008): 359–73; Angelides, "Inter/subjectivity, Power and Teacher-Student Sex Crime," *Subjectivity* 26 (2009): 87–108; and Angelides, "What's behind Child Sex Panics?" The feminist literature on girlhood and sexual agency is voluminous. For some prominent examples, see Deborah L. Tolman, "Doing Desire: Adolescent Girls' Struggles for/with Sexuality," *Gender and Society* 8, no. 3 (1994): 324–42; Feona Attwood, "Sluts and Riot Grrrls: Female Identity and Sexual Agency," *Journal of Gender Studies* 16, no. 3 (2007): 233–47; R. Danielle Egan and Gail L. Hawkes, "Endangered Girls and Incendiary Objects: Unpacking the Discourse on Sexualization," *Sexuality and Culture* 12 (2008): 291–311; Gail Hawkes and R. Danielle Egan, "Landscapes of Erotophobia: The Sexual(ized) Child in the Postmodern Anglophone West," *Sexuality and Culture* 12 (2008): 193–203; Kari Lerum and Shari L. Dworkin, "'Bad Girls Rule': An Interdisciplinary Feminist Commentary on the Report of the APA Task Force on the Sexualization of Girls," *Journal of Sex Research* 46, no. 4 (2009): 250–63; Emma Renold and Jessica Ringrose, "Schizoid Subjectivities? Re-theorizing Teen-Girls' Sexual Cultures in an Era of 'Sexualization,'" *Journal of Sociology* 47, no. 4 (2011): 389–409; Jessica Ringrose, *Postfeminist Education? Girls and the Sexual Politics of Schooling* (London: Routledge, 2013); Egan, *Becoming Sexual*; and Renold, Ringrose, and Egan, *Children, Sexuality and Sexualization*, 7. There are also a number of special journal issues dedicated to the topic, such as "Making Sense of the Sexualization Debates: Schools and Beyond," special issue, *Gender and Education* 24, no. 3 (2012): 249–356; "Feminisms, 'Sexualisation' and Contemporary Girlhoods," special issue, *Feminist Theory* 14, no. 3 (2013): 247–360; and *Sex Roles* 73, nos. 7–8 (2015): 269–369.

29. Renold and Ringrose, in "Schizoid Subjectivities?," 391, summarize the critical feminist literature on girls and suggest that the neglect of sexual agency is one of "the effects of the sexualization discourse." What I am gesturing toward is an argument about the neglect of agency being one of the primary *aims* of sexualization and other sex panic discourses. Hawkes and Egan, in "Landscapes of Erotophobia," 195, highlight the important place of agency in anxieties around child sexuality between 1830 and 1940, arguing that "it is the features of sexual agency—most especially conscious choice and resistance—that underpin the associations of youthful sexual volition with danger and disruption." See also Egan and Hawkes, *Theorizing the Sexual Child*; and Egan and Hawkes, "Endangered Girls and Incendiary Objects."

30. With a different, and psychoanalytic, take, R. Danielle Egan makes a compelling argument about what she sees as the anger, suspicion, and resentment subtending popular feminist texts on sexualization. See Egan, "Lost Objects: Feminism, Sexualisation and Melancholia," *Feminist Theory* 14, no. 3 (2013): 265–74.

31. I scarcely need to remind readers of Judith Butler's influential theory of performativity, as that "reiterative and citational practice by which discourse produces the effects it names." Butler, *Bodies That Matter: On the Discursive Limits of "Sex"* (New York: Routledge, 1993), 2.

32. At the other end of sex panic discourses that neglect issues of agency are the feminist discussions and debates about what some see as the recent emergence in advertising and popular culture of a neoliberal, postfeminist discourse of "compulsory (sexual) agency." See Rosalind Gill, "Empowerment/Sexism: Figuring Female Sexual Agency in Contemporary Advertising," *Feminism and Psychology* 18, no. 1 (2008): 35–60. In "Critical Respect: The Difficulties and Dilemmas of Agency and 'Choice' for Feminism," *European Journal of Women's Studies* 14, no. 1 (2007): 72, Rosalind C. Gill has argued that "a particular kind of sexualized (but not too sexualized) self-presentation

has become a normative requirement for many young women in the West." See also Angela McRobbie, *The Aftermath of Feminism: Gender, Culture and Social Change* (London: Sage, 2009); Linda Duits and Liesbet van Zoonen, "Headscarves and Porno-Chic: Disciplining Girls' Bodies in the European Multicultural Society," *European Journal of Women's Studies* 13, no. 2 (2006): 103–17; and Ringrose, *Postfeminist Education?*, chap. 5. As Ringrose points out in *Postfeminist Education?*, 67, Gill's "analysis remains at the level of media representations of women in advertising and popular culture." The same is true, I think, of Laina Y. Bay-Cheng's more recent analysis. In "The Agency Line: A Neoliberal Metric for Appraising Young Women's Sexuality," *Sex Roles* 73 (2015): 288, Bay-Cheng claims: "Young women continue to be confined within a prescribed normative space, now divided and disempowered even further by the neo-liberal pretense of sexual agency." Bay-Cheng is critiqued in the same issue of *Sex Roles* in Kari Lerum and Shari L. Dworkin, "Sexual Agency Is Not a Problem of Neoliberalism: Feminism, Sexual Justice, and the Carceral Turn," *Sex Roles* 73 (2015): 319–31. Lerum and Dworkin argue that Bay-Cheng's "theoretical claims both over-generalize about (all) young women and under-generalize non-agents or victims" (319). I agree with Ringrose's and Lerum and Dworkin's critiques and argue that, when such generalized claims are made about meanings and imperatives of sexual agency in the absence of empirical research, the result is often the erasure of young people's unique and specific (not general) subjectivities.

33. For an argument about the way childhood innocence has been "raced white" in US history, see Robin Bernstein, *Racial Innocence: Performing American Childhood from Slavery to Civil Rights* (New York: New York University Press, 2011).

34. For my argument about the importance of accounting for age as an intersecting axis of analysis, see Angelides, "Feminism, Child Sexual Abuse, and the Erasure of Child Sexuality," 163–68. I suggest age is not primordially determinative of child sexualities and subjectivities, but age and other experiences of difference such as race, ethnicity, class, gender, and so on, are *mutually* constitutive of child sexualities and subjectivities. I am not arguing for a return to the pre-1980 sexualizing and othering of working-class and nonwhite children; only that each young person's experiences of intersecting differences are unique in shaping their specific subjectivities.

35. Steven Angelides, *A History of Bisexuality* (Chicago: University of Chicago Press, 2001).

36. See Justin Richardson and Mark A. Schuster, *Everything You Never Wanted Your Kids to Know about Sex (But Were Afraid They'd Ask): The Secrets to Surviving Your Child's Sexual Development from Birth to the Teens* (New York: Crown, 2003); and Lenore Buth, *How to Talk Confidently with Your Child about Sex: For Parents* (St. Louis: Concordia, 2008).

37. Historical, sociological, medical, and anthropological works on children and sexuality have been important in dispelling ignorance and fear and raising understanding. Some notable and groundbreaking texts include: Jackson, *Childhood and Sexuality*; Ronald Goldman and Juliette Goldman, *Children's Sexual Thinking: A Comparative Study of Children Aged 5 to 15 Years in Australia, North America, Britain, and Sweden* (Boston: Routledge & Kegan Paul, 1982); Goldman and Goldman, *Show Me Yours: Understanding Children's Sexuality* (Ringwood: Penguin, 1988); Floyd M. Martinson, *The Sexual Life of Children* (Westport: Bergin & Garvey, 1994); Theo G. M. Sandfort and Jany Rademakers, eds., *Childhood Sexuality: Normal Sexual Behavior and Development* (New York: Haworth, 2001); and John Bancroft, ed., *Sexual Development in Childhood* (Bloomington: Indiana University Press, 2003).

38. Eve Kosofsky Sedgwick, *Epistemology of the Closet* (Berkeley: University of California Press, 1990), 8.

39. Sedgwick, *Epistemology of the Closet*, 8, 4.
40. See Freedman, "'Uncontrolled Desires'"; John D'Emilio, "The Homosexual Menace," in Kathy Peiss, Christina Simmons, and Robert A. Padgug, eds., *Passion and Power: Sexuality in History* (Philadelphia: Temple University Press, 1989), 226–40; George Chauncey, "The Postwar Sex Crime Panic," in *True Stories from the American Past*, ed. William Graebner (New York: McGraw-Hill, 1993), 160–78; and Philip Jenkins, *Moral Panic: Changing Concepts of the Child Molester in Modern America* (New Haven, CT: Yale University Press, 1998).
41. Freedman, "'Uncontrolled Desires,'" 87.
42. Jenkins, *Moral Panic*, 9.
43. On child sexualization panics as proxies for other agendas, such as the defense of white, middle-class sexuality and gender norms, see Renold and Ringrose, "Schizoid Subjectivities?"; Egan and Hawkes, "Endangered Girls and Incendiary Objects"; and Ringrose, *Postfeminist Education?* Egan and Hawkes argue in "Endangered Girls," 299, that the model of childhood central to sexualization discourse—the child as "incomplete," "innocent," "passive," and "processual"—"may help foster an exaggerated sense of peril."
44. R. Danielle Egan and Gail L. Hawkes, "Imperiled and Perilous: Exploring the History of Childhood Sexuality," *Journal of Historical Sociology* 21, no. 4 (2008): 365.
45. Roger N. Lancaster, *Sex Panic and the Punitive State* (Berkeley: University of California Press, 2011), 2.
46. Kincaid, *Erotic Innocence*, 17. James R. Kincaid, in "Producing Erotic Children," in Bruhm and Hurley, *Curiouser*, 9, also argues that "erotic children are manufactured—in the sense that we produce them in our cultural factories."
47. Richard D. Mohr, "The Pedophilia of Everyday Life," in Bruhm and Hurley, *Curiouser*, 28–29. For psychoanalytic readings of sex panics, see also Sheila L. Cavanagh's *Sexing the Teacher: School Sex Scandals and Queer Pedagogies* (Vancouver: University of British Columbia Press, 2007); and Egan, *Becoming Sexual*.
48. Kincaid, *Child-Loving*, 62.
49. Kincaid, *Erotic Innocence*, 17.
50. Jacqueline Rose, *The Case of Peter Pan, or The Impossibility of Children's Fiction* (London: Macmillan, 1984).
51. Lancaster, *Sex Panic and the Punitive State*, 232–33.
52. Lee Edelman, *No Future: Queer Theory and the Death Drive* (Durham, NC: Duke University Press, 2004), 11.
53. Kevin Ohi, *Innocence and Rapture: The Erotic Child in Pater, Wilde, James, and Nabokov* (New York: Palgrave Macmillan, 2005), 7.
54. Bruhm and Hurley, "Curiouser," ix.
55. Eve Kosofsky Sedgwick, "Paranoid Reading and Reparative Reading; or, You're So Paranoid, You Probably Think This Introduction Is about You," in *Novel Gazing: Queer Readings in Fiction*, ed. Eve Kosofsky Sedgwick (Durham, NC: Duke University Press, 1997), 1–40.
56. Henry Jenkins, ed., *The Children's Culture Reader* (New York: New York University Press, 1998), 23.
57. Levine, *Harmful to Minors*, xxxiv.
58. Lancaster, *Sex Panic and the Punitive State*, 256.
59. Renold, Ringrose, and Egan, *Children, Sexuality and Sexualization*, 7. See also n28, above, for references to influential feminist literature on girlhood and sexual agency.
60. Stockton, *The Queer Child*, 121.

61. Stockton, 119.
62. The lack of attention to boys in research, government reports, and media discourses concerning sexualization is striking. See, for example, Jessica May Clark, "Passive, Heterosexual and Female: Constructing Appropriate Childhoods in the 'Sexualisation of Childhood' Debate," *Sociological Research Online* 18, no. 2 (May 2013), http://www.socresonline.org.uk/18/2/13.html; and Sara Bragg, "What about the Boys?," in Renold, Ringrose, and Egan, *Children, Sexuality and Sexualization*, 89–104.
63. My use of *he or she* is not meant to exclude nonbinary personal pronouns (such as *they*), and I do not consider gender to be a binary opposition. However, when I use *he or she* I am doing so only when referring to the case studies of this book, none of which involve trans or nonbinary young people.
64. Steven Angelides, "Historicizing Affect, Psychoanalyzing History: Pedophilia and the Discourse of Child Sexuality," *Journal of Homosexuality* 46, nos. 1/2 (2003): 79–109.
65. Okami, "Child Perpetrators of Sexual Abuse," 116. Scholars of sex education in the anglophone West have, at least since the 1980s, been lamenting the tendency for sex education programs to be fear-based, moralizing, and unnecessarily focused on deficit models and negative outcomes of teenage sex. See, for example, Laina Y. Bay-Cheng, "The Trouble of Teen Sex: The Construction of Adolescent Sexuality through School-Based Sexuality Education," *Sex Education* 3, no. 1 (2003): 61–74; Dennis L. Carson, *The Education of Eros: A History of Education and the Problem of Adolescent Sexuality* (New York: Routledge, 2012); and Louisa Allen, *Young People and Sexuality Education: Rethinking Key Debates* (Basingstoke: Palgrave Macmillan, 2011).
66. Lancaster, *Sex Panic and the Punitive State*, 232, 240.
67. Lancaster, 2.
68. Chapter 5 offers a detailed post-Foucauldian model of power for thinking through agency and sexual consent in which I consider power to be relationality itself, or what Karen Barad calls "intra-activity" (see n69, below). As Foucault famously says in critiquing notions of sovereign power as something individuals or groups possess: "Power must be analysed as something which circulates, or rather as something which only functions in the form of a chain. It is never localised here or there, never in anybody's hands, never appropriated as a commodity or piece of wealth. Power is employed and exercised through a net-like organisation. And not only do individuals circulate between its threads; they are always in the position of simultaneously undergoing and exercising this power. They are not only its inert or consenting target; they are always also the elements of its articulation. In other words, individuals are the vehicles of power, not its points of application." Michel Foucault, "Two Lectures," in *Power/Knowledge: Selected Interviews and Other Writings 1972–1977*, ed. Colin Gordon (New York: Pantheon Books, 1980), 98.
69. Karen Barad, *Meeting the University Halfway: Quantum Physics and the Entanglement of Matter and Meaning* (Durham, NC: Duke University Press, 2007), 178. For Barad, the concept of "intra-action," which replaces that of "interaction," is central to her reformulation of agency. As she explains: "'Intra-action' *signifies the mutual constitution of entangled agencies*. That is, in contrast to the usual 'interaction,' which assumes that there are separate individual agencies that precede their interaction, the notion of intra-action recognizes that distinct agencies do not precede, but rather emerge through, their intra-action. It is important to note that the 'distinct' agencies are only distinct in a relational, not absolute, sense, that *agencies are only distinct in relation to their mutual entanglement; they don't exist as individual elements*" (33). In short, agency is possible only on account of this relational interdependence.

70. Egan and Hawkes, in *Theorizing the Sexual Child*, 155, also argue that the "shape of children's sexuality cannot be known, defined, or supposed in advance" and that "we should especially avoid cultural parameters that produce a singular vision."
71. Gilbert Herdt, "Introduction: Moral Panics, Sexual Rights, and Cultural Anger," in *Moral Panics, Sex Panics: Fear and the Fight over Sexual Rights*, ed. Herdt (New York: New York University Press, 2009), 1. See also Charles Krinsky, ed., *Moral Panics over Contemporary Children and Youth* (Farnham: Ashgate, 2008); and Breanne Fahs, Mary L. Dudy, and Sarah Stage, eds., *The Moral Panics of Sexuality* (Basingstoke: Palgrave Macmillan, 2013).
72. For some useful critiques and reformulations of moral/sex panic theory, see Herdt, *Moral Panics, Sex Panics*; Irvine, "Transient Feelings"; Suzanne Fraser, JaneMaree Maher, and Jan Wright, "Between Bodies and Collectivities: Articulating the Action of Emotion in Obesity Epidemic Discourse," *Social Theory and Health* 8 (2010): 192–209; Angela McRobbie and Sarah Thornton, "Rethinking 'Moral Panic' for Multi-mediated Social Worlds," *British Journal of Sociology* 46, no. 4 (1995): 559–74; Charles Krinsky, ed., *The Ashgate Research Companion to Moral Panics* (Farnham: Ashgate, 2013); Sean P. Hier, "Thinking beyond Moral Panic: Risk, Responsibility, and the Politics of Moralization," *Theoretical Criminology* 12, no. 2, (2008): 173–90; and Angelides, "Historicizing Affect, Psychoanalyzing History."
73. Adam Phillips, *Terrors and Experts* (London: Faber and Faber, 1995), 47.
74. See Angelides, "Historicizing Affect, Psychoanalyzing History." Other scholars diagnosing the psychological dynamics of sex panics who have been influenced by Kincaid are Joanne Faulkner (*The Importance of Being Innocent: Why We Worry about Children* [Cambridge: Cambridge University Press, 2011]); and R. Danielle Egan (*Becoming Sexual*).
75. Irvine, "Transient Feelings," 3.
76. Irvine, 25.
77. Lancaster, *Sex Panic and the Punitive State*, 10.
78. Wendy Hollway and Tony Jefferson, "Panic and Perjury: A Psychosocial Exploration of Agency," *British Journal of Social Psychology* 44, no. 2 (2005): 150. Or, as Roger Lancaster highlights in *Sex Panic and the Punitive State*, 11-12: "Sociological truths are compounded by the accumulation of individual cases to yield . . . statistics . . . but aggregated facts cannot tell us anything about the facts of a particular case."
79. Janet Halley, *Split Decisions: How and Why to Take a Break from Feminism* (Princeton, NJ: Princeton University Press, 2006). Halley talks about the ways that feminism has been so successful that, in many areas such as child sexual abuse law, feminism is, as she says, "running things" (20) by virtue of its ideas being integrated into the state. She is not suggesting this is a wholly negative thing, but she questions any presumption that feminism in these domains is necessarily right.
80. Carolyn Cocca, in *Jailbait: The Politics of Statutory Rape Laws in the United States* (Albany: State University of New York Press, 2004), provides a very useful exploration of the introduction of age-span provisions in statutory rape laws in the United States in the 1980s and 1990s and the ways this reflects a broader shift in thinking about adolescent sexuality and vulnerability. Age-span provisions highlight the growing disapproval toward "intergenerational" sex in the latter part of the twentieth century and offer a legal instantiation of the norm of close-in-age sexual relations as the only form of legitimate adolescent sexuality.
81. See Laura Kipnis, *Unwanted Advances: Sexual Paranoia Comes to Campus* (New York: Harper, 2017).

82. I have borrowed the phrase "displaced conversation" from Carole S. Vance, "Thinking Trafficking, Thinking Sex," *GLQ* 17, no. 1 (2011): 135–43.

CHAPTER ONE

1. Miranda Devine, "Moral Backlash over Sexing Up of Our Children," *Sydney Morning Herald*, May 22, 2008, http://www.smh.com.au/news/opinion/moral-backlash-over-sexing-up-of-our-children/2008/05/21/1211182891875.html.
2. On developments in the United States, see American Psychological Association, *Report of the APA Task Force on the Sexualization of Girls* (Washington, DC: American Psychological Association, 2007).
3. David Marr, *The Henson Case* (Melbourne: Text Publishing, 2008), 17.
4. Quoted in Marr, *The Henson Case*, 21.
5. The Henson scandal is preceded by only a matter of a few months by the police raid in Finland of an exhibition in the Kluuvi Gallery by artist Ulla Karttunen, entitled "Ekstaattisia naisia" (Ecstatic women). Although the exhibition was critical of child pornography and the eroticization of children, Karttunen was herself investigated and convicted for possession and dissemination of child pornography. See Juulia Jyränki and Harri Kalha, *Tapaus Neitsythuorakirkko* (The case of Virginwhorechurch) (Oslo: Like Publishing, 2009). Thanks to Annamari Vänskä for alerting me to this case. Notably, scandals surrounding artistic depictions of nude minors have been a feature especially in the North American context since the advent of the anti-child-pornography movement in the late 1970s and 1980s. For an account of this period, see Lawrence A. Stanley, "Art and 'Perversion': Censoring Images of Nude Children," *Art Journal* 50, no. 4 (Winter 1991): 20–27. For numerous other anglophone examples, see Robert Atkins and Svetlana Mintcheva, eds., *Censoring Culture: Contemporary Threats to Free Expression* (New York: New Press, 2006).
6. Clare Masters and Justin Valleyo, "Who Would Call This Art?," *Daily Telegraph*, May 23, 2008, 4.
7. Masters and Valleyo, "Who Would Call This Art?," 4.
8. Masters and Valleyo, 4.
9. Jayne Margetts, "Charges Likely over Bill Henson Exhibition," transcript, Australian Broadcasting Corporation Transcripts, May 23, 2008.
10. Margetts, "Charges Likely over Bill Henson Exhibition."
11. Marr, *The Henson Case*, 59.
12. Tim Dean, *Beyond Sexuality* (Chicago: University of Chicago Press, 2000), 159. Dean's comment is being made in the context of a discussion of promiscuity; however, he also seems to be making a general point about the psychic forces underpinning volatile reactions generally.
13. Marr, *The Henson Case*, 44.
14. Andrew Bolt, "When Shame Turns to Fame," *Herald-Sun*, June 18, 2008, 18.
15. Quoted in Marr, *The Henson Case*, 127.
16. Quoted in Marr, 69.
17. Quoted in Marr, 69. Richard Mohr argues that "society needs the pedophile: his existence allows everyone else to view sexy children innocently." Mohr, "The Pedophilia of Everyday Life," in *Curiouser: On the Queerness of Children*, ed. Steven Bruhm and Natasha Hurley (Minneapolis: University of Minnesota Press, 2004), 20.
18. Quoted in Marr, *The Henson Case*, 106–7.
19. James R. Kincaid, *Erotic Innocence: The Culture of Child Molesting* (Durham, NC: Duke University Press, 1998).

20. Gareth Griffith and Kathryn Simon, "Child Pornography Law," executive summary, Briefing Paper no. 9/08 (Sydney: NSW Parliamentary Library Research Service, August 2008).
21. Tom Iggulden, "NSW Police to Drop Bill Henson Case," transcript, Australian Broadcasting Commission, June 6, 2008.
22. Quoted in Marr, *The Henson Case*, 123.
23. Quoted in Marr, 123.
24. Clive Hamilton, "Henson Fracas: Art the Victim of Child S-xualisation," *Crikey*, May 23, 2008.
25. Alison Groggon, on behalf of the Creative Australia 2020 Summit representatives, "Open Letter in Support of Bill Henson," reprinted in *Age*, May 27, 2008.
26. Quoted in Marr, *The Henson Case*, 7.
27. Steve Biddulph, "Art or Not, It's Still Exploitation," *The Age*, May 28, 2008, 13.
28. Quoted in Cheryl Critchley, "Pic On Your Own Size," *Herald-Sun*, June 7, 2008, 21.
29. Quoted in Masters and Vallejo, "Who Would Call This Art?," 4.
30. Joanne McCarthy, "Debate about Art Ignores Children's Privacy," *Newcastle Herald*, May 27, 2008, late edition, 9.
31. Biddulph, "Art or Not," 13.
32. Leslie Cannold, "Shame on Adults for Paranoia over Adolescence," *Sun Herald (Sydney)*, extra ed., June 1, 2008, 8.
33. Cannold, "Shame on Adults for Paranoia," 8.
34. Andrea Burns, "Innocence Is Bliss, Perversity in the Beholder's Mind," *Sunday Herald Sun*, July 13, 2008, 107.
35. Catherine, "Poetic Imagery Not Porn," letter, *MX*, May 29, 2008, 14.
36. Terry Lane, "Why Henson's Work Is Art," *The Age*, June 5, 2008, 23.
37. Christopher Kremmer, "The Naked Truth about Religious Art," *Sydney Morning Herald*, July 9, 2008, 11.
38. Kremmer, "The Naked Truth," 11.
39. Of course, according to Kincaid, *Erotic Innocence*, it is through the very category of *innocence* that we have eroticized children and childhood.
40. "Beauty and Grotesquerie Are in the Eyes of Beholders," *Sydney Morning Herald*, July 11, 2008, 16.
41. "On Purity and Shame," New Matilda, May 28, 2008, http://newmatilda.com/2008/05/28/purity-and-shame.
42. Marr, *The Henson Case*, 44.
43. Unfortunately, I did not receive permission to use the Henson photograph. I refer readers to Marr's *The Henson Case*, which has a cropped version of the full-body image on the front cover and also the full-body image itself in the book.
44. Silvan S. Tomkins, *Affect Imagery Consciousness: The Complete Edition*, vol. 2 (New York: Springer, 2008), 360–61.
45. Thanks to JaneMaree Maher for pointing out N's rosy cheeks. Abigail Bray, in "Governing the Gaze: Child Sexual Abuse Moral Panics and the Post-feminist Blindspot," *Feminist Media Studies* 9, no. 2 (2009): 182, offers a different reading of shame in the image, connecting it to her own heterosexual pedophilic objectification. The "photograph reminds me of the paralysis of a childhood shamed and silenced by the intrusive attention of men on the streets, at school, in my home. Her withdrawn frozen body reminds me of the numbing impact of sexual objectification, of the unspeakable grief of a stolen dignity, of the silencing humiliations of looks, touches, and comments from adult men." That N and her family agreed to have the photos feature

centrally in the exhibition, made a statement in support of Henson (and continue to support him), (see Marr, *The Henson Case*, 99–112), and then agreed to allow David Marr to publish the photos in his book after the controversy erupted at the very least points to a very different set of relationships, affective relations, and gazes. I would also note that it is important to acknowledge a range of forms of shame. There is a world of difference between a shame tethered to sexual interest and that resulting from a sense of traumatizing sexual objectification of which Bray speaks.

46. Tomkins, *Affect Imagery Consciousness*, 1: 106.
47. See Tomkins, *Affect Imagery Consciousness*, 1: 163–64.
48. Following Tomkins, I am here considering shame to be part of an affective constellation or spectrum that includes various forms, or densities, including shyness, guilt, embarrassment, and humiliation.
49. Sally Munt, *Queer Attachments: The Cultural Politics of Shame* (Aldershot, UK: Ashgate, 2008), 2.
50. See, for example, Karin A. Martin, *Puberty, Sexuality, and the Self: Boys and Girls at Adolescence* (New York: Routledge, 1996).
51. This is not to suggest that sexual desire, pleasures, orientations, and identities emerge only at puberty, only that the development of sexual self-identity categories often coincides with puberty and adolescence.
52. Donald L. Nathanson, *Shame and Pride: Affect, Sex, and the Birth of the Self* (New York: W. W. Norton, 1992), 145.
53. Nathanson, *Shame and Pride*, 259.
54. Tomkins identifies nine primary affects, with eight of these originally conceptualized as a spectrum by way of a joint name: interest-excitement, enjoyment-joy, surprise-startle, distress-anguish, fear-terror, shame-humiliation, contempt-disgust, and anger-rage. Each of the terms in the polarity is distinguished only with regard to density, with the left term signifying the affect experienced at low density and the right at high. In the period between publishing volumes 2 and 3 of *Affect Imagery Consciousness*, Tomkins separated contempt—which he renamed dissmell—and disgust as distinct affects. See Silvan Tomkins, "What Are Affects?," *Shame and Its Sisters: A Silvan Tomkins Reader* (Durham, NC: Duke University Press, 1995), 74.
55. Tomkins, *Affect Imagery Consciousness*, 2: 353.
56. Janice M. Irvine, "Shame Comes Out of the Closet," *Sexuality Research and Social Policy* 6, no. 1 (March 2009): 71.
57. Norbert Elias, *The Civilizing Process*, rev. ed. (Malden, MA: Blackwell Publishing, 2000 [1939]), 142, quoted in Irvine, "Shame," 71.
58. Joanne Faulkner, in *The Importance of Being Innocent: Why We Worry about Children* (Cambridge: Cambridge University Press, 2011), 125, also comments on the allusion to sexuality: "The budding breast refers obliquely to a budding sexuality and the stirrings of a desire we cannot control."
59. For the concept of "intra-acting," see Karen Barad, *Meeting the Universe Halfway: Quantum Physics and the Entanglement of Matter and Meaning* (Durham, NC: Duke University Press, 2007), 33.
60. Michel Foucault, *The History of Sexuality, Volume 1: An Introduction* (London: Penguin, 1990), 155.
61. Sigmund Freud, "The 'Uncanny'" (1919), in *The Standard Edition of the Complete Works of Sigmund Freud*, 24 vols., ed. James Strachey (London: Hogarth Press, 1953–74), 17:219.

62. Nathanson, *Shame and Pride*, 145.
63. This quote is from Freud, "The 'Uncanny,'" 224, where he is citing Schelling's theory of the uncanny.
64. There is a further way in which shame and the uncanny might intersect in the works of Freud and Tomkins: both are shot through with an abiding ambivalence. Again, shame is "literally an ambivalent turning of the eyes away from the object toward the face, toward the self" (Tomkins, *Affect Imagery Consciousness*, 2: 360–61). We are ashamed in the face of, but retain our interest in, the other. The uncanny, however, is the ambivalent reemergence in the present tense of repressed unconscious contents or residually held beliefs; that is, ideas and desires once consciously held. It is the ambivalent, divided self facing its self-other. For an extended reading of shame and the uncanny, see Steven Angelides, "The Uncanny Sexual Child," in *Erogenous Danger Zones: Effective Productions of the (Infantile) Sexual*, ed. Insa Haertel (Berlin: Kulturverlag Kadmos, 2013), 105–21.
65. Freud, "The 'Uncanny.'" See also Nicholas Royle, *The Uncanny* (Manchester: Manchester University Press, 2003), 1–38.
66. Freud, "The 'Uncanny,'" 220.
67. Carl D. Schneider, "A Mature Sense of Shame," in *The Many Faces of Shame*, ed. Donald L. Nathanson (New York: Guildford Press, 1987), 194–213.
68. Tomkins, *Affect Imagery Consciousness*, 1: 163–64; Teresa Brennan, *The Transmission of Affect* (Ithaca, NY: Cornell University Press, 2003).
69. Biddulph, "Art or Not," 13.
70. Silvan S. Tomkins, "Shame," in Nathanson, *The Many Faces of Shame*, 145.
71. Germaine Greer, "Through a Lens Darkly," *The Age*, June 2, 2008, 13.
72. If, as Tomkins argues, shame is broadly speaking a turning away from that which causes it, there are several forms that this turning away might take. Nathanson, in *Shame and Pride*, 305–77, identifies four broad major defensive strategies, or "scripts," of shame management: withdrawal, avoidance, attack-self, and attack-other. Notice how readily applicable they are to many of the affective reactions to the Henson images I have been discussing. To take a few obvious examples, Hetty Johnston, Kevin Rudd, and Morris Iemma employed the attack-other script, attacking Henson directly. Leslie Cannold, in contrast, enlisted the attack-self script when appealing to N that "we" adults are at fault. Other possible psychical dynamics may too be operative within this mode: a displaced effort to attack the others who made Cannold feel ashamed of her body as a teenager; self-contempt projected as envy for not being as beautiful or daring as N. Many other commentators who felt disturbed by the images also withdrew from any public debate, perhaps in order to contemplate the issues or to avoid taking any position in the scandal. There are also a number of possible combinations of these defensive strategies.
73. Quoted in "Artworks Feature: Bill Henson," *Radio National*, August 15, 2010, https://www.abc.net.au/radionational/programs/archived/artworks/artworks-feature-bill-henson/3020240. See also Marr, *The Henson Case*, 69.
74. Royle, *The Uncanny*, 1.
75. Faulkner, *The Importance of Being Innocent*, 123, 126.
76. Allan Lloyd Smith, "The Phantoms of *Drood* and *Rebecca*: The Uncanny Reencountered through Abraham and Torok's 'Cryptonymy,'" *Poetics Today* 13, no. 2 (1992): 285.
77. Kylie Valentine, "Innocence Defiled, Again? The Art of Bill Henson and the Welfare of Children," *Australian Review of Public Affairs*, June 2008, http://www.australianreview.net/digest/2008/06/valentine.html.

78. Paul Sheehan, "We Live in a Sexual Twilight Zone," *Sydney Morning Herald*, October 13, 2008, https://www.smh.com.au/national/we-live-in-a-sexual-twilight-zone-20081013-gdsyky.html. An article in the *Sunday Telegraph* defended the hysterical response, even in those very terms: "If the community can't get 'hysterical' about naked pictures of a 13-year-old, what can it get hysterical about?" Quoted in Marr, *The Henson Case*, 138.
79. Marr, 62.
80. Quoted in "Panel Weigh In on Art versus Porn Debate," transcript, Australian Broadcasting Corporation, May 30, 2008, http://www.abc.net.au/worldtoday/content/2008/s2260436.htm.
81. Paul Sheehan, "Country-wise—the Commentators," *The Australian*, May 31, 2008, 29.
82. Michael Coulter, "Henson Leaves Moral Issues of His Art Unexposed," *The Age*, August 8, 2010, http://www.brisbanetimes.com.au/opinion/society-and-culture/henson-leaves-moral-issues-of-his-art-unexposed-20100807-11peb.html.
83. Coulter, "Henson Leaves Moral Issues Unexposed."
84. American Psychological Association, *On the Sexualization of Girls*, 2.
85. Ann J. Cahill, *Overcoming Objectification: A Carnal Ethics* (New York: Routledge, 2011), x, xii.
86. Alison Groggon's letter of support of Henson, on behalf of the Creative Australia 2020 Summit representatives, is exemplary of this defense.
87. Faulkner, in *The Importance of Being Innocent*, 130, notes that "Henson's model was an object lesson for Australia's youth, who are liable to be branded 'revolting' by no less than the prime minister if they publicly display their agency and vulnerability."
88. See the preface for a discussion of the notion of Foucauldian strategies.
89. Quoted in Margaret A. McLaren, "Foucault and Feminism: Power, Resistance, Freedom," in *Feminism and the Final Foucault*, ed. Dianna Taylor and Karen Vintges (Urbana: University of Illinois Press, 2004), 231n13. On power as intentional and nonsubjective, see Foucault, *The History of Sexuality*, 94–95.
90. Another "strategy" is the attempt to regulate what can and cannot be said in relation to these matters.
91. Valentine, "Innocence Defiled, Again?"; emphasis added.
92. Quoted in Marr, *The Henson Case*, 65.
93. Biddulph, "Art or Not," 13; emphasis added.
94. McCarthy, "Debate about Art Ignores Children's Privacy," 9; emphasis added.
95. Bray, in "Governing the Gaze," 175, argues that claims that the Henson scandal is indicative of a moral panic are themselves part of a normative discourse of neoliberal tolerance that governs the public gaze. This discourse erases feminist critiques of pedophilia and depoliticizes child sexual abuse (CSA). She suggests that, within this reactionary moral panic discourse, "CSA moral panics are often argued to perform a puritanical erasure of children's sexual agency through an irrational focus on children in general as potential victims of sexual abuse." A central feature of this "neoliberal narrative," she argues, "is a celebration of children's sexual liberation and agency as a form of individual self-empowerment that triumphs over the reactionary victim politics of CSA moral panics." Strikingly, *no* examples from the Henson scandal are given to support this claim; indeed, Bray merely refers to a strain of what she calls academic "radical liberation discourses" represented by Slavoj Zizek, Michel Foucault, Guy Hocquenghem, and Ellis Hanson, among others. The (*non*)connection to the Henson commentary is explained thus: "The 2008 media celebration of Bill

Henson's photographs of naked girls can be read in the context of this reification of the sexual child as an emblem of radical sexual politics" (178). In fact, in the context of the Henson media response, as myself and others have shown (e.g., Valentine, "Innocence Defiled, Again?"; Faulkner, *The Importance of Being Innocent*), and as is glaringly obvious when reviewing the scores of media reports and discussions, there was *no celebration of the sexual child whatsoever*. As we saw from media reports, there was barely a mention of the sexual child. In attempting to reclaim a feminist critical gaze, Bray herself has reified an objectifying adult gaze and remained silent on the question of the subjectivity of N and other young people. There is a huge difference between celebrating the sexual child and asking us to inquire, as I am here, into our avoidance of her (and him) and calling for her (and his) substantive recognition. Brian Simpson also argues that child sexuality was obscured in the scandal. See Simpson, "Sexualizing the Child: The Strange Case of Bill Henson, His 'Absolutely Revolting' Images and the Law of Childhood Innocence," *Sexualities* 14, no. 3 (2011): 209–311.

96. Valentine, in "Innocence Defiled, Again?," notes that the "Henson photos represent . . . a particularly thorny area of children's agency insofar as it evokes a particularly thorny area of *women's* agency." I am here making a somewhat stronger claim: it is this issue of children's agency that not only is evoked by Henson's images, but that in large measure drives the scandal behind the scenes.

97. Freud, "The 'Uncanny,'" 243.

CHAPTER TWO

1. John Kobler, "Sex Invades the Schoolhouse," *Saturday Evening Post*, June 29, 1968, 27, quoted in Jeffrey P. Moran, *Teaching Sex: The Shaping of Adolescence in the 20th Century* (Cambridge, MA: Harvard University Press, 2000), 167–68.
2. Michael G. Schofield with John Bynner, Patricia Lewis, Peter Massie, *The Sexual Behaviour of Young People* (Harmondsworth: Penguin, 1969), 23. This text was first published in 1965.
3. "The Pundits," editorial, *Sydney Morning Herald*, June 5, 1967, 2.
4. In the 1960s, the "youth problem" was very widely referred to. Jeffrey Weeks, in *Sex, Politics and Society: The Regulation of Sexuality since 1800* (London: Longman, 1989), 252, notes that the "problems of youth were dominating themes in the sexual debates of the 1960s."
5. American Medical Association, "Venereal Disease Task Force," *Journal of the American Medical Association* 193, no. 10 (September 6, 1965): 174.
6. American Medical Association, "Venereal Disease Task Force," 174; emphasis added.
7. See British Medical Association, *Venereal Disease and Young People* (London: British Medical Association, 1964).
8. See "Venereal Disease and Young People," book review, *Probation Journal* 11 (1965): 32; emphasis added.
9. Child Welfare Advisory Council (CWAC) of NSW, "Social Problems Arising in Relation to Premarital Intercourse," *Medical Journal of Australia* (June 3, 1967): 1146–50.
10. "Morals: The Second Sexual Revolution," *Time*, January 24, 1964, South Pacific edition, 40.
11. For examples of reports that took a more measured approach to the "problems" of adolescent sex and even challenged some of the alarmist responses, see Craig McGregor, "Sex and the Adolescent: Are We Growing into a Hedonist Society?," *Sydney Morning Herald*, November 24, 1965, 2; Harry Robinson, "Sex and the Teenager,"

Sydney Morning Herald weekend magazine, June 10, 1967, 15; Robb Wallace, "Student Sexual Morality," *Australian Humanist*, Summer 1967–68, 23; and Beatrice Faust, "S-E-X, Sex," *Australian Humanist*, July 1969, 6–9. Schofield, in *Sexual Behaviour of Young People*, 233–34, argues: "In face of much of the uninformed criticism about teenage sexual activities, it is tempting to spend too much time in pointing out that many of the generalizations are without factual information, that there are no signs of moral collapse, that more thought should be given to adult immorality, that many teenage attitudes are refreshing and stimulating, that there are many serious young people with great intellectual curiosity and high aspirations. But these assertions of good sense are not a substitute for factual information." Unfortunately, however, the moral-panic pushers chose pretty much to ignore this report. Faust, in "S-E-X, Sex," 6, offers an interesting reading of this in comparison to furor over the Kinsey reports: "Perhaps Kinsey told a breathless world that adults were worse than ever suspected—which is consoling, while Schofield found teen-agers better than they had been painted—which challenged popular prejudice" and, I would add, adult power structures.

12. On the notion of Foucauldian strategies, see the preface.
13. British Ministry of Education, *The Youth Service in England and Wales* (London: Her Majesty's Stationery Office, 1960), 29.
14. The term *permissiveness* was usually employed as a term of abuse, as Weeks, in *Sex, Politics and Society*, 249, notes, and as some commentators at the time noted; see Ian Edwards, "Guiding Children on Sex," *Australian Humanist*, July 1969, 12.
15. See, for example, Malcolm Muggeridge, "The Sexual Revolution," *Bulletin*, April 17, 1965, 28; McGregor, "Sex and the Adolescent"; Faust, "S-E-X, Sex"; and Schofield, *Sexual Behaviour of Young People*.
16. For prominent examples, see "Morals: The Second Sexual Revolution," 40–45; "The Morals Revolution on the U.S. Campus," *Newsweek*, April 6, 1964, 44–49; and Brian Buckley, "Morals: The Sexual Revolution," *Bulletin*, May 14, 1966, 19–24.
17. Weeks, *Sex, Politics and Society*, 250.
18. *Time*, "Morals: The Second Sexual Revolution."
19. See Buckley, "Morals: The Sexual Revolution."
20. "The Problem of Juvenile Delinquency," *New Life: Australia's Weekly Evangelical Newspaper*, October 28, 1965, 10; "Life without a Purpose," editorial, *New Life: Australia's Weekly Evangelical Newspaper*, August 11, 1966, 2; "The Fight against Moral Pollution," *New Life: Australia's Weekly Evangelical Newspaper*, May 10, 1973, 4.
21. For a comprehensive survey of these well-recognized changing social and material contexts for 1960s adolescents, see British Ministry of Education, "The Changing Scene," *The Youth Service in England and Wales*, 13–28. The phrase *bulge generation* is taken from this report, 13. For a few of the countless examples of reports decrying hedonism and narcissism, see Muggeridge, "The Sexual Revolution," 28–32; "The Tyranny of the Materialistic Majority," *New Life: Australia's Weekly Evangelical Newspaper*, December 1, 1962, 2; *Time*, "The Second Sexual Revolution"; *Newsweek*, "The Morals Revolution"; CWAC, "Social Problems Arising"; McGregor, "Sex and the Adolescent"; "The Sub-teens," *Bulletin*, February 10, 1968, 22–25. Religious groups and publications were particularly critical of this trend. On reports of the decline of religiosity, see Gregory Smelters, "Patterns of Religious Decay," *Australian Humanist*, December 1967–68, 26–28.
22. *Newsweek*, "The Morals Revolution," 48. The article goes on to argue that, despite the apparent truth of the claim about guilt, "it is unreasonable to believe that Victorian guilt will soon disappear."

23. Buckley, "Morals: The Sexual Revolution," 19.
24. The phrase *storm and stress* is G. Stanley Hall's description of what he saw as the inherent tempestuousness of adolescence. Hall was the famous developmental psychologist who, at the turn of the nineteenth century, popularized the very concept of adolescence. See Hall, *Adolescence*, 2 vols. (New York: Appleton, 1904).
25. British Ministry of Education, *Youth Service in England and Wales*, 29.
26. McGregor, "Sex and the Adolescent," 2.
27. McGregor, 2.
28. For just a few of the innumerable examples of concern over youth alienation, see *Newsweek*, "The Morals Revolution"; "Life without a Purpose," *New Life: Australia's Weekly Evangelical Newspaper*, August 11, 1966, 2; Ian Davidson, "The Generation Gap," *Australian Humanist*, April 1968, 10–17.
29. For example, McGregor, in "Sex and the Adolescent," 2, noted that "nowhere are the effects [of the sexual revolution] seen more clearly than in the much-maligned group, Australian adolescents."
30. See Moran, *Teaching Sex*; and Janice Irvine, *Talk about Sex: The Battles over Sex Education in the United States* (Berkeley: University of California Press, 2002).
31. "VD Upsurge in the West: Too Many Drive-Ins?," *Bulletin*, August 29, 1964, 20.
32. "VD Upsurge in the West," 20.
33. Of course, for defenders of "traditional morality," liberalization and tolerance were the problems responsible for teenage sex.
34. McGregor, "Sex and the Adolescent," 2.
35. Weeks, *Sex, Politics and Society*, 251–52.
36. G. Logan, *Sex Education in Queensland: A History of the Debate 1900–1980* (Queensland: Department of Education, 1980), 38.
37. Jeffrey Weeks, *Sexuality*, 2nd ed. (London: Routledge, 2003), 108.
38. *Time*, "Morals: The Second Sexual Revolution," 42. See also *Newsweek*, "The Morals Revolution on the U.S. Campus."
39. CWAC, "Social Problems Arising," 1146.
40. CWAC, "Social Problems Arising," 1146.
41. Schofield, *Sexual Behaviour of Young People*, 225. For an example of similar reports in a US context, see Elizabeth B. Hurlock, *Adolescent Development* (New York: McGraw Hill, 1973).
42. John K. Collins, "Sex Education: By Whom, When, and Where," *Medical Health in Australia* 4, no. 1 (1970): 4–10.
43. Collins, "Sex Education," 9.
44. "Sex Education," editorial, *Sydney Morning Herald*, January 6, 1967, 2.
45. "More Than the Facts," editorial, *Sydney Morning Herald*, January 11, 1967, 2.
46. Schofield, *Sexual Behaviour of Young People*, 226; see also Collins, "Sex Education." On the United States, see Hurlock, *Adolescent Development*, 274–77.
47. Quoted in "More Than the Facts."
48. "More Than the Facts."
49. Peter Bowers, "Some Will Be Frank: Sex Lessons," *Sydney Morning Herald*, January 30, 1967, 6. This was in response to comments made by the director of physical education a few days prior regarding a committee he headed that had developed the pilot. See "Preparation for Marriage Part of School Course," *Sydney Morning Herald*, January 26, 1967, 1.
50. On the US context, see Irvine, *Talk about Sex*; and Moran, *Teaching Sex*; on British context, see James Hampshire and Jane Lewis, "'The Ravages of Permissiveness': Sex

Education and the Permissive Society," *Twentieth Century British History* 15, no. 3 (2004): 290–312; and for a comparative US, UK, and Australian account, see Nicole Vitellone, *Object Matters: Condoms, Adolescence and Time* (Manchester: Manchester University Press, 2007), 13–21.
51. Irvine, *Talk about Sex*, 132–34.
52. "Sex Education for Young People," *New Life: Australia's Weekly Evangelical Newspaper*, June 29, 1967, 2.
53. "The Pundits," editorial, *Sydney Morning Herald*, June 5, 1967, 2. On the recommendation about contraceptive techniques, see CWAC, "Social Problems Arising," 1147.
54. "Sex Lessons at Primary Level Urged," *Sydney Morning Herald*, June 3, 1967, 1.
55. "Sex Lessons at Primary Level Urged," 1.
56. "Need in Sex Education," letter, *Sydney Morning Herald*, January 31, 1967, 2.
57. "Sex Education of Children," letter, *Sydney Morning Herald*, June 7, 1967, 2.
58. For instance, Collins's study of parental attitudes to sex education seems to confirm this. As we will see below, a majority of principals responding to a 1972 Department of Education survey on sex education supported the introduction of comprehensive sex education, further lending weight to this observation. See "Principals 'Favour Wider Sex Education,'" *Sydney Morning Herald*, January 9, 1973, 3.
59. Alison Bashford and Carolyn Strange, "Public Pedagogy: Sex Education and Mass Communication in the Mid-twentieth Century," *Journal of the History of Sexuality* 13, no. 1 (2004): 71–99.
60. Not all the major churches were opposed to comprehensive sex education. For example, the Presbyterian Church of Australia Church and Nation Committee in New South Wales backed the CWAC report, although not without criticism from within its ranks. See "Minister Critic of Sex Report," *Sydney Morning Herald*, July 31, 1967, 4; "Sex and the Church," letter, *Sydney Morning Herald*, August 4, 1967, 2; and "Church and Sex," letter, *Sydney Morning Herald*, August 7, 1967, 2.
61. For a discussion of these strategies of communication by the anti-sex education lobby during the 1970s in NSW, see Steven Angelides, "'The Continuing Homosexual Offensive': Sex Education, Gay Rights, and Homosexual Recruitment,'" in *Homophobia: An Australian History*, ed. Shirleene Robinson (Annandale: Federation Press, 2008), 172–92.
62. Janice Irvine, "Transient Feelings: Sex Panics and the Politics of Emotions," *GLQ* 14, no. 1 (2008): 1–40. Irvine conceptualizes the contagion of mass emotion as "scripted and situationally produced rather than instinctively aroused, authentic sentiments. This perspective on emotions as social does not mean they are not 'real'" (17).
63. Quoted in "School Sex Proposal Rejected," *Sydney Morning Herald*, June 6, 1967, 4. The minister went on to say, "[The] decision was mine, but [it] was not taken without consultation with senior officers of my department." Presumably, this consultation would have involved serious consideration of much of the negative community response.
64. "Sex Instruction Report Backed by Church Group," *Sydney Morning Herald*, July 2, 1967, 4.
65. Moran, *Teaching Sex*, 156–93; Irvine, *Talk about Sex*, 17–62.
66. Weeks, *Sexuality*.
67. See "Humanist Manifesto," excerpt from the International Humanist and Ethical Union's *Humanist Manifesto*, quoted in *Australian Humanist*, June 1967, 40.
68. I. S. Edwards, "Sex Education in Schools," letter, *Sydney Morning Herald*, March 2, 1967, 2.

69. B. Trump, "Humanists and Society," letter, *Sydney Morning Herald*, March 9, 1967, 2.
70. John A. McCluskie, "Sex and the Humanists," letter, *Sydney Morning Herald*, March 14, 1967, 2.
71. McCluskie, "Sex and the Humanists."
72. Faust, "S-E-X, Sex," 6.
73. Faust, 7.
74. I. S. Edwards, *Sex for Modern Teenagers* (Adelaide: Rigby, 1969).
75. Robinson, "Sex and the Teenager," 15.
76. Faust, "S-E-X, Sex," 9.
77. Schofield, *Sexual Behaviour of Young People*, 106.
78. Edwards, *Sex for Modern Teenagers*, 5.
79. "Crisis for Teenagers" was a highlighted subheadline of a news story about violent sex crime and the need for sex education. "School Sex Education Essential—Committee," *Sydney Morning Herald*, August 8, 1969, 1, 8.
80. "School Sex Education Essential—Committee," *Sydney Morning Herald*, August 8, 1969, 1.
81. "School Sex Education Essential—Committee," 1. See also *Report from the Select Committee on Violent Sex Crimes in New South Wales* (Sydney: NSW Government Printer, 1969), esp. xxii.
82. *Report from the Select Committee*, xvi.
83. "Why Girls Leave Home," front cover feature, *Bulletin*, January 6, 1968, 15–17; "Why Students Drop Out," *Bulletin*, June 15, 1968, 33–34; "Anarchism: What Do the Students Want?," front cover feature, *Bulletin*, July 6, 1968, 24–29; "The Thinking of Modern Youth: 'Why You Can't Understand Your Teenager,'" editorial, *New Life: Australia's Weekly Evangelical Newspaper*, May 14, 1970, 2.
84. See Schofield, *Sexual Behaviour of Young People*; Hurlock, *Adolescent Development*.
85. See John K. Collins, "Adolescent Sex Education," *Australian Journal of Social Issues* 7, no. 2 (1972): 124–31. This study was reported in "Pupils Give Views on Sex Lessons," *Sydney Morning Herald*, July 11, 1972, 3; David Dale, "Catching Up on Sex Lessons," *Sydney Morning Herald*, August 16, 1972, 7; and "Teach It at School Say Youngsters," *Daily Mirror*, September 24, 1973. This last newspaper clipping is held at State Records NSW, "Sex Education Reactions to Draft Policy on Sex Education in Schools," item no. 72/46591. The clipping does not have a page number.
86. "Committee to Review Sex Education," *Sydney Morning Herald*, November 12, 1971, 9.
87. Quoted in Stefania Siedlecky, "Sex Education in New South Wales: The Growing Up Film Series," *Health and History* 8, no. 2 (2006): 114.
88. Siedlecky, "Sex Education in New South Wales"; David Dale, "School Pupils Report on Sex Education," *Sydney Morning Herald*, May 31, 1972, 12.
89. Dale, "Catching Up on Sex Lessons," 7.
90. Dale, 7.
91. "Teach It at School Say Youngsters."
92. Dale, "Catching Up on Sex Lessons," 7.
93. New South Wales Department of Education, *Personal Development in Secondary Schools: The Place of Sex Education, A Statement of Principles* (Sydney: New South Wales Department of Education, 1974), 5.
94. Dale, "Catching Up on Sex Lessons," 7.
95. Dale, 7.

96. Government school principals were overwhelmingly in favor of the report. See "Principals 'Favour Wider Sex Education,'" *Sydney Morning Herald*, January 9, 1973, 3. The final report, *Personal Development in Secondary Schools*, 4, also noted that, in spite of the controversial issues mentioned above, there was "substantial approval of the principals on which the report was based and the recommendations it contained."
97. *Personal Development in Secondary Schools*, 9.
98. "Sex Education," editorial, *Sydney Morning Herald*, May 29, 1974, 6.
99. See, for example, "Sex Course—No Restrictions Plea: Women Concerned," *Sydney Morning Herald*, June 5, 1974, 13.
100. Lyn Harrison and Lynne Hillier, "What Should Be the 'Subject' of Sex Education?" *Discourse: Studies in the Cultural Politics of Education* 20, no. 2 (1999): 279–88.
101. Letter to Marion C. Linley from J. D. Buggie, director general of education, NSW, February 28, 1973. This letter is held at the State Records Office of NSW but is not itemized.
102. See Michel Foucault, *The History of Sexuality, Volume 1: An Introduction* (London: Penguin, 1990), 94–95.
103. For example, see Schofield, *Sexual Behaviour of Young People*, 82–97, where it was suggested that young people's knowledge of birth control and venereal disease was "sketchy."
104. CWAC, "Social Problems Arising," 1147.
105. Schofield, *Sexual Behaviour of Young People*, 14, 230.
106. *Personal Development in Secondary Schools*, 5.
107. Angus Gordon, *Plastic Identities: Adolescence, Homosexuality, and Contemporary Culture* (PhD diss., University of Melbourne, Australia, 1997), 9.
108. "School Sex Education Essential," 8.
109. Nancy Lesko, "Time Matters in Adolescence," in *Governing the Child in the New Millennium*, ed. Kenneth Hultqvist and Gunilla Dahlberg (New York: RoutledgeFalmer, 2001), 39.
110. Moran, *Teaching Sex*, 35.
111. Moran, 216.
112. Presumably, there were also caring and accepting conservative and Christian people, although such voices were not a feature in the public and media debates.
113. Collins, "Sex Education," 9, 5. Not all champions of the repressive hypothesis held such simplistic views of shame vis-à-vis sexuality. For instance, Herbert Marcuse, one of the more famous proponents of the repressive hypothesis, specifically argued against the notion of therapeutic "de-shaming" of individuals. In response to an interviewer on this question of de-shaming, he said: "I would say that shame is something positive and authentic. There are qualities and dimensions of the human being that are . . . his own and he shares them only with those whom he chooses. They do not belong to the community and they are not a public affair." Quoted in Carl D. Schneider, "A Mature Sense of Shame," in *The Many Faces of Shame*, ed. Donald L. Nathanson (New York: Guildford Press, 1987), 197.
114. See, for example, Isobel Allen, *Education in Sex and Personal Relationships* (London: Policy Studies Institute, 1987); Michelle Fine, "Sexuality, Schooling, and Adolescent Females: The Missing Discourse of Desire," *Harvard Educational Review* 58, no. 1 (1988): 29–51; L. Measor with Coralie Tiffin and Katrina Miller, *Young People's Views on Sex Education: Attitudes and Behaviour* (London: Routledge/Falmer, 2000); Judith Levine, *Harmful to Minors: The Perils of Protecting Children from Sex* (Minneapolis:

University of Minnesota Press, 2002); Michelle Fine and Sara McClelland, "Sexuality Education and Desire: Still Missing after All These Years," *Harvard Educational Review* 76, no. 3 (2006): 297–338; Vicki Strange, Simon Forrest, Ann Oakley, Judith Stephenson, and the RIPPLE Study Team, "Sex and Relationship Education for 13–16 Year Olds: Evidence from England," *Sex Education* 6, no. 1 (2006): 31–46; Gillian L. S. Hilton, "Listening to the Boys Again: An Exploration of What Boys Want to Learn in Sex Education Classes and How They Want to Be Taught," *Sex Education* 7, no. 2 (2007): 161–74; Jessica Fields, *Risky Lessons: Sex Education and Social Inequality* (New Brunswick: Rutgers University Press, 2008); Lisa Trimble, "Transformative Conversations about Sexualities Pedagogy and the Experience of Sexual Knowing," *Sex Education* 9, no. 1 (2009): 51–64; Louisa Allen and Moira Carmody, "'Pleasure Has No Passport': Re-visiting the Potential of Pleasure in Sexuality Education," *Sex Education* 12, no. 4 (2012): 455–68; and Sharon Lamb, Kara Lustig, and Kelly Graling, "The Use and Misuse of Pleasure in Sex Education Curricula," *Sex Education* 13, no. 5 (2013): 305–18.

115. Allen and Carmody, "'Pleasure Has No Passport,'" 458.
116. Lamb, Lustig, and Graling, "Use and Misuse of Pleasure," 316.
117. Allen and Carmody, "'Pleasure Has No Passport,'" 462. Lamb, Lustig, and Graling also make the point in "The Use and Misuse of Pleasure," 316.
118. Celia Roberts, "Early Puberty, 'Sexualization' and Feminism," *European Journal of Women's Studies* 20, no. 2 (2013): 138–54.
119. Howard Sercombe, "Risk, Adaptation and the Functional Teenage Brain," *Brain and Cognition* 89 (2014): 62. See also Howard Sercombe and Tomas Paus, "The 'Teen Brain' Research: An Introduction and Implications for Practitioners," *Youth and Policy* 103 (Summer 2009): 25–37.
120. Sercombe, "The Functional Teenage Brain," 64. For another useful critique of neuroscientific work on executive function, see Patricia H. Miller and Ellin K. Scholnick, "Feminist Theory and Contemporary Developmental Psychology: The Case of Children's Executive Function," *Feminism and Psychology* 25, no. 3 (2015): 266–83.
121. Sara B. Johnson, Robert W. Blum, and Jay N. Giedd, "Adolescent Maturity and the Brain: The Promise and Pitfalls of Neuroscience Research in Adolescent Health Policy," *Journal of Adolescent Health* 45 (2009): 220.

CHAPTER THREE

1. Linda Gordon, "The Politics of Child Sexual Abuse: Notes from American History," *Feminist Review* 28 (1988): 56–64.
2. Philip Jenkins, *Moral Panic: Changing Concepts of the Child Molester in Modern America* (New Haven, CT: Yale University Press, 1998), 130.
3. Dorothy Scott and Shurlee Swain, *Confronting Cruelty: Historical Perspectives on Child Protection in Australia* (Melbourne: Melbourne University Press, 2002), 162.
4. Jenkins, *Moral Panic*, 129.
5. On the "rediscovery" of child sexual abuse, see Erna Olafson, "When Paradigms Collide: Roland Summit and the Rediscovery of Child Sexual Abuse," in *Critical Issues in Child Sexual Abuse: Historical, Legal, and Psychological Perspectives*, ed. Jon R. Conte (London: Sage, 2002), 71–106; and Scott and Swain, *Confronting Cruelty*, 154. On the issue of "reinterpretation," see Gordon, "The Politics of Child Sexual Abuse," 60.
6. Gordon, in "The Politics of Child Sexual Abuse," 56, notes how "radical feminist consciousness pulled incest [and child sexual abuse more generally] out of the closet." There are, of course, multiple feminist positions regarding child sexual abuse

and child sexuality. In this chapter, when I speak of the "feminist discourse of child sexual abuse" or "child sexual abuse feminism," I am not referring to feminism in general (an impossibility, given the inherent diversity of feminisms) but to that loose assemblage of feminist psychologists, social workers, sociologists, and other health care professionals and practitioners working in the area of child sexual abuse, whose discursive fields are united around a radical feminist-inflected model of power and consent. Under this model, feminist assumptions join forces with the conventional liberal state position in what has become the hegemonic cultural perspective that sees children as without the power or knowledge to give informed consent for sex until certain arbitrarily-defined ages (usually between sixteen and eighteen). For an analysis of radical feminist and antipornography feminist assumptions regarding child sexuality and intergenerational sex, see Pat Califia, "The Aftermath of the Great Kiddy-Porn Panic of '77," in *Public Sex: The Culture of the Sex Radical* (San Francisco: Cleis Press, 1994), 53–70. For alternative feminist readings of the interlocking issues of child sexuality and child sexual abuse, see Gayle S. Rubin, "Thinking Sex: Notes for a Radical Theory of the Politics of Sexuality," in *The Lesbian and Gay Studies Reader*, ed. Henry Abelove, Michèle Aina Barale, and David M. Halperin (New York: Routledge, 1993), 3–44.

7. Sterling Fishman, "The History of Childhood Sexuality," *Journal of Contemporary History* 17, no. 2 (1982): 270.
8. Jenkins, *Moral Panic*, 14.
9. For a summary of research on child sexuality until 1983, see L. L. Constantine, "Child Sexuality: Recent Developments and Implications for Treatment, Prevention, and Social Policy," *Medicine and Law* 2 (1983): 55–67. For discussion and references to child sexuality in decades prior to the 1980s, see Jenkins, *Moral Panic*, and Fishman, "History of Childhood Sexuality."
10. L. Bender and A. Blau, "The Reaction of Children to Sexual Relations with Adults," *American Journal of Orthopsychiatry* 7 (1937): 514.
11. Myre Sim, *Guide to Psychiatry*, 3rd ed. (London: Churchill Livingstone, 1974), 778; emphasis added.
12. Quoted in Florence Rush, *The Best Kept Secret: Sexual Abuse of Children* (New York: McGraw-Hill, 1980), 98. For an analysis of victim blaming in child sexual assault cases between the 1930s and 1960s, see Lindy Burton, *Vulnerable Children: Three Studies of Children in Conflict* (London: Routledge & Kegan Paul, 1968), 87–98.
13. Clelland S. Ford and Frank A. Beach, *Patterns of Sexual Behavior* (New York: Harper & Row, 1951), 197.
14. Alfred C. Kinsey, Wardell B. Pomeroy, and Clyde E. Martin, *Sexual Behavior in the Human Male* (Philadelphia: Saunders, 1948), 180.
15. Kinsey et al., *Sexual Behavior in the Human Male*, 161; emphasis added.
16. Alfred C. Kinsey, Wardell B. Pomeroy, Clyde E. Martin, and Paul H. Gebhard, *Sexual Behavior in the Human Female* (Philadelphia: Saunders, 1953), 121.
17. Kinsey et al., *Sexual Behavior in the Human Female*, 121.
18. J. Weiss, E. Rogers, M. R. Darwin, and C. E. Dutton, "A Study of Girl Sex Victims," *Psychiatric Quarterly Supplement* 29 (1955): 2.
19. See Burton, *Vulnerable Children*.
20. See A. Salter, *Treating Child Sex Offenders and Victims: A Practical Guide* (Newbury Park, CA: Sage, 1988), 25–42; Gordon, "Politics of Child Sexual Abuse," 56–64; and Estelle B. Freedman, "Uncontrolled Desires: The Response to the Sexual Psychopath, 1920–1960," *Journal of American History* 74 (1987): 83–106.

21. See, for example, F. M. Martinson, *Infant and Child Sexuality* (St. Peter, MS: Book Mark, 1973); W. Pomeroy, *Your Child and Sex* (New York: Delacorte, 1974); Pomeroy, "A New Look at Incest," *Best of Forum* (1978): 92–97.
22. See, for example, Pomeroy, "New Look at Incest."
23. See, for example, E. and J. Oremland, *The Sexual and Gender Development of Young Children: The Role of Education* (Cambridge, MA: Ballinger, 1977).
24. Hal M. Wells, *The Sensuous Child* (New York: Stein & Day, 1978), 152. In fact, he claimed that "most of this sexual trauma stuff is nonsense."
25. See Larry L. Constantine and Joan M. Constantine, *Group Marriage: A Study of Contemporary Multilateral Marriage* (New York: Macmillan, 1973); and Pomeroy, "New Look at Incest."
26. Alayne Yates, *Sex without Shame* (New York: William Morrow, 1978), 90, 98. She goes on to say that "childhood is the best time to learn, although parents are definitely *not* the best teachers" (98). Yates differentiates between incest in early childhood and incest involving adolescents. "Incest that commences in adolescence is different and devastating," she says. "Unlike the younger child, the adolescent girl has already comprehended and incorporated the moral standards of society" (97).
27. D. J. Henderson, "Incest," in *Comprehensive Textbook of Psychiatry*, 2nd ed., ed. Alfred M. Freedman, Harold I. Kaplan, and Benjamin J. Sadock (Baltimore: Williams & Wilkins, 1975), 1536. Yates, in *Sex without Shame*, 90, said that "many youngsters do respond erotically within the incestuous liaison, and some become frankly seductive."
28. Paul H. Gebhard, John H. Gagnon, Wardell B. Pomeroy, and Cornelia V. Christenson, *Sex Offenders: An Analysis of Types* (New York: Harper & Row, 1965), 54, 276.
29. Gebhard et al., 54.
30. Robert S. de Ropp, *Sex Energy* (New York: Delta, 1969), 111–12.
31. Jenkins, *Moral Panic*, 156–63; Rush, *Best Kept Secret*, 187–90.
32. Edwin J. Haeberle, "Children, Sex, and Society," *Hustler*, December 1978, 124.
33. James R. Kincaid, *Erotic Innocence: The Culture of Child Molesting* (Durham, NC: Duke University Press, 1998).
34. Gordon, "Politics of Child Sexual Abuse," 56.
35. Gordon, 56.
36. Gordon, 63.
37. See, for example, Susan Brownmiller, *Against Our Will: Men, Women and Rape* (New York: Bantam Books, 1975); Judith Herman and Lisa Hirschman, "Father-Daughter Incest," *Signs: Journal of Women in Culture and Society* 2 (1977): 735–756.
38. David Finkelhor, "What's Wrong with Sex between Adults and Children? Ethics and the Problem of Sexual Abuse," *American Journal of Orthopsychiatry* 49, no.4 (1979): 694.
39. With this phrase Finkelhor is actually referring to the situation of sex between therapist and client, not between adult and child. However, he uses this example as an analogy of the adult-child sexual encounter.
40. Rush, *Best Kept Secret*, 193.
41. Herman and Hirschman, "Father-Daughter Incest," 751, 748.
42. Judith Lewis Herman and Lisa Hirschman, *Father-Daughter Incest* (Cambridge, MA: Harvard University Press, 1981), 27.
43. Herman and Hirschman, *Father-Daughter Incest*, 27.
44. Ann Wolbert Burgess and Nicholas Groth, "Sexual Victimization of Children," in *The Maltreatment of the School-Aged Child*, ed. Richard Volpe, Margot Breton, and Judith Mitton (Lexington, MA: Lexington Books, 1980), 79.

45. Burgess and Groth, "Sexual Victimization of Children," 79.
46. Burgess and Groth, 79.
47. Roland C. Summit, "The Child Sexual Abuse Accommodation Syndrome," *Child Abuse and Neglect* 7 (1983): 183.
48. Summit, "Accommodation Syndrome," 182.
49. For a compelling analysis of the rhetoric of power in relation to child sexuality and intergenerational sex, see James R. Kincaid, *Child-Loving: The Erotic Child and Victorian Culture* (New York: Routledge, 1992), 16–33.
50. For an example of the use of the metaphor of the slave, see Herman and Hirschman, *Father-Daughter Incest*, 27; and for an example of the use of the metaphor of the prisoner, see Finkelhor, "What's Wrong with Sex," 695.
51. Finkelhor, "What's Wrong with Sex," 696.
52. Burgess and Groth, "Sexual Victimization," 79.
53. Burgess and Groth, 79; emphasis added.
54. Summit, "Accommodation Syndrome," 182.
55. Herman and Hirschman, *Father-Daughter Incest*, 206. Finkelhor, in "What's Wrong with Sex," 696, at least concedes that "implicit coercion is present in many, if not most, sexual encounters in our society." However, in relying on a rather unexamined notion of "free will" and by making a spurious distinction between coercion and power, he ends up reaching the same conclusion—namely, that where there is an "inherent power differential," the sexual encounter is wrong.
56. Kincaid, *Child-Loving*, 29.
57. Rex and Wendy Stainton Rogers, *Stories of Childhood: Shifting Agendas of Child Concern* (Toronto: University of Toronto Press, 1992), 191.
58. Terry Leahy, in "Sex and the Age of Consent: The Ethical Issues," *Social Analysis* 39 (1996): 30, argues that "to separate sexual contacts from other child/adult interactions a missing premise must be supplied that shows that sex is unlike other forms of interaction between adults and children and that this difference implies that differences of power and knowledge make interaction evil in the case of sex while in other cases adult/child interactions can be beneficial."
59. Margaret Jackson, "Sex Research and the Construction of Sexuality: A Tool of Male Supremacy?," *Women's Studies International Forum* 7 (1984): 50.
60. For an excellent rethinking of power relations and sadomasochistic sex, see Karmen MacKendrick, *Counterpleasures* (Albany: State University of New York Press, 1999).
61. Kincaid, *Child-Loving*, 16–33. See chapter 5 for a further interrogation of this model of power as it functions in contemporary sex offense (positions-of-authority) laws.
62. Kincaid, in *Child-Loving*, 25, seems to suggest something similar. With regard to intergenerational sex, he says the "question is not the redistribution of power but its adequacy in the first place, its limitations as a tool for understanding and for living."
63. Finkelhor, "What's Wrong with Sex," 696.
64. Herman and Hirschman, *Father-Daughter Incest*, 42.
65. For examples, see Finkelhor, "What's Wrong with Sex"; Herman and Hirschman, "Father-Daughter Incest"; Roland Summit and JoAnn Kryso, "Sexual Abuse of Children: A Clinical Spectrum," *American Journal of Orthopsychiatry* 48 (1978): 237–51.
66. For another example of the use of tropes such as play and experimentation, see Rush, *Best Kept Secret*, 149.
67. Burgess and Groth, "Sexual Victimization," 84.
68. In their influential text, *Betrayal of Innocence: Incest and Its Devastation* (New York: Penguin, [1978] 1981), Susan Forward and Craig Buck appear to rely heavily on aspects of

the Freudian theory of infantile sexuality. However, despite arguing that "incestuous desires are at the core of human psychology" (7), they seem to downplay or evade the inevitable and mutually constituting relationship between child and adult sexuality: "I believe Oedipal desires are symbolic emotional desires and indistinct physical urges, rather than specific incestuous scenarios. The very young child does not specifically want to have intercourse with his mother. He wants her undivided attention; he wants to possess her; he wants her to do the things that give him pleasure and that arouse him. If he were older these desires would be sexual urges, but in his infancy and early childhood they are unfocused" (7). While this may indeed be the case, it fails to address the ways in which such supposedly unfocused desires actually work to constitute adult sexuality. In other words, it is through the retranscription of these desires—that is, *through* infantile sexuality—that adult sexuality is formed. The two cannot be neatly separated.

69. See, for example, T. C. Johnson, "Child Perpetrators—Children Who Molest Other Children: Preliminary Findings," *Child Abuse and Neglect* 12 (1988): 219–29; H. Cantwell, "Child Sexual Abuse: Very Young Perpetrators," *Child Abuse and Neglect* 12 (1988): 579–82. For a critical analysis of the literature on child sexual abusers, see Judith Levine, *Harmful to Minors: The Perils of Protecting Children from Sex* (Minneapolis: University of Minnesota Press, 2002), 45–67.

70. Paul Okami, "'Child Perpetrators of Sexual Abuse': The Emergence of a Problematic Deviant Category," *Journal of Sex Research* 29 (1992): 114. Within the child sex abuser literature, normative child sexuality is poorly defined and often construed as "sex play." Again, this reflects an increasing desexualization of childhood. For example, as Cantwell, in "Child Sexual Abuse," 1988, 581, reveals, "It is not clear to what extent sexual play among children is normal. Normal might be better defined but includes 'looking,' curiosity about another child's genitalia with mutual undressing. However, oral-genital contact and penetration of the vaginal/anal opening with fingers or objects is probably abnormal."

71. Olafson, "When Paradigms Collide," 72, 77.

72. Sigmund Freud, "The Aetiology of Hysteria" (1896), in *The Freud Reader*, ed. Peter Gay (Vintage: London, 1995), 97–111.

73. Sigmund Freud, *The Complete Works of Sigmund Freud*, vol. 3, ed. James Strachey (London: Hogarth Press, 1955), 168.

74. See, for example, Rush, *Best Kept Secret*, 82–83; Herman and Hirschman, *Father-Daughter Incest*, 9–10.

75. Herman and Hirschman, *Father-Daughter Incest*, 9.

76. Herman and Hirschman, 10. The argument that Freud deliberately suppressed the truth of child sexual abuse reached its apotheosis in the work of Jeffrey Moussaieff Masson, *The Assault on Truth: Freud's Suppression of the Seduction Theory* (New York: Farrar, Straus and Giroux, 1984).

77. Rush, *Best Kept Secret*, 83.

78. Sigmund Freud, *Three Essays on the Theory of Sexuality* (1905), *On Sexuality: Three Essays on the Theory of Sexuality and Other Works*, ed. Angela Richards, trans. James Strachey, vol. 7 of Pelican Freud Library, (Harmondsworth: Penguin, 1977), 108; Sigmund Freud, *An Outline of Psycho-Analysis* (1938), ed. and trans. James Strachey (London: Hogarth Press, 1940), 44. Jean Laplanche and J. B. Pontalis, in *The Language of Psycho-Analysis*, trans. D. Nicholson-Smith (New York: W. W. Norton, 1973), argue that, Freud did not give up the seduction thesis entirely, and in fact he forever implicitly searched for a material basis for it: "Freud could never resign himself to treating phantasy as the pure and simple outgrowth of the spontaneous sexual life of

the child. He is forever searching, behind the phantasy, for whatever has founded it in its reality: perceived evidence of the primal scene . . . ; the seduction of the infant by its mother . . . ; and, even more fundamentally, the notion that phantasies are based in the last reckoning on 'primal phantasies—on a mnemic residue transmitted from actual experiences in the history of the human species. . . . Quite obviously, the first stage—the stage of the scene of seduction—simply must be founded in something more real than the subject's imaginings alone" (406–7).

79. Herman and Hirschman, *Father-Daughter Incest*, 9.
80. Sigmund Freud, "Female Sexuality" (1931), *On Sexuality*, vol. 7 of Pelican Freud Library, 379.
81. Freud, *Three Essays*, 108. Or as he said in *Introductory Lectures on Psychoanalysis*: "Phantasies of being seduced are of particular interest, because so often they are not phantasies but real memories." *Introductory Lectures on Psychoanalysis* (1917), trans. James Strachey and eds James Strachey and Angela Richards, vol. 1 of Pelican Freud Library (Harmondsworth: Penguin, 1975), 471.
82. Freud, "Aetiology of Hysteria," 102.
83. Freud, 106.
84. Sigmund Freud and Josef Breuer, "On the Psychical Mechanism of Hysterical Phenomena: Preliminary Communication [1893]," *The Standard Edition of the Complete Psychological Works of Sigmund Freud*, ed. and trans. James Strachey (London: Hogarth Press, 1953–1975), 2:7.
85. Freud, "Aetiology of Hysteria," 100.
86. Herman and Hirschman, "Father-Daughter Incest," 737.
87. Summit, "Accommodation Syndrome," 177–81, 189.
88. John W. Pearce and Terry D. Pezzot-Pearce, *Psychotherapy of Abused and Neglected Children* (New York: Guilford Press, 1997), 305.
89. Sandra Wieland, *Techniques and Issues in Abuse-Focused Therapy with Children and Adolescents: Addressing the Internal Trauma* (Thousand Oaks: Sage, 1998), 27. See also Suzanne M. Sgroi, *Handbook of Clinical Intervention in Child Sexual Abuse* (Lexington: Lexington Books, 1982), 129.
90. Sharon Lamb, "Treating Sexually Abused Children: Issues of Blame and Responsibility," *American Journal of Orthopsychiatry* 56 (1986): 305.
91. Pearce and Pezzot-Pearce, *Psychotherapy*, 306; emphasis added.
92. Herman and Hirschman, "Father-Daughter Incest," 751.
93. See, for example, Wieland, *Techniques*, 27.
94. Herman and Hirschman, in "Father-Daughter Incest," 751, argue that the child's "sense of malignant power can be understood to have arisen as a defense against the child's feelings of utter helplessness."
95. On the use of "infatuation" and "curiosity", see Wieland, *Techniques*, 27–28.
96. Wieland, 28.
97. Wieland, 28.
98. Lamb, "Treating Sexually Abused Children," 304.
99. Anna C. Salter, *Predators: Pedophiles, Rapists, and Other Sex Offenders: Who They Are, How They Operate, and How We Can Protect Ourselves and Our Children* (New York: Basic Books, 2003), 14.
100. Anna C. Salter, *Transforming Trauma: A Guide to Understanding and Treating Adult Survivors of Child Sexual Abuse* (Thousand Oaks, CA: Sage, 1995), 118.
101. Sharon Lamb, *The Trouble with Blame: Victims, Perpetrators, and Responsibility* (Cambridge, MA: Harvard University Press, 1996), 43.

102. Lamb, *The Trouble with Blame*, 35.
103. Silvan S. Tomkins, *Affect Imagery Consciousness: The Complete Edition*, vol. 1 (New York: Springer, 2008), 353.
104. Tomkins, 1: 353.
105. Lamb, *The Trouble with Blame*, 35.
106. Lamb, 43.
107. Gordon, "Politics of Child Sexual Abuse," 61.
108. For a discussion of the importance of theorizing the relationship between age and sexuality, see Steven Angelides, "Feminism, Child Sexual Abuse, and the Erasure of Child Sexuality," *GLQ* 10, no. 2 (2004): 163–68.

CHAPTER FOUR

1. Gay Left Collective, "Happy Families? Paedophilia Examined," *Gay Left: A Gay Socialist Journal* 7 (Winter 1978/79): 2.
2. Gay Left Collective, "Happy Families?," 2.
3. It is worth highlighting that the editorial by the Gay Left Collective was a very measured analysis of arguments for and against pedophilia. They did not conclude either in favor of or opposition to the practice. Instead, they highlighted, among other things, the shortcomings of a simple libertarian approach to the issue, as well the complexities of adult-child power relations as argued by feminists. Among their conclusions were that we ought to incorporate children into debates in order to provide them with a degree of autonomy at the same time as we recognize "the limitations of children's ability to be responsible for themselves." In sum, we "must avoid . . . a totally 'adult-centred' solution." Gay Left Collective, "Happy Families?," 5.
4. On the interlocking issues of child sexual abuse, homosexuality, and pedophilia in the United States, see Philip Jenkins, *Moral Panic: Changing Concepts of the Child Molester in Modern America* (New Haven, CT: Yale University Press, 1998), 118–63; and Fred Fejes, *Gay Rights and Moral Panic: The Origins of America's Debate on Homosexuality* (New York: Palgrave Macmillan, 2008). On the British context, see Jeffrey Weeks, *Sexuality and Its Discontents* (London: Routledge & Kegan Paul, 1985), 211–45.
5. In fact, this chapter's case study exhibits striking parallels with the public and legal campaigns against the Paedophile Information Exchange (PIE) in the United Kingdom in the late 1970s. See Lucy Robinson, *Gay Men and the Left in Post-war Britain: How the Personal Got Political* (Manchester: Manchester University Press, 2007), chap. 5.
6. For some notable examples, see Jenkins, *Moral Panic*, 145–63; Weeks, *Sexuality and Its Discontents*, 211–45; Ken Plummer, "'The Paedophile's' Progress: A View from Below," in *Perspectives on Paedophilia*, ed. Brian Taylor (London: Batsford Academic and Educational, 1981), 113–32; Pat Califia, *Public Sex: The Culture of Radical Sex* (Pittsburgh: Cleis Press, 1994), 29–70; Robinson, *Gay Men and the Left*, 123–53; Steven Angelides, "The Emergence of the Paedophile in the Late Twentieth Century," *Australian Historical Studies* 36, no. 126 (2005): 272–95; David T. Evans, *Sexual Citizenship: The Material Construction of Sexualities* (London & New York: Routledge, 1993), chap. 8; and James R. Kincaid, *Child-Loving: The Erotic Child and Victorian Culture* (New York: Routledge, 1992).
7. Danny Vadasz, "For Love or Money? Behind the Headlines, Who's Screwing Whom?," *Outrage*, May 1983, 3–5.
8. John Silvester, "'Delta' Probe Shock: The Kids on Our Streets," *Sun*, March 30, 1983, 1–2.
9. Silvester, "'Delta' Probe Shock," 1.
10. Vadasz, "For Love or Money?," 5.

11. Vadasz, 5.
12. Vadasz, 5.
13. Silvester, "'Delta' Probe Shock," 1. Pat Califia, in *Public Sex*, 42, notes a very similar displacement in the United States in 1977 when a CBS *60 Minutes* story broke about child pornography: "After a brief mention of adult males with interests in young girls, the program focused on magazines full of erotic pictures of young boys and footage of teenage male hustlers working the streets."
14. For a discussion of the crackdown on child pornography and pedophilia in the United States, see Jenkins, *Moral Panic*, 145–63. On the NAMBLA controversy as reported in Australia, see John Cozijn, "Is Boy Love a Gay Issue?," *Campaign*, June 1983, 12–13. On the UK pedophile panic, see Philip Jenkins, *Intimate Enemies: Moral Panics in Contemporary Great Britain* (New York: Aldine de Gruyter, 1992), 72–99; and Weeks, *Sexuality and Its Discontents*, 211–45.
15. Quoted in Danny Vadasz, "Court Dumps Delta in Conspiracy Case," *Outrage*, June 1984, 5.
16. Like the PSG, the Paedophile Information Exchange was a support group for self-identified pedophiles. After an eighteen-month investigation, five committee members had been charged with conspiracy to corrupt public morals. One defendant died before trial, three were acquitted, and one was sentenced to two years on retrial. See Jamie Gardiner, "The End for Conspiracy Trials," *Outrage*, June 1984, 5; Robinson, *Gay Men and the Left*, 129–37; and Jenkins, *Intimate Enemies*, 72–78.
17. "Child Pornography: Nine Arrested," *Sydney Morning Herald*, November 7, 1983, 2; "Nine Men on Child Moral Charges," *The Age*, November 7, 1983, 1.
18. Adam Carr, "Delta Squad's 'Child Sex Ring,'" *Outrage*, December 1983/January 1984, 6.
19. "Child Pornography: Nine Arrested," 2; "Nine Men on Child Moral Charges," 1.
20. "Child Pornography: Nine Arrested," 2.
21. Brett Wright, "Child-Sex Task Force Snared in Legal Web," *The Age*, July 2, 1984, 10.
22. Jenkins, *Intimate Enemies*, 84.
23. Quoted in Wright, "Child-Sex Task Force," 10.
24. Quotes from Wright, 10.
25. Wright, 10.
26. Quoted in Wright, 10.
27. Quoted in Wright, 10.
28. Vadasz, "Court Dumps Delta," 5.
29. Gail Mason and Anna Chapman, "Defining Sexual Harassment: A History of the Commonwealth Legislation and Its Critiques," *Federal Law Review* 31 (2003): 195–224.
30. Jenkins, *Moral Panic*, 135.
31. This term is taken from the work of Paul Gebhard and his colleagues in the 1960s, who prefigured the feminist child sexual abuse movement. See Gebhard, John H. Gagnon, Wardell B. Pomeroy, and Cornelia V. Christenson, *Sex Offenders: An Analysis of Types* (New York: Harper and Row, 1965), 71.
32. Alliance of Revolting Feminists, "Alliance of Revolting Feminists Manifesto," *Melbourne Women's Liberation Newsletter*, June 1984, 12–13.
33. Quoted in Jenkins, *Moral Panic*, 137.
34. Alliance of Revolting Feminists, "Manifesto," 12–13.
35. Diana E. H. Russell, *The Secret Trauma: Incest in the Lives of Girls and Women* (New York: Basic Books, 1986), 82. On the National Organization for Women, see Mark

Blasius and Shane Phelan, *We Are Everywhere: A Historical Sourcebook of Gay and Lesbian Politics* (New York: Routledge, 1997), 468-69.
36. Judith Lewis Herman and Lisa Hirschman, "Father-Daughter Incest," *Signs: Journal of Women in Culture and Society* 2 (1977): 751. See also Judith Lewis Herman and Lisa Hirschman, *Father-Daughter Incest* (Cambridge, MA: Harvard University Press, 1981); David Finkelhor, "What's Wrong with Sex between Adults and Children? Ethics and the Problem of Sexual Abuse," *American Journal of Orthopsychiatry* 49 (1979): 692-97; Florence Rush, *The Best Kept Secret: Sexual Abuse of Children* (New York: McGraw-Hill, 1980); Ann Wolbert Burgess and Nicholas Groth, "Sexual Victimization of Children," in *The Maltreatment of the School-Aged Child*, ed. Richard Volpe, Margot Breton, and Judith Mitton (Lexington, MA: Lexington Books, 1980); and Roland C. Summit, "The Child Sexual Abuse Accommodation Syndrome," *Child Abuse and Neglect* 7 (1983): 177-93.
37. Linda Gordon, "The Politics of Child Sexual Abuse: Notes from American History," *Feminist Review* 28 (1988): 58; Dorothy Scott and Shurlee Swain, *Confronting Cruelty: Historical Perspectives on Child Protection in Australia* (Melbourne: Melbourne University Press, 2002), 42, 69-71.
38. See, for example, "Hospitals Report an 'Astonishing' Rise in Sexual Abuse of Children," *Sydney Morning Herald*, July 24, 1986, 3.
39. "Scars of Sexual Abuse Heal Slowly," *Sydney Morning Herald*, September 6, 1986, 8.
40. Scott and Swain, *Confronting Cruelty*, 162.
41. "Scars of Sexual Abuse Heal Slowly."
42. "Campaign Opens to Counter Sexual Abuse of Children," *Sydney Morning Herald*, October 1, 1986, 21. Another special run on ABC Television in 1984 was *The Stranger's Not the Danger*, where it was noted that for every child who is sexually abused by a stranger four more are abused by close family or friends. It should be noted that the theme of "stranger danger" still operated alongside that of "intimate danger." In fact, at the same time as such television campaigns were appearing, the "Safety House Scheme" was also introduced. This was a scheme "designed to alert children to the danger behind approaches from strangers and give them an easily recognisable refuge from a potential child molester." See "'Stranger Danger' before Your Eyes," *Sydney Morning Herald*, June 25, 1986, 15.
43. Margaret Harris, "Child Sex Cases Divide British," *Sydney Morning Herald*, July 4, 1987, 29.
44. Richard West, "Seeing Child Abuse as a Feminist Plot," *Sydney Morning Herald*, July 4, 1987, 29.
45. Richard Coleman, "Child Abuse Documentary Lurched into the Tabloid Telly Trap," *Sydney Morning Herald*, November 14, 1987, 82. The same day the *Sydney Morning Herald* carried this piece by Coleman, they also reported on the NSW government's blitz on pedophilia. The article began by detailing the government's campaign against child sexual assault, only to dovetail into a discussion not of incest or intimate danger but of homosexual pedophilia. This was followed three days later by another article, "Pedophiles: We Love Children," *Sydney Morning Herald*, November 17, 1987, 3, which was specifically on a group of self-proclaimed homosexual pedophiles. Although I do not want to suggest that heterosexual men were *consciously* scapegoating homosexuals as perpetrators of child sexual abuse, the rhetorical association of homosexuality with child sexual abuse in the media seems to be inextricable from a form of male reaction to the feminist child sexual abuse movement.
46. Susan Faludi, *Backlash: The Undeclared War against American Women* (New York:

Crown, 1991); Michael Kimmel, *Manhood in America: A Cultural History* (New York: Free Press, 1996).
47. Quoted in Kimmel, *Manhood in America*, 299.
48. Quoted in Kimmel, 302.
49. Quoted in Kimmel, 302, 303, 302–3.
50. For typical media examples, see "The Sensitive New Man Now Wants to Like Himself More," *Sydney Morning Herald*, June 1, 1985, 39; "The Trials of the Sensitive New Man," *Sydney Morning Herald*, October 20, 1986, 13; "Malefactors in the Issue of Equality," *The Australian*, December 16, 1986, 9; Bob Connell, "There's More to Feminism than a Nice, New Man," *Sydney Morning Herald*, January 5, 1987, 7; "The Men: Quantity without Quality," *Sydney Morning Herald*, January 21, 1987, 12; "What Women Don't Tell Men at Work," *Sydney Morning Herald*, November 20, 1987, 21; "Are These the Blokes That Women Blame?," *Sydney Morning Herald*, November 24, 1987, 19.
51. This was quoted in Connell, "There's More to Feminism," 7.
52. Kimmel, *Manhood in America*, 292.
53. Kimmel, 292.
54. Kimmel, 292. For Australian media examples of the figure of the wimp, of "soft masculinity," and the negative framing of the "sensitive New Age guy," see the review of the James Bond film *The Living Daylights* in "Too Sensitive for Seduction?," *Sydney Morning Herald*, November 26, 1987, 18; and "Differences Remain, but Thanks for Calling," *Sydney Morning Herald*, November 26, 1987, 19.
55. Angelides, "The Emergence of the Paedophile in the Late Twentieth Century," 272–95.
56. A. Nicholas Groth and H. Jean Birnbaum, "Adult Sexual Orientation and Attraction to Underage Persons," *Archives of Sexual Behavior* 7 (1978): 175–81; K. Howells, "Adult Sexual Interest in Children: Considerations Relevant to Theories of Etiology," in *Adult Sexual Interest in Children*, ed. M. Cook and K. Howells (New York: Academic Press, 1981), 55–94; David Finkelhor, *Child Sexual Abuse: New Theory and Research* (New York: Free Press, 1984); Neil McConaghy, *Sexual Behaviour: Problems and Management* (New York: Plenum Press, 1993). I should point out that as early as 1964 John McGeorge, in "Sexual Assaults on Children," *Medicine, Science and the Law* 4 (1964): 245, argued that there is "a large homosexual component in his [the "true" pedophile's] behavior." However, this seems not to have been a common feature of dominant theories in the way it was in the late 1970s and 1980s.
57. Neil McConaghy, "Penile Response Conditioning and Its Relationship to Aversion Therapy in Homosexuals," *Behaviour Therapy* 1, no. 2 (1970): 312. For another well-known example of this distinction between regressed and fixated offenders, see Howells, "Adult Sexual Interest in Children," 78. A hebephile usually refers to someone with an erotic preference for adolescents between the ages of thirteen and sixteen.
58. In summarizing Groth's account of the causal factors involved in regressed offender behavior, Howells, in "Adult Sexual Interest in Children," 78, notes "the precipitating events as physical, social, sexual, marital, financial and vocational crises to which the offender fails to adapt." See also Kurt Freund, C. K. McKnight, R. Langevin, and S. Cibiri, "The Female Child as a Surrogate Object," *Archives of Sexual Behavior* 2, no. 2 (1972): 119–33.
59. Quoted in "Vic Child Sex Report Exonerates Gays, Slams Pedophiles," *Outrage*, June 1986, 7.
60. See Plummer, "'The Paedophile's Progress."
61. Bernard Lagan, "Pedophile Unit Below Strength as Blitz Begins," *Sydney Morning Herald*, November 14, 1987, 3. In terms of psychomedical definitions, those attracted

to prepubescent children are defined as pedophiles, but self-identified pedophiles attracted to pubertal and postpubertal children are defined as hebephiles; therefore, these men misnamed themselves.

62. Califia, *Public Sex*, 29–70, 136–47.
63. James R. Kincaid, *Erotic Innocence: The Culture of Child Molesting* (Durham, NC: Duke University Press, 1998); Kincaid, *Child-Loving*.
64. Califia, *Public Sex*, 44.
65. On the decriminalization of sodomy across the United States, see William N. Eskridge Jr., *Gaylaw: Challenging the Apartheid of the Closet* (Cambridge, MA: Harvard University Press, 1999).
66. On the sex education debates in the context of the decriminalization of homosexuality, see Angelides, "The Emergence of the Paedophile in the Late Twentieth Century"; and Steven Angelides, "'The Continuing Homosexual Offensive': Sex Education, Gay Rights, and Homosexual Recruitment," in *Homophobia: An Australian History*, ed. Shirleene Robinson (Annandale: Federation Press, 2008). David M. Halperin has argued that "teaching has an extended history of association with deviance" going as far back as ancient Greece. See his "Deviant Teaching," in *A Companion to Lesbian, Gay, Bisexual, Transgender, and Queer Studies*, ed. George E. Haggarty and Molly McGarry (Malden: Blackwell, 2007): 151. On this longer history of cultural concern about the sexual seduction of children through teaching, see Clifford J. Rosky, "Fear of the Queer Child," *Buffalo Law Review* 61 (2013): 607–97.
67. Anita Bryant and Bob Green, *At Any Cost* (Old Tappan, NJ: Fleming H. Revell, 1978), quoted in Jenkins, *Moral Panic*, 124.
68. Local Government Act 1988. See Joe Moran, "Childhood Sexuality and Education: The Case of Section 28," *Sexualities* 4, no. 1 (2001): 73–89.
69. New South Wales Parliamentary Debates (Hansard), March 9, 1982, 2231.
70. Crimes (Homosexual Behaviour) Amendment Bill, second reading, New South Wales Parliamentary Debates (Hansard), New South Wales, February 18, 1982, 2109.
71. Crimes (Homosexual Behaviour) Amendment Bill, 2127.
72. "The Little Red School Book," MILESAGO: Australasian Music & Popular Culture 1964–1975, accessed July 24, 2018, http://www.milesago.com/press/lrs.htm.
73. The *Young, Gay, and Proud* booklet was published by the Melbourne Gay Teachers and Students Group, 1978.
74. Daniel Marshall, "Young Gays: Towards a History of Youth, Queer Sexualities and Education in Australia," *La Trobe Journal* 87 (May 2011): 60–73. Marshall notes that "the numbers of young people involved in this group were never large" (62).
75. Quoted in Gary Jaynes, "Young Gay and Proud: 20 Years On," in *Young People and Sexualities: Experiences, Perspectives and Service Provision*, compiled by Michael Crowhurst and Mic Emslie (Melbourne: Youth Research Centre, University of Melbourne, 2000), 10.
76. Quoted in Jaynes, 11.
77. New South Wales Parliamentary Debates (Hansard), December 3, 1981, 1456.
78. Committee to Raise Education Standards, *The Continuing Homosexual Offensive: Next Target: Anti-discrimination*, pamphlet, 4. The pamphlet is held in the Australian Lesbian and Gay Archives.
79. Barbara Fih and Stephanie Bunbury, "I Didn't Call for Lower Sex Age: Teacher," *The Age*, November 11, 1983, 3.
80. Fih and Bunbury, "I Didn't Call for Lower Sex Age," 3.
81. Gay Left Collective, quoted in *Newsletter of the 5th National Homosexual Conference*, August 1979, 25.

82. Robinson, *Gay Men and the Left*, 131.
83. Fih and Bunbury, "I Didn't Call for Lower Sex Age," 3.
84. Fih and Bunbury, 3.
85. Paul Robinson and Owen Wood, "'Sex-at-10' Teacher Outrage," *Sun*, November 10, 1983, 1.
86. Robinson and Wood, "'Sex-at-10' Teacher Outrage," 1.
87. Quoted in Robinson and Wood, 1.
88. Quoted in Robinson and Wood, 1.
89. Quoted in Robinson and Wood, 2.
90. Barbara Fih, "Sex Talk Teacher Taken from Class," *The Age*, November 12, 1983, 3.
91. Quoted in "Thorne 'Not Fit to Teach': Cain," *Outrage*, January 1985, 5.
92. Quoted in "Thorne 'Not Fit to Teach," 5.
93. Victoria, "Report of the Equal Opportunity Board for the Year Ended 30 June 1987," Papers Presented to Parliament, Session 1987–1988, 7, no. 40, Equal Opportunity Board and Commissioner for Equal Opportunity—Reports, 1986–1987, 82–105.
94. Victoria, "Report of the Equal Opportunity Board," 99.
95. "Cain to Outlaw Thorne," *Melbourne's Star Observer*, December 5, 1986, 1.
96. "New Move to Ban Gay-Rights Teacher," *Advertiser*, November 29, 1986.
97. Parliamentary Debates (Hansard), Parliament of Victoria, Legislative Assembly, vol. 385, 1986.
98. Graham Willett, "'Proud and Employed': The Gay and Lesbian Movement and the Victorian Teachers' Unions in the 1970s," *Labour History: A Journal of Labour and Social History* 76 (May 1999): 78–94; see also Jaynes, "Young Gay and Proud."
99. See also Angelides, "'The Continuing Homosexual Offensive.'"
100. "Teaching Deal Ends Three-Year Thorne Saga," *Outrage*, January 1987, 8.
101. "Teaching Deal Ends Saga," 8. Tragically, Thorne never returned to secondary-school teaching.
102. Lee Edelman, *No Future: Queer Theory and the Death Drive* (Durham, NC: Duke University Press, 2004), 2.
103. Edelman, *No Future*, 4.
104. On homophobic parliamentary preambles and age-of-consent debates in Australian homosexual-law-reform campaigns, see Graham Willett, *Living Out Loud: A History of Gay and Lesbian Activism in Australia* (St. Leonards: Allen & Unwin, 2000).
105. The Queensland legislation set the age of consent for homosexual sex other than anal sex at sixteen but made anal sex for men and women under the age of eighteen illegal. Willett, *Living Out Loud*, 224.
106. At this time, in 1981, the age of consent for heterosexual sex in the state of Victoria was sixteen.
107. *Gay Community News*, February 1981, 5.
108. Jenkins, *Intimate Enemies*, 71–99; Jenkins, *Moral Panic*, 145–63.
109. Angelides, "The Emergence of the Paedophile in the Late Twentieth Century," 295. At the time, many gay groups, including the Australian Pedophile Support Group, argued that "gays have once again been used as scapegoats to misdirect attention away from the real exploiters of children who are commonly fathers and family members." Carr, "Delta Squad's 'Child Sex Ring,'" 6.
110. Kincaid, *Erotic Innocence*, also foregrounds a scapegoat model centered on the sexual predator. In fact, in suggesting that erotic children are manufactured as a result of denial and adult projections of desire, Kincaid's own framework perhaps unwittingly diverts attention from the specificity and subjectivity of the sexual child.

111. Jenkins, *Moral Panic*, 157. For an extended account of the Boston sex scandal, see John Mitzel, *The Boston Sex Scandal* (Boston: Glad Day Books, 1980).
112. Roger N. Lancaster, *Sex Panic and the Punitive State* (Berkeley: University of California Press, 2011), 59. Elsewhere I have argued that the emergence of the category of the pedophile is inextricable from the erasure of child sexuality. See Angelides, "Historicizing Affect, Psychoanalyzing History"; and my remarks in a roundtable discussion, "Sex Work (Part One): Sexuality Studies at the University of Melbourne," *Traffic* 6 (2005): 103–31.
113. Daniel Tsang, introduction to *The Age Taboo: Gay Male Sexuality, Power, and Consent*, ed. Tsang (London: Gay Men's Press, 1981), 8.
114. Plummer, "'The Paedophile's' Progress," 122–23.
115. "Pedophiles: We Love Children," 3.

CHAPTER FIVE

1. Joe Kovacs, "U.S. Teacher Sexpidemic Spreading across the Planet," WorldNetDaily, December 14, 2005, http://worldnetdaily.com/news/article.asp?ARTICLE_ID=47895.
2. William Saletan, "Teachers' Pets?" *Slate*, January 16, 2006, https://slate.com/technology/2006/01/are-teachers-who-sleep-with-boys-getting-off.html.
3. To give just a few examples of such news headlines: D. Longenecker, "The Epidemic of School Sex Abuse," *Crisis Magazine*, April 29, 2008, https://www.crisismagazine.com/2008/the-epidemic-of-school-sex-abuse; Associated Press, "Teacher Sexual Abuse on Rise," Auburnpub.com, October 20, 2007, http://www.auburnpub.com/articles/2007/10/21/news/state/state01.txt; D. Kupelian, "What's behind Today's Epidemic of Teacher-Student Sex," *Whistleblower* 15, no. 3 (2006): 4–10; Kovacs, "U.S. Teacher Sexpidemic"; S. Churcher, "Why Are So Many Women Teachers Having Affairs with Their Pupils?," *Mail*, January 15, 2006, 44; W. Koch, "More Women Charged in Sex Cases: In the Last 18 Months, 25 Cases of Teachers Molesting Boys," *Chicago Sun-Times*, November 30, 2005, 34; D. Hope and T. Ong, "Hey, Teacher, Leave Those Kids Alone," *The Australian*, December 17, 2005, 19; ABC News, "Teacher Sex Scandals: Why So Many?," *Good Morning America*, August 3, 2005; H. Gilmore and D. Andreatta, "Sextracurricular Perv-Teacher Crisis, 1 in 10 Schoolkids Molested: Study," *New York Post*, April 24, 2005, 22; J. Bone, "Women Reined In over Boy Sex," *Times*, December 1, 2005, 47.
4. Charol Shakeshaft, *Educator Sexual Misconduct: A Synthesis of Existing Literature* (Washington, DC: US Department of Education, Office of the Under Secretary, 2004).
5. Kovacs, "U.S. Teacher Sexpidemic." At the height of the sex panic, around 2004 and 2005, WorldNetDaily, the website on which this article appeared, was regularly updated.
6. Sheila L. Cavanagh, *Sexing the Teacher: School Sex Scandals and Queer Pedagogies* (Vancouver: UBC Press, 2007), 10.
7. Shakeshaft, *Educator Sexual Misconduct*.
8. Shakeshaft, 31.
9. Helmut Graupner, "Sexual Consent: The Criminal Law in Europe and Outside of Europe," in *Adolescence, Sexuality, and the Criminal Law: Multidisciplinary Perspectives*, ed. Helmut Graupner and Vern L. Bullough (Binghamton, NY: Haworth Press, 2004), 111–71.
10. Sexual Offences Act 2003 (UK); Crimes Act 1958 (Vic); Criminal Code (Canada); Colorado Revised Statutes 18-3-401.
11. Michel Foucault, *The History of Sexuality, Volume 1: An Introduction* (London: Penguin, 1990).

12. Greetje Timmerman, "Sexual Harassment of Adolescents Perpetrated by Teachers and by Peers: An Exploration of the Dynamics of Power, Culture, and Gender in Secondary Schools," *Sex Roles: A Journal of Research* 48, nos. 5–6 (2003): 232; emphasis added.
13. Shakeshaft, *Educator Sexual Misconduct*, 50.
14. Quoted in Susan Estrich, "Is Teacher-Student Sex OK If the Student Is 18?," Fox News, June 18, 2006, http://www.foxnews.com/story/0,2933,200004,00.html.
15. Estrich, "Is Teacher-Student Sex OK?"
16. A notion of pastoral care modeled on the therapist-client relationship within mental health professions also informs ideas about prohibition of teacher-student sexual liaisons. I wonder too whether in fact much of the rationale behind identifying teachers as figures of authority is a hangover from rather outdated notions of pedagogical practices and relations, wherein the teacher is assumed to *possess* the knowledge that is then *inscribed* on the pupil as tabula rasa.
17. Crimes Act 1958 (Vic), section 49C; emphasis added.
18. Teachernet, "Abuse of a Position of Trust," accessed August 23, 2008, http://www.teachernet.gov.uk/wholeschool/familyandcommunity/childprotection/usefulinformation/abuseoftrust/; emphasis added. For an example of a school policy modeled on this government policy advice, see "Safeguarding (Child Protection) Policy," Papplewick School (Ascot, UK), April 2013, http://www.papplewick.org.uk/assets/safeguarding.doc.
19. Another obvious tension here is the challenge that sexual transgressions by teachers pose to perceptions of parental power and control.
20. Pat Sikes, "Scandalous Stories and Dangerous Liaisons: When Female Pupils and Male Teachers Fall in Love," *Sex Education* 6, no. 3 (2006): 265–80. In his book *Sex and Harm in the Age of Consent* (Minneapolis: University of Minnesota Press, 2016), 7, Joseph J. Fischel importantly questions the utility of the concept of consent for "adjudicating sexual harm." However, he does not question normative socio-legal assumptions about power in relationships of so-called dependence and authority. He therefore accepts the utility of the *concept* of sovereign power for adjudicating harm and for accurately describing the dynamics of such relationships of so-called dependence and authority. In so doing, although he advocates "for the creation of adolescents as a discrete class under law," he also argues for "tighter regulations around relations of dependence and authority" (24). His argument is advanced via the explicit exclusion of an account of the female sexual offender and reiterates the unquestioned assumption that sexual relations between teachers and students are *necessarily* asymmetrical with regard to power (in favor of the teacher), and should therefore be blanketly and criminally prohibited.
21. Debbie Epstein and Richard Johnson, *Schooling Sexualities* (Buckingham, PA: Open University Press, 1998), 132.
22. Kate Myers, "Dilemmas of Leadership: Sexuality and Schools," *International Journal of Leadership in Education* 5, no. 4 (2002): 301.
23. Cavanagh, *Sexing the Teacher*, 28.
24. *The Queen v. Natalina D'Addario*, transcript of proceedings, Victorian County Court, Australia, July 25, 2006, 2.
25. *The Queen v. Natalina D'Addario*, 2.
26. *R v. D'Addario* [2007], Victorian Count Court, July 25, 2006, 48.
27. Quoted in Kate Legge, "Teachers' Pets," *The Australian*, Weekend Australian Magazine, November 11, 2006, 29.

28. Eve Kosofsky Sedgwick, *Epistemology of the Closet* (Berkeley: University of California Press, 1990), 4.
29. Janet Halley, *Split Decisions: How and Why to Take a Break from Feminism* (Princeton, NJ: Princeton University Press, 2006), 348.
30. *R v. D'Addario*, 45–46; emphasis added.
31. Of the female-teacher-and-male-student scandals Cavanagh studies in *Sexing the Teacher*, 22, she notes that, in "most cases, the students sought out the amorous attentions of the female teacher and did not experience remorse, regret, or nullifying side effects."
32. *The Queen v. Natalina D'Addario*, 16.
33. Kate Myers with Graham Clayton, David James, and Jim O'Brien, *Teachers Behaving Badly? Dilemmas for School Leaders* (London: RoutledgeFalmer, 2005), 58–62.
34. See chapter 6 for a fuller account of the psychical dynamics of recognition.
35. Quoted in Legge, "Teachers' Pets," 29.
36. *The Queen v. Natalina D'Addario*, 5, 8–9.
37. See Wendy Hollway, "Heterosexual Sex: Power and Desire for the Other," in *Sex and Love: New Thoughts on Old Contradictions*, ed. Sue Cartledge and Joanna Ryan (London: Women's Press, 1983), 124–40; Hollway, *Subjectivity and Method in Psychology: Gender, Meaning, and Science* (London: Sage, 1989); Hollway, "Recognition and Heterosexual Desire," in *Theorising Heterosexuality: Telling it Straight*, ed. Diane Richardson (Buckingham, PA: Open University Press, 1996), 91–108; Hollway, "Gender Difference and the Production of Subjectivity," in *Changing the Subject: Psychology, Social Regulation and Subjectivity*, ed. Julian Henriques, Wendy Hollway, Cathy Urwin, Couze Venne, and Valerie Walkerdine, 2nd ed. (London: Routledge, 1998), 227–63; Wendy Hollway and Tony Jefferson, "PC or Not PC: Sexual Harassment and the Question of Ambivalence," *Human Relations* 49, no. 3 (1996): 373–93; and Wendy Hollway and Tony Jefferson, "'A Kiss Is Just a Kiss': Date Rape, Gender and Subjectivity," *Sexualities* 1, no. 4 (1998): 405–23.
38. Hollway and Jefferson, "PC or Not PC," 387.
39. Michel Foucault, "The Subject and Power," in Hubert L. Dreyfus and Paul Rabinow, *Michel Foucault: Beyond Structuralism and Hermeneutics* (Chicago: University of Chicago Press, 1983), 208–26.
40. Hollway and Jefferson, "PC or Not PC," 387.
41. Robert C. Prus, *Beyond the Power Mystique: Power as Intersubjective Accomplishment* (New York: State University of New York Press, 1999).
42. Karen Barad, *Meeting the Universe Halfway: Quantum Physics and the Entanglement of Matter and Meaning* (Durham, NC: Duke University Press, 2007), 33.
43. *The Queen v. Natalina D'Addario*, 22.
44. Quoted in Legge, "Teachers' Pets," 29.
45. Karin A. Martin, *Puberty, Sexuality, and the Self: Boys and Girls at Adolescence* (New York: Routledge, 1996), 14.
46. On young men and empowerment through intergenerational sex, see Bruce Rind, Philip Tromovitch, and Robert Bauserman, "A Meta-analytic Examination of Assumed Properties of Child Sexual Abuse Using College Samples," *Psychological Bulletin* 124, no. 1 (1998): 22–53; Andrea Nelson and Pamela Oliver, "Gender and the Construction of Consent in Child-Adult Sexual Contact: Beyond Gender Neutrality and Male Monopoly," *Gender and Society* 12, no. 5 (1998): 554–77; Bruce Rind, "Adolescent Sexual Experiences with Adults: Pathological or Functional?," *Journal of Psychology and Human Sexuality* 15, no. 3 (2003): 5–22; Bruce Rind, "An Empirical

Examination of Sexual Relations between Adolescents and Adults: They Differ from Those between Children and Adults and Should Be Treated Separately," *Journal of Psychology and Human Sexuality* 16, nos. 2–3 (2005): 55–62; Bruce Rind and Max Welter, "Enjoyment and Emotionally Negative Reactions in Minor–Adult Versus Minor–Peer and Adult–Adult First Postpubescent Coitus: A Secondary Analysis of the Kinsey Data," *Archives of Sexual Behavior* 43, no. 2 (2014): 285–97; Cavanagh, *Sexing the Teacher*; and Thomas K. Hubbard and Beert Verstraete, eds., *Censoring Sex Research: The Debate over Male Intergenerational Relations* (Walnut Creek, CA: Left Coast Press, 2013).
47. *The Queen v. Natalina D'Addario*, 11.
48. Group for the Advancement of Psychiatry, *Power and Authority in Adolescence: The Origins and Resolutions of Intergenerational Conflict* (New York: Group for the Advancement of Psychiatry, 1978), 193–94.
49. See n46, above. See also Steven Angelides, "Subjectivity under Erasure: Adolescent Sexuality, Gender, and Teacher-Student Sex," *Journal of Men's Studies* 15, no. 3 (2007): 347–60; and Angelides, "Sexual Offences against 'Children' and the Question of Judicial Gender Bias," *Australian Feminist Studies* 23, no. 57 (2008): 359–73.
50. Martin, *Puberty, Sexuality, and the Self*, 46.
51. Martin, 46.
52. Martin, esp. 46.
53. On the difficulties of conducting research on such topics, as well as the ways research protocols reproduce certain norms of sexuality, see Pat Sikes and Heather Piper, *Researching Sex and Lies in the Classroom: Allegations of Sexual Misconduct in Schools* (London: Routledge, 2010).
54. In 1992, in a case commonly referred to as Marion's case, the High Court of Australia upheld a 1986 British common-law test for establishing a minor's competence to consent to medical treatment. Following the ruling in *Gillick v West Norfolk and Wisbech Area Health Authority*, which allowed a twelve-year-old girl to consent to contraceptive advice and treatment without the approval of her mother, the High Court of Australia held that "a minor is capable of giving informed consent when he or she achieves a sufficient understanding and intelligence to enable him or her to understand fully what is proposed." This has become known as the Gillick competence test. See *Department of Health and Community Services (NT) v JWB (Marion's case)* (1992) 175 CLR 218, 237–38. In the United States, there also have existed similar mature minor exceptions in some states. See Roger J. R. Levesque, *Adolescents, Sex, and the Law: Preparing Adolescents for Responsible Citizenship* (Washington, DC: American Psychological Association, 2006), especially chap. 4.
55. Interactional and relational sociological approaches to questions of agency dovetail with what I am here highlighting as far as the importance of people's perceptions and understandings of categories, relationships, and social structures in shaping action and interaction. See, for example, Mark Rimmer, "Music, Middle Childhood and Agency: The Value of an Interactional-Relational Approach," *Childhood* 24, no. 4 (2017): 559–73.
56. Graupner, "Sexual Consent," 130, 137–39.
57. See chapter 6 for a more detailed discussion of the psychological dynamics in intergenerational sex.
58. For useful discussions of the way binary oppositions are sustained by contradiction and internal incoherence, see Eve Kosofsky Sedgwick, *Epistemology of the Closet* (Berkeley: University of California Press, 1990); and Penelope Deutscher, *Yielding Gender: Feminism, Deconstruction and the History of Philosophy* (New York: Routledge,

1997). Thanks to Elizabeth Wilson for highlighting this point and for directing me to Deutscher's text.
59. I am here indebted to a phrase of Levesque's, which is the subtitle of his book *Adolescents, Sex, and the Law: Preparing Adolescents for Responsible Citizenship*.
60. Shakeshaft, *Educator Sexual Misconduct*, 49; emphasis added.
61. Deborah Hope and Tracy Ong, "Hey, Teacher, Leave Those Kids Alone," *The Australian*, December 17, 2005, 19.
62. Sharon Lamb, *The Trouble with Blame: Victims, Perpetrators, and Responsibility* (Cambridge, MA: Harvard University Press, 1996), 7–8.
63. Lamb, *The Trouble with Blame*, 43.
64. *R v. D'Addario*, 46.
65. *The Queen v. Natalina D'Addario*, 38.
66. Peter Coviello, "The Sexual Child; or, This American Life," *Raritan* 27, no. 4 (2008): 134–57.
67. Barad, *Meeting the Universe Halfway*, 208.
68. Annemarie Mol, *The Body Multiple: Ontology in Medical Practice* (Durham, NC: Duke University Press, 2002), 157.
69. See Laura Kipnis, *Unwanted Advances: Sexual Paranoia Comes to Campus* (New York: Harper, 2017).
70. See, for example, Denise Cuthbert and Fiona Zammit, "Universities Need to Rethink Policy on Student-Staff Relationships," *Conversation*, November 20, 2017, https://theconversation.com/universities-need-to-rethink-policy-on-student-staff-relationships-86623.
71. Samuel Burgum, Sebastian Raza, and Jorge Vasquez, "An Interview with Wendy Brown: Redoing the Demos," *Theory, Culture and Society* 34, nos. 7–8 (2017): 230.
72. K. C. Johnson and Stuart Taylor Jr., *The Campus Rape Frenzy: The Attack on Due Process at America's Universities* (New York: Encounter Books, 2017); Kipnis, *Unwanted Advances*.
73. As is the dominant cultural insistence on mandating close-in-age sex.
74. Of professor-student relations in her days (and mine) as a student, Laura Kipnis says: "But somehow power seemed a lot less powerful back then. The gulf between students and faculty wasn't a shark-filled moat; a misstep wasn't fatal. We partied together, drank and got high together, slept together. The teachers may have been older and more accomplished, but you didn't feel they could take advantage of you because of it. How would they?" See Kipnis, "Sexual Paranoia Strikes Academe," *Chronicle Review—Chronicle of Higher Education*, February 27, 2015, 2. See also Kipnis, *Unwanted Advances*; and Janet Halley, "The Move to Affirmative Consent," *Signs: Journal of Women in Culture and Society* 42, no. 1 (Autumn 2016): 257–79.
75. For my part-autobiographical elaboration of the experience of teacher/professor–student power relations that contradicts the presumptions of positions-of-authority model, see Steven Angelides, "Can Sex Be Educated in a Culture of Fear, Victimhood, and Trauma?," keynote address, Sex/Education conference, New Delhi, November 18, 2017.

CHAPTER SIX
1. Kate Legge, "Teachers' Pets," *The Australian, Weekend Australian Magazine*, November 11, 2006, 28–29.
2. William Saletan, "Teachers' Pets?" *Slate*, January 16, 2006, https://slate.com/technology/2006/01/are-teachers-who-sleep-with-boys-getting-off.html.
3. Had Dunbar reached the general age of consent, sexual relations with Ellis would have remained an offense because Ellis was a teacher. See Victorian Crimes Act 1958.

4. See *R v. Hopper* (2005) Victorian Supreme Court of Appeal (VSCA) 214: 1–41.
5. Sheila L. Cavanagh, in *Sexing the Teacher: School Sex Scandals and Queer Pedagogies* (Vancouver: UBC Press, 2007), 87, refers to the narrative of the "lucky bastard," and it is one that also has had a particular resonance in mainstream "Aussie" vernacular in recent decades. The phrase "lucky SOB"—that is, lucky son of a bitch—is another colloquialism to refer to this fantasy. See M. Smerconish, "Does the Punishment Fit the Look?" *Philadelphia Daily News*, March 22, 2007, 21.
6. The *60 Minutes* television interview was aired on November 20, 2005. All quotes from the interview are cited from the transcript. See *60 Minutes*, transcript, "Breach of Trust," November 20, 2005, http://sixtyminutes.ninemsn.com.au/sixtyminutes/stories/2005_11_20/story_1567.asp.
7. Quoted in *R v. Ellis*, Victorian County Court, 2004, 70.
8. Quoted in Farrah Tomazin, "I Pursued Teacher, Says Boy," *The Age*, September 1, 2004, http://www.theage.com.au/articles/2004/08/31/1093938921166.html.
9. *60 Minutes*, "Breach of Trust."
10. Quoted in "Tearful Teacher Jailed for Sex with Boy, 15," *Sydney Morning Herald*, May 5, 2005, http://www.smh.com.au/news/National/Tearful-teacher-jailed-for-sex-with-boy-15/2005/05/05/1115092602035.html.
11. "Support Groups Critical of Sentence in Teacher 'Affair' Case," transcript, *World Today*, Australian Broadcasting Corporation, November 11, 2004, http://www.abc.net.au/worldtoday/content/2004/s1241300.htm.
12. Quoted in Chee Chee Leung, "Outcry from Crime Victim Groups as Teacher Avoids Jail," *The Age*, November 11, 2004, 3.
13. Quoted in Gary Hughes, "Female Sex Offenders Let Off Lightly?" *The Australian*, July 26, 2006, http://blogs.theaustralian.news.com.au/garyhughes/index.php/the australian/comments/female_sex_offenders_let_off_lightly/.
14. *D. P. P. v. Ellis* (2005), Victorian Supreme Court of Appeal 105, 3.
15. *D. P. P. v. Ellis*, 7.
16. Two other judges formed the appeal panel for the case, each affirming Callaway's reasoning.
17. Sentencing Act 1991 (Vic).
18. *R v. Ellis*, 76.
19. Law Institute of Victoria, "Response to Sentencing Advisory Council's Interim Report on Suspended Sentences," submission, November 23, 2005, 5.
20. *D. P. P. v. Ellis*, 6.
21. Sentencing Act 1991 (Vic), S.5 [2c].
22. Sentencing Act 1991 (Vic), S.5 [2c].
23. Sentencing Act 1991 (Vic), S.5 [2c].
24. *D. P. P. v. Ellis*, 9.
25. It's also the case certain moral values are being imposed vis-à-vis the denunciation of conduct; however, it seems clear to me that moral denunciations are dependent on prior assumptions about harm.
26. *D. P. P. v. Ellis*, 3.
27. *R v. Ellis*, 70.
28. Andrea Nelson and Pamela Oliver, "Gender and the Construction of Consent in Child-Adult Sexual Contact: Beyond Gender Neutrality and Male Monopoly," *Gender and Society* 12, no. 5 (1998): 555.
29. Bruce Rind, "An Empirical Examination of Sexual Relations between Adolescents and Adults: They Differ from Those between Children and Adults and Should Be Treated

Separately," *Journal of Psychology and Human Sexuality* 16, nos. 2–3 (2005): 55. For further references on nontraumatic experiences of teenage boys in sexual relationships with women, see chapter 5.
30. Kay L. Levine, "No Penis, No Problem," *Fordham Urban Law Journal* 33, no. 2 (2006): 400.
31. Nelson and Oliver, "Gender and the Construction of Consent"; Bruce Rind, Philip Tromovitch, and Robert Bauserman, "A Meta-analytic Examination of Assumed Properties of Child Sexual Abuse Using College Samples," *Psychological Bulletin* 124, no. 1 (1998): 22–53.
32. See, for example, LeRoy G. Schultz and Preston Jones, "Sexual Abuse of Children: Issues for Social Service and Health Professionals," *Child Welfare* 62, no. 2 (1983): 99–108; and Gregory S. Fritz, Kim Stoll, and Nathaniel N. Wagner, "A Comparison of Males and Females Who Were Sexually Molested as Children," *Journal of Sex and Marital Therapy* 7, no. 1 (1981): 54–59.
33. Donald James West and T. P. Woodhouse, "Sexual Encounters Between Boys and Adults," in *Children's Sexual Encounters with Adults*, ed. C. K. Li, Donald James West, and T. P. Woodhouse (New York: Prometheus, 1993), quoted in Rind, Tromovitch, and Bauserman, "A Meta-analytic Examination," 43. For further research highlighting the voluntary and nontraumatic nature of many boys' experiences of sex with women, see also C. L. Nash and Donald James West, "Sexual Molestation of Young Girls: A Retrospective Survey," in *Sexual Victimization*, ed. West (Brookfield, VT: Gower Publishing, 1985); and Denise A. Hines and David Finkelhor, "Statutory Sex Crime Relationships between Juveniles and Adults: A Review of Social Scientific Research," *Aggression and Violent Behavior* 12, no. 3 (2007): 308.
34. Nelson and Oliver, "Gender and the Construction of Consent," 572.
35. Nelson and Oliver, 572.
36. Rind, "An Empirical Examination"; Hines and Finkelhor, "Statutory Sex Crime Relationships."
37. *R v. Hopper*.
38. Karin A. Martin, *Puberty, Sexuality, and the Self: Boys and Girls at Adolescence* (New York: Routledge, 1996).
39. In a more recent nationally representative sample of 820 US adolescents between fourteen and seventeen years of age, one study found that a significantly higher proportion of "males (73.8%) reported masturbation than females (48.1%)." Cynthia L. Robbins, Vanessa Schick, Michael Reece, Debra Herbenick, Stephanie A. Sanders, Brian Dodge, and J. Dennis Fortenberry, "Prevalence, Frequency, and Associations of Masturbation with Partnered Sexual Behaviors among US Adolescents," *Archives of Pediatric Adolescent Medicine* 165, no. 12 (December 2011): 1087.
40. See Robert C. Sorensen, *Adolescent Sexuality in Contemporary America (The Sorensen Report)* (New York: World Publishing, 1973).
41. *R v. Ellis*, 70.
42. Martin, *Puberty, Sexuality, and the Self*, 13–14.
43. *60 Minutes*, "Breach of Trust."
44. There was also clearly no shortage of pleasure, which is also a crucial factor to consider when theorizing recognition and harm.
45. Quoted in "Tearful Teacher Jailed."
46. See Cavanagh, *Sexing the Teacher*.
47. Quoted in Wendy Koch, "More Women Charged in Sex Cases," *USA Today*, November 30, 2005, http://usatoday30.usatoday.com/news/nation/2005-11-29-women-sex-crimes_x.htm.

48. Quoted in James Bone, "Courts Get Tough on Women Who Have Sex with Boys," *Times*, December 1, 2005, http://www.thetimes.co.uk/tto/news/world/americas/article 1999945.ece.
49. *60 Minutes*, "Breach of Trust."
50. Legge, "Teachers' Pets," 28.
51. Ian Munro, "The Harm When Women Prey on Boys," *The Age*, March 18, 2006, 4.
52. Munro, 4.
53. Legge, "Teachers' Pets," 28–29.
54. Quoted in Legge, "Teachers' Pets," 30.
55. See Nelson and Oliver, "Gender and the Construction of Consent," 554–77.
56. Mark Cowling and Paul Reynolds, introduction to *Making Sense of Sexual Consent*, ed. Cowling and Reynolds (Aldershot, UK: Ashgate, 2004), 5.
57. Hines and Finkelhor, "Statutory Sex Crime Relationships," 308. See also Levine, "No Penis, No Problem"; Lynn M. Phillips, "Recasting Consent: Agency and Victimization in Adult-Teen Relationships," in *New Versions of Victims: Feminists Struggle with the Concept*, ed. Sharon Lamb (New York: New York University Press, 1999).
58. Hines and Finkelhor, "Statutory Sex Crime Relationships," 303.
59. Phillips, "Recasting Consent"; Nelson and Oliver, "Gender and the Construction of Consent."
60. See, for example, Hines and Finkelhor, "Statutory Sex Crime Relationships"; Levine, "No Penis, No Problem"; Phillips, "Recasting Consent"; Nelson and Oliver, "Gender and the Construction of Consent."
61. Levine, "No Penis, No Problem," 400–401. Levine also cites Nelson and Oliver's study.
62. Levine, 399n191; emphasis added.
63. Levine, 364.
64. Hannah Frith and Celia Kitzinger, "Reformulating Sexual Script Theory," *Theory and Psychology* 11, no. 2 (2001): 211.
65. See John H. Gagnon and William Simon, *Sexual Conduct: The Social Sources of Human Sexuality* (Chicago: Aldine, 1973).
66. Nancy J. Chodorow, *The Power of Feelings: Personal Meaning in Psychoanalysis, Gender, and Culture* (New Haven, CT: Yale University Press, 1999).
67. Frith and Kitzinger, "Reformulating Sexual Script Theory," 213.
68. Frith and Kitzinger, 213.
69. Nelson and Oliver, "Gender and the Construction of Consent," 573.
70. Quoted in Mark Bracher, *Lacan, Discourse, and Social Change: A Psychoanalytic Cultural Criticism* (Ithaca, NY: Cornell University Press, 1993), 10; emphasis added.
71. Also operating, I suspect, is a certain uneasiness about this "script" of masculine sexual prowess.
72. Thanks to Jane Connell for helping me understand this point about agency in relation to myself, and thus being able to think through it here.
73. Nelson and Oliver, "Gender and the Construction of Consent," 556.
74. Nelson and Oliver, 557.
75. Nelson and Oliver, 573.
76. Discussion with Barbara Baird has been helpful in thinking through this idea about the colonization of discursive space. Roger N. Lancaster, in *Sex Panic and the Punitive State* (Berkeley: University of California Press, 2011), 11, argues that the "tethering of punishment to imagined risks and anticipated future victimizations, as opposed to actual deeds and proven harm, would seem to set the law on a slippery slope." For

examples of female-teacher-and-male-student sex scandals in which boys have taken the initiative, see Cavanagh, *Sexing the Teacher*.

77. Quoted in Legge, "Teachers' Pets," 28.
78. Nelson and Oliver, "Gender and the Construction of Consent," 571.
79. Discussion with Marion J. Campbell has been helpful in formulating this point. See Campbell, "Fixing Consent," paper delivered at the Cultural Studies Association of Australasia National Conference, University of Technology, Sydney, November 26, 2005.
80. Nelson and Oliver, "Gender and the Construction of Consent," 572.
81. Roger J. R. Levesque, *Adolescents, Sex, and the Law: Preparing Adolescents for Responsible Citizenship* (Washington, DC: American Psychological Association, 2000), 42.
82. Quoted in Sam B. Garkawe, "The Effects of Victim Impact Statements on Sentencing Decisions," paper delivered at the Sentencing: Principles, Perspectives and Possibilities conference, Canberra, February 10–12, 2006, https://epubs.scu.edu.au/law_pubs/41/, 2.
83. Sentencing (Further Amendment) Act 2005 (Vic), S.1(a).
84. *D. P. P. v. Ellis*, 7.
85. *D. P. P. v. Ellis*, 12.
86. A. Sanders, C. Hoyle, and R. Morgan, "Victim Impact Statements: Don't Work, Can't Work," *Criminal Law Review* (June 2001): 451.
87. Sharon Marcus, "Fighting Bodies, Fighting Words: A Theory and Politics of Rape Prevention," in *Feminists Theorize the Political*, ed. Judith Butler and Joan W. Scott (New York: Routledge, 1992); Nicola Gavey, "'I Wasn't Raped, but . . .': Revisiting Definitional Problems in Sexual Victimization," in Lamb, *New Versions of Victims*.
88. Quoted in Craig Binnie and Elissa Hunt, "Sex Teacher Kept Contact to Very End," *Hobart Mercury*, May 6, 2005, 4.
89. Quoted in "Appeal Fails in Teacher Sex Case," *The Age*, September 9, 2005, http://www.theage.com.au/news/national/appeal-fails-in-teacher-sex-case/2005/09/09/1125772671345.html.
90. I would argue further, of course, that competent consent ought to be a defense in positions-of-authority laws.
91. Crimes (Sexual Offences) Act 1980 (Vic), 859; emphasis added.
92. Joan W. Scott, "Deconstructing Equality-versus-Difference: Or, The Uses of Poststructuralist Theory for Feminism," *Feminist Studies* 14, no. 1 (1988): 38.
93. Scott, "Deconstructing Equality-versus-Difference," 48.
94. Quoted in Regina Graycar and Jenny Morgan, *The Hidden Gender of Law*, 2nd ed. (Annandale: Federation Press, 2002), vii.
95. See, for example, Ann J. Cahill, *Rethinking Rape* (Ithaca, NY: Cornell University Press, 2001), 34.
96. Law Reform Commission of Victoria, *Sexual Offences against Children* (Melbourne: Commission, 1988), 18. See also Hines and Finkelhor, "Statutory Sex Crime Relationships."
97. *60 Minutes*, "Breach of Trust."
98. *R v. Ellis*, 70.
99. Sentencing (Further Amendment) Act 2005 (Vic), S.1.
100. "Hulls: No More Suspended Sentences for Serious Crimes," media release, Victorian Attorney-General's Office, August 22, 2006.
101. "Hulls: No More Suspended Sentences."

102. Sentencing (Suspended Sentences) Act 2006 (Vic), 1.
103. Sentencing Amendment Act 2010; Sentencing Amendment (Abolition of Suspended Sentences and Other Matters) Act 2013.
104. Sentencing Act 1991, S.5 (2).
105. It scarcely needs reiterating that, in our zeal to prosecute young people for adult crimes, we are certainly willing to bestow them with agency and responsibility.
106. Cavanagh, in *Sexing the Teacher*, 19, offers a different argument for the media focus on female teacher offenders. She sees it as a cultural defense of white, "reproductive, heterosexual futurity." Cavanagh argues that the white female teacher is issuing a direct challenge to central pillars of heteronormativity: marriage, the nuclear family, "human reproduction for racial and national betterment," childhood sexual innocence, appropriate age-stratified and age-concordant sexual interactions, and the repudiation of "unproductive pleasures." One of the primary social anxieties, according to Cavanagh, is that "boys will be feminized" (75). Without disputing this as one aspect of the sex panic, I argue that the "lucky bastard" is as central a target, perhaps even more. For a comparison of Cavanagh's arguments and mine, see Steven Angelides, "Hot for Teacher: The Cultural Erotics and Anxieties of Adolescent Sexuality," *Media International Australia* 135 (May 2010): 71–81.
107. "People are different from each another" is, of course, the first of Sedgwick's famous "axioms." Eve Kosofsky Sedgwick, *Epistemology of the Closet* (Berkeley: University of California Press, 1990), 22.
108. John Law, "What's Wrong with a One-World World," paper presented at the Center for the Humanities, Wesleyan University, Middletown, Connecticut, September 19, 2011, http://www.heterogeneities.net/publications/Law2011WhatsWrongWithAOneWorldWorld.pdf, 3.
109. R. Danielle Egan and Gail Hawkes argue something similar in "The Problem with Protection: Or, Why We Need to Move towards Recognition and the Sexual Agency of Children," *Continuum: Journal of Media and Cultural Studies* 23, no. 3 (2009): 397.
110. Karen Barad, *Meeting the Universe Halfway: Quantum Physics and the Entanglement of Matter and Meaning* (Durham, NC: Duke University Press, 2007), ix.
111. Annemarie Mol, *The Body Multiple: Ontology in Medical Practice* (Durham, NC: Duke University Press, 2002); Law, "What's Wrong with a One-World World."
112. See Elizabeth A. Wilson, *Psychosomatic: Feminism and the Neurological Body* (Durham, NC: Duke University Press, 2004).
113. On ontological politics, see Mol, *The Body Multiple*, viii; and Annemarie Mol, "Ontological Politics: A Word and Some Questions," *Sociological Review* 47 (May 1999): 74–89.

CHAPTER SEVEN
1. *Miller v. Skumanick*, 605 F. Supp. 2d 634 (M.D. Pa. 2009), 2.
2. *Miller v. Mitchell*, 598 F.3d 139 (3d Cir. 2010), 8–9.
3. *Miller v. Skumanick*, 3.
4. According to the families of these three girls, Skumanick did not send letters to those who originally disseminated the pictures (*Miller v. Skumanick*, 3).
5. *Miller v. Mitchell*, 6.
6. There had been other sexting-related charges and criminal cases in the United States prior to this one, with a few resulting in convictions. These cases went largely unnoticed in the media.

7. Liz Porter, "Malice in Wonderland," *The Age*, August 10, 2008, http://www.theage.com.au/news/technology/malice-in-wonderland/2008/08/09/1218139163632.html. See also Lucy Battersby, "Sexting: Fears as Teens Targeted," July 10, 2008, http://www.smh.com.au/articles/2008/07/10/1215282979671.html.
8. Elizabeth C. Eraker, "Stemming Sexting: Sensible Legal Approaches to Teenagers' Exchange of Self-Produced Pornography," *Berkeley Technology Law Journal* 25 (2010): 573.
9. "'Sexting' the Result of Porno-Drenched Society," *USA Today* [magazine] 138, no. 2770 (July 2009): 8.
10. Kimberlianne Podlas, "The 'Legal Epidemiology' of the Teen Sexting Epidemic: How the Media Influenced a Legislative Outbreak," *Pittsburgh Journal of Technology Law and Policy* 12, no. 1 (2011): 1–48.
11. R. Richmond, "Sexting May Place Teens at Risk," *New York Times*, March 26, 2009, http://gadgetwise.blogs.nytimes.com/2009/03/26/sexting-may-place-teens-at-legal-risk/; D. St. George, "Sending of Explicit Photos Can Land Teens in Legal Fix," *Washington Post*, May 7, 2009, http://www.washingtonpost.com/wp-dyn/content/article/2009/05/06/AR2009050604088.html; D. Searcey, "A Lawyer, Some Teens and a Fight over 'Sexting,'" *Wall Street Journal*, April 21, 2009, http://online.wsj.com/article/SB124026115528336397.html.
12. St. George, "Sending of Explicit Photos."
13. Battersby, "Sexting: Fears as Teens Targeted."
14. *Law & Order: Special Victims Unit*, season 10, episode 20, "Crush," aired May 5, 2009. Additionally, *The Early Show* on CBS, *Nightline* on ABC, and *Today* on NBC each ran features on sexting in 2009. See Clay Calvert, "Sex, Cell Phones, Privacy, and the First Amendment: When Children Become Child Pornographers and the Lolita Effect Undermines the Law," *Commlaw Conspectus* 18 (2009): 21–22.
15. Quoted in St. George, "Sending of Explicit Photos."
16. By *judicialization* I mean simply that the phenomenon of teenage sexting is currently inextricable from discussions about the law and criminality.
17. I have borrowed the phrase *displaced conversation* from Carole S. Vance, "Thinking Trafficking, Thinking Sex," *GLQ* 17, no. 1 (2011): 135–43. On Foucault's notion of strategies as features of power relations, see Michel Foucault, *The History of Sexuality, Volume 1: An Introduction* (London: Penguin, 1990), 94–95.
18. Philip Jenkins, *Moral Panic: Changing Concepts of the Child Molester in Modern America* (New Haven, CT: Yale University Press, 1998), 6. Janice M. Irvine, in "Transient Feelings: Sex Panics and the Politics of Emotions," *GLQ* 14, no. 1 (2008): 19, argues something similar when she says of sex panics that they "rely heavily of tales about sexual groups or issues that use distortion, hyperbole, or outright fabrication." On moral panics and exaggerations, see also Stanley Cohen, *Folk Devils and Moral Panics*, 3rd ed. (New York: Routledge, 2011), xxxix, 25–34.
19. NSW Government, "Safe Sexting: No Such Thing." The brochure is no longer available on the NSW government website; however, it is easy to find with a Google search of the title (see, for example, https://web3.canterburg-h.schools.nsw.edu.au/Documents%20for%20Uploading/Ongoing%20Files/Technology%20and%20Laptop%20Related/Sexting%20Fact%20Sheet.pdf). For another variation on this theme, see the iPad app designed by an Australian secondary school: "There's No Such Thing as Safe Sexting!," Echuca College, May 26, 2014, http://www.echucacollege.vic.edu.au/general-news/there-s-no-such-thing-as-safe-sexting/.

20. National Crime Prevention Council (NCPC), "Sexting: How Can Teens Stay Safe," accessed August 9, 2018, http://archive.ncpc.org/resources/files/pdf/internet-safety/NCPC-FactSheet1.pdf.
21. Podlas, "'Legal Epidemiology' of Sexting Epidemic," 16; National Campaign to Prevent Teen and Unplanned Pregnancy (NCPTUP), *Sex and Tech: Results from a Survey of Teens and Young Adults*, October 3, 2008, https://drvc.org/pdf/protecting_children/sextech_summary.pdf.
22. A Cox Communications/Harris survey of 655 teens between thirteen and eighteen years of age found that 19% had sent or received sexually suggestive pictures, and an MTV/Associated Press online survey found that 24% of fourteen- to seventeen-year-olds were involved in some form of sexting. See Podlas, "'Legal Epidemiology' of Sexting Epidemic," 18. A 2015 study in Pennsylvania of 6,021 teenagers found that 29% of ninth- to twelfth-grade students had consensually sexted. See Anne S. Frankel, Sarah Bauerle Bass, Freda Patterson, Ting Dai, and Deanna Brown, "Sexting, Risk Behavior, and Mental Health in Adolescents: An Examination of 2015 Pennsylvania Youth Risk Behavior Survey Data," *Journal of School Health* 88, no. 3 (March 2018): 190–99.
23. Amanda Lenhart, "Teens and Sexting: How and Why Minor Teens Are Sending Sexually Suggestive Nude or Nearly Nude Images via Text Messaging" (Washington, DC: Pew Research Centre, December 15, 2009), 2.
24. Kimberly J. Mitchell, David Finkelhor, Lisa M. Jones, and Janis Wolak, "Prevalence and Characteristics of Youth Sexting: A National Study," *Pediatrics* 129, no. 1 (2012): 17.
25. Jessica Ringrose, Rosalind Gill, Sonia Livingstone, and Laura Harvey, *A Qualitative Study of Children, Young People and "Sexting,"* report, National Society for Prevention to Children, May 2012, 11.
26. Jenkins, *Moral Panic*, 6.
27. NSW Government, "Safe Sexting: No Such Thing."
28. NCPC, "Sexting: How Can Teens Stay Safe."
29. Janis Wolak, David Finkelhor, and Kimberly J. Mitchell, "How Often Are Teens Arrested for Sexting? Data from a National Sample of Police Cases," *Pediatrics* 129, no. 1 (2012): 9.
30. For a critique of the way sexting is treated in media reports and social commentaries as a unitary phenomenon, see Jo Moran-Ellis, "Sexting, Intimacy and Criminal Acts: Translating Teenage Sexualities," in *Policing Sex*, ed. Paul Johnson and Derek Dalton (Abingdon, UK: Routledge, 2012), 115–32.
31. Irvine, "Transient Feelings," 23.
32. *Megan's Story* was developed by the organization ThinkUKnow, which is "an Internet safety program delivering interactive training to parents, carers and teachers through primary and secondary schools across Australia using a network of accredited trainers. . . . Created by the UK Child Exploitation and Online Protection (CEOP) Centre, ThinkUKnow Australia has been developed by the Australian Federal Police (AFP) and Microsoft Australia." ThinkUKnow, Australian Federal Police, accessed November 2018, https://www.afp.gov.au/what-we-do/campaigns/thinkuknow. South Eastern Centre against Sexual Assault (SECASA), *Sexting: Information for Parents*, September 30, 2011, https://www.secasa.com.au/assets/Documents/sexting-information-for-parents.pdf, also highlights the concern about jeopardizing job and university prospects. Notably, the lesson plans for *Megan's Story* are still available on the Victorian state government's website for download, https://www.parliament.vic

.gov.au/images/stories/committees/lawrefrom/isexting/subs/S57_-_AFP_-_Attachment_2.pdf.
33. Wolak, Finkelhor, and Mitchell, "How Often Are Teens Arrested for Sexting?" 9.
34. The risks are also much greater for the reputations of adult sexters, as attested by the high-profile sexting scandals surrounding sportspersons such as cricketer Shane Warne and golfer Tiger Woods.
35. Jenkins, *Moral Panic*, 7.
36. Cohen, *Folk Devils*, xxxix.
37. *Cynthia A. Logan and Albert M. Logan v. Sycamore Community School Board of Education, Paul Payne, and City of Montgomery*, civil complaint and jury demand, February 12, 2009, case no. 1:09-cv-885, U.S. District Court (S.D. Ohio).
38. Quoted in Katy Hastings, "Teenager Commits Suicide after 'Sexting' a Nude Photo to Her Boyfriend Made Her Life a Misery," DailyMail.com, March 11, 2009, http://www.dailymail.co.uk/tvshowbiz/article-1161112/Teenager-commits-suicide-sexting-nude-photo-boyfriend-life-misery.html.
39. *Logan v. Sycamore*, 7.
40. *Logan v. Sycamore*, 7. The civil suit was settled and Logan's parents received $154,000.
41. *Logan v. Sycamore*, 6–7.
42. Podlas, "'Legal Epidemiology' of Sexting Epidemic," 33.
43. "Sexting Youths Dial Up a Storm," *Sunday Times*, March 22, 2009, 12.
44. NSW Government, "Safe Sexting: No Such Thing"; emphasis added.
45. "ThinkUKnow Australia, "Sexting Education Video—Megan's Story," last accessed November 2018, https://www.parliament.vic.gov.au/images/stories/committees/lawrefrom/isexting/subs/S57_-_AFP_-_Attachment_2.pdf; emphasis added.
46. "Sexting Education Video," 2; emphasis added. There are five sample discussion questions in the teacher resource:

    1. Why do you think Megan took that photo and sent it on her mobile phone?
    2. What should her boyfriend have done with Megan's photo?
    3. How did Megan's classmates contribute to the problem?
    4. How will Megan's actions, and those of her classmates, affect her in the future?
    5. Would things have been different if a boy had sent an image of himself?

47. See Danielle Tyson, Amy Shields Dobson, and Mary Lou Rasmussen, "'Sexting' Teens: Decriminalising Young People's Sexual Practices," *Conversation*, September 28, 2012, http://theconversation.edu.au/sexting-teens-decriminalising-young-peoples-sexual-practices-8922; and Jessica Ringrose, Laura Harvey, Rosalind Gill, and Sonia Livingstone, "Teen Girls, Sexual Double Standards and 'Sexting': Gendered Value in Digital Image Exchange," *Feminist Theory* 14, no. 3 (2013): 305–23.
48. Amy Adele Hasinoff, *Sexting Panic: Rethinking Criminalization, Privacy, and Consent* (Champaign: University of Illinois Press, 2015).
49. NSW Government, "Safe Sexting: No Such Thing."
50. NCPC, "Sexting: How Can Teens Stay Safe."
51. NCPC.
52. They were each charged with "one count of producing, directing or promoting a photography or representation that they knew to include the sexual conduct of a child." *A. H. v. State*, 949 So. 2d 234, 235 (Fla. Dist. Ct. App. 2007).
53. Florida statutes § 827.071 (3). The Florida legal age of consent for sexual contact is eighteen years old. Close-in-age exemptions allow a person twenty-three years of age or younger to have sex with a minor age sixteen or seventeen. It is a second-degree

felony for a person twenty-four years of age or older to engage in sexual activity with a person sixteen or seventeen years of age.
54. *A. H. v. State.*
55. *A. H. v. State.*
56. *A. H. v. State.*
57. *A. H. v. State.*
58. Erich Goode and Nachman Ben-Yehuda, "Moral Panic," in *The Handbook of Deviant Behavior*, ed. Clifton D. D. Bryant (New York: Routledge, 2012), 47.
59. Family and Community Services, New South Wales Government, "Sexting and Cyber-Safety: Protecting Your Child Online," September 2011, http://www.community.nsw.gov.au/__data/assets/pdf_file/0006/319047/sexting_cyber_safety.pdf.
60. *A. H. v. State.* Florida statute § 827.071 (3) is being cited here.
61. Irvine, "Transient Feelings," 5.
62. Irvine, 2, 11.
63. Silvan S. Tomkins, *Affect Imagery Consciousness: The Complete Edition*, 2 vols. (New York: Springer, 2008), 1: 63.
64. Irvine, "Transient Feelings," draws on the work of Erving Goffman to talk about emotions as performed dramaturgically.
65. Phil Mollon, in *Shame and Jealousy: The Hidden Turmoils* (London: Karnac, 2002), 19–20, is among a host of psychoanalysts and psychologists who remind us that "shame and the fear of shame are amongst the most powerful of human aversive experiences." Perhaps it is little wonder, then, that the recruitment of fear and shame is often such a powerful mechanism for shaping behavior.
66. Again, I am referring here to Foucauldian performative strategies of power (as "both intentional and non-subjective"). See Michel Foucault, *The History of Sexuality, Volume 1: An Introduction*. (London: Penguin, 1990: 94–95).
67. Judith Duffy, "Police to Target the 'Sexting' Generation," *Sunday Herald* (Scotland), January 22, 2012, http://www.heraldscotland.com/mobile/news/home-news/police-to-target-the-sexting-generation.16547866?_=4a934273b8b55e10bc9ef5b13eae098792114786; emphasis added.
68. Irvine, "Transient Feelings," 21.
69. "A Youthful Mistake Shouldn't Be a Felony," editorial, *St. Petersburg* (FL) *Times*, May 1, 2011, 2P, quoted in Podlas, "'Legal Epidemiology' of Sexting Epidemic," 8–9n59.
70. National Center for Missing and Exploited Children (NCMEC), "Tips to Prevent Sexting for Parents." See also NCMEC, "Tips to Prevent Sexting for Teens," 2009, http://www.netsmartz.org/tipsheets (registration required).
71. Penny Marshall, "Generation Sexting: What Teenage Girls Really Get Up To on the Internet Should Chill Every Parent," *Daily Mail*, March 18, 2009, http://www.dailymail.co.uk/femail/article-1162777/Generation-sexting-What-teenage-girls-really-internet-chill-parent.html.
72. In the United States, some states have introduced diversionary programs for teenage sexters that are designed to protect them from harsh child pornography convictions. The youth are diverted into juvenile courts and/or an education program. Podlas, "'Legal Epidemiology' of Sexting Epidemic," 41–42. As Kath Albury and Kate Crawford note, in "Sexting, Consent and Young People's Ethics: Beyond *Megan's Story*," *Continuum: Journal of Media and Cultural Studies* 26, no. 3 (June 2012): 471, "The notion of diversionary education still frames teenage sexting as deviant and potentially shameful."

73. Albury and Crawford, "Sexting, Consent and Young People's Ethics," 471. See also Ringrose et al., "Teen Girls, Sexual Double Standards" for a discussion of gendered shaming.
74. SECASA, "Sexting: Information for Parents."
75. SECASA.
76. NCMEC, "Tips to Prevent Sexting."
77. NCMEC.
78. "To Deal with 'Sexting,' XXXtra Discretion Is Advised," *USA Today*, May 5, 2009, A10. Descriptions of teenage sexting as "stupid" are commonplace in the media.
79. "The Sex Toy Hiding in Your Purse," Cosmopolitan.com, June 17, 2008, http://www.cosmopolitan.com/sex-love/tips-moves/The-Sex-Toy-Hiding-in-Your-Purse. See also Jessica Leshnoff, "Sexting Not Just for Kids," AARP, August 29, 2016, https://www.aarp.org/relationships/love-sex/info-11-2009/sexting_not_just_for_kids.html.
80. Ample research has demonstrated that the cognitive capacities, the abstract reasoning, and the decision-making abilities of many minors as young as fourteen years of age equal those of adults. For some notable examples, see Daniel Offer, "In Defense of Adolescents," *Journal of the American Medical Association* 257 (1987): 3407–8; Daniel Offer and Kimberly A. Schonert-Reichl, "Debunking the Myths of Adolescence: Findings from Recent Research," *Journal of the American Academy of Child and Adolescent Psychiatry* 31 (1992): 1003–14; M. A. Males, *The Scapegoat Generation: America's War on Adolescents* (Monroe, MA: Common Courage Press, 1996); Males, *Framing Youth: 10 Myths about the Next Generation* (Monroe, MA: Common Courage Press, 1999); Roger J. R. Levesque, *Adolescents, Sex, and the Law: Preparing Adolescents for Responsible Citizenship* (Washington, DC: American Psychological Association, 2000); and Philip Graham, *The End of Adolescence* (Oxford: Oxford University Press, 2004). Graham argues that, with regard to emotional maturity, "early teens are much less emotionally mature than those in their late teens," but he goes on to claim that "all the evidence" indicates that early teens do not handle "emotionally demanding situations" as well as late teens not because of "immaturity of the brain" but because they are "not adequately prepared for the emotionally demanding experiences they may encounter" (20). Importantly, he also acknowledges what may seem like a commonsensical notion, that, at "any age, it is experience that matures us emotionally" (20).
81. *A. H. v. State.*
82. *A. H. v. State.*
83. In a number of court cases involving consensual sexting between close-in-age teenagers, where one (male) partner had reached the age of eighteen and the other was still a minor, the foreclosure of agency is neatly performed as a result of the statutory prohibition on intergenerational sex. In one of the first teen sexting cases in the United States, when a fourteen-year-old girl's request for a picture of her eighteen-year-old friend's penis was granted, her friend was convicted of "knowingly disseminating obscene material to a minor." The question of the girl's agency was not even considered. See *State of Iowa v. Jorge Canal Jr.*, 773 N.W.2d 528. Similarly, in the first Australian sexting case involving an eighteen-year-old boy, Damien Eades, and a thirteen-year-old girl, Eades was tried for "inciting a person under the age of 16 to an act of indecency" toward him after she sent him a photograph of herself nude. Because of her age, there was no question of consent and agency, and, indeed, both the defense and prosecution uncritically assumed that the girl had been "induced" to send the image. See *DPP v. Eades* [2009] NSWSC 1352; and *Eades v. Director of Public Prosecutions (NSW)* [2010] NSWCA 241.

INDEX

adolescence: and cognitive competence, 228n18; constructed as immature, xiv–xv, xxix–xxxiii, 14, 18–19, 23, 25, 30, 39, 128, 154, 160, 170–71, 174–76; as contradiction in law, 115–16, 117–19, 123, 147, 148, 153; and delinquency, 21–25, 34, 39; and gender differences in sexual development, 114; and mind/body mismatch, 39, 43–44; and neuroscience, 43–44; and premarital sex, 21–28; and premature sexualization, 24, 25, 39–40, 93; and puberty, 10, 11; rebelliousness of, 23; and sexual citizenship, 117–21; as third term, xv–xvi; as transitionality, 40, 43
Advertising Standards Authority, ix–x
agency: Barad on, 189n69; concept of, xxiii–xxiv, 124; gender differences and, 108, 109–10, 113, 123, 135–36, 144, 145; of young people, xi, xii, xiv, xv, xvi, xx, xxii, xxiii, xxvi, xxviii, xxix, xxx, xxxi, xxxiii, 3, 17–18, 35, 40–44, 87, 93, 94, 96, 112–19, 121, 123, 133–34, 136–37, 144, 148, 159, 170–72, 174–77, 185n18, 186n29, 186–87n32. *See also* under erasure
age of consent. *See under* consent
Albury, Kath, 172
Allen, Lindy, 15
Allen, Louisa, 42–43
Alliance of Revolting Feminists, 81
American Medical Association, 22
anxiety. *See* fear
Australian Pedophile Support Group, xxx, 77, 78, 80, 84, 97, 209n16

Barad, Karen, xxiii, 111–12, 124, 189nn68–69
Barber, Asa, 83
Bashford, Alison, 30
Bauserman, Robert, 134
Bay-Cheng, Laina, 187n32
Beach, Frank, 48
Bender, L., 47–48
Benjamin, Jessica, 136
Ben-Yehuda, Nachman, 168
Bernstein, Robin, 187n33
Biddulph, Steve, 6, 12
Blau, A., 47–48
Blum, Robert, 44
Bolt, Andrew, 4
Bravehearts, 2, 130
Bray, Abigail, 192–93n45, 195–96n95
Breuer, Josef, 61
British Medical Association, 22, 27, 28
Brown, Wendy, 125
Bruhm, Steven, xii, xix
Bryant, Anita, 74, 86
Buck, Craig, 205–6n68
Burgess, Ann Wolbert, 53, 54
Burns, Andrea, 7
Burton, Lindy, 49
Butler, Judith, 186n31

Cahill, Ann, 16
Cain, John, 92
Calderone, Mary, 33
Califia, Pat, 85, 86, 209n13
Callaway, Frank, 131, 132–33, 147–48, 149, 150

Cannold, Leslie, 7, 194n72
Cantwell, H., 206n70
Carmody, Moira, 42–43
Carr-Gregg, Michael, 138
Cavanagh, Sheila, 100, 105, 216n31, 219n5, 223n106
Chauncey, George, xvii
child pornography, xix, xxxiii, 3, 4, 5, 8, 46, 74, 75, 76, 77, 85, 86, 95, 157, 158, 162, 166–67, 168, 170, 172–74, 195n5, 209n13, 227n72
child prostitution, 75, 76, 77
child sexual abuse: children's sense of agency and, 64–66; historical reinterpretation of, 46; increase in reporting of, 45, 82; therapy for, 63–69; trauma of, 63–69
child sexual abuse movement: and childhood innocence, xxii–xxiii; and critique of masculinity, 80–81; and gender neutrality, 69–70; history of, xxii, 51–62; and male backlash, 82–84; model of power assumed by, xxii; 51–58, 203n6; politics of, 144, 145; rejection of Freud by, 59–62
child sexuality, x; adult contempt for, 171, 177; and adult voyeurism, 15–16; and child sexual abuse paradigm, xxiii, xxvi, xxix–xxx; emergence of, 9–11, 14, 15, 16; fear and shame of xi, xiv–xv, xvi–xvii, xxv, xxvi, xxxiii; 14–19, 41, 85, 153; as harmful, xi; history of, xxix, 47–51, 95–96; as innocent, xii, 58–59, 63; as multiple, 71, 146; signifier of, 75, 78, 86, 90, 93, 95–96, 97. *See also* under erasure
Child Welfare Advisory Council of New South Wales, 22, 27, 29, 31, 39
childhood: age as primary axis of, 153–54; and age stratification, xv, 187n34; fantasies of, xviii–xx; homogenization of, xi, xii, xv, xxvi, xxx, xxxiii, xxx, 19, 69, 123, 128, 154–55; innocence of, x, xi, xvi; xviii–xx, xxii–xxiii, 2, 3, 6, 7, 9; as multiple, 124, 146; and queer theory, xix–xxi; sexualized vs. sexual, xxii–xxiii, 15, 95
children: nude photography of, 1–3, 5, 6–13; objectification of, 16–17; as powerless, 52–53, 65, 81, 97, 102–3, 104; sexualization of, ix–x, xii, xiii, xiv, xviii, xx, xxii, 1–8; as sexually precocious, 47–49
Cocca, Carolyn, 190n80
Cohen, Lloyd, 83
Cohen, Stanley, 163, 167, 184n9

Coleman, Richard, 82, 84, 85
Collins, John, 27, 28, 34, 42
Committee to Raise Education Standards, 89
Concerned Parents Association, 89
consent: age of, xv, xxii, xxvii, xxx, xxxi, 50, 78, 85–86, 87, 90–91, 95, 97, 100–101, 103, 105, 115, 116–17, 118, 123, 127, 129, 144, 166, 167, 174, 213n105, 218n3, 226n53; children's capacity to, 15, 18–19, 46, 47, 51–53, 54, 63, 80, 81, 90, 93, 94, 97, 107, 116, 120, 121, 122, 133, 141, 145, 222n90; concept of, xxiii, xxv, 57, 58, 70, 96, 145, 146, 189n68, 202–3n6, 215n20, 217n54
Coulter, Michael, 16
Coviello, Peter, 123
Cowling, Mark, 141
Crawford, Kate, 172
Crime Victims Support Association, 130
Crowle, Elaine, 130
Curry, Norman, 91

D'Addario, Natalina, 105–14, 115, 116, 118–19, 121, 122
Dean, Tim, 3, 191n12
Deering, Rebecca, 138, 145
D'Emilio, John, xvii
de Ropp, Robert S., 50
Devine, Miranda, 1, 2
DiCaldo, Frank, xi, 185n16
Duggan, Lisa, 184n9
Dunbar, Ben, 127, 128–30, 132–33, 134, 135–37, 144, 145, 147–49, 150–51
Dworkin, Shari, 187n32

Edelman, Lee, xix, 94
Edmonds, Mike, 77, 90
Edwards, I. S., 31–32
Egan, Danielle, xi–xii, xvii, xx, 185n24, 186n29, 188n43, 190n70
Elias, Norbert, 11
Ellis, Karen, xxxii, 127, 128–34, 136–37, 138, 147, 148, 149, 150, 151, 152
emotion: performativity of, xi, xiii–xiv, xvii, xxiv–xxvi, xxix, xxxiii, 17–18, 23, 42, 95, 159, 160, 168–77
Epstein, Debbie, 104
Estrich, Susan, 102–3

Faludi, Susan, 82–83
Faulkner, Joanne, 13–14, 193n58, 195n87

Index / 231

Faust, Beatrice, 32, 197n11
fear: multiple forms of, xvii; Phillips on, xxiv–xxv; of sexual child, xxi. *See also* emotion; sex panic
Fine, Michelle, xii, 185n18
Finkelhor, David, 51–52, 53, 54, 57, 120, 134, 137–38, 141, 162, 204n39, 205n55
Fischel, Joseph, 215n20
Fishman, Sterling, 47, 51
Ford, Clelland, 48
Fordham, Robert, 90, 91
Forward, Susan, 205–6n68
Foucault, Michel, 155; on power relations, xiv, xxix, xxiii, 17, 23, 38–39, 185n27; on repressive hypothesis, 42; on sex as truth, 11; on sovereign power, xxxi, xxxii, 54, 101, 110, 189n68
Freedman, Estelle, xvii
Freud, Sigmund, xxix; on childhood sexuality, 47; and seduction theory, 59–62, 64, 207n81; on the uncanny, 11–12, 19
Frith, Hannah, 142, 143

Gagnon, John, 142–43
Gaudron, Mary, 149–50
Gavey, Nicola, 148
Gay Left Collective, 73–74, 90, 94, 208n3
Gay Legal Rights Coalition, 77, 89, 92
Gebhard, Paul H., 50
gender, as nonbinary, 189n63. *See also* adolescence; agency; sex crime; subjectivity
gender neutrality, xiv, xv, xxiii, xxxii, 69–70, 114–15, 127–28, 131, 132–33, 137, 139, 146, 147–50, 152, 153–54; and power, 14–15. *See also* sex crime
Giedd, Jay, 44
Gill, Rosalind, 186–87n32
Goode, Erich, 168
Gordon, Angus, 40
Gordon, Linda, 45, 46, 51, 71, 202–3n6
Graham, Philip, 228n80
Grech, Paul, 138
Greer, Germaine, 12–13
Groggon, Alison, 5
Groth, Nicholas, 53, 54
Grusovin, Deirdre, 87
guilt. *See* shame

Haeberle, Edwin J., 50
Hall, G. Stanley, 198n24
Hall, Janet, 6

Hall, Stuart, 184n9
Halley, Janet, xxvii, 125, 190n79
Halperin, David, 212n66
Hamilton, Clive, 4, 5
Hawkes, Gail, xii, xvii, 186n29, 188n43, 190n70
Hayes, Liz, 128–29, 138
Henson, Bill, xxvii–xxviii; art scandal involving, 1–19
Herdt, Gilbert, xxiv
Herman, Judith Lewis, 53, 54, 58, 60, 61–62, 65, 207n94
Hinch, Derryn, 4, 90
Hines, Denise, 134, 141
Hirschman, Lisa, 53, 54, 58, 60, 61–62, 65, 207n94
Hollway, Wendy, xxvii, 110–11, 112
homosexuality, equality campaigns for, 85–87, 89–90, 94–95
Hopper, Gavin, 127, 130, 131, 132, 133, 134, 135, 141, 144, 148, 150
Howells, K., 211n58
Hurley, Natasha, xii, xix

Iemma, Morris, 2, 194n72
intergenerational sex: and deferred trauma, 144–46; and gender differences, 114, 134; and harm to child, xxvii, 31, 48–49, 50, 66, 83, 84, 101, 102, 117, 128, 129, 131, 138, 139–42, 152–53; and shame, 153
Irvine, Janice, xiii, xxv, 11, 26, 29, 30, 160, 162, 168–70, 171, 185n23, 199n62, 224n18

Jackson, Margaret, 55–56
Jefferson, Tony, xxvii, 110–11
Jenkins, Henry, xix–xx, xxi
Jenkins, Philip, xvii, 78, 85, 95, 96, 161
Johnson, Richard, 104
Johnson, Sarah, 44
Johnston, Hetty, 2, 4, 5, 8, 12, 17, 130–31, 194n72
Jona, Walter, 91

Kennett, Jeff, 89
Kimmel, Michael, 82–83
Kincaid, James, xviii, xix, xxi, xxv, 4–5, 55, 56, 85, 188n46, 192n39, 205n62, 213n110
Kinsey, Alfred, 48–49
Kipnis, Laura, 125, 218n74
Kitzinger, Celia, 142, 143

Kobler, John, 21
Kovacs, Joe, 99
Kremmer, Christopher, 7

Lamb, Sharon, 64, 65, 67, 120–21
Lancaster, Roger, xviii, xx, xxii, xxvii, 97, 190n78, 221–22n76
Land of Giants, ix
Lane, Terry, 7
Laplanche, Jean, 206–7n78
law: harm of, 117, 122–23, 149, 150; performativity of, 116–17
Law, John, 154, 155
Leahy, Terry, 55, 205n58
Leary, Patrick, 138
Legge, Kate, 113, 127, 138
Lerum, Kari, 187n32
Lesko, Nancy, 40
Letourneau, Mary Kay, 99, 100
Levesque, Roger, 147
Levine, Judith, xx
Levine, Kay, 141–42
Little Red Schoolbook, The, 87

Mann, Sally, xxviii
Marcus, Sharon, 148
Marcuse, Herbert, 201n113
Marr, David, 3, 4, 9, 15
Marshall, Daniel, 212n74
Marshall, Penny, 172
Martin, Karin, 113, 135–36
Masson, Jeffrey Moussaieff, 206n76
Mayne, Stephen John, 78–79
McCarthy, Joanne, 6
McClelland, Sara, xii, 185n18
McCluskie, John, 32
McConaghy, Neil, 84
McElhenney, Amy, 102
McGeorge, John, 211n56
McNamara, Noel, 130
Medcraft, Steve, 131
Megan's Story (educational video). *See under* sexting
Melbourne Gay Teachers and Students Group, 87, 89–90, 93
Mitchell, Kimberly, 162
Mitzel, John, 96
Miu Miu, ix, x
Mohr, Richard, xviii, xxv, 191n17
Mol, Annemarie, 155
Moran, Jeffrey, 26, 41

Munro, Ian, 138
Munt, Sally, 10
Myers, Kate, 104, 109

NAMBLA. *See* North American Man/Boy Love Association
Nathanson, Donald, 10, 194n72
National Centre for Missing and Exploited Children, 172, 174
National Crime Prevention Council, 160, 162, 167
National Organization of Women, 81
Nelson, Andrea, 133, 134, 139–46
Nile, Fred, 86–87
North American Man/Boy Love Association, 77, 78, 80, 81, 85, 96, 97

objectification, definition of, 16. *See also* child sexuality
O'Farrell, Barry, 2
Ohi, Kevin, xi, xix, 185n25
Okami, Paul, xxii, 59
Olafson, Erna, 62
Oliver, Pam, 133, 134, 139–46
ontology, xiv, xxvii, 16, 55; as multiple, 71, 124, 146, 154

Paedophile Action for Liberation, 74, 78
Paedophile Information Exchange, 74, 78, 85, 97, 208n5, 209n16
Parents Victoria, 130
Pearce, John, 63, 64
pedophilia: emergence of support groups for, 74, 78; vs. hebephilia, 84–85, 94, 97, 211–12n61; medical definition of, 84; social alarm about, 73–79, 84, 89–91
People against Lenient Sentencing, 131
Pezzot-Pearce, Terry, 63, 64
Phillips, Adam, xxiv–xxv
Plummer, Ken, 97
Podlas, Kimberlianne, 161, 164
Pontalis, J. B., 206–7n78
power: epistemology of, 146; as intra-activity, 122; as multidimensional, 110–14, 115, 116, 117, 122, 124; and recognition, 112; as relational, xxiii, xxxii, 110–11, 125; sovereign model of, xxxi, xxxii, 54, 102–5, 108, 109–10, 128; sovereign model of, critique of, 108–18, 119, 125; strategies of, 3, 17
Prus, Robert, 111

Renold, Emma, xii, xx, 186n29
Reynolds, Paul, 141
Rind, Bruce, 133, 134
Ringrose, Jessica, xii, xx, 186n29, 187n32
Rose, Jacqueline, xix
Royle, Nicholas, 13
Rubin, Gayle, 184n9
Rudd, Kevin, xxviii, 3, 194n72
Rush, Florence, 53, 60, 62
Russell, Diana, 81

Saletan, William, 99
Salter, Anna, 66, 68
Schneider, Carl, 12
Schofield, Michael, 21, 27, 28, 33, 39–40, 197n11, 201n103
Scott, Joan, 149
Sedgwick, Eve Kosofsky, xvi–xvii, xix, 107, 154, 155
Sercombe, Howard, 44
sex crime: and gender differences, 131–54; and judicial gender bias, xxxi–xxxii, 114–15, 127–28, 130–33, 139; and positions-of-authority laws, xxxi, 100–104, 105; and sentencing, 105–6, 130–33, 139, 147–48, 149, 151
sex education, xxviii–xxix; comprehensive curriculum for, 29, 42–43; and homosexual equality, 85–95; and humanist movement, 26, 31–34, 36, 41; and instrumentalism, 41; as response to sexual revolution, 22, 25–26; shame and, 27–28, 29; teenage views of, 34–36
Sex for Modern Teenagers (Edwards), 32, 33–34
sex panics, x–xi; and adolescence, xv–xvi; and childhood innocence, xviii; and mobilization of negative affect, xii, xiii–xiv, xvii, xxiv–xxv, 17–18, 23, 95; sociology of, 160, 161, 162, 163, 165, 166, 167, 168–69, 184n9; strategies of, xi–xiii, xiv, xv, xvi, xxiv, xxv–xxvi, xxix, xxxiii, 3, 17, 23, 38–44, 96, 159–60, 170; theory of, xxiv
sexting: and criminal cases 158, 162, 167–68, 175, 228n83; danger of, 160–61, 162, 164; media coverage of, 158–59, 160, 171–72; and *Megan's Story* educational video, 162, 165–66, 171, 225n32, 226n46; prevalence of, 161; and shaming, 165–66, 170–73; and suicide, 163–64; Tunkhannock High School scandal over, 157–58
sexual revolution, 23–25; and private morality, 26–27, 31, 33, 36
shame, xiv, 121; and defensive scripts, 194n72; performativity of, 153, 165–66, 170–73; and sexuality, 8–11, 25, 67–69, 201n113. *See also* child sexuality; emotion
Sheehan, Paul, 14, 16, 17
Shoop, Robert, 138
SIECUS (Sexuality Information and Education Council of the United States), 33
Sikes, Pat, 104, 105
Sim, Myre, 48
Simon, William, 142–43
Skumanick, George, Jr., 157–58
Smallwood, John, 129, 130, 132, 133, 147
Smith, Allan Lloyd, 14
social constructionism, xvii, 81, 139–44
Sorensen, Robert, 135
South Eastern Centre against Sexual Assault, 173
Stainton Rogers, Rex, 55
Stainton Rogers, Wendy, 55
Steinberg, Leo, 7
Stockton, Kathryn Bond, ix, xi, xii, xix, xx
Strange, Carolyn, 30
Sturges, Jock, xxviii
subjectivity: and agency, 135–36, 144; of children and young people, xii, xv, xxvi, 11, 16–18, 34–42, 65–69, 71, 101; gender differences and, 133, 135–66, 135–36; and intersubjective dynamics, 110–14; and multiplicity, 153–55; and recognition, 111–12, 113, 114, 116, 136–37; and sexual experience, 114, 135–36, 142; and social scripts, 142–44; as subject-act-ivity, 114
Summit, Roland, 53, 54

Thorne, Alison, 77–78, 87, 89–94
Timmerman, Greetje, 102
Tomkins, Silvan, 9–10, 12, 68, 169, 193n54, 194n72
Tromovitch, Philip, 134
Tsang, Daniel, 97

uncanny, the, and the sexual child, 11–14; shame and, 11–12, 194n64; as crisis of meaning, 13–14 under erasure: child sexuality and agency as, xi–xii, xv, xx–xxi, xxiii, xxx, 3, 17, 23, 57–58, 65, 171, 172, 174; concept of, xi; Derrida and, 184n14

Vadasz, Danny, 76
Valentine, Kylie, 14, 17–18, 196n96
Vance, Carole, 184n9, 191n82, 224n17

Warner, Michael, xii
Watney, Simon, 184

Weeks, Jeffrey, 24, 26–27, 184n9, 196n4, 197n14
Wells, Hal M., 50, 204n24
West, Donald James, 134
Wieland, Sandra, 63, 65
Wolak, Janis, 162
Woodhouse, T. P., 134

Yates, Alayne, 50, 204nn26–27
Young, Gay, and Proud, 87–89
Young, Jock, 184n9